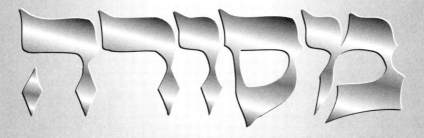

ArtScroll® Series

Rabbi Nosson Scherman / Rabbi Meir Zlotowitz

General Editors

Yemima

Words of Torah.
Words of chizuk.
Words you have to hear.

Adapted by Shiffy Friedman

Published by
ARTSCROLL
Me'sorah Publications, ltd

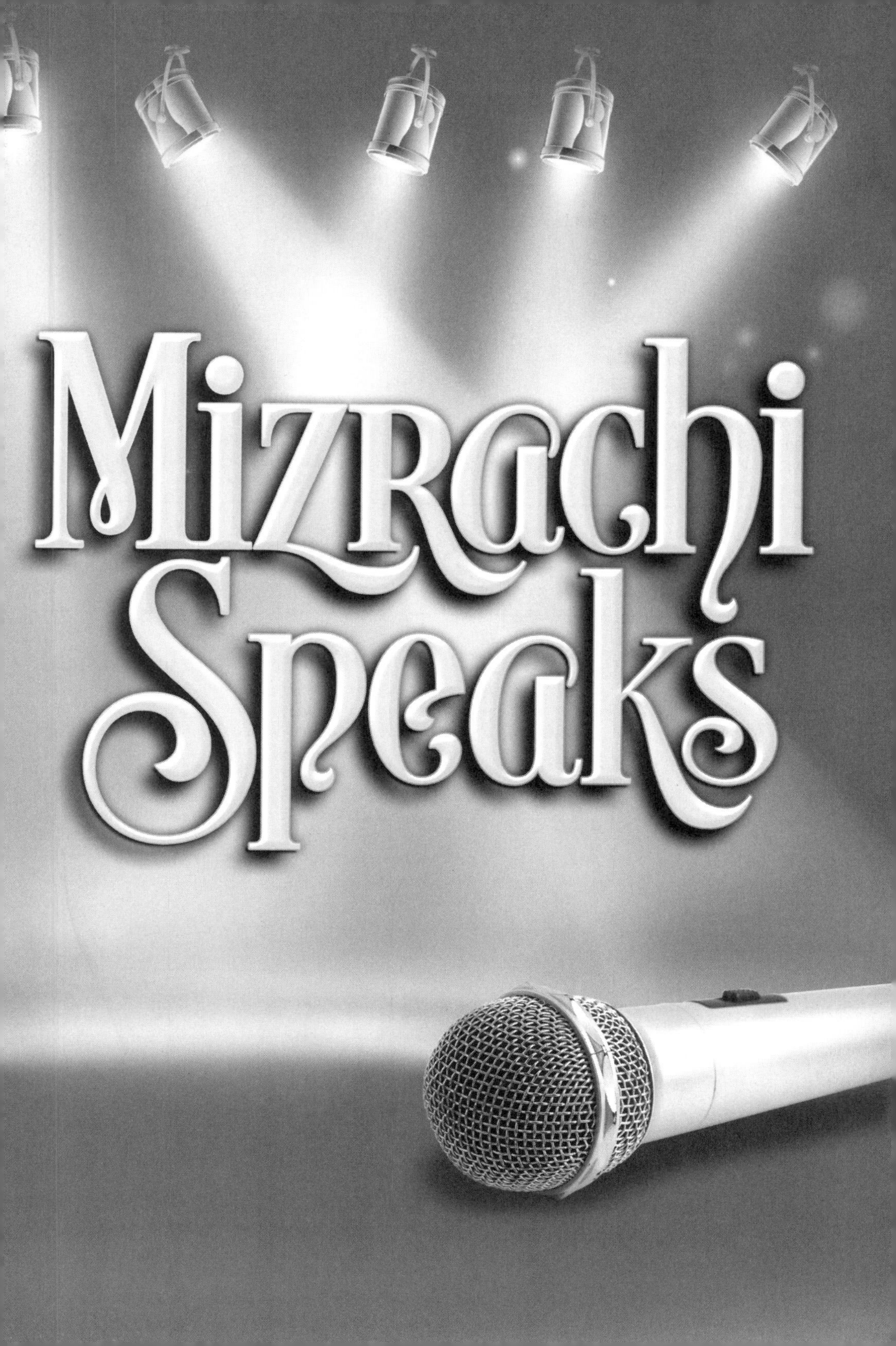
Mizrachi
Speaks

FIRST EDITION
First Impression … November 2016

296.7
Mizrachi
2016

Published and Distributed by   3 1712 01555 0760
MESORAH PUBLICATIONS, LTD.
4401 Second Avenue / Brooklyn, N.Y 11232

Distributed in Europe by
LEHMANNS
Unit E, Viking Business Park
Rolling Mill Road
Jarow, Tyne & Wear, NE32 3DP
England

Distributed in Australia and New Zealand
by GOLDS WORLDS OF JUDAICA
3-13 William Street
Balaclava, Melbourne 3183
Victoria, Australia

Distributed in Israel by
SIFRIATI / A. GITLER — BOOKS
Moshav Magshimim
Israel

Distributed in South Africa by
KOLLEL BOOKSHOP
Northfield Centre, 17 Northfield Avenue
Glenhazel 2192, Johannesburg, South Africa

ARTSCROLL® SERIES
YEMIMA MIZRACHI SPEAKS
© Copyright 2016, by MESORAH PUBLICATIONS, Ltd.
4401 Second Avenue / Brooklyn, N.Y. 11232 / (718) 921-9000 / www.artscroll.com

Segments of this book originally appeared in Ami Magazine.

ISBN 10: 1-4226-1840-4 / ISBN 13: 978-1-4226-1840-0

Typography by CompuScribe at ArtScroll Studios, Ltd.
Bound by Sefercraft, Quality Bookbinders, Ltd., Brooklyn N.Y. 11232

Table of Contents

SEFER SHEMOS

SEFER VAYIKRA

SEFER BAMIDBAR

SEFER DEVARIM

Author's Acknowledgments

Thank you, first of all, to my Ima, Mrs. Tirtza Rothchild, who would read the *parashah* with the *truppen* to us every single Shabbos, the way her mother had taught her. I grew up on this music. All week long, this majestic woman worried about cakes and cleaning, but on *erev Shabbos* she sat and read the words of Torah to us.

My father, Rav Elinosson Rothchild, has always been a chassid of Torah and *derech eretz*. Women should learn as much as they can in thefir own way, he believed. The *ko somar l'beis Yaakov* was very important to him. Every Shabbos, we learned all of Torah, Nevi'im, and Kesuvim with him. A fierce follower of Rav Samson Rafael Hirsch's teachings, he instilled in me a love of Torah. Whenever I see him, he is always with a *sefer* in his hand. It's his most precious possession in the world.

I owe a debt of gratitude to my husband, Rav Chaim, who enables me to spread the words of Torah that he lives by and teaches. To my holy children who go to sleep almost every evening without Ima, I say, *"todah rabbah."* They have such a tremendous *zechus*. A special thank-you to my daughter Shira Conu for her help in the collection procedure.

Vetalmidosai yoseir mikulam. I learn so much from my students. From them, I learn what it means to have courage, to stand up for what's right, to live for Hashem. Thank you!

Thank you to my right-hand woman, Osnat Hirschenson, who is always at my side to help me in my mission of spreading words of Torah to women everywhere, and to my Hebrew editor Yikrat Friedman, who collects my words like diamonds.

A special thanks to Rebbetzin Fuchs for her tireless effort in helping me spread the beauty of Torah.

Thank you to Ami Magazine for serving as the international English platform for my words. Many of the thoughts shared in this book were first published in your pages. You are the medium through which thousands of women have received *chizuk*, guidance, and comfort.

I am deeply grateful to my English writer Shiffy Friedman, who struggled with my Hebrew, with my lack of time, with my erratic schedule. You were the one who had trust in this from the very beginning. It's easy to critique feminine Torah, but you made it so beautiful, rich, and warm.

Yemima Mizrachi

Cheshvan 5777

Editor's Acknowledgments

Dear women,

Eretz Yisrael nikneis be'yissurim, living in Eretz Yisrael is accompanied with hardship, our Sages teach in *Berachos* (5a). When my husband and I first merited to move from New York to Eretz Yisrael upon our marriage, I struggled to understand how those words would play out in my life. Except for missing family, of course, life was so idyllic, so rich and satisfying and beautiful. But then the ache awakened: this deep desire to continue teaching Torah, to once again enter a classroom and transmit the magnificent words of our Sages to wide-eyed students. How I missed those teaching days!

But in His kindness, Hashem heeded to my yearning. Teaching, He showed me, need not only occur in a brick-and-mortar classroom. It can happen through the pen, through spreading Torah messages across the world to women of all stages. I am eternally grateful to HaKadosh Baruch Hu for orchestrating this unique arrangement on my behalf. Through spreading the messages that Rabbanit Yemima Mizrachi relates to me, I have merited to help shed light and clarity to thousands of English-speaking women around the globe. *Odeh Hashem Elokai bechal levavi.*

Every writer carves off slabs of time to dedicate herself to a project that is close to her heart. But life does happen during that precious writing time: the children grow, the clock ticks, the seasons change. I am deeply grateful to my partner in life, Ezra, for being there for me, always, but especially when I was immersed in the preparation of this book or required assistance with Torah sources, and to my precious children, Yosef Mordechai, Chana, and Yehudis, for bearing with a mother who has been living a dual life for months now. I hope you always felt the way I do: that you come first.

To my dedicated parents, Reb Dovid and Mrs. Suri Kahan, thank you for believing in me, always, for rooting for me, for showing me that nothing stands in the way of willpower. I live by those lessons every day.

To my in-laws, Reb Aron Yida and Mrs. Devoiry Friedman, I owe a debt of gratitude. In addition to your appreciation for Torah and your gracious support, your incredibly positive feedback on every project I've ever undertaken means so much to me. A special thanks to my grandparents, siblings, and siblings-in-law for your support and encouragement in my work.

Once upon a time, I was an essay writer. The extent of my writing was the essays I wrote back in high school, encouraged by a master English teacher, Mrs. Breina Biller, whose enthrallment with the written word was contagious. But it was Mrs. Leah Klein, and her husband Joel, who trusted me blindly with my very first position as a syndicated columnist. I am eternally grateful for your faith in me.

Through the recommendation of Rabbi Shlomo Schwimmer I was led to Ami Magazine, then only a project in the making, not the flourishing publication that it is today. I have enjoyed a wonderful relationship with Rechy Frankfurter, the editor at Ami Living, who has taught me so much about writing, editing, and life. Thank you, Rechy, for being a remarkable encouraging editor and friend. Through my work for Ami Living, where I first partnered with Rabbanit Yemima

Mizrachi to facilitate her popular weekly column, I have had the blessed opportunity to meet with women who have truly changed my life, women like Mrs. Tammy Karmel whose clarity and *emunah* have transformed my *avodas Hashem*. To the readers who've reached out to me over the years I extend a special thanks. Your words have touched me. As I continue to write in my solitary space, the positive feedback motivates me further.

How do I thank Rabbanit Yemima Mizrachi? You have trusted me with a treasure trove of lessons on parenting, marriage, and life as a Jewish woman, which I pray will guide me as I raise my growing family, *b'ezras Hashem*. And thank you to your daughter, Shira Conu, and your dedicated secretary, Osnat Hirschenson for helping me along this illuminating journey.

To Miriam Zakon of ArtScroll, you are the dream editor. Ever so understanding and accommodating, your excitement about this project was infectious. It was a true pleasure to work with you. Thank you to Reb Shmuel Blitz of ArtScroll, for your guidance and assistance in this important project. Thank you to Suri Brand, for an impeccable copyediting job. My thanks also to Rabbi Pinchas Waldman, for meticulously checking the sources, and to Eli Kroen, for designing the magnificent cover; Mrs. Judi Dick, for her editorial review; Mrs. Faygie Weinbaum, for her meticulous proofreading; and Mrs. Estie Dicker, for paginating the book.

To the readers of this book, I offer my thanks. For women like you, I've merited to delve into the sweet words of Torah, to live and breathe its messages day in, day out. You have put me through an experience that I hope has left its imprint on my soul. In this merit, may this book serve as a balm, a guide, a source of light and joy for you.

Shehecheyanu v'kiyimanu lazman hazeh!

Shiffy Friedman

Yerushalayim/ Cheshvan 5777

Introduction: *Toras Imecha* – The Torah of Women

To my dear sisters,

You hold in your hands a book for women, by a woman. It is a book that transmits true Torah messages to hearts that are thirsty for spiritual comfort. I am just the *shaliach*, the messenger, bringing you the words of Toras Moshe that have given me such clarity, peace, joy, and love. My goal in my lectures and this book is for Jewish women around the world to hear the words of our Sages and understand how they impact on our lives as women. In the past, *Toras imecha* was traditionally passed from mother to daughter, a *mesorah* that is still very important. But for many, this wasn't enough. I pray to Hashem that I merit to fill this void.

What makes the Torah for women so unique? Every morning, after Modeh Ani, we say, *"Shema beni mussar avicha v'al titosh toras imecha,* listen, my son, to your rebuke of your father, and don't veer from the Torah of your mother"

(*Mishlei* 1:8). What stunning words! Please, my dear son, we cry, please, my darling daughter, don't abandon what I have worked so hard to instill in you. Don't stray from the path. Today, we hear those words repeated so many times to so many of our wandering children.

What can bring back a lost child who has gone so far? It is the *Toras imecha*. The responsibility and incredible merit lies on the shoulders of us women.

What is this Torah? Time and again, I observe the answer in the yeshivah that my husband has for *bachurim* who are stumbling in their search for the truth. On Purim, these boys came to celebrate with us in our home. At the beginning, I was worried how they would conduct themselves once they'd become intoxicated. While we women were enjoying the festivities in the kitchen, a heavyset young man came in from the dining room, crying. "Rabbanit," he said, "I want to call my mother." But his mother lives in Monsey, where it was still night. When I told him we'd have to wait and he kicked up a fuss, I decided to give her a ring. She picked up right away. "Mommy," he cried, "I love you!" Then he said to me, "Rabbanit, can you tell her that I'm a good boy? She never heard anyone say it to her."

Why was this brokenhearted young man desperate for me to tell this to his mother? In his *sefer* Aish Kodesh, the Piaseczna Rebbe provides an answer. A person can transmit to the next generation whatever it is that he is obligated to do. For example, the man's obligation is to learn Torah, so he has the ability to give over whatever he learns to his child. A woman, on the other hand, does not have an obligation to learn Torah, so when she does it, she does it from a place of love. *That*, says the Aish Kodesh, is what she can pass forward: the *geshmak*, the love, the warmth, so that even when her child rejects his obligation to learn Torah, he can still feel its sweetness within him, the sweetness his mother has on her face when she reads a Rashi, the glow in her eyes when she sits at a *shiur* and, yes, her excitement as she reads a book such as this. That's what's ingrained in his heart. No matter how far he's gone, the love for Torah and mitzvos—his desire to be a "good boy" — will still be burning within him.

The Gemara in *Shabbos* (89a) tells of the incident in which *Am Yisrael* was dancing around the golden calf. When the Satan observed this, he came to Hashem and said, "The Torah You gave, do You know where it is?" "I gave it to the land," Hashem answered. So the Satan trekked out to the land in his search for the Torah, but couldn't find it. Next he went to the sea, and then the lower spheres, but still he could not find it. "I looked for the Torah everywhere and I couldn't find it," he declared. So Hashem sent him to *ben Amram*. Satan approached Moshe and asked him, "Where is the Torah that Hashem gave you?" Moshe cried, "Who am I that Hashem should give me the Torah?"

And now Hashem intervened. "You are deceitful!" Moshe answered, "You have such a treasure! How can I take credit for it [that You gave it all to me]?"

And what was Hashem's response to Moshe's answer? "Since you made yourself small, the Torah will be named for you." And indeed, we are told *"Zichru Toras Moshe,"* remember Moshe's Torah (*Malachi* 3:22).

Satan's name can be associated with the word for desertion, *natash* (which has all three letters of the word Satan). He's the one who goes to Hashem and says, "Look, where is the Torah You gave them?" He's the one who rejoices when a Jew deserts the ways of the Torah, running off excitedly to report to HaKadosh Baruch Hu, "Look what he's doing. Look what she's doing."

When that happens, Hashem goes to Moshe Rabbeinu and demands, "*Nu*, what did your children do to the Torah?" And Moshe answers so beautifully, as he did centuries back, "The Torah is so huge that it can't be mine. I'm not worthy of its greatness." And that's what this person is feeling now.

When the nation sinned with the calf, they simply felt that the Torah was too holy for them. They didn't know how to deal with such holy stuff, so they made an *eigel maseichah*, a molten calf (*Shemos* 32:4). The *masach*, dear women, which is Hebrew for screen, is simply a means of escaping a reality that is too holy, when people feel they are not worthy enough of something bigger.

Do you think that all of the children who've left the Torah did so because the Torah was too small, because the Internet and the secular world are bigger? No. They left because *they* felt too small. The Torah was too big to be observed by someone who perceived himself as so small.

This is the reason, dear women, that the ultimate *tefillah* of a mother is *vezakeini legadeil*. Please, Hashem, we beg at the Shabbos candles, give me the capacity to make them feel big, to uproot the disease of this generation, this feeling of littleness, so they can feel worthy of observing the holy Torah.

When you make your children feel big, feel capable, and you show them how happy you are with every word of Torah, they say, "I can do this." And that, too, is part of *Toras imecha*.

What's the *chiddush* in this book, dear readers? Thousands of women are learning Torah today. It's become a movement even in the secular world, but they learn Torah the way men learn it. What does HaKadosh Baruch Hu request of us? *Ko somar le'veis Yaakov v'sageid li'vnei Yisrael (Shemos* 19:3). It's the same Torah for both, but we both need a different approach. The emphasis is so different.

One thing that a woman always needs is comfort: before she gets married, before she gives birth, as she builds her home, when she marries off her child… always. Who can provide this comfort to us? *Anochi*, the first word of the *Aseres HaDibros*, the Ten Commandments, alludes to a verse in *Yeshayahu* (51:12), "*Anochi anochi Hu menachemchem*, I, only I, am your consoler." When you learn My Torah, Hashem tells us, you will find comfort.

When I open a *sefer*, before I prepare a *shiur*, I always look for the face I want to speak to, the woman I am out to comfort. And I try to prepare a *shiur* especially for her: for that one woman. Only the Torah can provide comfort. It's a caress on a hard day. It's the only source that can truly tell us that everything will be all right. Every *parashah* is called a *Sidrah*. It's all *b'seder*, dear sisters, when we learn the *parashah*.

What we women need to hear is the Torah that will open our eyes to the greatness of Hashem, to the wisdom of His ways, to the beauty of His world to provide us comfort. It is my deep *tefillah* that this book will do that for you.

Fondly,
Yemima Mizrachi

Yerushalayim, Cheshvan 5777

If you have comments or questions, please email me at:
Yemimamizrachispeaks@gmail.com
I look forward to hearing from all my friends.

Sefer Bereishis

Boundaries:
A Curse or a Blessing?

We initially meet the world's very first couple in the most beautiful place on earth, in Gan Eden. Adam and Chavah are blessed with the harmony every couple strives for *b'Gan Eden mikedem*, in the Garden of Eden that once was. What was so special about Eden, dear sisters? What was so unique about the place to which we refer when we bless every new couple under the *chuppah*? We find the answer in the word *eden*, which can be read as *ad heinah* — "up to here" (*Ibn Ezra, Koheles* 4:2). The secret blessing of Gan Eden and the entire Creation were the boundaries that HaKadosh Baruch Hu put forth.

When Hashem created the waters and the land on the second day of Creation, the sea wanted to flow onto the ground. Because this lack of boundaries would wash away the earth, Hashem established borders. "Up until here is your territory," He told the sea. The moon, too, wanted to impinge on the sun's boundaries, but Hashem made order in the creation.

Every creature has an innate desire to erupt past its borders, and the same was true of Adam and Chavah. How they wanted to taste of the forbidden fruit! But that was the blessing of Eden: the borders that Hashem had erected for them. When they crossed the line, the border that appeared restrictive and unappealing, they unleashed the curses from which we suffer until this very day.

Dear Jewish women, we are blessed and privileged to lead a life of Eden, a sweet Torah life that provides us the boundaries for a life of paradise. Yes, the borders may appear restraining at times. How we want to taste just a tiny bit from the forbidden fruit! We sometimes wonder: Why does every detail of my life have to be directed by something other than my heart and mind? But remember, dear beautiful women, that the secret of blessing is boundaries. *Ad heinah* — up to here, my child. Don't cross the line.

If there is any time in history when we've seen the repercussions of a boundary-free life, it is today. In a world that celebrates hedonism and liberalism in the most cowardly of ways, it's not hard to understand why the epitome of Eden is limitation. The curse that a life of "Everyone can do whatever they please" engenders makes the Torah's clear boundaries so sweet, so precious, in our eyes.

When Crossing the Line Is Crucial

As beautiful as a life of boundaries is, however, there are four exceptions that every Jewish woman must make. When are the four times that we must step over the line for the sake of Hashem?

Gan Eden was a self-contained paradise that provided Adam and Chavah with everything they needed. The only creations that flowed out of this beautiful place were four rivers: Pishon, Gichon, Chidekel, and Peras (*Bereishis* 2:10–14). According to the Ben Ish Chai, the names of these bodies of water offer insight into the four exceptions, the times when we must say, "I've done so much, but I will flow one bit more."

The first river listed in the Torah is Pishon, which hints at *chesed*. (The root of Pishon, *pashah*, means "add" or "grow" and can be associated with "additional" *chesed*.) "I helped her enough," you may be tempted to say. "Now let her stand on her own two feet. It's time that she made a life for herself." No, dear sister, do one more bit for a fellow Jew in need. Take that extra step, cook one more soup, smile one more time, make one more phone call. Stretch yourself one bit more for another human being.

What does Gichon allude to? Your throat. (*Gachon* means the part of a reptile that crawls on the ground, which includes its throat.) When you feel that you've davened enough, dear sister, daven one bit more. Break the borders and offer one more prayer to Hashem. "But I've cried so much already and nothing changed!" One more *tefillah*, dear sister. Just one more.

Chidekel encapsulates the power to forgive. It combines the words *chad*, sharp and smooth, and *kal*, easy, and it represents letting things pass over *b'chadus u'bekalus*, smooth and easy, as if they were unseen. Let it go, dear woman. Instead of saying, "I'm so hurt right now. I will never speak to her again!" give her one more chance. Give him one more opportunity to make it right.

And the last situation for which transcending borders will bring you blessing is Peras, similar to *peru*, which refers to fertility. Children are a blessing, dear women. One more child in your life will only amplify the light in your home.

Borders are a *berachah*. Children need them, adolescents even more, and even we adults must have borders in order to lead rich, satisfying lives of structure and truth. But when it comes to one more *chesed*, one more prayer, trying for peace one more time, and bringing one more child into the world, let yourself flow like a fountain, free and unrestricted.

Achieving a Balance in Your Home

A Torah life is all about balance. On the one hand, we have the boundaries set up for us. The mitzvos provide us with incredible structure and clarity. But on the other hand, Hashem expects us to make exceptions, to loosen up for the sake of peace, for the sake of connection, for the sake of blessing. In your home, dear women, the balance of love and boundaries is crucial. As we learn in *Parashas Bereishis*, *shalom bayis* can only be achieved through that delicate balance.

Essentially, a man and woman have the greatest potential to bring the *Shechinah*, the Divine Presence, into their midst. The root of both *ish*, man, and *ishah*, woman, in Lashon HaKodesh is *eish*, fire. While a *yud* is added to *eish* to create the word *ish*, man, a *hei* is added to *eish* to create the word *ishah*, woman. Those two letters, *yud* and *hei*, comprise the Divine Name: the only way a couple can bring Hashem into their home is when both husband and wife work together for the sake of peace. If this does not happen, G-d forbid, they are left with *eish*, a destructive fire that will only harm their own relationship, but will also affect the rest of their home (*Sotah* 17a, and *Rashi* there). If creating a home of harmony is what brings Hashem's Presence into our midst, why is it so hard? What keeps getting in the way of a couple's blessed peace?

After Adam and Chavah stepped over the one boundary that Hashem had set forth for them, after they caved in to their impulse and tasted from the *eitz hada'as*, they were penalized. Hashem cursed the woman, "I will greatly increase your suffering and your childbearing; in pain shall you bear children" (*Bereishis* 3:16). For generations to come, women would be cursed with not only the physical pain of bearing children, but also the burden of raising them. And Adam's curse was "through suffering shall you eat of the ground all the days of your life" (ibid. 3:17). Every man would suffer the burden of earning a livelihood. What a curse!

But the greatest curse of all, dear women, is that these punishments have become an obstacle for peace between husband and wife. The wholeness and depth of the world's first couple's relationship, for which we all strive, would be forever marred by the issues that crop up as a result of the curses.

The husband is so preoccupied with his curse of earning a living that he can't be there for his wife when she needs to discuss their difficult child. The child's mother will stay awake all night wondering what will be with her erring son, while her husband will stay awake all night figuring out how to cover the monthly expenses. They are each so busy with their own *kelalah* that it's hard for them to connect, to enjoy the true beauty of a wholesome marriage. This, dear women, is the greatest curse of all.

So what can we do to make way for Hashem's Presence in our home? How can we do this when we're both bogged down by our own punishments, heading in different directions? Here is the secret to true blessing in your home: Daven for each other. When a woman prays for her husband's worries, and the man prays for hers, they can achieve true peace in the home. Instead of telling your husband, "Can you stop talking about the bills already? I don't want to hear about it, that's your job" — pray for him! It's tough to carry the burden of *parnassah* all day, every day. The more concern you express for his plight, and the more you express that concern toward Hashem, the more you are preparing the way for the beautiful marriage that Adam and Chavah enjoyed before they sinned.

If you don't daven for each other, the ideal relationship just won't happen. You can read the world's most incredible marriage manuals, you can take the most exquisite vacations together, but what will happen when you finally sit at the top of a glorious mountain sharing an ice cream? You will find yourself asking, "Why are you talking about money now?" And he will question, "We're five thousand miles away from the kids. Can we talk about this a different time?" We live and breathe our curses. If you want to express and cultivate true love, the only way to do so is to share them, by davening for one another.

Throughout *Sefer Bereishis*, we find several references to the importance of davening for one another. Sarah Imeinu, for instance, was upset at Avraham because he didn't daven for her. Commenting on the words *Chamasi alecha* — "The outrage against me is because of you" (ibid. 16:5), Rashi explains that it bothered Sarah that Avraham only prayed for his own ability to have children, which led to the birth of Yishmael. Earlier, the verse tells us *U'leAvram heitiv ba'avurah* — "Avraham's life became better because of her" (ibid. 12:16). Commentators explain that Avraham's blessing for livelihood was in Sarah's hands. As soon as she prayed on his behalf, he was helped.

Look at Yitzchak and Rivkah, how they each davened with the other in mind. Yitzchak prayed *l'nochach ishto*, on his wife's behalf (ibid. 25:21), and they merited their salvation.

The curses that befell Adam and Chavah all the way back at the beginning of time plague us until this day. However, if we want to enter the blessed Gan Eden that they merited at first, we have the ability to do so despite our pains. Daven on your husband's behalf, and you will merit bringing Hashem's Presence into your home.

Again and Again and Again

I've davened for him yesterday and the day before, you may be thinking. *But when will this end?* Our repeated attempts to bring peace into the home can sometimes leave us feeling depleted. How can you make your home a beautiful, loving resting place for the *Shechinah*? *Parashas Bereishis* gives us a sense of the newness that we try desperately to hold on to, the sense of newness we experienced at the start of our marriage. How can we truly experience this wonderful sense of newness, of feeling like that flawless newborn child, every day in our lives?

The *sefer Tikkunei Zohar* offers seventy possible word combinations culled from the letters that make up the word *bereishis*. Of the seventy, let's talk about the one that pertains most to us Jewish women. *Bereishis* contains the letters that can be rearranged to *rosh bayis*. That is you, the vanguard of the home. You, dear women, are responsible for creating the feeling of newness in your own little world. The *teshukah*, the passion with which you approach your *avodas Hashem*, will set the tone in your home. What is *teshukah*? It is the enthusiasm you inject into duties and roles that are otherwise routine. With your *binah yeseirah*, with your special insight (*Niddah* 45b), dear Jewish woman, you can transform seemingly humdrum tasks into exciting, novel projects.

The quality of *teshukah* is unique to women. Of course, a man could have *cheishek*, but there's a subtle difference between the two approaches. *Cheishek* is the desire to tackle something new, while *teshukah* is drawing a sense of newness from the familiar. It's looking at the same old, same old with new eyes.

You can transform your home into a Gan Eden through this very passion. The word *teshukah*, we learn, is composed of two words: *tash kavah*, you look forward to that which tires you. Imagine that! As a woman, you have the ability to actually anticipate chores and duties that exhaust your body and drain your energy. You have the capacity to approach your obligations with a sense of newness even if you've done them too many times to count. That is your unique quality of *teshukah*.

You're tired from listening to so many *shidduchim*, but you await them nevertheless. Sometimes, you're tired from davening so much, from begging for that same *yeshuah* time and again. But, oh, how you look forward to opening that siddur in the morning! You're tired from tending to the needs of your children, but you look forward to the birth of your next baby.

This is the power of a Jewish woman. When she awakens in

the morning, eager to tackle her duties, her passionate zeal is contagious. Only she has the capacity to give her family the feeling of "Wow! This world is a wonderful place! What a magnificent day today!"

Our matriarchs, Sarah and Rivkah, whom we meet in *Chumash Bereishis*, merited three symbols of Hashem's Presence in their home: the cloud that hovered above their tent, the dough that was blessed, and the candle that burned from Shabbos to Shabbos (*Rashi, Bereishis* 24:67). The cloud, the dough, and the candle all usually have a temporary existence. Eventually, the wind blows the clouds away, a candle is extinguished, and dough goes sour. So how did these women merit these extended blessings? Because they had the power of renewal, of passion. Because our matriarchs had the capacity to infuse fresh life into their repetitive tasks, they merited these signs of Hashem's Presence.

The passion with which a woman approaches her role fills her home with a sense of excitement toward *avodas Hashem*. Commenting on the words *V'el isheich teshukaseich v'hu yimshol bach* — "Your craving shall be for your husband, and he shall rule over you" (ibid. 3:16), the Bnei Yissaschar explains that the woman's husband will follow his wife's *mashal*, example. If he sees that she wakes up with a smile in the morning, her sparkle will carry into his approach as well. If she speaks to the children in a gentle, loving manner, he'll think, *That seems to work really well*, and he'll follow suit.

Yet this verse was actually describing woman's punishment. How is this a punishment for the woman? It puts her in a tight position. Her every action is under scrutiny, and it is only through her enthusiasm that her home will be a happy place. Without her passion, the environment starts to wilt. How is this her rectification for the first sin in Gan Eden? How was Chavah successful in having Adam partake from the fruit of the *eitz hada'as*? When a man senses his wife's feelings toward something, even if he's aware that Hashem instructs him otherwise, he feels drawn to it. It's an element inherent in every couple since the time of Adam and Chavah.

Chavah was culpable for the first sin, generating the punishment of death, but she was also the one who started anew and planted hope in this world. She laid the foundation of a new world. She named her son Sheis *ki shas li Elokim zera acher* — "because Hashem provided me another child in place [of Hevel]" (ibid. 4:25). Chavah says to us, "My dear daughters, it's always possible to return to Gan Eden."

Yes, dear sisters, you have the ability to renew your relationship: with your husband, with your children, with Hashem. Infuse your life with enthusiasm, awaken every morning with a desire to tackle your duties with joy, and you will merit to live in your own Gan Eden, every day.

L'Mishpechoseihem: Family Is the Glue

Parashas Noach is always read at a time when the winter starts to crawl into our bones. When this season comes upon us, we have the opportunity to spend many quality hours with our dear family. On the long, dark evenings when the blustery winds howl outside, we have the chance to connect, to come closer to the people who mean the most to us in the world.

In *Parashas Noach*, we learn about how precious family is. The time lapse between *Parashas Bereishis* and *Parashas Noach* spans over 1,500 years, yet the Torah, contrary to the detail it offers for other time periods, chose to fast-forward to the time of Noach and the flood. Only once the world came to appreciate the concept of family, as happened following the *mabul*, did the Torah find it noteworthy to delve into the events in depth.

The term for family, *mishpachah*, the root of the word *l'mishpechoseihem*, appears for the first time after most of the world was wiped out in the flood: "Every living being, every creeping thing, and every bird, everything that moves upon the earth, came out of the ark by their families" (*Bereishis* 8:19). It took the world that many years and a calamity so disastrous to value this incredible asset.

Parashas Bereishis concludes with the words *V'Noach matza chein b'einei Hashem* — "Noach found grace in the eyes of Hashem" (ibid. 6:8). How did he merit this grace that saved him and his brood from the colossal flood?

When a person chooses to focus on growing closer to those dearest to him, when he learns to exercise kindness and self-lessness to his flesh and blood, he merits acquiring true *chein* in the eyes of Hashem. Noach was the epitome of a family man. He was *noach*, calm as the waters of a brook. During the *mabul*, he remained inside the ark, tending to the needs of his family (and the animals), while the world was turning over outside.

Following the storm that wrecked the entire world, Noach emerged unscathed with his entire family and all of the animals he had gathered inside. As the verse tells us, *l'mishpechoseihem yatzu min hateivah* — "they came out of the ark 'to' their families." It's hard to understand: to which family did they go? There *were* no other creatures in the world after the destruction. Our Sages tell us something beautiful, that the animals went to establish their own new families because it was now that they finally appreciated the value of family. When they observed Noach's devotion to his relatives, they grasped the deep connection that only family provides.

Family is the glue, the key to success that holds us all together. It's impossible for a person to survive the tempestuous storms of her life without this source of comfort and energy. Often, we think we're managing just fine with friends. But then, when a *mabul* happens, it is the family that surrounds us and provides us with the warmth and comfort we desperately need. There is no greater asset in which to invest.

The Beauty of Selflessness

Not always is giving to the family so rewarding. After a long day of giving to the little charges in your home, it's normal to feel drained and depleted. Sometimes it can be challenging to give so selflessly, to exercise self-restraint, to work on your *middos* all the time. You just want to sit down and stay seated instead of running around and tending to everyone's needs at every hour of the day and night. But investing in family, working to bring them together, building a home for Hashem, dear women, is what gives you energy in the long run.

What happened when the world chose to disregard the value of family, when they decided that life was meant to be lived for selfish pleasure? *Vatimalei ha'aretz chamas* — "The earth became filled with robbery" (*Bereishis* 6:11). Rav Dessler explains that *chamas* only happens when a person thinks that he is in this world to receive. Everything he sees, then, becomes his.

A Jewish woman who wants to help her family emerge unscathed from the storms in life must have her mind and heart set on giving. It is not enough to simply provide her husband and children with their needs. It must be done with a happy heart. If a woman says, "Just one moment. Where does it say that I must cook for Shabbos with joy? Can't I just stand at the pot and stir the soup? Where does it say that I have to hug my children? That I have to greet my husband with a happy face?"

This is the unwritten Torah, dear sisters. "Why do I have to do everything? And what happens if I don't? I washed the dishes, I went to work, and I returned in a sour mood. Is that an *aveirah*?"

No. It's not an *aveirah*. It's worse than that. Do you know what the Torah calls this attitude in *Parashas Noach*? *Chamas*. You rob your husband and children of joy. You rob yourself of merits. You rob the world of your shining countenance.

Why is giving without joy considered *chamas*? Robbery is one offense that can be committed without it falling into the category of a full-fledged sin. The *Talmud Yerushalmi* (*Bava Metzia* 4:2) tells us that in Noach's day, people would commit despicable acts that were not in the parameters of an explicit *aveirah*. For instance, people would go to the market and taste some peanuts. "Mmm, this is good!" And then they would taste the carob. "This is great!" The quantity they sampled didn't add up to even one cent. It wasn't an amount for which they were able to pay, but every person did this. It's true that it isn't a big deal, but one sampling from this one and one from the other adds up. One drop and one drop and then a flood.

No, you're not obligated to smile, dear women. Where does it say that your eyes have to shine all day long? You don't have to feel overwhelmed with excitement when Shabbos comes. But when you don't do this, you're robbing your children of the joy of *Yiddishkeit*. If you can't do it for yourself, do it for your family.

Cry Now

In a book that is geared to the Jewish woman, the epicenter of her family, it is crucial to discuss the importance of this asset right at the beginning. Of course, it is marvelous for a woman to carve out time to devote herself to *chesed*, to give *shiurim*, to care for another Jew. But as the *akeres habayis*, the homemaker, the first and foremost role is to nurture the family.

Every child has only one mother, dear women. On so many evenings, when I leave the house to give a *shiur*, I feel a pinch in my heart as I pass the bedrooms where my children sleep peacefully. I look at their beautiful faces. They look like angels (when they're sleeping, of course!), and I can't stop the questions in my mind. Did I give them enough today? It's true that the women waiting at the *shiur* are thirsty for words of Torah, but first I have to make sure that my children are satiated with my love.

But how can we always give with joy? How can we keep the stream of selflessness alive and bursting with love? Sometimes it gets stuffy in the ark. We feel like we need air to breathe, we need to escape. There are the children, the children who wake you up at all hours of the night, who never stop being hungry. If dinner isn't ready right on time, you risk a tantrum that leaves you scarred. You feel like you're drowning in the deep waters. Is that how you feel sometimes?

The greatest enemy of prayer is "*noach*," when the waters are too calm. The Midrash tells us that in Noach's time, there were no seasons (see *Malbim, Bereishis* 9:13–4). All year long, the weather was beautifully pleasant. Rain fell only once in forty years. Imagine! There was never a cloudy day. What a dream! But then, the people forgot about Hashem. Everything was just so perfect they had nothing to cry about.

It's not for naught that both Noach and Rachel are mentioned with the words *Vayizkor Elokim* — "And Hashem remembered": *Vayizkor Elokim es Noach* (*Bereishis* 8:1); *Vayizkor Elokim es Rachel* (ibid. 30:22). What's the connection between the two? Rachel tells you, dear women.

"I was like Noach. My entire future was planned out for me so I had no reason to pray. I missed out on so many years of *tefillah*! I was a beautiful girl. I was the girl everyone knew would marry Yaakov, the saint. My sister, Leah, the one with the bloodshot eyes, she was supposed to marry Esav. But she was the one who didn't stop praying, and I was the sanguine, content one."

In Cheshvan, the month of Rachel's *yahrtzeit*, our mother begs us to cry now. Yes, when the house feels stuffy with the adorable little kids and their arts and crafts all over the place, that's the time to pray. When the daily routine and the endless demands weigh heavy on your heart and eyelids, remember that everything is from Hashem and connect to Him. Tell Him how badly you want to give of yourself with joy. Express your pain at how sour you feel. The connection that *tefillah* engenders will make you feel so much better. This is what will fill you with the capacity for giving with joy.

Often women come over to me after a *shiur* and they say, "Rabbanit, how did you know that that's exactly what I needed to hear?" And I tell them that it's not me. It's Moshe Rabbeinu and the holy Torah.

As long as we seek to give of ourselves to our family, as long as we're ready and willing to forgo our personal comfort and pleasure in order to make those around us more comfortable and happy, the glue that holds our families together will become stronger and stronger. If we choose to be the calm, selfless oasis in the storm, like Noach our forefather, we will merit to emerge from the tests of life, unscathed. And then, we'll be *zocheh* to look around and see the beautiful family we've established by our devoted efforts.

The Pain
of the Waiting Game

In *Parashas Lech Lecha*, we begin to read about the *nisyonos* with which Hashem challenged Avraham, and how he victoriously emerged from each one. The Torah portion begins with the command *Lech lecha* — "Go!" — according to some opinions the very first *nisayon*. Hashem commands Avraham to leave his home, his birthplace, his father's house, and wander until Hashem will lead him to his destination.

The final *nisayon* that Avraham experienced, in *Parashas Vayeira*, was *Akeidas Yitzchak* — Hashem's command that he sacrifice his precious only son on the altar.

The *Midrash Tanchuma* (*Vayeira* 22) compares the first and the last tests, and notes that they both contain the words *lech lecha*. The question is raised: Which of Avraham Avinu's *nisyonos* was more difficult: the first or the last?

What a strange question! How can these two tests be compared at all? Can one compare the challenge of slitting a precious son's throat to that of wandering as a nomad for a while?

But if our Sages ask this question, there's a reason. They want to teach us something that may not be clear to us from the outset.

Yes, sacrificing a child is a challenge of great magnitude, but *lech lecha* was nowhere near easy either: Avraham had no idea when the *nisayon* would end, and a waiting game is a challenge of tremendous magnitude as well.

The Gemara (*Taanis* 23a) relates that the great Choni HaMe'agel was never able to understand how *Am Yisrael* would endure the harrowing wait for the *geulah*. "*Kol yamai hayisi mitzta'er al hapasuk,*" he would say. "All my life I've found it hard to understand the verse *V'shuv Hashem es shivas Tzion hayinu k'cholmim* — that when the redemption will finally come, all of our previous anguish will seem like a dream (*Tehillim* 126:1). I can't believe that," he would say, "I can't wait that long."

Choni was accustomed to standing in the circle that he formed with his stick, asking Hashem for rain, and watching it happen instantaneously; he didn't appreciate the concept of waiting, until he fell into a seventy-year sleep, that is.

When he saw that the carob sapling whose planting he'd observed immediately prior to falling asleep had grown into a gigantic, fruitful tree, he realized that he had slept for seventy years. When he came to people and introduced himself as Choni HaMe'agel, they refused to believe him. He said to Hashem, "If no one believes me, then I don't want to live anymore."

It was at that moment that Choni came to the realization that he hadn't understood the beauty of *lech lecha* until then. He could not wait, so he slept. But sleep is not the way to deal with a challenge. We must push ourselves through this *lech lecha* in order to emerge victorious. Like our forefather Avraham, we must persevere and trudge along the road whose end is not in sight if we want to reap its benefits.

Jewels Along the Journey

What are the benefits of this arduous *lech lecha* journey? Of course, we constantly beseech Hashem, *lo al yedei nisa-yon* — we don't want to be tested — but if, *lo aleinu*, Hashem chooses to do otherwise, what do we stand to gain from thrusting the walking stick into the ground and carrying on?

First, we discover the good people in our lives. During a time of challenge, who our real friends are becomes clear to us.

Before he was confronted by Hashem with the ten *nisyonos*, Avraham had three friends: Aner, Eshkol, and Mamrei. Why did Hashem choose to speak to him at Eilonei Mamrei and not near the others? Because Mamrei was Avraham's only true friend, as Avraham discovered through his challenges.

Mamrei was the only one to encourage Avraham to perform a bris milah, as is evident in his name. While Mamrei's name contains the letters standing for *Mul maher rofacha Elokim* — "Hurry to circumcise; Hashem will be your doctor," Aner is the acronym for *Inui nefesh ra* — "Circumcision is torture. Stay away," similar to Eshkol's reaction of *Ein shaveh klum lamul* — "Milah is not worthwhile."

A challenge brings those who care for you to your side. You cherish their presence and their closeness.

Yet another benefit from the arduous challenge of *lech lecha*, of waiting endlessly with *emunah*, is what it does to marriage. After much wandering, Avraham turned to Sarah and said, *Hinei na yadati ki ishah yefas mareh at* — "I have now discovered that you are a woman of beautiful appearance" (*Bereishis* 12:11). Only then did he see her beauty for the first time?

Explains Rashi that Avraham turned to Sarah and said that during a long *lech lecha* journey a woman usually loses her beauty, but you, my wife, stayed beautiful because *"yafah"* — which means *"Yah poh,"* Hashem is here with you.

"Because you spoke to Hashem all this time," Avraham said to Sarah, "you came out strong from this challenge and you're so much more beautiful in my eyes."

Unfortunately, a challenge can easily unravel the threads of a marriage, especially when fingers are pointed. But when a husband and wife transcend their pain and strengthen themselves with *emunah*, trust in Hashem, working together to encourage and support each other during those difficult, anguished moments, the relationship reaches heights that would otherwise be unattainable.

And the last precious jewel a wanderer can find during her *lech lecha* travails we learn from our Mother Rachel, whose *yahrtzeit* falls around the time *Parashas Lech Lecha* is read. There is no woman in the world who traveled a longer journey than she. First, she waited for her true *zivug*; then, for the birth of her first child. Nothing came easily to our Mother Rachel — not even her burial. For every gift in her life, Rachel had to wait; who if not she could teach us about the power of *Tefillas HaDerech*, the prayer for traveling?

When the Kohen Gadol entered the Kodesh Kodashim on Yom Kippur, the holiest day of the year, he said a short *tefillah* for *Am Yisrael*: that no woman miscarry, that the nation be blessed with bounty, and *shelo tikaneis lefanecha tefillas ovrei derachim*, that Hashem should not answer the prayers of those travelers who are asking for the rain to desist (*Yoma* 53b). On the holiest day of the year, these are the requests for which the Kohen Gadol found it so important to pray?

Yes, because the *tefillah* of someone who's on the *derech*, journeying along the road, is so precious in the eyes of the Ribbono shel Olam. The prayer of someone who is being challenged with *lech lecha*, of a Jew who's subjected to the pain of indefinite waiting — be it for a *zivug*, a child, the return of a lost son, *parnassah*, a *refuah*, or a *yeshuah* of any kind — reaches a special place in *Shamayim*.

Rachel Imeinu's message is so profound. Keep praying, my

dear children, she says to us. Don't forget that the *tefillah* of a "traveler" has enormous power! And when you are on your *lech lecha* journey, groping in the dark, she reminds us, don't worry. As Hashem promises: *yesh sachar lif'u'laseich* — "there is reward for your work" (*Yirmiyahu* 31:15). You will see that your prayers will not only help you, but they will help all of *Am Yisrael*.

Learning How to Wait

We Jews are no strangers to the waiting game. For every good deed we perform, we know that we will receive a reward in the World to Come. Instead of expecting instant gratification, we live with the knowledge that we are working toward a return that we will only later enjoy.

Yehi ratzon, may it be His will, that all of those who are traversing long winding roads will finally reach their *menuchah*, their comfort. And, as Hashem promised our mother Rachel, *v'shavu vanim ligvulam* — "the children will return to their boundaries [from their exiles]" (ibid. 31:16).

Back From the Dead

In *Parashas Vayeira*, we read about several instances of *techiyas hemeisim*, revivification of the dead. The first case is Sarah Imeinu, a barren ninety-year-old woman who gave birth to a son. Rachel Imeinu described it when she said, *Havah li vanim v'im ayin meisah anochi* — "Give me children — otherwise, I am dead" (*Bereishis* 30:1). Barrenness is akin to death. Similarly, the angels told Avraham Avinu before they informed him of the impending miracle of Yitzchak's birth, *Ka'eis chayah*, which can be interpreted as "Now you will merit life" (ibid. 18:10).

When Yishmael was dying of thirst, and his mother Hagar abandoned him, she said, *Al er'eh b'mos hayaled* — "Let me not see the death of the child" (ibid. 21:16). Suddenly, Hashem opened her eyes, and she saw a well of water. When she gave Yishmael to drink, he was miraculously revived.

In yet another episode of *techiyas hameisim* in *Parashas Vayeira*, Yitzchak lay on the altar, prepared to be sacrificed as an *olah*, a burnt offering to Hashem. At the last second, when the knife was on his throat, an angel called to Avraham, *Al tishlach yadcha el hana'ar* — "Do not stretch out your hand against the lad" (ibid. 22:12), and Yitzchak lived. The *Zohar* (addenda, *Bereishis* 252b) says that Yitzchak's name is composed of two words: *keitz chaya* — he was at the threshold of death, but then he came back to life.

In the haftarah to *Vayeira*, Elisha the prophet blessed the barren Shunami woman, who hosted him when he passed through her town, that she would bear a child. The miracle was indeed realized, but years later, when he returned to the family, the child fell dead. Utilizing his supernatural powers, Elisha brought the child back to life.

From death to life. From one instant to the next, everything changed.

Nothing Is Set in Stone

In the Talmud, Rabbi Yochanan tells us that *ein mazel l'Yisrael* — "the Jewish people's fate is not predetermined" (*Shabbos* 156a). Because we don't have a predetermined *mazel*, our fortunes and destiny can change at any time. In Hebrew, the word for nature is *teva*, the root of the word *matbei'a*, coin. *Teva* is Hashem's imprint, how nature usually manifests itself. A coin has two imprints, heads and tails. A coin that is tossed can fall on either side. By the flip of a coin, everything can change.

The Midrash (*Lekach Tov, Lech Lecha* 2) tells us about three very special coins that can be used to depict the concept of *ein mazel l'Yisrael*. One of these coins, used during the times of Avraham and Sarah, depicted an elderly couple on one side and a young couple on the other.

The second coin, which was used during the times of King David, showed a shepherd carrying a stick and a sack on one side. On the other side was a tower fortress, symbolizing the Temple that King David was promised that his son, Shlomo HaMelech, would build.

In the same vein, the third coin, which was used in the days of Mordechai and Esther, also depicted a miraculous change in nature that occurred during that time. While one side showed the *sak v'eifer*, the sackcloth and ashes of mourning that Mordechai donned after learning of Haman's nefarious plot, the other side featured the golden crown that adorned Mordechai's head after the Purim miracle.

All three coins were meant to deliver one message to the nation: the *mazel* of a Jew can change in the blink of an eye (or the toss of a coin!).

Tzechok: The Power of Holy Laughter

What is the secret to flipping our *mazel* from one side of a coin to the other? *Parashas Vayeira* shows us many ways to transform our *mazel*, including *tefillah*, tears, and *chesed*. After Avraham pleaded for his nephew's rescue, Lot was miraculously saved from the hands of his captors. So, too, when Hagar cried to Hashem for her child's recovery, he merited his salvation: *Vayifkach Elokim es eineha vateire be'er mayim* — "G-d opened her eyes, and she perceived a well of water" (*Bereishis* 21:19). As a result of her tears, Yishmael didn't succumb to dehydration.

However, I want to share with you the greatest secret of all. The real game-changer, we learn in *Parashas Vayeira*, is *tzechok*, laughter.

Laughter is a central theme in *Parashas Vayeira*. First, when Avraham hears that he'll be blessed with a child, he laughs (ibid. 17:17). When Sarah hears the news, she exhibits a similar reaction: *Vatitzchak Sarah* (ibid. 18:12). She says, "Whoever hears this will laugh at me" (ibid. 21:6). The very name Yitzchak personifies laughter.

Yishmael, too, is *metzacheik*, mocking (ibid. 21:9). And when Lot instructs his family to leave Sedom prior to its destruction, the *pasuk* tells us, "He was a laughingstock in the eyes of his sons-in law" (ibid. 19:14).

The word *tzechok* can be split into two, *tzei chok* — "go out of the laws." To experience true laughter, we must be able to transcend the laws of nature. For Jews, there's no such thing as being bound to the laws of nature; there is no defined *mazel*. Thus a Jewish home owns the capacity for real laughter, thanks to the knowledge that any situation can always change — and improve.

In the wicked city of Sedom, people mocked freely. What is the fundamental difference between the *tzechok* of *emunah* and the *tzechok* of Sedom? Holy laughter is meant to declare Hashem's greatness, indicating that we believe in His power to change our lives, whereas the cynical laughter of Sedom is intended to make Hashem less significant.

When you express your deepest emotions through laughter, dear women, you give yourself a chance to see the greater picture, to internalize the reality that you're in the Hands of Hashem, no matter what you're enduring. By allowing yourself to bask in the comfort of *emunah*, you're emulating our *Imahos* in the greatest of ways, transforming your home into a happy, peaceful place. Our faith allows us to see beyond the limitations of *mazel*, and into the joyous place of infinite possibility, because we are in the Hands of our infinite Creator.

How can we revive that lost laughter, especially when *tzei chok* seems like an impossibility to us? How can we learn to laugh the holy laughter that will work miracles in changing our *mazel* for the better?

Rav Wolbe gives us a beautiful answer in *Parashas Vayeira*. When women are productive, he suggests, when they use their potential to accomplish and perform, they become truly happy individuals. Because Avraham Avinu understood this well, he explains, he told Sarah that something good was about to happen, and he instructed, *Mahari…lushi va'asi ugos* — "Hurry up…knead the dough, and bake cakes for our guests" (ibid. 18:6).

When the angels asked about Sarah's whereabouts upon

their arrival, Avraham said to them, *Hinei va'ohel* — "Behold, in the tent" (ibid. 18:9). One commentary explains that due to her barrenness, Sarah was ashamed to go out among people. She was afraid people would say, "Here comes the barren woman." How does Avraham try to counter her feelings of sadness? By requesting that she bake cakes, that she do something productive to increase her positive energy.

Rav Wolbe says that when a woman bakes challah, she becomes happy. She looks at what she has created, those loaves that were a mere lump of flour and water just an hour earlier, and she realizes that thanks to her productivity, her loved ones will be well nourished.

I will never forget the massive challah bakes I attended in London and South Africa that were conducted as part of the worldwide Shabbos Project initiative. When I looked around the room in London filled with 4,000 women, I thought to myself, *Would all of these women show up if they knew I'd be addressing, say, the topic of tznius?* It was the movement of those 8,000 hands kneading, kneading, kneading that gave those women power. It filled them with a sense of mission like nothing else. It brought back their lost laughter.

When we believe that HaKadosh Baruch Hu can bring salvation in the blink of an eye, that nothing is beyond His reach, and that no matter what situation we are in we rise up like yeast, fill our homes with the aroma of challah, and keep accomplishing without losing faith, then we will merit that HaKadosh Baruch Hu will bring true laughter into our lives.

No Fear

"Yemima, how can you tell me to laugh when I'm suffering so much?" When a woman is in pain, she just can't see beyond the challenge that weighs down heavily on her heart. It's so hard to laugh then! But for this, too, the Torah portion of *Vayeira* offers a solution.

In *Parashas Vayeira*, we find many references to the Hebrew root for sight, *reish alef hei*. Even in the very first *pesukim*, the word *vayar* is used twice in one sentence. *Vayisa einav vayar v'hinei sheloshah anashim nitzavim alav vayar vayaratz likrasam* — "He lifted his eyes and he saw: behold, three men were standing over him; he perceived, and he ran toward them" (*Bereishis* 18:2).

Why is the word *vayar* repeated? Rashi explains that the first "he saw" means that he simply *saw* the angels coming. From the second *vayar* we learn that he *perceived*. He didn't only see three people at face value. He perceived that the reason they stopped at a distance was because they didn't want to trouble him in his weakened state.

Upon first glance, when Avraham saw three people approaching from the distance — three scruffy pagans — he was worried that their intent was to harm him. The first *vayar* can be vowelized into the Hebrew word for fear, *yirah*. Upon further observation, however, Avraham came to a new conclusion. They're hungry and thirsty, he suddenly perceived. They're guests.

Every first encounter stirs up fear within. Singlehood? I'm afraid. Marriage? I'm terrified. Pregnancy? How will I get through this? Birth? I can't even think about it. A difficult child, issues in school, and later, *shidduchim*. The first moment has us cowering in fear.

However, dear Jewish women, there's no reason to fear. The Torah teaches us that the secret to a good life is not to take things at face value. Only the first glance invokes fear. Wait a moment. If you only take the time to look again, a new scene will unfold before your eyes. Instead of seeing an Arab idolater, you will see a hungry guest. You will see a holy angel who's coming to impart an exhilarating message. If you zoom out of your challenge, you will discover a clearer, more pleasant picture. This vantage will fill you with the energy and clarity to laugh despite the hardship, dear women. It will help you become unstuck from the pain that feels so unbearable, the pain that makes every breath an ordeal.

The *Nisayon* – and the Lesson – of the *Akeidah*

When I go to comfort a woman who has lost her husband or child to an illness, I usually say to her, "You've suffered a double loss. You didn't only lose your husband or child. You also lost a part of HaKadosh Baruch Hu. You prayed to Him, you relied on Him, you put your faith in Him. You said, '*Hashem rofeh cholim,*' with such intensity. And now you're wondering, *How did this happen, Ribbono shel Olam?*"

This is the *nisayon* of *Akeidas Yitzchak.*

"Come," HaKadosh Baruch Hu had said to Avraham as He led him outside. "Gaze now, toward the heavens, and count the stars if you are able to count them" (*Bereishis* 15:5). In the same way the sky is studded with countless stars, Hashem had indicated, Avraham's offspring would be plentiful. And what happened in *Parashas Vayeira*? Suddenly Hashem instructed Avraham, "Please take your son, your only one, whom you love" (ibid. 22:2) — and bring him as an offering on the altar.

How could this be happening? What suddenly happened to the promise that Avraham had held on to with so much hope, with so much joy?

Often, women who are struggling with a challenge will say to me, "I don't understand. For this I reached this point? I got so many promises, and suddenly everything turned around on me. It seems to me that Hashem forgot about me. How can I manage this *nisayon*?"

It is then that we have to take a step back and take a second look.

Let's hear what Reb Nosson, the disciple of Rebbe Nachman of Breslov, the great consoler, says on this subject. Why was the *nisayon* of the *akeidah* so difficult?

"To a person of Avraham's level of righteousness, the challenge wasn't all that great. To me it seems that even simple people would withstand the challenge if Hashem would instruct them explicitly to sacrifice their only child on the altar."

If you would hear Hashem's command in your ears, would you think twice before fulfilling His wish? But, continues Reb Nosson, the essence of the *nisayon* lies in Avraham's words, said as he led his son off toward the altar: "Stay here by yourselves with the donkey, and I and the lad will go yonder — *ad koh*" (ibid. 22:5).

At that point, Avraham was able to remember a conversation he had had with Hashem, when Hashem said to him, *Ki veYitzchak yikarei lecha zara* — "For through Yitzchak will be called your offspring" (ibid. 21:12). And now, suddenly, he was instructed to sacrifice the child from whom he was promised to merit plentiful offspring. That was the crux of the challenge! How could the promise of *koh yihyeh zarecha* — "So will be your offspring" (ibid. 15:5) be fulfilled (*Midrash Tanchuma, Vayeira* 23)?

When he was told to sacrifice his son, Avraham said to his servants, "I and the lad will go yonder — *ad koh*." The blatant conflict of the two usages of *koh* had the potential to undermine all of his confirmations of faith.

However, this was exactly when Avraham reached the zenith of his faithfulness. He strengthened himself and proclaimed, "Even if I don't understand His ways, I am obligated to do my part and walk my son toward the altar. Despite all this, I believe that Hashem will fulfill His oath to me because He is capable of reconciling two opposing commands."

"Avraham raised his eyes and *perceived* the place from afar" (ibid. 22:4). This is the challenge of faith: to take a step back and observe the scene from a distance.

Reb Nosson continues to explain a most poignant concept. He notes that it's written in the Gemara that all the prophets prophesied using the word *koh: Koh amar Hashem* — "So says Hashem." Only Moshe Rabbeinu prophesied with the words *Zeh hadavar* — "This is the Word." Only Moshe's generation had the ability to experience the clarity of Hashem from up close, with a point of the finger. The other prophets expressed their *nevuah* with the word *koh:* it will be what it will be, but it is still in the distance.

As believing Jews, it is incumbent upon us to believe that only Hashem sees the end of the challenge. Only He perceives the full picture. For this reason, Avraham chose to name the site of the *akeidah* Hashem Yireh — "Hashem will see" (ibid. 22:14). When the total picture is taken into account, you are able to state, "Hashem, I understand that what You are doing is all good."

One day soon, Hashem will give us the ultimate clarity, but until He does so, we have to take a step back and try our best to take in the scene from a distance. The more we remove ourselves from a situation, the easier it will be for us to see the full picture — and to laugh despite the pain.

Living a Double Life

Parashas Chayei Sarah commences with the verse *Vayihyu chayei Sarah meah shanah v'esrim shanah v'sheva shanim shnei chayei Sarah* — "Sarah's lifetime was one hundred years, twenty years, and seven years; [these were] the years of Sarah's life" (*Bereishis* 23:1). The Ba'al HaTurim explains that the word *shnei*, years, can be defined as "two," as in *shnei chayei*, "two lives": her life before and after giving birth.

This can also allude to Sarah Imeinu's "double life." What type of double life did Sarah Imeinu lead? If we think of the challenges that she faced throughout the 127 years of her life, we would imagine that the life she led was one of sadness. First, she was barren. And the wandering! Imagine packing up and settling down, packing up and settling down the way they did. Isn't a forced nomadic lifestyle sufficient reason to sulk? Kidnaping, a husband at war with great kings... A difficult, struggle-filled life. Despite it all, however, the pious Sarah made a conscious decision to be happy, busying herself with outreach even in times of great distress.

Although her life circumstances theoretically entitled her to be embittered and depressed, she chose instead to move beyond her pain and create for herself a productive, satisfying life. Pain and happiness: a double life.

Through the Eyes of Faith

Says the Ben Ish Chai, every woman has the capacity to lead a double life: the natural life that she's handed from Above, and then the life she *chooses* to live. This is the life of a woman with faith. He tells a very special parable of a pair of Siamese twins who were embattled in a serious quarrel: while one twin wanted to get married, the other one insisted she wouldn't. In order to resolve their issue, they decided to consult with the scholar in their town.

"It's a very serious problem," the wise man said to them. "So what will we do? Now both of you sit on the floor," he commanded. He turned to the twin who didn't want to marry and said to her, "Stand up." Of course, she couldn't; her sister's weight was dragging her down. Then the scholar turned to the twin who was determined to get married and requested the same of her. This time, thanks to her utmost determination, the girl tore herself apart with much strength, and she was finally free to get married and lead an independent life.

Every morning, says the Ben Ish Chai, we women wake up attached to a Siamese twin. When we announce, "I want to be productive. I want to do so much today!" she counters, "No way! Today is not the day." What can we do, dear women, to push our way through to a beautiful independence? It is our duty to tear ourselves apart, to extricate ourselves from this negative voice of excuses that seeks to pull us only lower and lower.

This was the life of our mother Sarah: the life of a woman who insisted on seeing everything through eyes of faith. How did she do it? How did she pull off this elusive feat with such grace and dignity?

This is the million-dollar question. Rashi reveals her secret to us. Why, he asks, does the Torah list every digit of her life separately? Rashi famously answers that when Sarah was 100 years old, she was like a 20-year-old concerning her pious behavior, and when she was 20 years old, she was as beautiful as a 7-year-old. *Kulan shavin l'tovah* — "All of her days were equally good," he explains (*Rashi, Bereishis* 23:1).

What does it mean that every day was equally good? Sarah Imeinu possessed a rare characteristic that the famed Rav Yisrael Salanter spoke of often: she was a role model in the *middah* of *hishtavus*, seeing everything equally. When a situation was bad, she took it the same way as when it was good. When something negative happened in her life, it was *b'seder*. When something good came her way, it was *b'seder* too.

In this vein, the *mussar* giants explain Rashi's words *bat kuf k'bat chaf*, referencing Chapters *Kuf* and *Chaf*, 100 and 20, in *Tehillim*. While Chapter 100 opens with *Mizmor l'sodah*, a song that is sung to express gratitude and joy, Chapter 20 says, *Ya'ancha Hashem b'yom tzarah*, a chapter that is recited in times of pain and distress. When Sarah was in a situation represented by Chapter 20, when she was stricken with a challenge, "*b'yom tzarah*," she continued to serve Hashem and lead her life with the same positive attitude and acknowledgment of Hashem's kindness as when she was in Chapter 100 mode, a time of gratitude.

Everything for Good

This is the challenge. How can we always be connected to Hashem in the same way? How can we emulate Sarah in being "*bat kuf k'bat chaf*"? Answers the Sfas Emes, our mother Sarah lived with the word *l'tovah* — *kulan shavin l'tovah*. To her, everything that happened was for the good. When something good happened in her life, she saw it as a vehicle through which she could become a better person. And when a challenge came her way, she accepted it with the same clarity. Wow! Dear women, this is our work in this world — to take whatever Hashem sends us with grace and with clarity.

In *Parashas Chayei Sarah*, we read that *vaHaShem beirach es Avraham bakol* — "Hashem blessed Avraham with everything" (*Bereishis* 24:1). Interestingly, the interpretations for the word *bakol* are not only varied, but also clearly contradictory. While one commentary states that Bakol was the name of the daughter Avraham was blessed with, another says that the blessing was that he did *not* have a daughter because finding a husband for her would have been too arduous in the immoral generation in which he lived. Yet a third explanation for the word is that *bakol* has the numerical value of 52 — the same as the Hebrew word for "son," *ben* — meaning that Avraham was blessed with a son.

How can we understand these conflicting interpretations? We could, says the Sfas Emes, if we know who Avraham and Sarah were. The incredible blessing that Hashem blessed them with was that they had the capacity to say, *Kol d'avid Rachmana l'tav avid* — "Whatever Hashem does is for the good" (*Berachos* 60b). No matter what the blessing was, they felt blessed.

As a couple, Avraham and Sarah underwent so many painful challenges together, so many *nisyonos* that tested their faith, but because they worked toward leading this "double life" — looking at whatever happens and saying, "this too is for the good" — they were indeed blessed with a rich, fulfilling life. A positive person is the luckiest of all. What greater blessing can there be than seeing everything as a *berachah*?

Esther and Sarah

In his *sefer Pri Tzaddik*, Rav Tzadok HaKohen of Lublin offers a beautiful thought on this topic. He quotes the Midrash, which relates that Rabbi Akiva was once delivering a lesson, and his students fell asleep. In an attempt to wake them, he asked a question: "What message did Queen Esther see from the fact that she was the queen of 127 provinces? She saw that she was a descendant of Sarah Imeinu, who lived for 127 years" (*Midrash Rabbah, Bereishis* 58:3).

Now, let's stop for a moment to ask the obvious questions: How could the students of the esteemed Rabbi Akiva all fall asleep while he was teaching? This is Rabbi Akiva we are talking about! And, furthermore, how did the question he asked stir them awake?

When Queen Esther found herself in the unfamiliar, foreign palace of Achashveirosh, she cried to Hashem, "Sarah Imeinu can't be my role model. She was only in the palace of Pharaoh for one night, after which You struck him and she was able to leave. I'm here for five years, and I don't see a way out. This is so hard for me!"

These were her thoughts for a long, long time, until one day, in desperation, she decided to talk directly to Sarah. "Why don't you help your daughter?" she cried. And then she heard Sarah Imeinu's answer. "Do you think it was easy for me?" she heard her say. "It's true that I was in a foreign palace for only one night, but do you know that Avraham grew up in a place of idol worship and yet he chose to make a life for himself? I was surrounded by immorality all my life, but I chose to transcend it. Esther, dear, you could still be a queen. You have my blood. You could lead a double life."

That's when it happened: *Vatilbash Esther malchus* — "She clothed herself in her queenly robes" (*Esther* 5:1). She realized she *could* lead a double life.

The *talmidim* of Rabbi Akiva struggled with a similar issue as Esther. They looked at their rebbi and saw only his purity, his righteousness. "How are his words relevant to me?" they wondered. "He's way beyond me." By telling them the story of Esther, Rabbi Akiva was wisely imparting the message "You can be a Rabbi Akiva. You can lead a double life."

Yes, the situation that Hashem sent your way may not be ideal, dear sisters. But that does not have to deter you from leading a *"shnei chayei Sarah,"* a double life that is filled with *emunah* and joy.

When It Hits Home

But still, you may argue, at least Sarah was married to the most pious man in her generation. She may have struggled with insurmountable challenges, but she truly had a life partner, someone who understood her pain and walked the arduous path with her together. What if I'm in this alone because my husband and I are simply not compatible? For that too, dear women, we find consolation in *Parashas Chayei Sarah*.

One of the most charming *pesukim* in the Torah is in this portion. When Rivkah's family members asked her whether or not she would be willing to accompany Eliezer on his journey and to marry Yitzchak, the young girl answered with one word: *Eileich!* — "I will go!" (*Bereishis* 24:58).

Rivkah's quick response is quite contrary to the response I hear often from girls who are awaiting their *bashert*. The usual response is one of "How will I know that I didn't make a mistake?" I feel that specifically because girls are so anxious about *shidduchim* today they are at risk of actually making the very mistake of which they're so fearful. Even once a girl feels that the young man in question might be interesting for her, she then has to answer to too many other parties, involving herself in an awful lot of unnecessary contemplation and deliberation. Wouldn't it be so simple if we'd all learn from our mother Rivkah and say, "I will go"?

Rivkah's response doesn't only serve as a lesson for young women of marriageable age. It's instructive to every one of us, including those who already merited building a Jewish home. When a woman thinks, *I made a mistake in my choice…* she's dismissing Hashem's place in her marriage.

We know that finding one's partner is as hard as splitting the sea (*Sanhedrin* 22a). What happened at the splitting of the Red Sea? Two opposite entities, the water and the earth, allowed the other to infringe on their space. What a miracle! That's the only way a *shidduch* can happen and a marriage can last.

The Ba'al HaTanya tells us that the only way any *shidduch* ever occurs is because of a mistake in our logic. In his words, "All *shidduchim* happen through the lies of the matchmaker, and not according to the truth…because the power of logic would never allow us to finalize a match." To our human eyes, it seems like *we're* the ones making a choice — he looks good to her, she to him, so why not? And then, Yaakov wakes up in the morning and sees *v'hinei hi Leah* — "it is Leah," not Rachel (*Bereishis* 29:25). She's not the girl he'd intended to marry. Despite all the rigorous research and interrogations, you will always find that impossible flaw in your spouse. Always. How is that? Because of the mistake in the logic that the Ba'al HaTanya tells us about.

The Chizkuni notes in *Parashas Bereishis* that Adam understood that Chavah was his wife when he realized that one of his ribs was missing. And where did he find it? In her. The sign that you and your husband were meant for each other is when you complement each other: he has what you don't and you have what he doesn't. That's the perfect marriage.

You know you're for each other if you love to spend and he counts every penny; if you're a social butterfly and he's a hermit, always seeking peace and quiet; you live by early to bed, early to rise, and he has no relationship with the clock; you're super-family-minded, and he can forget to talk to his brother for months.

The stark differences between you and your husband are precisely the areas that can make your marriage shine.

In Hebrew, the word for match is *hatamah*, and people err by thinking that they have to be like *te'umim*, twins. Of course, we're so alike! We're meant to be a carbon copy of each other.

How can that ever be possible? Even twin sisters, who were

born to the same mother and were raised in the same home, are never exactly alike. The beauty of marriage is to build a relationship, to grow closer to each other, by having each party contribute his or her unique attributes.

Often, when a woman's marriage exasperates her, she asks two questions. In the back of her mind, the issues niggle at her and don't allow her any rest. She wonders, *Why didn't I see this before?* And, of course, *Is there a way for me to make this work?*

Celebrate the Differences

In this *parashah*, *Parashas Chayei Sarah*, the Ben Ish Chai writes that Eliezer was that "*shadchan* — the *shakran*." It's crystal clear to us that Yitzchak and Rivkah had opposing personalities. While his entire essence was one of *gevurah*, Rivkah's core was one of *chesed* and selflessness. How would Rivkah's family give the go-ahead? Eliezer, in his brilliance, created signs for himself. He said to Hashem that he'll know that he has met the right one when "the young woman to whom I will say, 'Please tip your pitcher and I will drink,' will say to me, 'Drink, and I will also give water to your camels'" (*Bereishis* 24:14).

It may seem that Eliezer worked according to a method that's against the Torah. How did he know that this was truly the way to determine who the right one for Yitzchak would be? Isn't this similar to when a girl and boy determine their suitability based on handwriting analysis or the verdict of a palm reader? Of course not. Avraham transmitted several signs to Eliezer, which Eliezer saw in Rivkah, and this was only one sign that he added to that list. However, the fact that he added this sign to his list is still another proof that HaKadosh Baruch Hu runs the world. He has us think in ways that may be against logic in order to bring us to our destined match.

If Hashem would allow us to think logically before finalizing a *shidduch*, this world wouldn't be perpetuated. He has to blind us for that moment, keep secrets from us, have us ask the right people at the right time, only because this world must have continuity. Of course, once the couple builds a solid marriage, the husband and wife will be smart enough to choose to ignore the differences, but until then, it would only work to move them apart.

As the good wife you want to be, learn to celebrate your differences and to appreciate how your strengths and his strengths can contribute to the beautiful blend that is a Jewish marriage. Like Rivkah, choose to jump into it and tackle the situation with a readiness that only a Jewish woman knows: *Eileich!*

It is my deepest wish that all of us merit to lead a double life, a noble existence with a deeper purpose, in spite of everything that life throws our way. Just like our righteous foremothers, buried in Me'aras HaMachpeilah, the "double" cave that symbolizes their mastery at leading double lives, may we merit to tear ourselves away from that voice of negativity and find the strength to say "*l'tovah*" all of our days. And when the differences between you and your husband are glaring, carry on smiling and know that, like Adam and Chavah, together you can make up a beautiful whole.

Recognition: The Greatest Need of All

arashas Toldos starts off with the birth of Yitzchak and Rivkah's twin sons, Yaakov and Esav, whose personalities and mind-sets were at two ends of the spectrum. From the age of thirteen, the essential differences between the two became apparent, with Esav turning to idols and Yaakov spending his day in the study halls. Esav was not only a hunter in the literal sense. He knew how to slyly trap his father by asking questions that made him appear unusually pious. Yaakov, on the other hand, was morally wholesome, saying what he thought and spending all his time immersed in Torah study. How did two children—twins! —turn out so strikingly different?

Commenting on the words *veRivkah oheves es Yaakov* — "Rivkah loved Yaakov" (*Bereishis* 25:28), Rav Shamshon Rafael Hirsch writes that perhaps Esav sensed this. Perhaps he felt that his mother's heart tugged in his twin's direction.

The very first need a child has upon his birth is that his existence be acknowledged. For this reason, HaKadosh Baruch Hu blessed every newborn child with a voice that doesn't befit his tiny size; you simply can't ignore a newborn's cry! Once he grows a little older, Hashem equips him with a charming smile so that his caregivers will feel the need to stay with him as much as they can. Later, this same child's need to feel acknowledged can unfortunately present itself through his rebellious behavior or provocative clothes. When Esav grew up, the clothes he wore were Nimrod's: clothes of *mered*, mutiny. This was his way of telling the world, "I am I. I'm an existing human being."

Why would a child feel the need to go to such defiant lengths in order to fulfill this innate need? Because every child, no matter what shell he constructs around his delicate soul, must feel that he is a "somebody." This is one way we can read the prayer we recite at a bris milah immediately before the child's name is announced: *Elokeinu v'Elokei avoseinu kayeim es hayeled hazeh l'aviv u'le'imo* — HaKadosh Baruch Hu, make this child feel that he exists in the eyes of his parents.

How can parents accomplish this critically important task? It's not enough for them to know in their hearts that they love the child. They need to transmit this love for him in as many ways as possible, via the use of all five senses.

Parenting: A Multisensory Experience

Rav Yonasan Eibeshitz tells us that it's amazing to observe from *Parashas Toldos* how our forefather Yitzchak mastered this task. He transmitted his feelings of love to his sons despite his blindness by making use of the other four senses. When Rivkah clothed Yaakov in Esav's garb, Yaakov immediately reacted by saying, *Ulai yemusheini avi* — "Perhaps my father will feel me" (*Bereishis* 27:12), because his father's embrace was something he was accustomed to, something he expected.

As Rav Yonasan points out, this is exactly what transpired. As soon as Yaakov entered his father's chamber, Yitzchak said to him, "Come close, if you please, so I can feel you, my son" (ibid.

27:21). When Yitzchak said, *Hakol kol Yaakov* — "The voice is Yaakov's voice" (ibid. 27:22), he again bonded with Yaakov, this time through his sense of hearing.

Then he connected to Yaakov through his sense of taste by eating the foods he brought to him. "Serve me and let me eat of my son's game," he requested of Yaakov (ibid. 27:25). "Come close, if you please, and kiss me, my son," the passage continues. And later, we read, *vayarach es rei'ach begadav* — "he smelled the fragrance of his clothes" (ibid. 27:27).

See on how many levels our holy forefather connected to his child!

For Yitzchak, parenting was clearly a multisensory experience despite his failing eyesight. In today's day and age, *multisensory* is a buzzword in the field of education. Teachers are instructed to provide their students with as many sensory experiences as possible during class in order to make the lesson most absorbable and everlasting. What lesson is more important for us to impart to our precious children than letting them know how much we love them, how much they mean to us?

Says Rav Yonasan, "How important it is to be a sensitive parent — a parent who uses all of the senses to connect to his children!" Only a child who receives enough loving touch, for which the Hebrew root is *masheish* (as in "*yemusheini*"), from her parents, feels that she has a *mamashus* — a presence. The role of a parent is not only to provide food and clothes for a child. More critically, it is to form a deep connection, one that is reinforced through all five senses.

Unfortunately, I find myself consoling mothers of fallen soldiers all too often. I remember one particular time when I went to comfort the mother of a young soldier who had been brutally stabbed to death in Tel Aviv. When I sat with his mother, she cried so hard, and I tried to console her by telling her that he's still with her. "He's here with you," I said to her. But do you know what she kept saying? "No, but I want to *touch* him!" Being able to touch our children, to envelop them in a warm embrace, is such a privilege. It's a merit we should not take for granted.

The pain of those children who are missing out on connecting to their parents through all of the senses may unfortunately lead them toward fulfilling this need from other undesirable sources. When a child does not receive a listening ear at home, he will manage to find someone who will listen. Sadly, when a child is not hugged and kissed as she grows up, she may seek out other sources to receive the loving physical touch she is sorely lacking.

Of course, as Jewish mothers, our lives are one long tale of flurry and frenzy. Between taking care of the basic needs of the children, and the basic upkeep of the home, there isn't much time left to connect. But we must keep in mind that this is of paramount importance. Dear Jewish mothers, your child will appreciate your loving embrace so much more than an elaborate dinner. He will cherish the quality time you spend with him infinitely more than the latest gadget. Your child's physical needs are almost petty when it comes to fulfilling his emotional needs. If you want him to feel that he is *mamashus*, a "somebody," there is no one in the world who can transmit this message to him better than you.

Bless Your Child

Even more important than transmitting your love via your five senses — such as looking into the child's eyes, embracing him, and listening to his concerns — is the last part of Yitzchak's interaction with Yaakov: *vayevarcheihu* — "and he blessed him" (*Bereishis* 27:23).

There is nothing like the blessing a parent gives her child. When Esav entered the room to learn that the blessings had already been given to his brother, he cried, *Halo atzalta li berachah* — "Have you not reserved a blessing for me?" (ibid. 27:36). The letters of the word *atzel* can also be read as *eitzel*, near. A pained Esav asked his father, "Am I not close enough to you to merit receiving your blessings?" To a child, his parent's blessing is a sign of closeness.

Every time we speak to our children with positivity, every time we point out their strengths, we are bestowing them with blessings, and this is the ultimate closeness they crave. To start off a rebuke with derogatory, critical words, or to use them ever, gives the child an unspoken message that he is not beloved. Even when we must rebuke our children, if we do so in a positive way, if our children sense that we want only the best for them and we speak from a place of love, they will welcome our words.

Do You Believe in Your Child?

Utilizing the five senses to express love, however, is only a manifestation of the love you must feel inside. The only way your interactions of bonding can be authentic is if you truly appreciate your child in your heart. It's easy to feel that bond if your child is sweet, happy, and obedient. Of course you love him! But let's understand how we can reach that connection when dealing with a difficult child, the child who keeps pushing your buttons.

In *Parashas Toldos* and the Torah portions preceding it, it's difficult to understand the stories we read. Why does life have to be so trying? Avraham and Sarah waited for decades to have a child of their own. Finally, when they merited raising a child together, Sarah didn't merit to live to see *nachas* from him. When Yitzchak married Rivkah, the troubles started all over again. For years, they yearned for a child of their own, and when Hashem answered their prayers, Rivkah, the new mother, was appalled to see that her baby son was covered in a blanket of red. Why does everything have to be so *complicated*?

I would like to teach you something about *berachah*, what

blessing truly means. When something comes to you through toil, realize that it's a blessing. If you receive something *b'kalut*, easily, that's a *klalah*. Whatever comes easily can also depart from us easily.

Our Sages teach us that after Rivkah instructed Yaakov to don Esav's clothes and perform deeds that went directly against the integrity of his character, he told her, "This is how you want me to accept the blessings from my father? If I deceive him, he is liable to even curse me." She answered, "Listen, my child. This is how we receive blessings. They don't come easily. *Alai kilelascha* — 'Upon me shall come your curse' (*Bereishis* 27:13)." We have to accept the risks and hardships in order to receive blessings.

Children are a blessing, and that's why children are accompanied by challenge from the very start. Right after Yitzchak blessed Yaakov, whom he was sure was Esav, Esav suddenly entered the room. As soon as Yitzchak grasped what had occurred, he realized he'd made a mistake. His immediate reaction was *Vayecherad Yitzchak charadah gedolah* — "Yitzchak trembled in very great perplexity" (ibid. 27:33). He was instantly overcome with anxiety because, according to Rashi, he saw Gehinnom open up before his feet when Esav stepped into the room. He couldn't believe that the child who he thought was pious was indeed wicked. The challenge of raising children!

This very same anxiety gripped the heart of our mother Rivkah. When she was carrying her two children, every time she passed the non-Jewish house of worship, Esav would move vigorously, and when she'd pass a *beis midrash*, Yaakov would move. This confused and frightened Rivkah, thinking she was carrying one child with interests in idolatry as well Torah, and she cried, *Lamah zeh anochi* — "Why am I like this?" (ibid. 25:22). She didn't understand why she would be given such a child.

Later, Yitzchak and Rivkah learned the answer. As parents, we often ask ourselves, *Where did we go wrong? How did I make a mistake like that?* But then we discover the truth. Children, the greatest blessing of all, are accompanied by sorrow, by guilt, by confusion. *Vayecherad Yitzchak charadah gedolah.* When Yitzchak realized that the child who he thought was pious was indeed wicked, he trembled with anxiety. But then what did he do? He blessed him too.

Children can bring us *tza'ar*, children could bring us pain, but children are a blessing nevertheless. Why does it have to be this way? Why can't we merit miracles: to receive children who fill our hearts with only joy from the very first moment? Why does every step of the way entail such hardship?

If we want to merit miracles, we have to work toward receiving them. We can't be like Esav, who came home tired and hungry and couldn't be bothered to cook his next meal, selling his birthright, instead, for a bowl of lentils. In order for Yaakov to receive the blessings, he was charged with a difficult task: to risk his spiritual essence of truth and perpetrate a falsehood against his father.

It isn't easy to raise a child, not in previous generations and definitely not today. But at the times when *chinuch* seems hardest, when the child is taking us to Gehinnom and back, that's when miracles happen.

As mothers, we were blessed with the task of *giddul banim*, raising children. It is our duty to bring our precious children into the world, and to nurture their bodies and souls in order for them to grow into the best servants of Hashem they can be. Along the path to this ideal goal, our children will be faced with challenges, some of which we will guide them through and others that they'll be forced to overcome on their own. The greatest gift we can give our children is the knowledge that we are there for them, that even when they're not in our presence, we *are* there, and we know that they'll make us proud. Because when a child feels that his parents believe in him, he will eventually come back to prove it to them. Believe in your children, dear mothers, believe in them! And in the merit of your hard work, may you see miracles.

The Plants Need Water Too

In *Parashas Toldos*, we confronted Rivkah's untold distress of *Lamah zeh anochi* — "Why am I like this?" (*Bereishis* 25:22). Why did You choose me, Hashem? Why do I have to be the one to raise a child who has aspirations for idol worship in my home?

Do you know that look of *Lamah zeh anochi* that you some-times spot in a weary mother's eye? Let's learn from another of our mothers, Rachel Imeinu, how a mother can deal with that emotion.

The Midrash (*Midrash Aggadah, Bereishis* 53:1) tells us that there are seven barren women in *Tanach*: Sarah, Rivkah, Rachel, Leah (secondary infertility), Chanah, the mother of Shimshon, and Zion (as it says, *Sos tasis v'sageil ha'akarah* — "Bring intense joy and delight to the barren one [Jerusalem]"). Why seven? Each of these women represent one day of the week: Sarah represents Sunday, Rivkah Monday, and so on.

Which aspect of Yom Sheini personifies Rivkah's unique pain? On Monday, HaKadosh Baruch Hu created the skies; He decid-ed that this body of water will always be above, and this one will always be below. Why, asks Rivkah, do you give a mother two children with such divergent paths? One son is above: he's sitting and learning, growing closer to You, and living with truth. The other is so low, so stuck in the depths of the *tehom*, the abyss. Why did You create these profound differences between them?

Our Sages offer an exquisite explanation for Rivkah's bafflement. The waters below are known as *mayim bochim*, the weeping waters. These waters cry because they also crave to be close to Hashem. When Hashem gives you a child who is not like the others, *lo aleinu*, not like his "Yaakov" brothers, He's doing so in order to transform you into *mayim bochim*, into a crying *ima*. This child is there to teach you something about tears. And this lesson speaks to so many of us mothers: I know hardly a family today in which HaKadosh Baruch Hu hasn't put such a child.

You may wonder: Is it right for Mommy to cry in front of her children? Shouldn't we be strong and assertive to reassure them that they have someone to lean on always? Let's learn the true meaning of a crying *ima* from our mother who's been crying for thousands of years, Rachel Imeinu.

In *Parashas Vayeitzei*, Rachel appears before Yaakov: *V'Rachel ba'ah im hatzon asher l'aviha ke ro'ah he* — "Rachel had arrived with her father's flock, for she was a shepherdess" (*Bereishis* 29:9). In Lashon HaKodesh, this verse reads strangely because *rachel* also means "sheep." So what did Yaakov see: a flock of sheep or their shepherd?

The Sages explain that Rachel was both: she was the paradigm of a mother. On the one hand, she was that loving, caring shepherd who gave her sheep the sense of security they craved. On the other hand, she was also an *ima-a-a-a*, a crying and helpless sheep. In her feminine depth of understanding, she recognized the importance of both approaches.

When I speak of a crying mother, I don't refer to the times when life circumstances are trying. Of course that would bring a mother to tears. I'm speaking about crying when life is normal.

I have such fond memories of my grandmother, *aleha*

hashalom, who would cry so often in front of us grandchildren. When we came, she cried. When she watched us eat and enjoy her food, she cried. When we left, she cried again.

Rav Shlomo Wolbe, *zt"l*, the renowned *chinuch* giant, was known to say that when he was growing up in prewar Europe, he would watch his mother cry while lighting the candles every Friday night. He would say to her, "Mama, I'm okay. Why are you crying?" And without fail, every time, she would answer softly, "Shloimele, I'm crying for your future. I want you to have a good life." Rav Wolbe said that every time he faced a *nisayon*, he would tell himself, *You will be okay. Mama cried for you.*

Today this concept may seem foreign to mothers. At the parenting classes, the focus is on being positive, that shining light in your child's life. Dear mothers, the sunshine is definitely crucial for your saplings, but where is the rain? Your children need water, water, water.

It's Okay to Look Helpless, Ima

How can a crying mother help her children flourish as individuals and grow up to be healthy, independent adults?

During the time when Eretz Yisrael was hit by a wave of knife attacks, I heard a prominent *rav* lecture on the topic. He noted that what made the volatile circumstance so unique was that until then people were able to pacify themselves by saying, "The army will take care of it," "The police will keep the peace." This time, however, it was a one-on-one battle — one that each individual victim was left to fight with his own two hands — which is why we started seeing some rather strange sights: women holding rolling pins as they made their way to work, or people walking with oversize umbrellas when the sun was bright and cheerful. In this war, people knew that no one would do the work for them. They had to do it themselves.

And this is the challenge of our generation worldwide. The

challenge of *chinuch* is immense. All it takes is an iPhone, a few minutes of access, and the battle is lost. It's a one-on-one struggle, and by then we have no way of saving the souls of our children.

My husband had the merit of opening a yeshivah, which he named Avnei Kodesh, inspired by the words of a verse in *Eichah*: *Tishtapheichnah avnei kodesh b'rosh kol chutzos* — "The sacred stones are scattered at the head of every street" (*Eichah* 4:1). It breaks the heart to see how these diamonds, who often come from beautiful families and top yeshivos, are forced to wage this one-on-one battle.

A boy will come to my husband and say, "Take my iPhone for one week," or "Hide it from me for one month." What suddenly happened that this young man was able to disconnect from his dangerous lifeline? From where did he have this *ko'ach*? Maybe, I think, it happened because for the first time in his life, when his parents brought him to this place, he saw them helpless. And maybe, when he saw his *ima* looking like a little sheep, so dependent on her Shepherd to show her the way, he thought to himself, *Even Ima can't help me now. I must protect myself. Of course, she can daven for me. She can even prepare clean clothes and nutritious meals, but it's my yetzer hara, and I will fight it.*

When these diamonds see their *ima* shedding tears, when they observe her unabashed helplessness, they learn to take the reins.

Rashi teaches us in several instances, *Lameid leshoncha lomar eini yodei'a* — "Train yourself to admit, 'I don't know.'" Dear Jewish mother, teach yourself to say, "I do not know. Yes, I am a shepherd, but, like Rachel Imeinu, I am also a *rachel*, a lost sheep looking for a way to her child's heart, hoping for him and waiting for the day when my child won't be in the lower waters, but rather in the upper waters, the waters that merit closeness to Hashem and His Torah."

Where Did My Tears Go?

What happens when you do your best to storm the heavens, but you feel that the gates haven't opened? Like Rachel, you may be praying desperately to be granted a child, or, like Rivkah, you may be beseeching that the child you bore come closer to Hashem and His Torah, but you don't see that your *tefillos* were answered.

Why hasn't Hashem answered you yet? In *Parashas Vayeitzei*, we're let in on a secret regarding the way Hashem runs His world: "Hashem prolongs the salvation for the righteous and supplies it immediately to the wicked" (*Bereishis Rabbah* 68:5). The one who is truly righteous must fight her way to her *zivug*, fight her way to fertility, to prosperity, to shed a few pounds.

But it doesn't seem fair! Why does it seem that only the wicked ones enjoy such a smooth life? What would be wrong if we'd receive blessings and trials according to our deeds?

The Yefeh To'ar enlightens us with a stunning explanation. A righteous person desires to see everyone in a positive light. She wants to say, "Hashem, she's a good person, she's a good person, and she's a good person." Hashem doesn't want the cause and effect to be so evident in this world so that when one person receives a blessing everyone will know she did a good deed and if, G-d forbid, she is stricken with a challenge, everyone will know that she had committed a sin. If a young woman has a hard time finding her *zivug*, she would berate herself for being no good. And everyone around her would think the same. If that would be the case, it would be a difficult, almost impossible task to view people, including ourselves, as righteous.

Because of the righteous person's desire to see everyone in a good light, Hashem instituted a system that challenges the *tzaddik's* own life: a system that can end up filling his life with trials and tribulations. Only because the *tzaddik* does not want to be aware of the shortcomings of the people around him, Hashem decreed that life's happenings should not be associated with the person's deeds, good or bad.

So, dear beautiful women, if you are suffering, you can stop berating yourself right now. Not only are you not the bad person you've been telling yourself you are, but you are indeed a *tzaddeikes*!

Danger: Jealousy!

The Rebbe of Izhbitz says that we must realize that when we suffer deeply, the emotion that withholds blessings from us is jealousy. The pain in itself, he says, awakens envy within. Even a righteous person who otherwise *"fargins"* others involuntarily experiences jealousy when he is suffering. *Vatekanei Rachel ba'achosah* — "Rachel envied her sister" (*Bereishis* 30:1) — even the pious, loving sister Rachel was jealous of Leah. Says the Rebbe of Izhbitz, sometimes a person's entire fortune may be withheld because of the jealousy she feels toward those who were already blessed.

How hard it is to stand at your younger sister's *chuppah* and pray on her behalf! How very, very hard. But, dear Jewish daughter, battle the jealousy in your heart. You must, says the Rebbe of Izhbitz. You must! A jealous woman, he says, is like a woman who wants to enter a house. She knocks on the roof and she knocks on the walls, but she doesn't knock on the door. Sometimes we're so busy with what others have that we lose focus on knocking on the door that will generate our own blessings.

Instead of envisioning how good and beautiful the life of your friend or sister or neighbor is, instead of knocking on her door and prying it open in your creative mind, you can knock on the gates of Heaven. That's where your focus should be.

It's so hard not to feel jealous, and it's so easy to fall into the trap when you're in pain. In general, I consider myself a person who is gracious to others. I was sure that this was my strength, until I learned that it isn't. After my young son Yosef Chai passed away due to heart disease, I was happy for every mother whose child left the Intensive Care Unit alive. Still, I couldn't rid myself of the thought, *Why couldn't my child come out of here alive? Why didn't he merit a refuah sheleimah?*

So what can we do? We all want the best of everything, don't we? If you're waiting for your salvation, dear women, know that jealousy is the last barrier you must break before the light enters your life. And you can battle it by starting with one word, *todah*. Every time you thank, the jealousy in your heart downsizes one tiny bit. The more you keep saying it, the smaller and smaller it will become. This is a promise from Rav Chaim Palagi. It is your secret pass to your *yeshuah*. The more you focus on the gifts you have, the less you'll think about what's missing.

Often a blockage does not allow the birth you're waiting for to happen. Be it the birth of a child, the birth of a *shidduch*, the birth of hope. What can you do to merit the "*toldah*"? Accustom yourself "*l'todah*," to thank. (*Toldah*, "children," and *l'todah*, "to thank," have the same Hebrew letters.) Even if it seems to you that your prayers haven't been answered, the positivity this practice will engender in your heart and home will make your life rich and beautiful. And with a grateful heart, you will see salvation everywhere you turn.

Lessons From the Martyrs

We live in a time of *hester panim* — G-d's Presence is concealed from us. In such trying times, who can bring the *geulah*? The Maharal explains beautifully that only the people who are very *nistar*, very concealed, can reach the crevices in which HaKadosh Baruch Hu hides.

In *Parashas Vayishlach*, we read about Yosef's behavior for the sake of *tznius:* he hid his mother Rachel's beauty so that Esav wouldn't lay his eyes upon her (*Rashi, Bereishis* 33:7). What was he doing? Yosef foresaw that his descendant would be Mashiach ben Yosef, and he understood that a being so pure and holy could only emerge in the merit of *tznius*, from the hidden strength of his mother, Rachel.

In the infamous Har Nof massacre, our nation lost four *kedoshim*, all of whom were particularly exemplary in the characteristic of modesty. These were people you probably never have heard of, if not for this horrific tragedy.

When I went to console Chaya, the holy wife of Rav Kalman Levine, may Hashem avenge his blood, she said to me that she waited for her *zivug* for quite some time. When she finally met her future husband, he said to her, "If you plan to have a famous *rav* for a husband, it won't happen with me. I want to be the man who sits in the corner seat of the *beis midrash* — the one nobody knows."

Rav Levine made one exception to this rule of living in modesty: the only occasion when he went against his unassuming nature and spoke to the public was after terrorist attacks. Then, even his children knew that Abba would be giving what they called his "*pigua* (terrorist attack) speech." What was the topic of this talk?

"He would tell everyone around him," reminisced Chaya, "that they please not miss out on this auspicious time. 'Whenever a *pigua* happens,' he would say, 'we start asking questions: What happened? To whom? Where? But this is not the time for these questions. It is the time to ask for Mashiach. It is the time when we could storm the heavens because even Hashem is angry at these moments.' This was the only occasion when my husband would talk to the public."

Yaakova, the holy wife of Rav Aryeh Kupinsky, may Hashem avenge his blood, who was also cruelly murdered while davening in the *beis midrash*, said to me that her husband's main message was *achdus*. This virtuous couple lost their daughter Chana Chaya two years ago when she simply did not wake up from her sleep one morning. "Yemima," Yaakova said to me when I went to sit with her, "I want to tell you what my six-year-old son asked me the other day."

When this young child learned of his father's passing, he said to his mother, "Since Abba was killed *al kiddush Hashem*, his soul merited to reach a high place in Gan Eden, but Chana Chaya died a natural death. So will he get to see her up there?"

What did the brilliant Yaakova answer her son, mature beyond his years? She said to him, "Up there there's only *achdus*. Yes, my dear child, Abba can see Chana Chaya once again."

One Big Picture

Let's speak about *achdus*, the virtue of this exalted *kadosh*. After Rachel gave birth to Binyamin, she passed away. And where was she buried? Along the way, so that her future children would have a place to pour their hearts out, so that she could cry along with them. Rachel cries that we should love each other; she waits for the day when we'll unite as one so that the *Geulah* can finally come upon us.

How can we do it? How can we finally beat Esav and win this endless war? Through love.

What is love? The numerical value of *ahavah* is 13, which is the *gematria* of the word *echad*. When we feel true love, we see everything as *echad*, as one. Yaakov worked for his beloved wife Rachel for a total of fourteen years. Fourteen years is a long, long time. But how did he see these years? *K'yamim achadim* — "as a few days" (*Bereishis* 29:20), because of his deep love toward her.

Often, we mentally draw up long lists of issues we have with the people around us. It's so easy for us to find reasons to be unhappy, especially with those dearest to us. But, dear women, if we feel true love toward these people — toward our husbands, our children, our in-laws, our friends — then it all becomes one; we don't see the nitty-gritty details that had bothered us before. We say, "So what?" and we move on.

Once, on my return trip from the States to Eretz Yisrael, a wise elderly man said to me during the plane ride, "Did you ever wonder why the way back to Eretz Yisrael is shorter than the way to America?" He explained that when we travel toward the States, we're traveling against the wind, but when we return, we're traveling in the same direction. Then he added, "It goes faster because we love Eretz Yisrael." When we love something dearly, we don't fret over the details anymore. Everything becomes one big picture.

In my previous experiences as a lawyer involved in divorce

cases, I realized something very interesting. When the *kesubah* is read at the *chuppah*, the couple does not pay attention to all the details this document discusses. When the love is there, the marriage contract is seen as one whole picture: as a part of the matrimonial ceremony. However, when, G-d forbid, strife breaks out and divorce happens, the husband and wife suddenly concentrate on every detail. It's not one long document anymore.

The holy widows said to me, "People from all stripes of *Yiddishkeit* came to comfort us." When so many different Jews come together for one cause, they realize that we are only different on the surface because when there's love, when there's *achdus*, we don't see the details anymore.

Every attribute or characteristic that Hashem grants us, dear women, can be used as a tool for growth or decline. There are times when we must shy away from the limelight and lead a life of privacy and times when we must speak up. There are times when we must be oblivious to the details, but then there are times when we must make it our business to notice them.

Focus on Those Details

When true love exists between two people, they focus on the tiny details of good in each other. When you choose to love your husband, your children, your students, you will find that there is so much beauty you hadn't seen before. Dear sisters, this is the secret to true *ahavah*, to true *achdus*: when the situation is negative, see everything as a whole, as *echad*. Don't fret over the small details. However, when you want to see the good, cherish every tiny detail. That's true love.

One of the holy widows, whose name I won't mention, told me that one of her greatest sorrows now that her husband was so tragically torn away from her is the memory of their mornings together. When her husband would return home from shul after Shacharis, she recalled, he would be in the greatest of moods, while she would be nervous and irritable until she had her first cup of coffee.

"The first thing I want to do when I get up from the *shivah*," she said to me, "Is go to his *kever* and ask him for forgiveness. I should have cherished those special moments with him, but instead I let my negativity get in the way."

The winter is an excellent time to cherish every tiny detail about those we love. Huddled on the couch with a hot cocoa, or even sitting around the Shabbos table on a long Friday night, gives you a beautiful opportunity to focus deeply on every precious member of your family. When you focus on the details of good in your loved ones, the love and warmth will spread.

Rivkah and Rachel: Fearless Women

In *Parashas Vayishlach* we encounter several instances of fear and anxiety. First we meet Yaakov, who fears for his life and the life of his family at the thought of meeting his brother Esav. His fear stems from two opposing sources.

On the one hand, Yaakov understands that he stands to lose something infinitely precious. When we're gifted like that, we tend to think, *Ribbono shel Olam, You've given me so much. How can I be guaranteed that these blessings will remain with me forever?* We especially experience this kind of fear after a birth or a long-awaited *simchah* that fills our hearts with an unusual mix of joy and anxiety. *Katonti mikol hachasadim*, says Yaakov. "I have been diminished by all of the kindnesses" (*Bereishis* 32:11). This is the fear of the wealthy. Yaakov is concerned that perhaps the time has come for him to "pay" for the blessings in his life.

What's the antidote for this unpleasant fear? We find the answer in this Torah portion. Every time the thought of *Will I have to pay for this?* worms its way into your mind, take the initiative to pay back— with good.

After Yaakov's battle with the angel and his problems with

Dinah and the people of Shechem, HaKadosh Baruch Hu reminded him to fulfill the *nedarim* he'd pledged earlier. *Ma'aser*, *tzedakah*, and a *seudas hoda'ah*, a meal of thanksgiving, undoubtedly help toward warding off the fear that stems from feeling undeserving of blessings. Indeed, this is one of the reasons why a woman would offer a post-birth *korban* in the times of the Beis HaMikdash. Giving something back to Hashem does something to us; it allows us to breathe more freely, to know that we've paid back, albeit in a small way.

This, tells us the Ben Ish Chai (*Re'eh* 17), is why a person should host a celebratory meal on his birthday. In the exquisite words of David HaMelech, the one person who knew fears like no one else did, *Nidru v'shalmu laShem Elokeichem kol sevivav yovilu shai lamora* — "Make vows and fulfill them to Hashem, your God; all who surround Him will present gifts to the Awesome One" (*Tehillim* 76:12). The *mora*, which also means the "fear," will be obliterated through the *shai*, the gifts. When you feel overwhelmed with gratitude, take the opportunity to give back. Do something for Hashem; something small, but something significant.

When you offer a sacrifice, when you step out of your comfort zone for His sake, you are bringing the greatest *korban* that you can. Dear women, when you bring an offering to Hashem, your home is transformed into your Holy of Holies, your Kodesh Kodashim.

The second kind of fear is quite the opposite. It is the fear of remaining in the dark forever. When a woman experiences a stressful challenge, she's wont to entertain the thought of *Will I stay stuck here until the end? Will the sun never rise for me again? Will I never meet my bashert? Will the baby never come? Will this child never bring us any nachas?* This is an enormously draining type of fear that leaves us feeling both frustrated and hopeless.

For this fear, too, we find the solution in *Parashas Vayishlach*. This is the fear that disappears when the sun rises, when the morning star illuminates the sky.

The Midrash tells us that two men experienced fears: Yaakov and Moshe (*Bereishis Rabbah* 76:1). The women in *Tanach*, on the contrary, were generally fearless.

Indeed, it was Rivkah's fearless approach that accompanied Yaakov during his battles with his brother. He held on to her promise of *Alai kilelascha beni* — "Your curse will be on me, my son" (*Bereishis* 27:13) like a rescue line. The letters of the word *alai*, "on me," can be seen as an abbreviation of the names of the three people in his life who would trigger Yaakov's intense anxiety: Esav, Lavan, and Yosef. Through it all, he heard the voice of his mother in his ears: "I am with you, my son!"

However, at the time Yaakov needed his mother's strength most, Rivkah had passed away. He received the news under the tree called Alon Bachus, and he cried, "Ima, Ima, how will I manage without your *ko'ach*?"

The second woman in his life who taught Yaakov not to fear was Rachel. Sadly, at the age of thirty-seven, she, too, passed away. Later, in *Parashas Vayechi*, when Yaakov recalled this period in his life, he said to his children, *Va'ani b'vo'i miPadan meisah alai Rachel* — "As for me, when I came from Padan, Rachel died on me" (ibid. 48:7). There, too, *alai* alluded to the *ko'ach* of his mother Rivkah and his wife Rachel to ward off his fears. After Rachel's passing, he found himself grappling with a fear he hadn't encountered earlier: he was now alone.

The Jewish woman has the power of fearlessness in her genes: *Lo sira l'veisah* — "She fears not for her household" (*Mishlei* 31:21). She has no fear for her family. She has the ability to remain strong, to keep moving ahead.

Banish the Unfounded Fears

In today's era of constant anxiety, we are plagued with the reality of fear and terror. Of course, when tragedy strikes and we find ourselves surrounded by hordes who would prefer that we didn't exist, it's only normal that our hearts be filled with fear. But when we find ourselves in a fearful place, we should utilize the opportunity to reignite our belief in Hashem. *Will I ever marry off this child?* With the help of Hashem, you *will* see the light at the end of the tunnel. *Will all these blessings in my life last?* Very soon, you will see that this fear was all but a fantasy: a fear with no basis.

When the *Sar shel Esav*, Esav's angel, approaches Yaakov, ready for battle, Yaakov asked, "What's your name?" to which the angel replied, "I have no name. There is no name for fear." Baseless anxiety has no name because it's all in the mind. "But you, who won this battle, will receive a new name, Yisrael." Because Yaakov banished his fear and did what he had to despite his fearful nature, he received a name that personifies victory. *Ki sarisa im Elokim v'im anashim vatuchal* — "For you have striven with the Divine and with man and you have overcome" (*Bereishis* 32:29).

Every *shachor*, darkness, is followed by *shachar*, morning. *Vayizrach lo hashemesh* — "The sun rose for him" (ibid. 32:32). Very soon, all your fears will be obliterated. Once the morning star will rise in the sky, you will see that you aren't Yaakov anymore. You are Yisrael: the one who won the battle with the angel, the one who conquered his fear in order to come closer to Hashem.

Yamim Rabim: The Ability to Wait?

Let's discuss the term *vayeishev*, the beauty of living with *yishuv hada'as*, peace of mind, to be able to sit, calm and settled, when the world around you is a *balagan*, a mess. What is it like to have the peace of mind of Yosef HaTzaddik, or of Tamar, even in the darkest, loneliest moments? How did they do it?

Parashas Vayeishev is steeped in tragedies and unpleasant events. In this one Torah portion, Yosef was sold by his brothers, Potifar's wife slandered Yosef's name, the righteous Tamar's wicked husbands died, and she became involved in a problematic relationship with her father-in-law, Yehudah. Still, these heroes were like candles, giving off light even when their situations were utterly bleak. How did they do it? How did they remain unaffected by their plight?

The key to living a life like this is a beautiful expression we find in *Parashas Vayeishev*: *yamim rabim* — "many days." Both Yosef and Tamar knew the secret: to wait, wait, wait with patience. Yes, it may take time for the salvation to come, but to wait with patience is the secret to survival.

When Yosef was imprisoned on false charges, he didn't know how long it would be before he'd be a free man again. Still, he chose to wait patiently. For twelve years he sat behind bars, thoughts of revenge never crossing his mind. When he saw other prisoners in distress, he approached them and asked, "Why do you appear downcast today?" (*Bereishis* 40:7). His perspective differed drastically from those of Pharaoh's foolish cupbearer and baker, who wanted immediate interpretations of their dreams. How many years had Yosef waited for *his* dreams to come true?

In the same vein, Tamar sat and waited. After the death of her two husbands, the eldest sons of Yehudah, she dreamed of the day when Yehudah would allow her to marry his third son, Sheilah, whose name alludes to the word for "illusion." Although this was all a dream in Tamar's mind, she waited patiently. *Vayirbu hayamim* — "Many days passed" — as she sat in her father's home and waited (*Bereishis* 38:12).

So, too, our father Yaakov knew the secret of "many days." *Vayisabel al bno yamim rabim* — "He mourned for his son many days" (ibid. 37:34).

Yamim rabim is power. If you want to see the light, the happy ending, be it with *shalom bayis, parnassah, nachas,* or *shidduchim,* you must learn to wait, dear Jewish women.

What can you do when the going gets tough? When Potifar's wife tried in vain to entice Yosef to sin, the visage of his father, Yaakov, appeared to him and encouraged him to remain strong and unrelenting (*Rashi, Bereishis* 39:11, quoting *Sotah* 36b). The challenge Yosef faced was profound, but it was this image that provided him with the proper perspective and a reminder of the long-term negative consequences that would result by giving in to his inclination.

Like the pious Yosef, visualize the image of our father Yaakov, of how he waited many days for his own salvation. Don't allow whatever difficult circumstances you are facing to cloud your clarity, your perspective of the larger picture. And let Yosef's words to his brothers (when they left him to tell Yaakov that Yosef was alive) ring in your ears: *Al tirgezu badarech* — "Do not become agitated on the way" (ibid. 45:24). Yes, it's a long journey, but do not give up. Draw closer to HaKadosh Baruch Hu and you will make it through.

The Greatest Pain in the World

The sorrows that Yosef and Tamar endured in *Parashas Vayeishev* share a common denominator: they both suffered the pain of abandonment by those who should have cared for them. The pain of feeling uncared for by your very own flesh and blood surpasses all other anguish in the world. How I cry for the young women who suffered at the hands of their father or mother!

A woman once sent me such a tragic message. "Yemima," she wrote to me, "how can I learn to love a husband or a child when I've never learned what it means to love? It is language I don't know. If you don't absorb love in the home, how can you ever feel it?"

I cried when I read her words because she so aptly described the deep, deep void in her life. There is nothing more excruciating than living with this loneliness.

When family members withhold their love or, even worse, express their hatred, the fire of love is extinguished in a child's heart. The saddest of all is when a child or sibling is treated like a stranger. The Ohr HaChaim interprets the verse "They saw him from afar" (*Bereishis* 37:18), to mean that Yosef's brothers perceived him as a stranger. At that moment, they closed the gates of love in their hearts. They suppressed their brotherly affection and chose instead to cause him untold harm.

Yosef, in his innocence, asked a passerby, who was actually the angel Gavriel, about the whereabouts of his brothers. "My brothers do I seek," he said. "Tell me, please, where are they pasturing?" (ibid. 37:16).

And Gavriel answered, *Nasu mizeh* — "They have journeyed from here" (ibid. 37:17). Yosef understood him in the literal sense, but Rashi gives a deeper interpretation to Gavriel's words that would have frightened Yosef greatly.

"You asked about your *brothers*, but they have gone away from the feeling of *achvah*, brotherhood." How tragic! The *Da'as Zekeinim MiBa'alei HaTosafos* explains (on *Bereishis* 37:17) that the *zeh* in the word *mizeh* has the numerical value of 12. *Nasu mizeh* — "They have journeyed from here" — means that the brothers have traveled away from their brotherhood of twelve brothers.

The angel implied to Yosef that he was no longer a part of a twelve-brother unit because his brothers weren't interested in him any longer. Instead, they had gone to Dosan, from the word *das*, law, to seek legal grounds to put him to death.

In his commentary on this painful verse, the Ohr HaChaim says something that always makes my innards curdle: "Your brothers have gone to find the grounds on which to justify their hatred, as if hatred comes from religion, from halachah,"

Dear sisters, how I cry when I read these words! How many parents and siblings distance themselves from a dear, broken family member "on the grounds of Torah." What can be further from the truth? To tear apart a Jewish heart because of jealousy, to preserve an image or to make your life easier — and to say it is on "Torah grounds" — that is nothing more than justifying unjustifiable hatred.

Tamar, too, suffered the pain of familial abandonment. After her husbands, the eldest sons of Yehudah, died for their sins, Yehudah promised her his third son, Sheilah. "Remain a widow in your father's house until my son Sheilah grows up" (*Bereishis* 38:11). In her innocence, Tamar waited patiently. But then she learned that Sheilah had grown and that she wasn't given to him as a wife.

When a person feels abandoned by the ones who should love and support her most, she often has to go to great lengths to survive. In order to fulfill her destiny, Tamar was forced to commit deeds that a modest woman such as she would never even contemplate. People who feel unloved know how to do this. They learn how to fight, how to scream, how to do anything in their power to pursue the dream of love that remains so elusive.

No one can give a child what a mother and father can. Dear mothers, if a child in not nurtured with love, if a child is not given the security that her home is an emotionally safe haven for her, *oy v'avoy* to her and her family. The pain that accompanies this child throughout life is indescribable.

Perfect Imperfection

If you meet someone who has undergone the terrible ordeal of living without parental security and love, what *chizuk*, what words of strength and comfort, can you offer her? And if you yourself have had that almost unbearable *nisayon*, how can you find the strength to carry on, to renew yourself and heal your broken heart?

Let's look at a lesson we learn from Chanukah, which often falls out right before this *parashah*.

The *Tanna* Hillel plays a prominent role on the Chanukah scene. Indeed, the Hebrew word *chanukah* is an acronym for *Ches neiros vahalachah k'Beis Hillel* — "Eight candles and the halachah is according to Hillel."

What was Hillel's beautiful lesson to us? We learn it from the famous story in the Gemara (*Shabbos* 31a), a tale of a fellow who came to pester Hillel while he was washing himself and scrubbing his head on *erev Shabbos*.

The first question the man had was, "Why do the Persians have oval-shaped heads?" With the utmost patience, Hillel answered, "What a great question! That's because the midwives there are not very professional [and they squeeze the heads in a way that causes this ugly shape]."

A while later, the nag came calling on Hillel again. Again Hillel commended the man for his brilliant question: "Why do the eyes of the people from Tarmud appear to be squinting"? Hillel answer patiently, "Because they live in a sandy country."

A while later the pest returned yet another time asking, "Why are the feet of the Africans so wide?"

"That's because they live near swamps," Hillel replied patiently. (In order to prevent them from drowning, Hashem created them with wide feet.)

The entire narrative is very strange. What was this man really asking with his many questions, and what was Hillel's message to him? The real question he had was, "Why did HaKadosh Baruch Hu create ugliness in His world? Why is there any kind of imperfection?" And Hillel answered him, "Everything that your eyes of flesh see as imperfection is really the secret of these peoples' survival. If the midwives wouldn't squeeze the babies' heads the way they do, if the Tarmudim would have wide open eyes, if the Africans wouldn't have wide feet, these populations would not survive."

This is Hillel's profound message to all of us, dear women. What we see as an imperfection, an obstacle may actually be the secret of our survival. As long as we remember that, and we work toward believing this with all of our hearts, the journey in the darkness will be transformed into a journey of light. And we will find the stamina to wait it out—patiently.

When I lost my beautiful baby son to heart disease several years ago, I felt so alone. The *nisayon* was so painful. However, because I knew what a broken heart meant, I was later able to better understand others with broken hearts. This was the silver lining behind my challenge.

Of course, none of us wants to be tried. We want life to be smooth sailing. But when it isn't, let us remember that the challenge we see as an obstacle may very well be the secret of our survival, the aspect that will make our lives so much richer and more beautiful. We have to pray to HaKadosh Baruch Hu that we be granted the perspective of Hillel, who was always *mehallel*, praising. Even when the *kallah* was not so beautiful, he would still sing, *Kallah na'eh vachasudah* — "The bride is beautiful and gracious" (*Kesubos* 17a).

No person in the world can take the place of your father or mother. It is this love that every child deserves that helps a child develop and blossom. But if this is the painful challenge Hashem is trying you with, the pain of abandonment, know, dear sister, that you are not alone. David HaMelech cried about this: *Ki avi v'imi azavuni* — "My father and my mother have abandoned me" (*Tehillim* 27:10). But how does the verse end, dear sister? *VaHashem ya'asfeini* — "And Hashem will gather me in." The profound yearning you have to connect to a parent gives you the opportunity to connect to Hashem with unsurpassed closeness.

The aspects of your life that look imperfect to your eyes, dear women, those will bring you the most growth. Both Yosef (progenitor of Mashiach ben Yosef) and Tamar (whose descendant will be Mashiach ben David) ultimately became ancestors of Mashiach as a result of their challenging situations — but they had to wait it out.

So wait, dear Jewish women. It might be *yamim rabim*, many days, but in the end you will hear Hashem's voice telling you, as Yehudah admitted to Tamar, *Tzadkah* — "You are a righteous woman" (*Bereishis* 38:26), because you didn't give up and you knew what the purpose of this *nisayon* was: to make you a more beautiful person. After the *yamim rabim*, you will be able to look back with pride and say, "It was all worth it."

Is Beauty a Torah Value?

*P*arashas *Mikeitz* is usually read during the time of year when all of the children in Eretz Yisrael are singing, *Chanukah, Chanukah, chag kol kach yafeh...* (the Hebrew version of *Chanukah, oh, Chanukah, ah yom tov ah sheina..."*). Chanukah is a *chag* of beauty, of *yofi*. What is beauty's place in the Jewish world? Does it have a place at all? We find the answer in this *parashah*.

First, let us define the word *beauty* as the Torah understands it. True beauty comes from something hidden beneath the surface that cannot easily be seen, and there is no nation in the world that acknowledges and appreciates this kind of beauty more than *Am Yisrael*.

What's Beneath the Surface

When Yaakov remembered how his son Yosef had been killed, and that now Binyamin was being forced to descend to Mitzrayim, he threw his hands up in the air and cried, "I can't anymore." He used the very unique word, *chulanah*, when he said, *Alai hayu chulanah* — "All [the pain in the world] has fallen upon me" (*Bereishis* 42:36). The Ba'al HaTurim reveals a fascinating insight. He explains that the only two places in *Tanach* where the word *chulanah* is used is in the case of Yaakov, and in *Mishlei*, where Shlomo HaMelech sings the praises of the *eishes chayil*, the woman of valor, proclaiming, *V'at alis al kulanah* — "And you, Jewish woman, have the capacity to rise above all [the pain in the world]" (*Mishlei* 31:29).

How does the *eishes chayil* do this? How can we, like the *eishes chayil*, rise above the pain that surrounds us? We can do it, because we believe that there is something beneath the surface that we cannot see. We believe that although we don't understand everything that happens in our lives, it is still beautiful. If we want to know true beauty, we have to learn to interpret everything that HaKadosh Baruch Hu sends our way in a positive light. We are the ones who have the incredible ability to grapple with even the most trying situation and extrapolate its beautiful lessons. We are able to see beneath the surface.

Why are women in particular blessed with this unique capacity? Because we are dreamers. Our Sages tell us, *Kol hachalomos holchim achar hapeh* — "All dreams follow their interpretation" (*Berachos* 55b). The way you interpret the dream, the way you interpret your life, is what it will ultimately be.

This is precisely the reason for Pharaoh's peculiar choice of wording when he talks about his dream: *Chalom chalamti u'foser ein oso* — "I dreamed a frightening dream, but I cannot find an interpreter for it" (*Bereishis* 41:15). Following his dream of the seven plump cows who were swallowed by the seven emaciated cows, and a virtual repetition of the dream with stalks of grain in place of cows, he didn't say, *V'pisron ein oso* — "And there is no *interpretation* for it" — because that was not the case. On the contrary, his advisers had too many interpretations to offer. One said, "You will give birth to seven daughters, and they will all die." Another offered, "You will conquer seven empires, and seven will rebel against you" (*Midrash Rabbah, Bereishis* 8:6).

In essence, Pharaoh was saying "No, no, I'm looking for someone who can solve this beautifully, someone who has the ability to see the good in everything. Is there someone out there who can do this for me?"

That's when Yosef, the one who appreciated beauty, came along. Pharaoh named Yosef Tzofnas Panei'ach (*Bereishis* 41:45); he had the ability to reveal what was hidden. And what does he say? That there would be seven years of plenty, and then seven years of famine, and in order to survive it the Egyptians must fill the storehouses with grain during the plentiful years.

So enthusiastic was Pharaoh with Yosef's interpretation that he chose to crown him as vice king (ibid. 41:43). Why? Because he recognized Yosef's wisdom; he saw that Yosef understood the importance of looking deeper to find what's hidden under the surface. When Yosef saw seven skinny cows, he looked at what they had swallowed: the abundance they contained within. In order to interpret the happenings in our lives, we must look for the hidden beauty, the *tzofnas panei'ach*.

Every Object of Beauty Must Be Covered

Let's speak of the hidden beauty. Where is its place in Judaism? We are prone to think that beauty belongs to Yefes, the third son of Noach, the forefather of the Greek nation. Yefes is not like Cham, who is corrupt and immodest, but he is not Shem either. What is the difference between Shem and Yefes? Both of them entered their father's room one day to find him drunk in an immodest manner; both wanted to do something to preserve his honor. However, while Shem chose to cover his father's shame, Yefes looked away. Yes, he conducted himself politely, but who benefited from the behavior? No one other than he; so that *he* would not see that which was not aesthetic. He didn't want to see imperfection, but he was not ready to take the proper measures to fix that imperfection and ensure that others did not see it.

We, the Jewish nation, are descendants of Shem, whose reward for covering his father is the beautiful article of clothing that our menfolk wear: tzitzis, a holy covering for their bodies.

Rashi teaches us that Yefes also received a reward for his actions: centuries later, in the War of Gog and Magog, the fallen bodies of his descendants won't be abandoned in the battle-fields; they will merit burial (*Midrash Tanchuma, Noach* 15).

While Yefes did not want to gaze at something that wasn't aesthetic, turning his back on the sight, Shem and his descendants, *Klal Yisrael*, have an entirely different understanding of why we seek to cover it. We don't cover the body because it is not pleasing to the eye; we conceal it because it is holy. It is so beautiful and so full of light that we don't want to blind the eyes of others.

How does HaKadosh Baruch Hu express His appreciation for beauty? By requesting that the *keilim*, vessels of the Mishkan, be concealed when they were traveling and exposed to the public. *Tznius* is about covering what's precious. Where do you keep the silverware and expensive jewelry? Are they safely stored away or out in the open? Something that is truly valuable to you, something that is precious, must be covered.

Yaft Elokim l'Yefes v'yishkon b'ohalei Shem — "Beauty was granted to Yefes, and He will dwell in the tents of Shem" (*Bereishis* 9:27). Women ask me, "Yemima, why do we need all of these halachos about covering the collarbone? Who cares about my collarbone?"

Tznius is not about covering something that is not beautiful; it's about covering something that is extraordinarily beautiful and precious.

Let's understand the words *ohalei Shem*. The Hebrew word *ohel* means a tent — a small dwelling that surrounds the person or family so that they can live in privacy and modesty, as in Bil'ams praise of the Jewish people, *Mah tovu ohalecha Yaakov* — "How goodly are your tents, Yaakov!" (*Bamidbar* 24:5). Even the entrances of their tents were not opposite each other, to preserve modesty (*Rashi, Bamidbar* ibid.).

When Yaakov's sons descended to Mitzrayim to purchase provisions, he requested that they all enter through different gates. "You are all so handsome," he told them. "I don't want an *ayin hara* to befall you." What was Yaakov's fear of *ayin hara*, an evil eye? It wasn't the fear that a non-Jew has: "Let's hide our beauty so that those who look at us won't hurt us." Instead, our patriarch Yaakov's fear was that the beauty of his sons would hurt *others*, that those who looked at them would feel imperfect in their presence.

Mind the Lampshade

It's not only covering the body that modesty necessitates. When we flaunt our perfection — be it talents, riches, or any gift we were graciously granted by HaKadosh Baruch Hu — we are hurting others. We are blinding them with our light. Why should we want to expose all that light? It is like a high beam that pierces through their eyes and disturbs them to no end.

You're probably familiar with the situation where you spend hours sifting through your closet before going to a wedding, desperate to find the clothes that actually zip up and look good on you. Finally, you enter the hall, holding your breath, but feeling good about yourself. You're reveling in the pleasure of spending the evening with family and friends, and all is just wonderful. But what happens next? Another woman enters the hall wearing that very same dress, only two sizes smaller. She gives the impression that the world was created just for her. And the way she carries herself! In a flash, your good feeling dissipates.

What does Hashem say to the other woman? Why? Why did I grant you the beauty? So that you can blind others? I want you to look beautiful and pleasant, but do it with caution.

Think of a lampshade, something that you place around the bulb so that people can look at the light and see how pleasant it is, so that they aren't blinded by its glow. Without the lampshade, the light becomes harsh, not pleasant. Be a person that others will enjoy looking at. You are too good of a soul to make others miserable with what Hashem has given you.

The greatest gift that you can give yourself and your children is to be mindful of the lampshade. Yes, appreciate your gifts and use them wisely. Don't hide them away, but don't expose them either. In a world that is all too connected, all too in the know about every detail of everyone else's life, this lampshade gives a message about the value within. It not only tells others that you understand the true value of a Jew, but also that you value your gifts. It gives you a chance to be human: to accept yourself with all your assets and imperfections because you are not on show all day, every day.

At the core of the Hellenistic culture was accepting only perfection and nothing less. If a child born to Greek parents had even a minor handicap, he was immediately eliminated. Unfortunately, this culture has infiltrated into our society as well. Parents only want that "perfect" *shidduch*, and yeshivos and schools want only *metzuyanim*. *Metzuyan* is a contraction of the words *matza Yavan*. This is what Yavan, our spiritual enemy, was all about. As Jews, we value imperfection. We see it as a facet of our humanness, our potential to grow and develop into something truly beautiful.

Like the light of the Chanukah candles, true beauty is the kind of light people can look at for hours without hurting their eyes. It's the kind of light that warms their hearts, that makes them want to come closer to Hashem and His Torah because it is so pleasant and accepting.

There is so much beauty hidden inside you, dear Jewish woman, and when you cover that light, it is so, so pleasant to look at you. When you remember that the gifts you were given are too beautiful to be revealed from behind the tent or from under the lampshade, you will merit *V'at alis al kulanah*, to rise above any pain in the world.

A Nation of Interferers

When we read *Parashas Vayigash*, we are in the darkest part of winter. The month of Teves also marks the beginning of the destruction of the Temple. Although we usually think of this month in bleak terms, HaKadosh Baruch Hu, in His kindness, sends us the *refuah kodem lamakkah*, the remedy prior to the pain: He tells us the secret to bringing about the third Beis HaMikdash. It's called "*vayigash*." "Enough with the '*hitgosheish*,' the fighting," He says. "Start with '*lageshes*,' drawing near to each other."

That is exactly what Yehudah did in *Parashas Vayigash*. Although to his brothers it seemed a dangerous, senseless step, he took the risk nevertheless: he offered to serve as the guarantor for Binyamin's release.

The Lashon HaKodesh word for "guarantor" is *areiv*, which also means to "mix." Yehudah chose to interfere on his brother's behalf in order to spare his father unnecessary pain. This is the nature of *Am Yisrael*. Yes, we tend to "mix in" to someone else's business because we have it in us to care. Here in Eretz Yisrael, you can't fall in the street without having five people bending over you to help you up. *Kol Yisrael areivim zeh bazeh* — "All of the Jewish nation are guarantors for each other" (*Shevuos* 39a). This is such an important characteristic of ours, and one which we should be proud; we are not of those who turn a blind eye when we see someone in distress. Like Yehudah, we should learn to say, "Now I'm going to interfere for my brother and father's sake. I will make it as if it is solely my problem."

I remember the time that I had the privilege of spending a few days in Antwerp, where the Jewish community welcomed me with such tremendous *hachnasas orchim*. They made my way in so pleasant. However, it was there that I learned of a new mitzvah, the mitzvah of *hotza'as orchim*, to help the guests on their departure.

Due to a strike at the Belgium airport, I was stuck miles from where I wanted to be: home. But I didn't need to worry for too long. A very kind Jew drove my secretary and me to Amsterdam so we could catch a flight from there. Finally, at two o'clock in the afternoon, we took off. It was then that we realized that we hadn't eaten anything since the night before, and the stewardess apologetically informed us that there were no more kosher meals available. So my secretary stood up and asked around our fellow Jews, "Does anyone have any food for two hungry Jewish women?" In no time, we were bombarded with goodies. It was the first time I understood why Israelis carry such enormous backpacks with them!

This is who we are, a nation of interferers, of people who are disturbed if your high beams are not on at night because they want you to arrive safely to your destination.

Just Be There

What did Yosef give his brothers when he saw their distress at the thought of returning to their father, Yaakov, without Binyamin at their side? *Vayitein es kolo bivchi* — "He gave his crying voice to them" (*Bereishis* 45:2). How did this help them in their deep anguish? Because when HaKadosh Baruch Hu sees that a Jew is involved in his brothers' pain, he gives him the capacity to truly help them. Says Rebbe Elimelech of Lizhensk in his renowned *sefer Noam Elimelech*, that the word *bechi*, "crying," is an acronym for *b'shem kol Yisrael* — "for the sake of the Jewish people." If you cry for something on behalf of the entire nation, Hashem will give you the capabilities to be of help.

It is our duty to show that we care, to intervene on any level that we can, be it by sending over a warm meal, making a phone call, or giving a smile — and then Hashem will intervene as well. "You do yours," He says, "and I will do Mine." You do whatever you can, dear women. Hashem understands that you can't save the situation entirely, but your seemingly small deed will spur His intervention.

When Yehudah spoke to Yosef in the palace, he said to him, *Adoni sha'al es avadav ...hayeish lachem av oh ach* — "My master asked his servants..., 'Do you have a father or a brother?'" (*Bereishis* 44:19). Commenting on this verse, the Nesivos Shalom of Slonim says that the word *Adoni* refers to Hashem, our Master, and we, His people, are the servants. HaKadosh Baruch Hu asks us every day, "Do you see your fellow Jew as your brother? Are you involved with *Am Yisrael*? Are you present in their pain?"

The greatest present you can give your fellow Jew is your presence. True, you can't cure her disease or change her *mazel* in her life, but you can be there for her. Says David HaMelech (*Tehillim* 46:2), *Ezrah v'tzaros nimtza me'od* — just being there for someone who is in pain already helps so much.

Dear women, each and every one of us should ask ourselves the question that Reuven asked after not finding Yosef in the pit: *Hayeled einenu v'ani anah ani va* — "The boy is not here, and I — where can I go?" (*Bereishis* 37:30). "Where will I run away," he was saying, "so as not to see my father's pain?" (see *Rashi* there). What did I do to help him out? It's very nice to lead a private life, but when it comes to seeing someone else's pain, when it comes to interfering from a place of caring, there are no limits. As a member of *Klal Yisrael*, my first concern should always be the plight of my brothers and sisters.

Cry for Your Fellow Jew

What is the power of tears? A cry actually marks the start of the salvation. Cries are a sign of faith, that the situation has become so desperate that the person finally chooses to lift his hands and give over the reins to a Higher Power. As long as the tears are kept in check, there's that inner voice telling us, "It's okay. We can manage this."

Who knew the power of a Jew's cries even better than we know ourselves? Nevuchadnetzar, the king of Bavel. When he forced the battered nation into exile, he forbade them to cry. Only after the Jews finally arrived in Babylon did they compose the well-known chapter of *Tehillim*, *Al naharos Bavel sham yashavnu gam bachinu* — "On the riverbanks of Babylon there we sat and also wept" (*Tehillim* 137:1). How cathartic it must have felt. Finally they could cry!

When you cry, dear women, as Yosef did for his brothers, you reveal your love for your fellow Jew. It is the antithesis of the hatred that brought about the destruction. One of the unwritten rules that accompany animosity is this: I won't cry for your pain. What did the brothers realize later — only too late? *Asheimim anachnu al achinu asher ra'inu tzaras nafsho b'hischaneno aleinu v'lo shamanu* — "We are guilty concerning our brother, inasmuch as we saw his heartfelt anguish when he pleaded with us, but we paid no heed" (*Bereishis* 42:21). Only once we realize the importance of empathy, the responsibility we all have to take to heart someone else's pain, can we finally create peace.

Is it hard for you to cry? Don't think that tears came easily to Yosef HaTzaddik, who was raised by a pillar of *gevurah*: his mother, Rachel, who exercised extraordinary self-control when she relayed the *simanim* to her sister, Leah, and who remained silent about her supernatural act of sacrifice. Rachel's *gevurah* was passed down to her descendants: Binyamin's descendant King Shaul did not tell a soul that Shmuel had chosen him as king, and Esther HaMalkah chose not to reveal her nationality and birthplace. These were people, Rachel's children, Yosef's family, who personified utter self-control, and yet their cries heralded the start of the salvation. Yosef broke his years of silence with a piercing cry, and our redemption will come about through the tears of our mother Rachel.

Allow yourself to cry, dear sisters. Tears have the power to soften the ground, to bring life to the seeds of salvation. When you cry for a friend, and especially when you cry for not-such-a-friend, you're exhibiting the greatest display of love.

Disagreements Are Not an Excuse for Inflicting Pain

No matter what type of disagreement we Jews may be involved in, be it political or personal, we must remember one thing: in *Parashas Vayeishev*, the *parashah* in which Yosef was sold, everyone thought they were so right. Yaakov knew he was right when he loved Yosef more than he loved his other sons; Yosef was convinced he was right when he spoke *lashon hara* about his brothers to his father; and, of course, the brothers were sure that they were right when they sold Yosef into slavery.

Our Sages tell us that even HaKadosh Baruch Hu, though He considered what the brothers did to be a sin, agreed with their decision not to reveal it to Yaakov. If so, why were they punished? Why are we suffering to this day because of their wrongdoing? Our Sages answer that they were guilty because they saw their brother in distress, *v'lo shamanu* (*Bereishis* 42:21)

— and they didn't care. Perhaps they were right, but there is no excuse for ignoring a brother's pain, and that is why they were punished. Yes, you may be one hundred percent right, even according to the halachah, but that does not give you permission to hurt your fellow Jew, to ignore his pain.

The greatest *machlokes* of all time began on Chanukah: the *machlokes* of Hillel and Shammai. Still, no matter how wrong one party felt the other was, they still married off their children with the other party (*Yevamos* 13b). Isn't that amazing? Especially because the disagreements were with regard to halachah, the people from one faction could have considered those from the others not worthy marriage material. But that was not the case, because the *machlokes* was in the name of Heaven. The fact that halachah is on your side does not give you the right to hate.

In *Parashas Vayigash*, we read about the moving scene in which Yosef and Binyamin finally embrace as brothers. When the verse tells us that one cried on the other's neck, the word for neck is written in the plural form, *tzavrei* (*Bereishis* 45:14). Rashi explains that Yosef was crying for the two Temples in Binyamin's *nachalah* that would be destroyed, and Binyamin cried over the destruction of Mishkan Shiloh in Yosef's *nachalah*. Doesn't this symbolize the pinnacle of who we should be as a nation: each crying, not for his own pain, but for the pain of his brother? These are the genes we inherited; we are a people that thinks first of the other before we think of ourselves.

A beautiful midrash on *Parashas Vayigash* (*Midrash Tanchuma, Vayigash* 7) fills us in on what happened behind the scenes. Part of the cruel act that Yosef put up for his brothers was that he accused Binyamin of stealing his cup, to which Binyamin replied, "I swear in the life of my brother Yosef that I did not take it." When Yosef asked him, "Do you remember your brother?" he said, "Of course! I am the father of ten sons, each of whom I named in my brother's memory: The name of my firstborn is Bela, because he was swallowed away from me. My second son is Mupim, because I learned Torah from his mouth, and the name of my third son is Chupim, because I did not merit to see his *chuppah*, and he did not merit to see mine." At this point of the conversation, Yosef could no longer control himself, says the Midrash, and that's when he revealed his identity.

The Midrash tells us that this episode alludes to our relationship with Hashem. When He hears us mention the name of someone else, when He sees that someone else is on our mind the way Yosef was always on Binyamin's mind, it is so precious in His eyes that He "gives in" and does His part to bring the salvation. When you take out your *Tehillim* and you daven for someone else, when you go through your list of names and you have them all in mind, even the ones you don't know, Hashem intervenes as well — on their behalf, and yours. As it is written in the Talmud, "Whoever prays for his friend, and he is in need of something similar, he will be answered first" (*Bava Kamma* 92a).

The Strength of Our Generation

Twelve heroes, the *shivtei Kah*, gathered around their dying father, Yaakov. All of them were strong, and so holy. When you read about this, you can't help but wonder, *When I reach my 120 years, will I get such nachas when I see my children gathered all around me?*

The *neshamos* of this generation, however, are not the *neshamos* of yesteryear. The souls we brought into this world are tired, oh, so weak and tired. Have you noticed how weary their faces look? I see girls of fifteen and boys of sixteen who look like they've gone through life's greatest traumas. They stuff themselves with vitamin C before a test, vitamin B after, and omega-3 during. *Kara ravatz k'aryeh* — "They sleep like the lions" (*Bereishis* 49:9) — a sleep that's deep and endless, and who can possibly wake them up? Why is that so? Why are the generations getting weaker and weaker?

Commenting on the verse that reveals Yaakov's age at his passing (ibid. 47:28), the Ohr HaChaim asks, "Why did those generations live longer lives?" Noach lived until 930, Moshe until 120, and the life span keeps diminishing.

The Ohr HaChaim explains his answer with a parable of a king who wished to have an exquisite crown. He gave his servants many precious stones and requested that they polish them with much care so that they would glisten to his liking. As time moved on, the king realized that his servants were working slower and slower; they could not manage with so many precious stones. He didn't want to get angry at them, so he decided to allot them smaller amounts so their workload wouldn't be too heavy. Says the Ohr HaChaim, "Every day is a diamond. Hashem has expectations from every day that He entrusts in our care. He sees how breathless and flustered we are, how sapped of energy our beings have become, and He doesn't want to burden us. So, He gives us only as much as He thinks we could handle."

As the generations move on, people are only getting weaker. When I was a young child, I used to jump in the streets for hours. Who still does that today? But we can still expect one thing from this new generation: Mashiach. From this tired generation Mashiach will come, and the Ohr HaChaim explains the reason beautifully. This new generation, he says, is aware of its weakness, and that gives it so much power.

When Yaakov (Yisrael) is about to die, the verse tells us, *vayischazeik Yisrael* — "Yisrael summoned his strength" (*Bereishis* 48:2). Yaakov was infused with a sudden surge of power, and he sat up in bed. In the same vein, the Shabbos on which we read *Parashas Vayechi*, the final *parashah* in *Sefer Bereishis*, is called "Chazak." Why attribute the power to the end? Wouldn't it be more appropriate to label the beginning as a time of strength? This teaches us that the real power comes to us when we see the end, when we relinquish control. At the point that a person acknowledges his weakness, he is filled with a surge of real power.

Ein shilton b'yom hamaves, Koheles tells us — "there is no authority on the day of death" (*Koheles* 8:8). Based on this verse, the Midrash (*Midrash Rabbah, Bereishis* 96:3) teaches us that toward the end of his life Moshe forgot a halachah and did not assert himself when Zimri sinned; instead, it was Pinchas who took control of the situation (*Bamidbar* 25:8; *Rashi, Bamidbar* 25:6). In their final days, the great David HaMelech was incredibly weak, and Yaakov bowed to his own son, Yosef. But that's what makes us *chazak*, strong. It is our perception that we're in control that weakens us, and when this distorted belief is no more, we become the strongest we will ever be.

We see an interesting pattern among some siblings throughout *Tanach*: the older siblings are weaker in their Torah observance than their younger counterparts — Hevel's offering is accepted, while Kayin's is not, and he ends up being the first murderer in history (*Bereishis* 4:8), Efraim is stronger than Menasheh (ibid. 48:19), Yitzchak is greater than Yishmael, Yaakov is holier than Esav, and Reuven loses both the *kehunah* and the *malchus*, which are given to his younger brothers. Why are the elder ones so much weaker? Because when their parents started out their journeys of parenthood, they had too much control. *Bechori atah kochi v'reishis oni*, Yaakov tells Reuven. "You are my firstborn, my strength and my initial vigor" (ibid. 49:3). You were born when I still thought I could change the world. And as long as a parent feels he has the power, that he is in control, he is essentially weak.

When we were growing up, we still thought we had power. We were embarrassed to ask for a private tutor when we needed help in school. Today's generation requests assistance at their own initiative! They want help in school, help in the kitchen, help with the kids. They say shamelessly, "I need help!" and because they've relinquished their control they are so much stronger than we were. They are the generation that will bring Mashiach. Strength is not, "I can do it." Real strength is, "Only You can do it."

The Big Day

And when will Mashiach come? We don't know. *Bikeish Yaakov legalos es hakeitz v'nistam mimenu* — "Yaakov desired to disclose when the end would come, but it slipped his mind" (*Rashi, Bereishis* 49:1, quoting *Midrash Rabbah, Bereishis* 96:1). Why doesn't Hashem reveal when the end will come? You'll get married in two years, own a house in five. Wouldn't it be such a relief for us? Perhaps it would, but the Midrash tells us that the more a generation waits in the dark, the more it depends on Hashem. Yes, we become weaker because of it, but we are becoming all the more powerful at the same time. We are slowly, slowly opening our fists and relinquishing control.

Lishuascha kivisi Hashem, says Yaakov in his final discourse. "For Your salvation do I long, Hashem" (*Bereishis* 49:18). On this powerful verse, the Midrash comments, *Hakol b'kivui* — a person can attain everything with longing, with hope (*Midrash Rabbah, Bereishis* 98:14). *Kivui* is when we feel powerless, when we are completely dependent on Hashem. We call the next generation passive, but they are really the *mekaveh* generation, the hoping generation that has thrown its hands up in the air.

When a new *mikveh* is constructed, a very deep pit must be dug in order for descending water to have a place to gather. It may seem rather low and empty to the eye, but it is really full and holy. This is the generation of today: it may look empty, but it has more than enough room for the rain, for the salvation, because it is *mekaveh*.

Dear Jewish women, how we must learn to be hopeful! As long as we think, *Everything is on my shoulders*, we are weak, but the moment we relinquish that control, we become infused with power, we are *chazak*. We have to remember that the strong ones are those who have lifted their hands up and given the power back to the Almighty. *Hashleich al Hashem yehavcha v'hu yechalkelecha* — "Cast upon Hashem your 'baggage,' and He will provide for you" (*Tehillim* 55:23).

Fill Yourself With Strength

How can we learn to have the kind of strength that brings salvation? *Parashas Vayechi* is essentially a portion that highlights human frailty. Yaakov Avinu, the crown of his family, lies listless on his deathbed. And the pain of separation that he'd endured weakened him so. Just reading Yosef's parting words from his dear father, without the interpretations or explanations, makes me cry. "Yosef fell on his father's face, he wept over him, and kissed him" (*Bereishis* 50:1).

Imagine the scene, dear women. Yosef falls on his father and cries, "Oy, Abba! How little time I merited to bring you joy! How little I saw of you. But when I stood before the wife of Potifar and was enticed to sin, it was your face, Abba, that I envisioned in my mind. I saw you telling me, 'No, my son, don't sin.' How I will miss that face of yours!"

The pain of separation is profound. Our Sages tell us that a woman endures this kind of suffering many times over the span of her life. She parts from childhood in no time, growing into an adolescent. Then she parts from her adolescence into adulthood. Before long, she parts from her singlehood. I will never forget sitting at home one Shabbos when I was newly married, telling my husband, "I want my mother!" To which my husband said, "What do you want? That I should bring *my* mother?" As much as we are grateful to have found our *bashert*, it's tough to transition into married life. Every child to whom she grows so attached over nine months is then separated from her. He grows and grows and grows some more, and then he is gone — off to yeshivah, to seminary, to build his own nest. And parting from the childbearing years is an immensely weakening challenge of its own.

What do these separations do to a woman? Do they sap her of her strength? Not at all. In their subtle way, transitions fill us with strength. Before a separation, the person is gifted with indescribable *kochos*. When Yaakov was at the threshold of death, the Torah tells us that he was suddenly filled with a surge of strength and he sat up in bed. This burst of energy is no surprise at all. If you've ever watched a candle burn out, you've witnessed how it bursts into a tall flame one last time before it's entirely extinguished.

Our Sages teach us that when a person experiences a separation and thus feels sapped of strength, Hashem stands at his side, at the side of his vulnerability, and strengthens him. This transforms the person into a strong, sturdy being who is able to endure the challenging phase with grace. Hashem says, "I want to stand at the side of this weak woman at the moment she acknowledges her vulnerability." It is the change that moves the ground from under our feet and makes us realize how little control we have over our own lives, how much of a puppet we are in the hands of Hashem. The Chafetz Chaim would say that when an adult loses a tooth, thoughts of repentance should enter his mind. These little transitions to old age are signs that we are not in control, which in turn make us all the more strong and resilient.

When we women are in our weakest moments, dear sisters, that's when Hashem strengthens us most. When we transition from mother-to-be to mother, we are filled with a sudden surge of energy that brings the precious child into this world. Hashem stands at our heads the way he did at Yaakov's deathbed, and holds our hands as we transition with grace.

How do I know this to be true? From the words of our Sages: *Shechinah l'ma'alah meirashosav shel choleh* — "Hashem's Presence rests at the head of a sick person" (*Shabbos* 12b). When you feel weakest, dear sisters, is when you become the strongest indeed. When your child makes your heart ache, when you ache for a child, when you ache for a salvation, and you feel that you can't bear the pain any longer, that's when you will feel the strongest. That's when Hashem stands at the side of His dear daughter and helps her.

Because our essence centers on transitions, on change, on weakness, we women are the strongest. If you're feeling sapped of your strength and unable to forge on, listen to the stunning words of our Sages. On the Shabbos that we read *Parashas Vayechi*, on Shabbos Chazak, they write, Hashem bestows His daughters with the strength of all the matriarchs in *Chumash Bereishis*. On this very Shabbos, you receive the collective *ko'ach* of Sarah, of Rivkah, of Rachel, of Leah: women who endured the weakest of moments, but also the strongest of moments. In the words of the famed Rav Tzvi Meir Zilberberg, *shlita*, "The *tzaddikim* of the previous generations revealed to us the great light of Shabbos *Parashas Vayechi*. On this Shabbos, we receive immense *kochos*. It is like Kol Nidrei, the opening, the beginning, for the weeks of *Shovavim* (Shemos, Va'eira, Bo, Beshalach, Yisro, Mishpatim — a propitious time for *teshuvah*) that follow. Whoever is stringent with the observance of Shabbos on this day merits an exalted *Shovavim* phase — a more elevated, spiritual experience" (*Sichos Hizchazkus*).

From Sarah, you receive the power to laugh. From Rivkah, the power to give birth and tend to your children. From Rachel, you receive the power to cry, and from Leah you receive the greatest power of all: the strength to wait. My dear sisters, the numerical value of the word *yechi* is *ko'ach*. You cannot fathom the strength that Hashem sends your way on this Shabbos.

What strength you have, dear women! *Chazak chazak v'nischazeik!*

Sefer Shemos

The Ivriyah:
A Defining Factor
in Every Jewish Woman

Commenting on the opening words of *Sefer Shemos*, *V'eileh shemos bnei Yisrael haba'im Mitzraimah* — "And these are the names of the children of Israel who were coming to Egypt" (*Shemos* 1:1), Rav Tzadok HaKohen MiLublin asks, "Since when does a new episode in history begin with the letter *vav*, 'and'?"

If not for this *vav*, he answers, we would not see the connection between *Sefer Bereishis* and *Sefer Shemos*. So vast is the gap between these two *sefarim* that it necessitated a *vav* to bridge it, to explain that despite the many differences between the two chronicles, one is a continuation of the other.

A significant aspect of the contrast between *Sefer Bereishis* and *Sefer Shemos* is related to the Jewish woman. In truth, *Bereishis* could have been subtitled "Book of the Barren." Much of the *sefer* revolves around the pain of the childless Sarah, then

Rivkah, and then Rachel. The women in *Sefer Shemos*, by contrast, *paru vayishretzu vayirbu vaya'atzmu bime'od me'od* (ibid. 1:7). They "multiplied fruitfully," bearing six children at one birth.

This is not the only significant difference between *Sefer Bereishis* and *Sefer Shemos*. The *sefer Zera Baruch* (vol. 3, *Seder HaYom* 2:4) tells us that the word *bereishis* is a combination of two words, *ashrei* and *bas* — "fortunate is the daughter." Sarah, Rivkah, Rachel, and Leah were privileged to be the daughters of Hashem, personally guided through every step in life by their Father's hand. As *Sefer Shemos* opens, however, the women were thrust into challenging roles and were seemingly left to fend for themselves; the *yad Hashem* was no longer visible.

Instead of being daughters, these women were now thrust into the role of mothers, fighting to preserve their family lives, feeling as if they were all on their own. Unlike Sarah, if a woman disagreed with her husband, her husband didn't hear the voice of Hashem, the Ultimate Mediator, steering them in the right direction. Unlike Rivkah, the women in Mitzrayim did not have Shem and Ever to turn to for clarity during a confusing pregnancy. In *Sefer Shemos*, the Jewish women were forced to search for their own solutions.

The Fortitude of the Jewish Woman

Being a mother presents a challenge because your role never ends. A neighbor of mine who was once a sought-after doctor but is now unfortunately incapacitated told me, "Yemima, my mother died twenty years ago, but in my greatest moments of pain I find myself still crying for her. I miss her so much."

In *Sefer Shemos*, we Jewish women are called by a new name, one we've never encountered previously: Ivriyah. When Pharaoh instructs the midwives, Shifrah and Puah, to kill the male infants born to Jewish mothers he says, *B'yaledchen es haIvriyos...im bein hu vahamiten oso* — "When you deliver the Hebrew women...if it is a son, you shall put him to death" (ibid. 1:16). *Lo chanashim haMitzriyos haIvriyos*, they reply. "The Ivriyos are not like the Egyptian women" (ibid. 1:19). Later, when Bisyah pulls baby Moshe from the water, Miriam approaches her and asks, "Should I go summon for you a wet nurse from the Ivriyos who will nurse the boy for you?" (ibid. 2:7).

The expert on language, Ibn Ezra, explains that the word *Ivri* is associated with the *emunah* of Avraham, who came from *eiver hanahar*, the "other side of the river." It is the name that says, "Listen, dear daughter, you are making a frightening transition right now, transitioning from daughter to mother. Can you cross this treacherous divide? It's a very narrow passage. Can you do it?"

And the answer is no. We cannot do it on our own. A Jewish woman's secret to crossing from one shore to the other, fighting her way toward marriage, toward marital harmony and *parnassah*, toward becoming a mother, lies in the word *Ivriyah* — a word that can be divided into the words *eiver Kah*, "turning toward Hashem." How can you be an expectant woman with hope, even as you trudge through the *ma'avar*, the transitioning phase? By putting your faith in the One Above.

A Labor of Love

In *Parashas Shemos*, Pharaoh proposed a devious plan to stem the astronomical Jewish growth. He told the midwives Shifrah and Puah that as soon as they determined a baby's gender from the crown of its emerging head, if he was a male they should kill him. "How can we determine the gender from the baby's head?" they asked. Explains Rabbi Chaninah that when a girl is born, *panehah l'ma'alah* — "her face is turned upward" — and when a boy is born, he faces downward (*Sotah* 11b).

What a beautiful manifestation of Ivriyah! The Jewish woman turns toward Hashem from the very moment of her birth.

These were the amazing women of *Sefer Shemos*. They knew that they couldn't preserve their family lives without facing upward.

The Tzemach Tzedek says that the souls of those women in Mitzrayim will be the souls of the generation of Mashiach. Both generations will be confronted with the same challenges and will not be able to cross the turbulent river without turning their faces upward.

What happens when your face turns toward Hashem? Suddenly, all the narrow passages open up for you. Yes, the passages are still *tzar*, narrow, but with Hashem at your side they are transformed into *tzirim*, contractions, that widen the spaces for you. You find yourself forging forward with a strength you didn't know you possessed.

Vayakam melech chadash al Mitzrayim asher lo yada es Yosef — "A new king arose over Egypt who did not know of Yosef" (*Shemos* 1:8). Of course, the obvious question is, How could this new king not know Yosef? Was there anyone who hadn't heard of this wise adviser who contributed monumentally to the country?

The Kli Yakar says that this new king knew Yosef, but he didn't know the "Yosef syndrome." He didn't know that Yosef's people insisted, "No, this is not the *sof*, the end. The more you will make life narrow for us, the more we will move forward."

It is precisely when people try to bring us down that we flourish. The more challenges we face, the more babies we produce.

I will never forget when I watched my eldest daughter become an Ivriyah herself. Standing by her side as she experienced the pangs of childbirth, I felt more than ever how powerless I was to guide her through this milestone. She, in her weakest state, was more powerful than I. It was now her turn to find the Ivriyah within. All I could do was hold her hand as I prayed, wishing I could do more. The highlight of becoming a grandmother for the first time was observing my daughter make the transformation, realizing with a depth she couldn't grasp before that life is all about turning to face Hashem.

When my precious grandson finally emerged into the world at noon, I closed my eyes tightly to thank Him not only for his birth, but also for the manifestation of the powers and the rebirth of an Ivriyah. And when a new mother finds her Father, she becomes a daughter again.

In the moments when we are weakest, we are the most powerful if we take the opportunity to turn to Hashem. When we allow Him to guide us, paths of comfort suddenly open up before our eyes, and we are blessed with the ability to see the good in everything.

Chassan Damim: Safeguarding the Holiness of Our Precious Sons

Let's talk about the bris milah that we encounter in *Parashas Shemos*, performed by the very first female *"mohel"* by the name of Tzipporah. The child was already eight days old, and when Tzipporah, Moshe's wife, saw that her husband did not circumcise the child, and she understood that the angel's attack on Moshe was because of his failure to do so, what did she do? *Vatikach Tzipporah tzor vatichros es orlas benah* — "She took a sharp stone and cut off the foreskin of her son" (*Shemos* 4:25), and she said to him, "You caused my *chassan's* bloodshed!" (ibid.). What does this mean? What does "You're my *chassan damim*" imply?

The Ibn Ezra explains that women call a newly circumcised baby a *chassan*. This is intriguing. You know of the concept of a *chassan bar mitzvah*, right? And of a *chassan Torah*. And, of course, you know of a *chassan* under his *chuppah*. But what is the concept of a *chassan* at a bris?

The Ibn Ezra tells us that every woman essentially assumes the role of Tzipporah, the circumciser of her eldest son, because she's the first one to call her son *"chassan."* A mother is the one to tell her child, "My dear son, you will one day grow up to be the *chassan* of some woman. Please take good care of yourself so you will grow up to be a loyal, dedicated husband."

The generation in which Tzipporah raised her firstborn was not unlike the world of impurity we live in today. The Mitzrayim she was going to live in was known as *ervas ha'aretz*, the most immoral of countries (*Bereishis* 42:9). This brilliant woman understood that if she didn't whisper this message into the ears of her tiny son, the word *chassan* while she circumcised him, who would guard him?

At the bris of every Jewish child, the congregants say, *K'sheim shenichnas labris kein yikaneis lasorah u'l'chuppah u'lema'asim tovim* — "Just as he entered the covenant of circumcision, may he [merit to] enter to [a life of] Torah, to the *chuppah*, and to good deeds." Why do we mention the child's marriage when he's little more than one week old?

Now that the child has been circumcised, we want to give him a blessing: that as this child grows, he will guard his purity and holiness in order to build a true Torah home.

Mother, dear, this is your role, just as much as feeding or diapering is. You're the one with the task of helping him safeguard his purity. It's your task to raise a trustworthy, loyal man. How crucial this lesson is for the world we live in, a world filled with more immorality than our grandparents could have ever fathomed. We live in a modern Mitzrayim, where the filth penetrates from every unsafe crevice.

How important her message is to our generation! All of us mothers must be starkly aware of the power we hold in keeping our children safe, even from a very young age.

Our Sages tell us that "after Pharaoh issued the decree that all Jewish baby boys be thrown into the sea, the pious mother of Moshe, Yocheved, constructed a special *chuppah* in his *teivah*" (*Shemos Rabbah* 1:24).

This conceivably could be interpreted that in essence she was saying to him, "My son, I built for you a *chuppah*, because I may never see you again. If someone saves you, remember: you are a *chassan*. Remember to preserve your purity."

What *chinuch*. Even in the darkest of times, these holy women didn't lose focus on the primary values in a Jewish home. They understood that if they didn't protect their generation, no one would. As the mothers of this generation, we too were given the exalted task of ensuring that our precious children's holiness remains intact. It's not easy, dear women. Not easy at all. And it starts as soon as the child is born.

I remember that our *rav*, Rav Tzion Bracha, *zt"l*, would whisper into the ears of every child at his bris, "*Chatan talmid chacham.*" Not everyone understood why he referred to the child with those words, but we do.

Ishto Hi Beiso:
How to Make Your Home a Safe Place

Parashas Shemos opens with the words *V'eileh shemos bnei Yisrael haba'im Mitzraimah eis Yaakov ish u'veiso ba'u* — "These are the names of the children of Israel who were coming to Egypt; with Yaakov, each man and his household came" (*Shemos* 1:1). What does the word *beiso* refer to? Our Sages teach us that *beiso zo ishto* — "his house refers to his wife" (Mishnah, *Yoma* 1:1). If only the men had ascended to Egypt, there would be no *Am Yisrael*.

Rav Yerucham Levovitz used to say that the souls of the women in Mitzrayim will be *megulgal*, reincarnated, in the generation of the Final Redemption. We are those heroic women, dear sisters. You're Shifrah. You're Tzipporah. You're Bisyah, the daughter of Pharaoh.

No, I'm not a proponent of female circumcisers, but I do believe that we women have the power to build the generation with *milim*, words. Not with the knife of *milah*, but with a good *milah*, a good word. What was Yocheved's first reaction when she saw her newborn son? *Vateire oso ki tov hu* — "She saw that he was good" (*Shemos* 2:2). A Jewish mother must work to see the good in her child, the light in his eye. When a woman is not an *arel sefasayim* — she doesn't keep her lips shut when it comes to doling out praise and words of positivity — she's safeguarding the purity of her children. When she chooses to accept the challenges that come her way instead of seeking someone to blame, she's giving her children a message that home is a safe place, a happy place, a place they want to be.

The more you seek to create that shell for your husband and children, and the more you utilize your Ivriyah power to turn to Hashem for guidance, the better you will be able to protect your precious ones from the filth of the modern Mitzrayim, by building strong, impenetrable walls in your beautiful Jewish home.

Are You a Victim of *Kotzer Ruach?*

"What's happening to us?" I once asked my daughter. "Why don't people believe me when I say that Hashem loves us?"

"Ima," she said to me, "maybe it's because we think that Hashem is like us, with the same character traits. We bear a grudge for a long time. We don't forgive so easily. We remember the bad much more than we remember the good."

These were the words of my sweet daughter, and when she said that, the first verses in *Parashas Va'eira* immediately came to mind. When Moshe complained that Hashem had sent him in vain to save the Jews, Hashem rebuked him and assured him that the redemption was at hand.

Chaval al d'avdin — "A pity about those who are gone," Hashem said, referring to our Patriarchs, who maintained their faith in Hashem without complaint (*Sanhedrin* 111a). Our forefathers understood that Hashem's ways are unfathomable. There's no way in the world that we can possibly comprehend the way He operates as a force that's filled with so much love.

Especially if we think unfavorably of ourselves and our deeds, or of others, this is hard to grasp.

Worthy of Redemption

When our battered nation was in the tough Egyptian exile, they also had a hard time grasping this reality. When Moshe came to inform them that their redemption was approaching, *v'lo shamu el Moshe mikotzer ruach u'mei'avodah kashah* — "they did not heed Moshe because of shortness of breath and hard work" (*Shemos* 6:9). The Midrash explains that *kotzer ruach* means that their spirits were so deflated that they felt undeserving of redemption. They were like the women who say to me, "Yemima, what are you talking about? We're not going anywhere anytime soon. Look at the *lashon hara*, the discord, the sins…"

The first phase of the redemption is to understand that you are Hashem's daughter and that you are worthy of being redeemed. How did Hashem choose to address his wilting nation? "Moshe," He said, "go to the children and tell them, *Beni bechori Yisrael* — 'My son, my firstborn, Yisrael' (ibid. 4:22)." You, dear sisters, are the daughters of Hashem, no matter how you feel about your *tefillah* or *tznius* — or lack thereof.

Let's imagine that a woman (no one you know!) has a teenaged daughter who is taking her to Gehinnom and back with her rebellious antics. One day this woman walks down the street when she suddenly hears the pleading voice of her daughter in the distance: "Mommy, I fell into a pit!" What would she do? Would she stop and say, "Daughter, dear, this happened because of your sins"? No way in the world, because this is the daughter you love. That's the fact. No matter how much we've sinned, Hashem is infinitely more loving than any parent we know.

Hashem says to us, "How many times must I remind you how much I love you?" If we don't grasp this message, we will never be redeemed, because a person who doesn't think he's deserving of liberation won't be liberated. Any woman who feels "I'm not good enough" is stuck in a pit. Depression doesn't allow for redemption; it only drags you deeper and deeper into a cavernous ditch.

You can see this when you're dealing with a dispirited child who thinks his life is not worth living. If you'll put him last in line, he'll say, "I knew they hated me." If you'll put him first in line, he'll say, "They just want to make fun of me." Nothing is good for him. Even when the redemption comes, he won't see it.

Low self-esteem robs a person of a good life in this world and a good life in the next. It's the reason so many of our dear children give up the values we try to instill in them. It's the reason people don't have the courage to do what they know is right.

What makes a person think unfavorably of herself? What's a cause for low self-esteem? The many challenges she faces. *Vayarei'u osanu haMitzrim Vai'anunu* — "The Egyptians mistreated us and afflicted us" (*Devarim* 26:6). The *metzarim*, the afflictions in your life, make you feel that you're *ra*, bad. If you don't have the livelihood you wish for, the children of your dreams, the perfect marriage, you start to feel that it's an indication of who you are, that you're no good.

This is the frustration Moshe Rabbeinu felt when he cried to Hashem, *Lama harei'osah la'am hazeh* — "Why did you bring the nation to a state in which they feel that they're evil?" (*Shemos* 5:22). A negative self-image is a dangerous hindrance to the redemption. It doesn't allow us to see the salvation when it finally comes. The more we see the bad, the more bad we'll see.

Blessings of Rain

Rebbi Nachman of Breslov tells us that Hashem comes to us in the month of Shevat — usually one of the rainiest months in Eretz Yisrael — with overflowing buckets. "Take *simchah*," He offers. "Take your *zivug*." "Take *parnassah*." "Take a new home." However, notes Rebbe Nachman, when you plant a good seed in decaying soil, the crop will rot. HaKadosh Baruch Hu tells the despondent woman, "I want to bestow abundant gifts upon you, but you're a sad woman. I'll give you a wonderful husband — and you'll squirm at his posture. I'll give you beautiful children — and you'll see their flaws. Nothing in the world will make you happy."

This is one reason why the month of Shevat precedes the month of Adar. During the month of Adar, we increase our happiness, and during the month of Shevat we decrease our sadness. In order to experience the true joy of Adar, we must first rid ourselves of negativity. In the month of Shevat, accustom yourself to saying, *Sheyiheyu besoros tovos* — "May there be good tidings," a phrase whose first letters compose the Hebrew word *shevat*. Only if you choose to see the abundance of goodness Hashem sends your way, the blessing in the rain, will you merit the redemption you're waiting for.

A great way to remind yourself of Hashem's love to you is when you see the rain. It's Hashem's way of letting you know that He's concerned about your well-being. He wants to ensure that you receive the proper nutrients to enjoy a satisfying, rich life. It's a sign of His love for us, sent straight from the heavens.

Especially for a Jewish woman, whose attitude and self-concept becomes the pulse of the home, it's crucial to develop a positive self-image. So many times I meet girls who tell me they feel undeserving of Hashem's kindness, and later, when I meet their mothers, I'm not surprised at their destructive perspective.

The home is the first place where a child develops an assessment of herself. *How am I doing?* she wonders from when she's a toddler. A confident mother can imbue confidence in her children. A positive mother can give her children the gift of self-assurance.

Take Notice of the Plagues

Although it's crucial for every Jewish woman to develop an appreciation for herself, it's equally important to keep in mind that only Hashem is perfect. Pharaoh chose to present himself as a god. For this reason, he relieved himself in the Nile in the early morning, when no one was around to observe him, and he'd control himself throughout the remainder of the day. With this behavior, he intended to impart a message to his nation: "I have no need to relieve myself." In other words, he wanted to be seen as a flawless being, perfect from the inside out.

Because of his extreme haughtiness, Pharaoh could not take a lesson from the *makkos*. To every thinking person, they were bold signs, signs that begged for attention and introspection, but to him, they were chance occurrences.

But we don't want to be like Pharaoh. We realize that everything Hashem sends our way is a message: from strep throat to a broken limb to the baby's ear infection. Nothing happens by chance. When Hashem sends you a *makkah*, it's not a call for a blame game — "I'm perfect, somebody else messed up here." It's a call for introspection — "What do You want to tell me, Hashem?" Especially if it returns time and again, don't turn a blind eye to the deeper reason — "What is it that You want me to fix?"

It's astounding to observe how some women react to the afflictions Hashem sends their way. While most women righteously follow the guidance of our Sages that when an affliction comes upon a person he should examine his deeds, others immediately seek a culprit.

Your children are watching, dear women. What kind of lesson are you imparting to them? Searching for a target to blame is a blatant expression of "It can't be me. I'm flawless." Who are we kidding when we think that?

Our Sages discuss the concept of suffering and its underlying message in the Gemara (*Arachin* 16b). They ask, "What is considered *yissurim*, pain?" And they answer that when a person sticks his hand into his pocket, intending to remove a dime, and he withdraws a nickel, he should take it as a sign from Hashem. Of course, many commentators ask a simple question: Such a slightly upsetting occurrence is considered *suffering*? And the Ba'al Shem Tov teaches us something so profound about how we should accept any kind of suffering.

He says that yes, removing a nickel instead of a dime *can* be all the pain a person will suffer, if she stops to think right then about what Hashem wants from her. If, at the slightest discomfort, we have the clarity to stop and introspect, that's where the pain will end. However, if we choose to be blind to the occurrences in our world, passing them off as chance incidents, His reminders will only become more and more outright, G-d forbid.

The Sfas Emes expounds on this subject with an enlightening notation. In the distant past, he writes, a *makkah* came upon a person as a message for him to rectify a deed of *avodah zarah*. He would proceed to rectify it, and the affliction would disappear. Later, an affliction came as a sign of indecency. When the person would rectify his behavior, it would vanish. In the generation of Mashiach, the Sfas Emes tells us, afflictions come upon a person for one reason: a lack of respect between one person and another.

The Be'er Mayim Chaim delves into every plague that struck the Egyptians, explaining how they each corresponded to a specific unkind behavior they exhibited toward the Jews. For instance, the Egyptians were stricken with the plague of blood because they didn't allow the Jewish women to purify themselves according to the halachah. They were afflicted with a deluge of frogs because they had forced the Jews to chase and capture insects and frogs every day, an order they regarded as a humorous entertainment for themselves. The plague of lice served as a punishment for the Egyptians' prohibition against the Jews' basic physical cleansing after a laborious day at work. For their cruel behavior to their fellow men, says the Be'er Mayim Chaim, the Egyptians were struck with ten *makkos*!

Rav Chaim Shmulevitz once shared that a woman came to him and said, "My husband broke his foot, and I feel that I must rectify my deeds because every morning I give him a drink before he davens and that's prohibited."

Said Rav Chaim incredulously, "How blind can a person be? Several weeks before, a young man with a slight limp was suggested to this woman's daughter, and she said, 'He's crippled. I don't want crippled people in the family.'"

When you try to discern what's going on, don't escape the truth. It's not because you don't say *Perek Shirah* every morning or that you don't take challah every Friday. Don't only look into your deeds between yourself and Hashem, advises the Sfas Emes. Make certain you are also looking into the deeds between you and your fellow man.

Rav Yitzchak Zilberstein tells the story of a respected bank manager who came to see him. "They fired me from my job, and I don't know why. What should I do now?" he cried.

Says the *rav*: This man could not know that two weeks earlier, a brokenhearted young man sat in that same chair, crying to the *rav* that the manager had dismissed him from his position in the bank because of his stutter. "It does not appeal to the customers," the manager had told him, stripping him of his livelihood and confidence

As much as it's important for us to value ourselves, we must pay close attention to the value of others. Every Jew should be held in high esteem. When Moshe Rabbeinu noticed an Egyptian beating his fellow Jew, he struck the Egyptian and buried him in the sand. No one was there to witness the episode, the verse tells us. "He turned this way and that and saw that there was no man" (*Shemos* 2:12). So how did this story surface? The Jew whom he saved went and informed on him!

Said Moshe Rabbeinu, *Achein noda hadavar* — "Indeed the matter is known" (ibid. 2:14). Now he understood the reason for this exile: because a Jew would inform on a fellow Jew.

Dear women, how we wish for this exile to end! How we wish to finally be redeemed. Here is the secret: believe that you're deserving of salvation and that your friend and sister and neighbor are worthy as well.

Raising Our Children: With Happiness and With Love

fter *Am Yisrael* miraculously were redeemed from the Egyptian exile, Moshe Rabbeinu discussed with them how they would commemorate this momentous event once they reached Eretz Yisrael: "When your children will say to you, 'What is this service to you?' you'll say to them, 'It is a Pesach feast-offering to Hashem, Who passed over the houses of the children of Israel in Egypt when He smote the Egyptians, but He saved our households'" (*Shemos* 12:26–27), When the nation heard this, the verse continues, the people "bowed their heads and prostrated themselves" (ibid. 12:27). Rashi explains that the entire nation bowed their heads in gratitude for the news that they would be freed, be given the land, and have future generations of children. The nation rejoiced that they would be fruitful.

Just a minute… Isn't this the very same verse that we quote at the Seder when speaking about the wicked son and how we should answer him when he says, with brazen chutzpah, "What is this service to you?" For this they were grateful?

Answers Rebbe Nachman of Breslov that the nation rejoiced because there is no such thing as a bad child. No such thing.

Children are saplings, and saplings have one incredible characteristic: if you plant them in rotten soil, they just won't grow. It's not the seed that's bad; it's the soil in which you planted it. A negative environment is rotten soil for a beautiful seed. You, dear Jewish mother, are your child's soil. If you're despondent, you have no power of *simchah* and no power of growth. A happy mother is one who says, "You're such a gift to me. I'm so happy just because I have you."

Every child deserves a happy mother. When a mother is happy, her children are instinctively drawn into the joyous attitude that permeates the home. What she does for herself inadvertently becomes a deed that she does for her children. *Ba'avur zeh asah Hashem li*, we're instructed to tell the wicked son. "Because of this, Hashem redeemed me." By virtue of you, the mother, experiencing the redemption, your child made it to freedom as well. Every move you take, dear mother, every thought that crosses your mind, has a powerful impact on your offspring.

The *Pri Tzaddik* explains that the reason the nation rejoiced even upon hearing that their children may be wicked is because they thought to themselves that if they, a nation of idol worshipers, was liberated by the hands of Hashem, then even a wicked child deserves to be loved. They understood that every human being is worthy of love and the showering of joy.

Child of *Geulah*

I remember attending the shivah home of Philippe Braham, may Hashem avenge his blood, who was killed in the Paris massacre at Hyper Cacher, a kosher supermarket. His widow, Valerie, sat there utterly shattered. Only one year earlier she'd lost a child to cancer, and several months prior her mother had passed away. "We were able to bear everything," she said sadly, "but now that Philippe is not here with us…"

At her side sat her eight-year-old daughter, Sandrine. She hovered over her mother like a butterfly, kissing her every few minutes. While I sat there, she gave me a look that said, "Don't you dare make my mother cry. She shouldn't cry because of you." She hugged her mother as if she was a little mother herself. Her mother turned to me and said, "Do you know, Yemima, who's keeping me strong? This little one here."

She continued, "On Friday, Philippe went to buy challos. He was the one to do our Shabbos shopping because he loved Shabbos so much. When I heard about the terrorist attack, I immediately phoned him and he didn't answer. I tried again and again. My heart! All I kept hoping was that he was only injured. But then the worst happened. About an hour before Shabbos, a psychologist came down to my home. She said to me that, number one, my husband had been killed and that, number two, I shouldn't tell the kids right away — that I should do it slowly, slowly."

Following the instructions of the psychologist, Valerie told Sandrine that her father wouldn't be with them for Shabbos, that he had been critically injured. "Mama," the young girl said to her mother, "don't you worry. Everything will be all right. Papa is a strong person; he'll get over it."

When Shabbos was over, the child kept asking, "What's with Papa? What's with Papa?"

"He's critically injured, Sandrine."

"I'm praying for him, Mama. Don't worry."

When Monday arrived, it was time for them to board a flight to Eretz Yisrael for the *levayah*. Valerie sat down with Sandrine and said, "Do you remember that I told you that Papa is critically injured?"

The young girl nodded, her eyes wide open.

"He's not with us anymore. He went up to Heaven."

Sandrine looked into her mother's eyes and said, "Don't worry, Mama. I'll raise the young ones with you. Now Papa went to watch over our brother, and you have nothing to worry about."

Valerie turned to me and said, "Yemima, I'm so worried. This child did not shed a tear from when I told her the news."

"Don't worry," I said to Valerie, "because these are the children of the *geulah*."

It's so true. Think about the young girl Miriam, who stood at the river and said to her mother, "Mama, you go. I'll watch over baby Moshe. I see that it's hard for you to be here, so I'll take over. It's too much for you."

She stood there and watched as Bisyah, Pharaoh's daughter, drew Moshe from the water and carried him away. I always imagine in my mind how this young girl ran to call her mother, saying, "Pharaoh's daughter is looking for a Jewish woman to nurse the baby." How brilliant a child she was. These are our children. They want only one thing from us: Mommy, be happy.

Unfortunately, I don't always manage to accompany my children to their after-school activities. One Sunday, my student Noa accompanied my daughter Ahuva to her ballet event. When they returned, I asked her, "So how was it, Ahuva?"

"Ima," she said in all honesty, "it was awkward, because at the end all the girls danced with their mothers and I danced with Noa. It was very nice, but I also wanted you to be there." (In other words: Ima, you abandoned me.)

The next week, of course, I made it my business to be a good mother. I canceled a lecture because my high school daughters were performing in a presentation. I know the program of these evenings in my dreams already — it's always either about the Cossacks or the Communists — but this time I was in for a surprise. This time, it was a happy performance. It was about Mashiach, about the *geulah*. I simply sat and cried. And my daughters couldn't believe that I was there. They kept coming to my seat and asking, "Ima, are you enjoying it?"

As I sat there, I thought about their happiness and how contingent it was on mine. If Ima was happy, so were they. That's all they wanted. *Ima*, I kept telling myself, *just be happy. You're the soil.*

Mercy, Mercy, Mercy

How do we raise loving, empathic children? When we treat them with empathy.

"Mommy, I had a hard day today."

"Come, my child. Tell me everything."

Today's mothers don't have the authoritative capacity that the mothers of yesteryear employed, and if Hashem took it from us, He had a reason. He doesn't want an authoritarian mother. He wants a merciful mother. How validating it feels to know that you don't have to be something you can't be.

I didn't make this up, dear sisters, to make you happy (although nothing is more important than a happy mother). According to Kabbalah, the *geulah* has a component of lack of order. When Hashem feels that it's time for our redemption, things happen in no particular order. In the same vein, in the time of the *geulah*, the younger ones have more authority than their elders (*Sotah* 49b). We rely on them much more than the parents of previous generations did. And we must treat them with mercy.

Hashem wants you to look at your children and see their sweetness. He wants you to realize that they were born into a virtual desert, the forces of impurity luring them from all sides. All they want is your warmth, the positive light that will light up their own lives. Just as Hashem was so full of mercy toward His children, who were at the forty-ninth level of impurity before they were redeemed from Egypt, be that merciful mother toward your child.

At a child's bris, the following blessing is recited: "Blessed is the One Who sanctified the beloved one in his mother's womb..." We may ask, "Why are we blessing the child as a fetus in its mother's womb after he was already born?" The Shem MiShmuel answers that this refers to the holiness of *all* Jewish fetuses, which don't have an evil inclination and are completely holy. It is to tell us that the holiness of a child emanates from its mother's womb! There is no such thing as a bad child.

The word for womb, *rechem*, is similar to the word for kindness, *racheim*. Before the child is born, the mother performs constant acts of kindness. The steps she selflessly takes to protect her child give him the opportunity to develop into a healthy, strong baby. But her compassionate deeds don't end at birth. After she committed the sin of the *eitz hada'as*, Hashem cursed Chavah and, in turn, every woman, with *harbah arbeh itzvoneich v'heironeich* — "I will greatly increase your suffering and your childbearing" (*Bereishis* 3:16). Rashi explains that *itzvoneich* refers to the woman's pain of rearing the child. Raising children is a herculean task: every step is another contraction, enabling the development of a more beautiful adult.

The Shelah HaKadosh expounds on the words *harbah arbeh*, noting that the plague of *arbeh*, grasshoppers, struck Egypt on Tu B'Shevat. In every child, you're able to see either *arbeh*, a destructive plague that has come to ruin everything, to sap your energy and resources, or you can see the *harbah*, the bounty, the beautiful crop. Says the Shelah, the word *arbeh* has the numerical value of the word *ben*, son, multiplied four times (*arbeh* = 208; *ben* = 52), alluding to the four sons we discuss in the Haggadah: the wise one, the wicked one, the simple one, and the one who doesn't know how to ask. Every child, he tells us, is a combination of all four sons. Never will your child be only wise or only wicked. The question is whether you'll see in him the crops we celebrate on Tu B'Shevat or the plague.

It's interesting to note that the plague of the grasshoppers is the only one for which Hashem commanded, *U'lema'an tesaper b'aznei vincha u'ven bincha...* — "And you should relate in the ears of your son and your son's son..." (*Shemos* 10:2). This is the sole plague that is associated with children and grandchildren because of its relevance to their upbringing. Do you feel the children just come to wreck the home you cleaned so carefully? Is that all you see: more and more destruction wherever you turn? Or do you see how they came to transform your life into an abundance of joy and happiness?

Choseich Shivto: Don't Withhold the Shevet From Your Loved Ones

Of course, you wonder, where is the discipline? Doesn't Yemima heed the words of Shlomo, the wisest of all men, *Choseich shivto sonei beno* — "One who withholds his staff is the enemy of his child" (*Mishlei* 13:24)?

Let's understand the multiple definitions of the word *shevet*. A *shevet* can mean a staff with which one strikes a child, the stick you employ when you're angry and impatient. This very same word, however, can mean a cane on which one leans. Do you employ rules in your home from a place of compassion because you want your children to have a structure to lean on?

No, I'm not a proponent of the "free-for-all" approach, but I strongly believe that rules and structure must come from a place of kindness.

There's a third way to understand the word *shevet*. The Chida, Rabbi Chaim Dovid Azulai, teaches that *shevet* relates to Shevat. *Chodesh Shevat* is the month that symbolizes the birth of a new season. When the child sees the beautiful blossoms of the month of Shevat, the brilliant sun in the month of Shevat, the goodness in his environment, he can't misbehave.

This is the most successful kind of parenting approach, dear mothers. The *chinuch* of Shevat: of blossoms and sunshine. That's how to raise our children. That is the *shevet* we must never withhold from them. It's not the stick your child needs; it's the warmth and sunshine. When he gets that, he gets the greatest *mussar shmuess* of all.

The plague that followed *arbeh*, the plague of darkness, had no negative repercussions for the Jews. During that time, the Torah teaches us, Hashem brought total light into the Jewish homes (*Shemos* 10:23). The light was so brilliant that it was then that the Jews finally realized the abomination of the place they'd inhabited for over two centuries with crystal-clear vision. The light purified them to a degree that they emerged entirely cleansed. When a person is showered with so much light, his negative facets shrivel away (see *Pri Tzaddik, Bo*).

When a home is full of light, when the mother's face is shining, no child wants to misbehave around her. Even when her children do the wrong thing, they feel bad for their mother. This is the home you want to have. This is the Torah-true parenting model: *U'lechal Bnei Yisrael hayah ohr b'moshvosam* — "For all the Children of Israel there was light in their dwellings" (*Shemos* 10:23). A home of light, dear women, is the antidote for the plague of darkness, of *tza'ar gidul banim*.

Dear mothers, you can be that light for your children. You can be that source of sunshine that generates beautiful blossoms and breathtaking gardens. See every child of yours as a source of bountiful blessings, and, with Hashem's help, he will be.

Elokei Avi:
What Kind of Parent Are You?

I n *Parashas Beshalach*, the Jewish nation sings to Hashem at the sea, praising and thanking Him for the incredible miracles they experienced. For this reason, the Shabbos on which we read this Torah portion is known as Shabbos Shirah, the "Shabbos of Song." Let's understand the inherent beauty of song and how we can incorporate it into our daily lives.

Let Your Children Blossom

When Shlomo HaMelech sought to praise the woman of valor, he wrote a poem whose first verse begins with the first letter, *alef*, and its last with the last letter, *tav: Tenu lah mipri yadeha* — "Give her from the fruits of her hand" (*Mishlei* 31:31). These hands that invested so much will eventually reap the fruits of her labor, the wise king tells us. However, we must first traverse the path from *alef* until *tav*; it's not an overnight occurrence.

The Alshich comments on the author's choice of words. Shlomo doesn't say, "Give her the fruits of her hands," but rather "*from* the fruits of her hands," which relays a deep message to the Jewish woman: you will only get to see a small part of your rewards in this world.

I always wondered, what kind of praise is this for the woman? Isn't it enough that Shlomo writes, *Kamu vaneha vaye'ashruha* — "Her children have risen and praised her" ("You're the best, Mommy!")? *Ba'alah vayehallelah*, he goes on to say. "Her husband will praise her" ("There's no one like you in the world, dear wife!"). *Rabbos banos asu chayil v'at alis al kulanah* — "Many women performed courageous deeds, and you surpassed them all" (*Mishlei* 31:28–29). What is the deeper, added message of this verse?

The Alshich's answer offered insight to my question. A woman is wont to say, "What do I gain from all this praise? It doesn't help me one bit. All I want is to see results from my efforts. How will these compliments help me if my children don't turn out the way I want?"

For this reason, the final, most consummate praise the woman receives from her husband is the wise writer's last verse: Yes, dear woman, what you see in the here and now is only *mipri*, *from* the fruits. It's not all of it. You deserve the world for the efforts you invest.

And we all know how much effort it takes.

I once read an incredible *chiddush* from the Divrei Yoel, the Rebbe of Satmar. He wrote that on the first day of Tishrei, Hashem judges us, the children, and we rely on the merits of our fathers. If you take a closer look at the words in the *machzor* of Rosh Hashanah, you'll realize that we constantly refer to the pious deeds of our forefathers in the hopes of garnering heavenly mercy in their merit. On Tu B'Shevat, says the Divrei Yoel, the parents are judged. You, dear women, are brought to trial regarding your parenting. What kind of mother are you for your children? On this day, the heavenly judges take a look at your fruits, your children. Are they satiated? Are they thirsty for your love? Are they protected from the sun? Did you prune the weeds?

Imagine! This is the day when Hashem discerns your parenting abilities. He examines the heart and soul you and your husband invest in the precious saplings in your care. If the fruit looks good, it means the soil is good. But if, G-d forbid, it isn't, HaKadosh Baruch Hu asks, "What kind of parenting power can I give her for the coming year?"

Hashem holds your maternal power in high esteem, dear women. He trusts you with His precious souls because He has faith in your ability to tend to their every need.

In this vein, Rashi offers an illuminating interpretation of the verse in the Song of the Sea, *Zeh Keili v'anveihu Elokei avi va'aromemenhu* — "This is my G-d and I will build Him a Sanctuary; a G-d of my father and I will exalt Him" (*Shemos* 15:2). My holiness does not start with me; it is my parent's holiness and G-dliness that was instilled in me. This verse tells me that the way I perform a commandment is a reflection of my father: whether Hashem was truly his G-d, "the G-d of my father," or if he performed the commandments by rote.

What kind of parent are you, dear mothers?

This is not a simple concept. It's so hard to raise children properly! Our Sages compare parenting to planting a tree (*Taanis* 5b–6a). In order to produce a strong tree, a farmer must devote himself with utmost care to the procedure. In the event of a storm, only a well-rooted tree will survive. The turbulent world we live in necessitates every ounce of our efforts in the planting process.

I know, dear women, it's so difficult to maintain a balance of discipline and love. On the one hand, we need to jump into the sea like Nachshon ben Aminadav, fearlessly tackling the issues at hand. But at the same time, oh how we need the sensitivity of Miriam: the gentle, loving approach. Give the plant a chance to blossom! Take a step back, dear mothers.

Parenting 101:
Raise Your Hands Heavenward

The most essential parenting role of the mother is prayer: to spread her arms like branches on a tree. This is the power inherent to the Jewish mother that is most needed for the child's success. This incredible power is also a responsibility of great magnitude. *Videi Moshe keveidim* — "And Moshe's hands grew heavy" (*Shemos* 17:12), we read in *Parashas Beshalach*. At the start of the frightening war between Amalek and the Jews, Moshe raised his hands to the sky in prayer. As he stood there, beseeching, his hands grew heavy and he needed the help of Aharon and Chur. You, dear mother, when it's hard for you, don't be afraid to ask for help.

The Gemara notes that when a tree sheds its fruit early, it's customary to dye it with red paint (*Chullin* 77b–78a). However, our Sages ask, isn't this an Amorite superstitious custom? No, they answer. The red paint is simply a conspicuous reminder of the tree's need for people's prayers. The same was true in Moshe's case; he stood like a tree with its branches upward. How did it work that when he raised his hands the Jews gained strength and when he dropped them the Amalekim's power intensified? Was Moshe employing magic? Not at all. When the Jews saw his hands raised to the sky, they turned their hearts to their Father in Heaven. His hands were merely a reminder of the direction in which they had to focus their hopes.

A tree is a sign of hope, dear women. In *Parashas Beshalach*, the Jews were thirsty; they had no water, and they were ready to give up. What did Hashem do when Moshe cried out to him? *Vayoreihu Hashem eitz* — "Hashem showed him a tree" (*Shemos* 15:25). Through the tree, Hashem conveyed a profound message to the disgruntled nation: "Aren't you embarrassed? Look at this tree, how thirsty it is, and how it stands with its arms outstretched to the sky as it waits for rain to fall."

When the nation stood at the shores of the sea, frozen with fright, they thought that this was the end. The Egyptians followed closely behind, armed and equipped to decimate them all. And what did Moshe say to them? What does Hashem say to you when you're at your wits' end, completely in the dark and unable to fathom how the salvation will ever come?

Hashem yilacheim lachem v'atem tacharishun — "Hashem will make war for you, and you shall remain silent" (*Shemos* 14:14). The magnificent words of this verse bring tears to my eyes every time I read them. Moshe Rabbeinu's message in the word *tacharishun* was that he showed them a *churshah*, a thicket of trees. The branches of all the trees, Moshe pointed out, raise their wings upward. Isn't that a beautiful description of a *beis knesses*? The trees teach us an invaluable lesson about hope, about focus (see *Likutei Moharan* 251).

The red paint is not the solution for an ailing tree. It's the means to the end; it's simply a way to attract attention from passersby so they can immerse themselves in prayer on its behalf. The end is *tefillah*.

Banish the Bitterness; Bring on the Music

Look at Miriam the prophetess. She left Mitzrayim and headed out on a long trek, her children in tow. "Ima, what filling are you putting into our sandwiches?"

"What sandwiches? Go paste the stickers on the drums I prepared."

"Drums? I want something good!"

Miriam and her peers didn't even prepare food for the journey. *V'gam tzeidah lo asu lahem* — "They didn't make provisions for themselves" (*Shemos* 12:39), tells us the verse in *Parashas Bo*. What did she do? She played the drums, and the women drummed after her. Even more important than the aroma of food that wafts through the home, dear women, is the sound of song in the air.

A house in which the woman doesn't sing in joy doesn't have the capacity to draw salvation. We see this phenomenon with *Am Yisrael* in the desert. They crossed the sea, witnessing miracles, and made their way to the other side. Before long, however, they were dissatisfied again: "They came to Marah, but they could not drink the waters of Marah because they were bitter. . . And the people complained against Moshe saying, 'What shall we drink?'" (*Shemos* 15:23–4). In the plain sense, the word *they* refers to the water and explains why the people couldn't drink it. The Baal Shem Tov, however, interprets the reference as applying to the people.

Was the water bitter? No. The *people* were bitter, and when a person is embittered, he sees everything negatively. Think about the miracles Hashem performed with *Am Yisrael*. He split the waters for them! But what happens when a person is bitter? *Vayamru al yam b'Yam Suf* — "And they rebelled about the sea while they were at the Reed Sea" (*Tehillim* 106:7). "For this we left Mitzrayim?" they cried. Dear sisters, when a woman chooses to be bitter, all the gifts Hashem sends her way will become reasons for complaint.

This is the war we must wage against Amalek. The word *Amalek* has the same numerical value as the word *mar*, bitter. A parable is told of a father who lifts his son onto his shoulders and they head out on a journey. The son says to his father, "Pluck that fruit for me from that tree," and the father fulfills his request. "Give me from this one," the son says again, and the father complies. As they continue on their way and the son starts to tire, he suddenly calls out to a passerby. "Excuse me," he says, "have you seen my father?"

"Aren't you ashamed of yourself?" the enraged father says. "I'm carrying you all this way and you don't even see me? I'm throwing you off my shoulder right now!"

Some people only know how to forge communication

through complaints. "It's so hard for me." "I'm so drained." This is the content of their prayers and the content of their conversation with others. To these women, Hashem says, "When it's good for you, you don't remember Me. Everything is perfect. When do you open up your lines of communication? When you have what to complain about. When you're a bitter woman."

Because of the embittered nature of *Am Yisrael* following their exodus from Mitzrayim, the Midrash of *Parashas Beshalach* is full of parables that convey great lessons to us. A king saves a woman from the hands of bandits and then requests to marry her. What's her reaction? She refuses to talk to him. When the king threatens to return her to the bandits, she starts to scream and he's overjoyed. "I want to hear your voice!" he says. *Hashmi'ini es koleich*, Hashem begs of us. "Let Me hear your voice!" (*Shir HaShirim* 2:14) — the voice that cried to Me from the depths of Mitzrayim.

What's Hashem's plea to us, His dear daughters? My princess, stop calling to Me only in times of bitterness. I don't want to make you suffer in order to hear your beautiful voice. Speak with Me. Thank Me. Share your life with Me, dear daughter.

Hashem wants to hear from you. Raise your voice to Him in song, like our role model Miriam. Build a positive, deep connection with Him that comes from a happy place. Hashem is *motzi asirim bakosharos* — "He releases the bound in the appropriate time" (*Tehillim* 68:7). Expounding on the word *bakosharos*, the Sfas Emes notes (*Beshalach* 5653) that every person has a choice of how to connect with Hashem: either through *bechi*, crying, or through *shirah*, song. You choose! Do you want your relationship to be one of tears and pleading or of gratitude and joy? And if you want to know which one Hashem prefers, here's your answer: *Habocher b'shirei zimrah* — He chooses the songs. Bring on the music!

No Complaints – Ever?

The fact of life is that things do get tough. Does this mean that we can never cry? How are you, the Jewish woman, supposed to transform your cry into a song? What a difficult task!

According to the Midrash on *Parashas Beshalach*, the pious Jewish women knew to sing even before the *geulah* unfolded. At the sea, they erupted into song even before the menfolk. Only after the men saw the Egyptians dead on the shores of the sea, *az yashir* — "then they started to sing" (*Shemos* 14:30, 15:1), whereas *vatikach Miriam haneviah achos Aharon es hatof b'yadah* — "Miriam the prophetess, the sister of Aharon, took the drum in her hand" (ibid. 15:20) while they were still *besoch hayam* — "in the middle of the seabed" (ibid. 15:19).

Despite the intense fear that gripped their hearts, Miriam and the women had greater faith than the men that there would be an eventual redemption, accompanied by miracles of great magnitude. This is why, the *Mechilta* teaches us, the song of the women — not the men — was accompanied by drums: they were so confident that Hashem would perform miracles that they prepared the drums in advance to use in singing Hashem's praise.

Vateitzenah chol hanashim achareha b'supim u'vimcholos — "And all of the women followed after her with drums and in dance" (ibid. 15:20). Regarding this wondrous song of the women, the Midrash comments, *Tashuru meirosh? Amanah* (*Shemos Rabbah* 23:5). Who is the woman with true *emunah*? The one who sings *meirosh*, from the start. Singing after the miracle unfolds and the Hand of Hashem is revealed is also beautiful, but the song that you sing when you're in the seeming darkness is all the more noteworthy.

Are we expected to sing always? What happens when things are *truly* hard for us? HaKadosh Baruch Hu says, *Am zu yatzarti li tehillasi yesapeiru* — "I created this nation for Myself, in order for them to sing My praises" (*Yeshayahu* 43:21). And yet, especially the Book of *Tehillim*, a *sefer* of *tehillos*, is full of complaints! *Hashem mah rabu tzarai...* — Hashem, my sorrows are so great..." (*Tehillim* 3:2). Is this considered praise?

In the days of old, I used to be strict with my students. "Don't complain!" I would admonish. "It's forbidden!" But over time, I gained some clarity on the balance. HaKadosh Baruch Hu didn't create us women with nine measures of speech (*Kiddushin* 49b) solely in order for us to tell Him, "Thank You, thank You," all day!

Parashas Beshalach comes along to clarify this concept exquisitely. We read countless times that Hashem revealed Himself to *Am Yisrael* following their litany of complaints. *Shamati es telunos Bnei Yisrael* — "I heard the complaints of the Jewish people" (*Shemos* 16:12). The Sfas Emes offers a most relieving point, noting that a complaint is a phrase that expresses a subconscious belief in Hashem. After all, why would you bother fussing to someone who doesn't have the capacity to help you anyway? Imagine! Your complaint is actually a manifestation of your belief.

If so, *Parashas Beshalach* lets us in on a remarkable secret: your complaint is specifically evidence of your faith, but that's if you complain the right way. How do we do that? How do we draw the line between a grievance that's forbidden and one that's welcome? Three main differences lie between them: the target of the complaint, the tone of it, and its content.

Let's talk about the target of the complaint. *Vayilonu kal adas Bnei Yisrael al Moshe v'al Aharon bamidbar* — "The entire assembly of the Children of Israel complained against Moshe and Aharon in the Wilderness" (ibid. 16:2). Immediately upon hearing this complaint from the nation, what did Moshe Rabbeinu instruct them to do? Direct your complaints toward the only One Who has the capability to help you: Hashem. *Lo aleinu selunoseichem ki al Hashem* — "Your complaints are not against us, but against Hashem" (ibid. 16:8).

How foolish we are when we direct our complaints toward our husbands, our children, *ourselves*. Directing our fusses toward any target other than Hashem is a futile effort that generates only further negativity.

Rashi explains that when the nation was standing at the brink of the sea screaming, HaKadosh Baruch Hu said to Moshe, *"Mah titzak eilai! Alai hadavar talui v'lo alecha* — "Why do you cry out? To Me!" (ibid. 14:15). Rashi explains, Let them know that the outcome depends on Me and not on you (ibid. 14:15 and *Rashi* there). Let the nation cry to Me. Rightfully so. When Rachel Imeinu complained to Yaakov about her barrenness, he answered her, *Hatachas Elokim anochi* — "Am I in place of Hashem?" (*Bereishis* 30:2). Turn to the One Who can help you.

Unloading your complaints to your poor husband will only defeat the purpose of your complaint. Instead, heed the words of our Father in Heaven: *B'tzel Shakai yislonan* (*Tehillim* 91:1) — he shall dwell in My protective shade, My dear child, direct complaints this way, He says.

Equally important is the tone of your complaint. How do you express your frustration? The challenge in life is to speak pleasantly, even in times of pressure. That's where the nation failed when begging for water in the desert, he notes. Hashem *wants* to hear our voice. *Hashmi'ini es koleich*, but make it *koleich areiv*, a sweet voice. If, in a stressful situation, you turn to Hashem and make a request in a sweet, pleasant tone, He will listen to your complaint. How beautiful it is to start a sentence with the word *please*. Isn't this what we teach our children from when they say their first words?

The third condition of a welcome complaint is its content. The Midrash (*Yalkut Shimoni, Chukas* 764) tells us that *Klal Yisrael* was never able to sing *shirah* on the manna because if they first complained about something, they were later unable to give thanks for it. So how is it that on the water, about which they first complained when it was lacking, they were eventually able to sing the *Shiras HaBe'er*, the Song of the Well?

The answer lies in the contrast between the two complaints. When the nation was desperate for even a drop of water to wet their parched throats, their complaint only emphasized their dependence on HaKadosh Baruch Hu. "We can't survive without You!" they cried. However, when the nation complained about the manna, the content of their complaint was one of criticism. They looked at this queer creation, which they dubbed *halechem haklokeil* — "inferior bread" (*Bamidbar* 21:5) — and criticized its quality and taste, hence losing their chance at later singing a song of thanks to Hashem for this wondrous gift.

Even when you are intensely dissatisfied with a particular aspect of your life, dear women, remember that complaining about your situation in a critical manner will G-d forbid put a negative stamp on it forever. Your children, your husband, your livelihood — they will all come around. Until they do, turn your complaint into a prayer for the future.

The woman who takes her *bechi*, her complaints, and turns them into *shirah*, song, is a pious woman indeed. If you want to be that woman, you could continue complaining — but to Hashem, in a sweet voice, and with positivity. Every one of those complaints is yet another testimony to your genuine faith, your true belief that only Hashem can make your life the life you desire.

Can Love Be Commanded?

Parashas Yisro is the Torah portion that focuses on the pivotal moments when the Jewish nation received the Torah at Har Sinai. What were the *luchos*, the Tablets on which Hashem's commandments were inscribed? *V'haluchos ma'aseh Elokim heimah v'hamichtav michtav Elokim hu charus al haluchos* — "The Tablets were Hashem's handiwork, and the script was the script of Hashem, engraved on the Tablets" (*Shemos* 32:16). The Tablets are Hashem's very own script to us.

Oh, how we wish to receive a letter from Hashem, even a very brief one. When we don't know why things are happening in our lives, we crave a little clarity, a clue that will connect causes and effects to our human eyes. The Torah is Hashem's script to us, dear women. It's His letter to His children. So what are You writing to us, Ribbono shel Olam? What do you want us to know?

Rav Shlomo Wolbe, *zt"l*, notes that from *Yetzias Mitzrayim* until the nation received the Torah, the Torah continually discusses their *bechirah*, their choices: to leave the exile, to jump into the sea, etc. Suddenly, in *Parashas Yisro*, Hashem thrust the Torah into their hands. The Gemara cites the astounding words *kafah aleihem har kagigis* — "Hashem suspended the mountain over their heads" (*Shabbos* 84a), and He told them that if they didn't accept the Torah, this would their burial place. So where was the nation's choice?

Rav Wolbe's answer to this glaring question offers a magnificent insight into the ways of Hashem. From one moment to the next, Hashem performed astounding miracles for the Jews. The skies opened before their eyes: seven heavens tore open when the nation stood at Har Sinai. After being exposed to miracles of such magnitude, the Jews simply couldn't understand what it would be like *not* to follow the words of Hashem's Torah.

What is the deeper meaning of the words *kafah aleihem har kagigis*? There are times when things become so obvious to you that you feel like you're being led in a certain direction. That's what happened at *mattan Torah*. The startling clarity of Hashem's greatness and oneness impelled them to follow Him, to accept the yoke as His chosen nation.

Let's understand this on a simple level. When you hear a powerful *dvar Torah* that highlights the importance of a certain commandment, how do you feel about fulfilling it? You're suddenly filled with a conviction that this is the right thing to do, and you simply can't see yourself doing otherwise. It's essentially your own drive, inspired by an external power, that's urging you in that direction.

Rav Wolbe expounds on his explanation with an awe-inspiring message. In the future, he wrote, there will live a generation that won't have the stamina to withstand the evil inclination. They simply won't. The yetzer hara will lure them in with new tactics at every moment, with sounds, with sights, with thunder and lightning. We cannot judge the people of this generation because they just won't have the power to overcome their temptations. On one thing, however, we will be able to judge: Why didn't you immerse yourself in Torah? To read even one verse, even with no motivation or fervor, is to fill yourself with meaning. There's no way that a person will learn the Torah and walk away from it unchanged, because the Torah has the power of persuasion. It has the ability to impel you in a new direction.

In the times heralding the coming of Mashiach, the times we live in today, the *yetzer hara* is so enormous, so dazzling and alluring. He infiltrates every facet of our lives, allowing us no peace. The only armament we have in our defense is an opposing force that is even greater, even more enormous and dazzling and touching, and that is the Torah. When we live according to the Torah, we develop an inner conviction to follow it of our own will.

In his discussion on this topic, Rav Wolbe refers to the *Ma'aseh Merkavah*, the Vision of the Chariot, citing the *Sefer Yechezkel*. The prophet Yechezkel was shown a chariot in which the angels sat. Sitting in a chair on the chariot was the form of a person. Says Rav Wolbe, this sight teaches us that in the higher spheres, the prophet was able to see the true greatness of man. The essence of man is exquisitely holy, even more so than the angels. The evil inclination is only an external force that tries to lure him away from his true essence.

Citing the words from *Koheles* (9:14–15), Rav Wolbe continues to explain that man is essentially a "small city with few people. One day, a famous king encircles the city and builds large fortified towers on top of it. The king finds one wise person inside." The city refers to the person's body, and the king symbolizes the evil inclination, who tries to fashion dazzling towers and arouse our fantasies. Who is the smart inhabitant who dwells inside the city? That's the *yetzer hatov* (*Nedarim* 32b). He dwells inside each of us, dear women! He's not a power that we have to cultivate.

We are truly holy beings. It's our job to keep the evil inclination where he belongs: outside our holy vessel. The only way to do that, dear sisters, is through Torah.

But I'm a Woman: What Does Torah Mean to Me?

The commandment of learning Torah is relegated to the menfolk of our nation. But does that mean that we women are doomed to be unable to absorb its untold power to keep the evil inclination at bay?

Not at all! The Torah has the ability to inspire us, to trigger our emotions, stirring our feminine, emotion-based psyche. That's Hashem's "letter" to us. As women, our role is to perform our special commandments with the fervor and vigor that only we have the capacity to experience. When we approach the mitzvos with our trademark awe and excitement, we're fulfilling the Torah to its utmost degree, the woman's way.

Indeed, the Torah was first given to the women. Moshe was commanded, *Koh somar l'Veis Yaakov* — "So shall you say to the House of Yaakov" (*Shemos* 19:3), which refers to the women (*Mechilta*), and only then, *v'sagid livnei Yisrael* — "relate to the Children of Israel," the men (ibid.). Why did Hashem choose to convey the Torah's message to women first? Women set the tone of the home, and we are the ones responsible for inculcating love of Torah in our husbands and children, a task to which our loving nature is most suited. In a home where the mother has a love for Torah, the walls radiate with purity. Her fire and enthusiasm for Hashem's mitzvos course through the blood of her children until they establish an independent conviction to observe the mitzvos of their own volition.

We have the capacity to apply Hashem's "script" to our daily lives with true joy. In his deep wisdom, Hashem chose to approach the women first because He understood how well they do with His instruction. *Challah? Of course I'll bake challah! Three batches every week, and I'll distribute them to all the needy families in the neighborhood. Shabbos? What a blessing!*

I'll do whatever it takes to fulfill Your wishes. And, of course, I won't speak any lashon hara. How can I? I'm a Torah Jew!

Where is the love that poured forth from those pious women's hearts when they accepted the Torah with open arms, their eyes shining? Where is that excitement we once had?

Let me share with you a most touching discourse from the Tiferes Shlomo of Radomsk on *Parashas Yisro*, a piece that's saturated with love. In preparation for *mattan Torah*, "Moshe brought the people forth from the camp toward Hashem, and they stood at the bottom of the mountain" (*Shemos* 19:17). Commenting on this verse, Rashi notes that the *Shechinah* came out to the nation like a *chassan* goes out toward his *kallah*.

Our Sages famously analogize *mattan Torah* to a wedding, where *Am Yisrael* is the *kallah*, Hashem is the *chassan*, and the Torah is the *kesubah*, the marriage contract. Love must come from the heart. So then how can Hashem command us, *V'ahavta eis Hashem Elokecha* (*Devarim* 6:5), to love Him? What can I do if I just don't feel connected to the Torah or its mitzvos?

Answering this question, the Tiferes Shlomo explains that before we recite *V'ahavta eis Hashem Elokecha*, in Shema, we first say a most touching prayer *Ahavah Rabbah/Ahavas Olam*. In this prayer, we constantly make reference to Hashem's love toward us; concluding with the blessing: *Habocher b'amo Yisrael b'ahavah* — "Who chose His nation, Israel, with love." According to the Tiferes Shlomo, through observing the marriage contract between Hashem and us, we give ourselves the capacity to absorb that very love. The more connected we are to Hashem's "script," the more inspired we become by His passionate *ahavah* toward us. *Kamayim hapanim lapanim* — "like water that reflects a face back to a face" (*Mishlei* 27:19), we can turn into vessels of love and warmth.

At first, the Jews did not want to accept the Torah. The *kallah* didn't want to be burdened with the prospect of marriage. It's work, after all. She has to constantly ensure that she doesn't break her *chassan's* heart, that she doesn't disappoint him. So what did HaKadosh Baruch Hu, the *chassan*, say? "I love you, I love you, I love you. I prepared something very special for you."

Note the brilliance of the *Krias Shema* blessing, the Tiferes Shlomo tells us. Before we read the command of *V'ahavta eis Hashem Elokecha,* that we love Hashem, we launch into a monologue saturated with love: *Ahavah rabbah ahavtanu…chemlah gedolah viyeseirah chamalta aleinu…* — "With an abundant love You have loved us…; with exceedingly great compassion You have had compassion on us…" Only after this display of love, which is so intense, do we say, *Shema Yisrael.* . .

In every person, Hashem implanted a desire to be recognized. Infinitely more than you want to love, you have a deep desire to be loved. The Torah is your vehicle to experience that emotion to the highest degree. There is no way for you not to feel Hashem's deep love toward you when you keep His commandments, when you connect to Him through our *kesubah.* When you recite *Ahavah Rabbah* every morning, give yourself the opportunity to internalize the depth of the words, Hashem's message of overflowing love to you, His dear daughter, and when you reach the words of *V'Ahavta,* you will no doubt be impelled to reflect that love as well.

How to Cultivate the Love

Let's take Hashem's message about love into the marriage domain.

The *kesubah,* like the *luchos,* details the responsibilities of both parties in a marriage. This is what the husband will provide, and this will be the wife's role. Interestingly, it makes no mention of the emotional relationship between husband and wife. Why not? Why is the concept of *ahavah* not mentioned in either the *luchos* or the *kesubah?*

The Torah is conveying something beautiful: there are two dimensions to every relationship. First, there's the technical dimension, decisions about who will take the children to school, who will wash the dishes on *motza'ei Shabbos*, who will provide the livelihood and who will pay the bills. That's the practical aspect of the partnership, which every couple arranges according to their situation and needs. But there's a second, more crucial, aspect of the relationship, and that is *V'ahavta l'rei'acha kamocha* — "Love your friend like you love yourself." For this, no signatures are needed. It's a given.

We are accustomed to thinking that love is voluntary; we can either love someone or choose not to. But in *Parashas Yisro*, we learn something novel. When HaKadosh Baruch Hu offered the Torah to *Am Yisrael*, He lifted the mountain above their heads like a roof. "Either you accept the Torah," He said, "or you will be buried here." In other words, there was no choice for the nation. When there's no love in a home, it loses all of its vitality. When the unwritten clause of the *kesubah* is neglected, the house becomes a factory, a business that packs the children's lunches and sends them off to school.

What if you just don't feel love? How can you be forced to love if you just don't feel it? There must be an answer, and the answer we find in our Role Model of love, the Ribbono shel Olam. When a woman says, "What else does he want from me? I cook, bake, and clean the house," she must know that all of these tasks belong to the first part of the *kesubah:* the part on which she signed. But what happens to the unwritten clause, the one that's a given?

The Ohr HaChaim enlightens us in *Parashas Yisro*. In order to ignite *ahavah*, it's not enough to take care of the home and the children. It's important to do what Hashem does, to be verbal in our expression of love. When you do for your husband and children, point out the meaning of these acts: "See what I am doing for you. I'm doing this only because you are so dear to me."

Let's examine what Hashem said before giving *Am Yisrael* the *Aseres HaDibros*. *Atem re'isem asher asisi b'Mitzrayim* — "You have seen what I did to Egypt." My beloved nation, do you realize how dear you are to Me? *V'esa eschem al kanfei nesharim* — "I have borne you on the wings of an eagle." I am choosing you; you are My nation. *V'avi eschem eilai* — "and I brought you to Me." It is only Me and you. From Hashem's loving words, we learn about the attitude we must foster in relationships.

It can't be only about you. As much as you deserve commendation for fulfilling the technical part of your contract, it is much more important to focus on the injunction to love the other as yourself — the dimension that is a given. When HaKadosh Baruch Hu expressed His closeness to *Am Yisrael*, He revealed Himself to them on a beautiful mountain adorned with greenery. A request for *ahavas Hashem* would have been superfluous; it was understood that the nation would react in kind.

When it comes to the unwritten clause of your *kesubah*, remember *Parashas Yisro*. Remember the unwritten clause of the *luchos*, the *klal gadol baTorah*. Hashem did not deem it necessary to mention *ahavas Hashem* or *ahavas haTorah* in the *luchos* because it is not a choice. It is a consequence of work. By investing in this aspect of your relationship, by extending yourself to express positive feelings to your loved ones, you are following in the ways of Hashem.

Replenishing Your Foundation

This is the *parashah* of true *simchah*! It's not merely a list of dry laws; it's the code that's saturated with advice on every aspect of living. Often a student will ask me, "Are you a therapist? A *shalom bayis* counselor?" And I say, "I live by the Torah." The Torah, dear women, contains all the information we need to lead a rich, fulfilling life. The Sfas Emes (*Mishpatim* 5636) tells us that in every letter of the Torah every person can find what he needs at that moment! Are you looking for your *bashert*? For happiness? For *parnassah*? Everything is right there.

It's not easy, being happy for the long term. When you buy a new sweater, you're happy. It's so exciting to come home and gently remove the tissue paper. The fabric is still soft and delicate and the embroidery so perfect. But what happens when you've worn it several times? It's over. It brings you no more joy.

A child — oh, how you wish for one! And when you finally hold that infant, all day you want to kiss its tiny feet. Why don't you feel the same way about your seventeen-year-old son? "Pick your towel up from the floor" is all you have to say to him.

Where's that twinkle in your eye that you had under the

chuppah? Is your husband not the same man you knew then, that *chassan* who stirred your heart?

When the novelty of something new wears off, it's hard to maintain that original joy. The very same item that ignited a surge of emotion suddenly does nothing to your heart.

So how do we make newness a constant reality? Here is where the Torah's depth lies. *Parashas Mishpatim* hinges around one notion: giving, giving, giving. Give to the convert, give to the orphan, to the widow, to the servant: just keep giving. There's a very sweet book titled *Have You Filled a Bucket Today?* that teaches children the importance of making others happy. The author focuses on a point that is so clearly expressed in the Torah: when you fill another person's bucket, you fill your own. When you give to others, you instill true joy in your own heart.

The equation is simple. If joy comes from newness, by pouring forth your inner abilities and allowing them to flow, you give the new spirit its space and you feel more and more joy! The more you give, the more newness you experience. Giving fills you with that rush of energy that emanates from the newness it engenders. What a blessing!

The *shefa*, abundance of material possessions, that is especially prevalent in America today doesn't lead to joy. The Maharal teaches us that the Hebrew letters of the word *shefa* can be rearranged to create the word *ipush*, decay. If you don't express your inner capacity to give, this power will shrivel up inside you, sucking out the joy of living. True joy emanates from giving, dear women. The moment you start giving, you will see how Hashem infuses you with new *kochos*, new spirits, a novelty that won't wear off as long as you keep giving.

Think about this for a moment and you will realize how true it is. How do you feel after you've done something for another person? You could spend a whole tiring day visiting the sick and the elderly, yet come home feeling invigorated. You exerted yourself so much, but when you give, you fill yourself with newness. You replenish your fountain with new, pure water.

I find that the reason many people are broken inside is because they have this aching desire to give of themselves, but they have no recipients. Either they have no family, no spouse, no children, or they feel that their recipients won't appreciate their deeds and they thus stop giving.

Im Kesef Talveh es Ami: Lend to My Nation

I want to share with you an astounding midrash (*Tanchuma*, *Mishpatim* 12) on lending. All of Hashem's creatures, tell us the Midrash, borrow from one another. The day borrows from the night, the night from the day, the light from the sun, and the sun from the light. Wisdom borrows from intelligence and intelligence from wisdom.

Our Sages expound on this concept, adding that intelligence is acquired from the teacher and wisdom from the student, who comes to conclusions based on his teacher's teachings. How enlightening! A teacher needs his students. This is my opportunity to thank you, dear students. If not for your reading my words, I wouldn't be worth anything.

For forty days, Yehoshua, Moshe's disciple, stood at the foot of the mountain, waiting for Moshe to descend with the Torah (*Rashi*, *Yoma* 76a). Why did he wait all that time? Yehoshua feared that if Moshe would descend and find that no student was anticipating his arrival, he wouldn't be Moshe Rabbeinu. He would be Moshe, but he wouldn't have the *talmidim* that rendered him a rebbi.

Going back to the Midrash, Hashem joins in and adds, "I, too, borrow *ko'ach* from you, as it says, *Tenu oz Leilokim* — 'Give strength to Hashem' (*Tehillim* 68:35). You're My other half! I am only a King because I have a nation. I, too, am dependent on you."

We see that this is a universe based on lending and borrowing freely. And when a person lends to his friend in order to ensnare him with *ribbis*? To such a person, the Midrash tells us, Hashem says, "Aren't you ashamed of yourself? See how much I've lent, and I don't take *ribbis*. I water the land, I make the plants grow, I light up the celestial spheres, I blow life into your soul — see how much I've lent!"

Yes, this is a world of lending, dear sisters, a world that revolves around giving. *Im kesef*, commands Hashem, "if you have money," *talveh es ami*, "that you will lend to My nation," *es he'ani imach*, "to the poor person who is with you," ...*lo sesimun alav neshech*, "you shall not charge him interest" (*Shemos* 22:24) — this money was originally designated for the poor person, who has always been with you; it was given to you so that you should give it to him and perform a mitzvah when giving it (*Ohr HaChaim, Shemos* 22:24).

But this doesn't only pertain to money. Whatever Hashem bestowed on you, share it freely with others. That's the reason you have it! What are you worth without it? *You don't feel like giving shiurim? What will you do all day, Yemima?*

Kabeid es Hashem meihonecha — "Serve Hashem from your treasure" (*Mishlei* 3:9), advises Shlomo HaMelech. If you know how to do something, do it for others. What is your treasure? Are you blessed with grace? Dance in a *tzedakah* production. Know how to draw? Paint pictures for your children. If you're a storyteller, enthrall children in a preschool. Love to swim? Work with special kids in the pool. Do you know how to give advice? Become a coach. If you have the potential, don't let it rot inside you — "lend" it to others!

Conflicting Opportunities to Give: Which One Should You Choose?

So we already understand that giving is the best thing we can do for ourselves and others. It's a win-win situation. But what happens when you're conflicted about whom to give to?

Parashas Mishpatim starts with words that are directed toward men and women alike: *V'eileh hamishpatim asher tasim lifneihem* — "These are the ordinances that you shall put before them" (*Shemos* 21:1). As Torah Jews, we are constantly commanded to make judgments.

Subconsciously and consciously, we're always weighing our options. Do I want to have a cleaner house or be a calmer mother? Invest more hours at work to bring in more money, or be a more available wife? Sometimes the speculations seem minor, but the decisions are incumbent upon us nevertheless. Should I prepare another dish for dinner or take a short nap? Should I do homework with this child or play Rummikub with that one? No one will make that decision for you, and you want to do it right.

The difficulty of the decision-making process is compounded by the knowledge that in many cases both choices are technically sound. You're not weighing the consequences of a mitzvah over an *aveirah*; it's the choice between two apparent mitzvos that throws you off. Should you volunteer for the local *chesed* organization or spend more time with your loved ones? Which act of giving outweighs the other?

What can you do when you find yourself weighing the pros and cons of one duty over another, trying desperately to determine what's right for you at that moment? Let's look into *Parashas Mishpatim* for guidance.

Our Torah has established for us a crystal-clear guide, and with this we can achieve peace and happiness in the heart and home. The *mishpatim* in the Torah increase peace among people. Thus, we're permitted, and even encouraged, to forgo a mitzvah if doing it will detract from peace in the world.

Let's use the example of *tza'ar ba'alei chaim* to explain this concept. The *parashah* gives us a scenario in which a person encounters two men; one is about to load his donkey, and one is in the middle of unloading his donkey. Faced with this choice, the person is required to help the latter so that the animal will not suffer unnecessarily. However, if the other person, the one loading the donkey, is an enemy of his, he is obligated to assist him first in order to conquer his *yetzer hara* (*Bava Metzia* 32b). Imagine that: the person you loathe is the one you should help first!

But what happens to the important mitzvah of *tza'ar ba'alei chaim*, inflicting pain on an animal? By choosing to help load the donkey first, the other donkey sags under his burden for a longer time. But *Parashas Mishpatim* shows us that promoting peace can sometimes mean leaving another *chesed* undone.

What does *oneg Shabbos* mean to you? Many women (myself included) envision a lavish spread with three main-course options and fifteen dips. It sounds so lovely, so royal! But what happens to your home in the process? Is the plan all about pots and pans? Why shouldn't your husband and children enjoy a calm, pressure-free — and, yes, peaceful — environment?

That's where decision-making can get tough, because the *yetzer hara* has a wickedly clever way of getting to us women; he knows exactly how to speak our language, how to say the words that will influence us most. But with our clarity, we can always remind ourselves that the highest rung in our ladder of values is the imperative to keep the peace.

As Jewish women, we are constantly inundated with difficult decisions. How do we know which ones to choose? Volunteering for the organization or staying home for your husband? The answer is to take a step back and see the whole picture. If we look ahead and see what each choice of giving will bring about, we will know what's right for us at the moment.

In *Parashas Mishpatim*, the Torah tells us, *Lo sateh mishpat...v'shochad lo sikach* — "Do not pervert judgment...and do not accept a bribe" (*Shemos* 23:6–8). It's not only judges who can be bribed: it's all of us, as we make our day-to-day judgments or choose our *chesed* priorities. How can we know if we are bending the truth? How can we determine if we are guilty of "bribing" ourselves during the decision-making process? Only by being true to ourselves and by stopping to kid ourselves will we know what are our true intentions for giving.

When we opt to look the other way and choose the more glamorous *chesed* option just because it feels better (or looks better to others!), we are withholding the truth from ourselves and our loved ones. And when we bribe ourselves into thinking that the supplementary paycheck will help pay tuition, who are we kidding?

When you're in a quandary regarding two obligations, think hard. Think deep. Which duty will promote more peace in this world? *Yes, Yemima, I know you love to give shiurim, to have your Torah spill forth and light up the eyes of your students, so it's hard to turn down a last-minute request, but do your children need you more?* Dear women, your children will surely be so proud to have the most exquisite birthday party or Purim costume, your chance to express your gift of creativity. But will they want a calm mother first? How about your husband? When you give of yourself with honesty, choosing the duty carefully, you will promote more peace in your home.

A Torah life is all about clarity. It's all about peace. And when you fulfill your personal *na'aseh v'nishma*, doing what you know is right for you to do, you will merit *na'aseh v'nismach*, experiencing true joy.

The Mishkan: Drawing Joy to Your Heart

The Torah portions of *Terumah, Tetzaveh, Ki Sisa*, and *Vayakhel* all focus on the Mishkan, the Tabernacle. What was so unique about this resting place for Hashem? We find the answer in the root of the Hebrew word *mishkan* — *mem shin chaf* — which means that people were drawn to it (*mashach* means "to attract"). It had an incredible power of attraction, this holy site, drawing people toward it like a magnet.

The Gemara (*Kesubos* 8a) teaches us that when there is a wedding or *sheva berachos*, we say before Birkas HaMazon *she-hasimchah bim'ono* — "that this celebration is in His dwelling place." Where Hashem dwells, there we find joyous celebration. What can we deduce from this? If we want to bring joy into our lives, dear women, we need to create a magnet for it. It doesn't just happen on its own. You can't wake up in the morning and expect to feel happiness, to walk around the house and experience a palpable joy in the air. It's not a natural state of being, but we need it so badly. So how can we draw *simchah* toward us and our home?

The Mishkan: Drawing Joy to Your Heart / 165

In order for you to live a life of happiness, you must invest. Simply put, Hashem says, *V'asu li mikdash v'shachanti besocham* — "They shall make a Sanctuary for Me, so that I may dwell among them" (*Shemos* 25:8). It's your job to first create that space, that sanctuary, for happiness.

Especially for women, happiness is not a reflex. On the contrary, after Chavah sinned, Hashem's curse to the woman was *harbah arbeh itzvoneich* — "I will greatly increase your pain" (*Bereishis* 3:16). How, then, will we learn to draw happiness toward us?

The *Zohar* teaches a riveting concept regarding *simchah*. It explains that in the lower spheres, which are called the *avna tova*, the "good stone," a person constantly wants to receive from the higher spheres. However, the only way he is able to draw bounty and light from Heaven is if his countenance is lit up. If he lives a sad existence, he will receive accordingly. *Tehillim* (100:2) states, *Ivdu es Hashem b'simchah* — "Serve Hashem with joy," because a man's *simchah* in this world draws *simchah* from Above.

What a magnificent approach to *simchah*! We see from this teaching that your every effort to live a joyous life will reflect on the light you receive from Above.

Let's start with understanding what the "good stone" implies. It's the most basic level of *simchah* in this world. You take a dirty diamond and you polish it until it sparkles; you take a tough situation and make it shine. Somehow, this is so much simpler to achieve outside the home. At the workplace or with your friends, it's easy to take a situation and laugh at it. It's easy to polish up stress and turn it into a joke. But what happens in your own personal Mishkan? That's where the challenge lies; it's in the home where you've got to do the most serious work.

The Gemara teaches a famous concept: *Kasheh tarbus ra'ah b'beiso shel adam* (*Berachos* 7b), which can be interpreted to mean that situations that cause stress but can be tolerated outside the home become *kasheh*, hard to deal with, when they happen inside the home. In the office, you can endure a colleague's frequent tardiness, her habit of leaving dirty coffee cups in the sink, her endless, annoying talking. When your husband or child does the same thing, where's that tolerance?

Always Anticipating: The Secret to Joy

We find a most exquisite description of the curtains of the Sanctuary. Rashi (on *Shemos* 26:9) compares the covering at the entrance of the Mishkan on the east side to a modest *kallah* whose face is concealed by a veil. The Gemara offers another comparison for the back portion, the west side, which was completely covered in fabric, with curtains reaching down to the ground: it was like a woman who walks in the marketplace, her train trailing behind her, her royalty impressing everyone (*Shabbos* 98b).

What we are hearing here is that you, the woman, can be a Mishkan wherever you are. You can exude royalty even in the marketplace because you're the *bayis*. *Ishto — zu beiso*. The woman is the home. Even in the market, even when you don't yet have a physical home of your own, you have the capacity to be a Mishkan, an edifice that draws joy.

How can you draw joy into your heart? The Pri Tzaddik, Rav Tzadok of Lublin, brilliantly elucidates the concept of *simchah*. He notes that there's a difference between *tzechok*, laughter, and *simchah*, joy. You engage in laughter only *after* you hear or see something comical. You experience *simchah*, on the other hand, in *anticipation* of something that will take place in the future, something that hasn't yet happened.

The son of Yaakov who represents the month of Adar, who epitomizes joy, is Naftali. Of Naftali, Moshe said, *Naftali seva ratzon* — "Naftali is satiated with favor" (*Devarim* 33:23). Fertile with desires, he was always looking for more. He always awaited more good. How is an insatiable amount of desires *simchah*?

The Ba'al HaTanya explains that a broken heart and a bitter spirit are not considered *atzvus*, sadness. *Atzvus*, he notes, is when the heart is cold like a stone and has no life. Bitterness and a broken heart, however, are signs of life, and the person can transform them into true joy. In other words, the Ba'al HaTanya is teaching us that as long as we hope, as long as we have a desire for something to happen, even if we are bitter about it right now, we have the capacity for joy. The main thing is that you're not a wooden board. Something is still stirring inside that heart of yours. To hope is to feel joy! To anticipate is *simchah*!

Atzvus, on the other hand, is apathy. It's when the person is like a statue. *Atzabeihem kesef v'zahav ma'aseh yedei adam* — "Their idols [or their '*atzvus*,' sadness] are [lifeless] silver and gold, the handiwork of man" (*Tehillim* 115:4); as long as you're crying, you're kicking, you're screaming, you can feel true *simchah*.

A Magnet for Joy

But what can you do if your home is not a happy place? How can you become a magnet for *simchah*? The first thing you must understand is that every day is precious. Even the pain you're experiencing today is building the Beis HaMikdash.

When Hashem instructed Moshe to command the nation to bring contributions for the Mishkan, He said, *V'yikchu li terumah mei'eis kol ish asher yidvenu libo tikchu es terumasi* — "Let them take for Me a portion; from every man whose heart motivates him you shall take My portion" (*Shemos* 25:2). Using another definition of the word *yidvenu*, "motivates," the Kli Yakar remarks that Hashem wants a portion from every man whose heart is *throbbing*, every man who is in pain. We can't fathom how our pain builds the Beis HaMikdash. The only way we can come to a place of joy is if we first allow ourselves to feel, to stop numbing the pain.

Rav Shalom Sharabi said that no prayer is identical to the prayer a person previously offered. Every day, when you daven another *tefillah*, it is elevated by the *tefillah* you offered the day before. One *tefillah* piles upon the other, until it finally reaches the heavens. Through prayer, you're building. Construction doesn't start anew every day, it is an ongoing process.

This is true for every one of your deeds, dear women. Everything you do builds up to create a most magnificent edifice. As much as you don't always see the results of your labor, know that none of your efforts are in vain. Every day is a new opportunity to continue the process.

From our precious children we can learn to find excitement in every day. Haman wanted to kill the Jewish children first because he couldn't tolerate their purity, their easily excitable personas. See how your daughter's eyes twinkle with excitement when she comes home with a "Shabbos Mommy" note. Something so seemingly trivial sparks children's joy in a real way. Their hearts are so alive!

Esther Klein, a venerable woman who was stricken with a degenerative disease, used her one functional finger to write about her daily struggles and challenges. Once, she wrote about the house she was forced to move to because the one she'd lived in wasn't on the ground level. She wrote about how sad it was for her to part from the home where she raised her family, where she invested so much. And then, when she was wheeled into her new apartment, she wanted to cry at the hospital look it had, filled with all her medical paraphernalia.

"When I saw the special chair that awaited me," she writes, "my spirits fell." Just then, one of her granddaughters walked into the room and exclaimed, "Look at this chair! Look at the regal throne they prepared for Savta!"

Esther burst out crying, pondering the power of a child. Look how this child saw a dreaded chair as a kingly throne. We must beg Hashem that He grant us the eyes of children. Oh, how they know to find joy. In nothing, they find something to be excited about. This is one secret to joy: always anticipate. Even when the situation is painful, embrace every new day with shining eyes, with the eyes of a child.

Defying Limits: *Kiton Echad Asei Li*

Another secret to *simchah* is finding it in tiny spaces. Yes, the house is tiny. You feel like you're losing your mind from the mess all around you. The children, may they be well, don't stop moving. In your mind, you keep wishing that you'd have more space.

Do you know what Hashem says about a small space? *Kiton echad asei li she'adur etzlechem* — "Make for Me a small room so I can live with you" (*Shemos Rabbah* 33:1). In the small space, that's where *simchah* happens.

Shlomo HaMelech asks Hashem, "*Hinei hashamayim u'shemei hashamayim lo yechalkelucha* — 'The Heavens and the highest heavens cannot contain You' (*Melachim I* 8:27) — so how can You want such a small place?" The answer? Because true joy emanates from lack.

One of the tips nutritionists give to women who want to lose weight is to eat from a small plate. The portion suddenly looks much bigger on a small plate. A woman really has this power: to take a small lot and make it accommodate so much. She could take one toffee and split it between five kids. She could find two carrots and onions in the refrigerator and cook up a delicious soup. She can say, "Look what I managed to do in these ten minutes! I organized this whole closet!" "Look how many clothes I was able to buy for a hundred dollars!"

What is it about creating so much from so little that imbues us with such joy? It's the thrill of victory, *nitzachon*. This is what fuels a woman, who is an *eizer kenegdo*, who relishes the challenge against the limits of time, of money, of space. We women understand this joy best.

This is precisely the power of the moon, to whom the woman is often compared. Compared to the sun, the moon is tiny and yet she is able to light up the world. How does she do that? She lives by the premise of *me'at hamachazik es hamerubah* — "the small that contains the many." A woman has the capacity to defy all boundaries, to exceed even her own expectations for success — and that fills her with true joy.

The less you have, dear women, the more joy you have the capacity to experience. Allow the little pleasures in life to excite you. Make them huge in your eyes, and your children will live by your example. Even a trip to the park is reason to celebrate. The fact that you woke up this morning and everyone in the house was breathing — on top of each other, maybe, but breathing nonetheless — is cause for joy.

Don't spare your words when you want to express your joy, dear sisters. Commenting on the words *V'yikchu li terumah* — "Let them take for Me a portion" (*Shemos* 25:2), the *Panim Yafos* notes that the word *v'yikchu* also implies "taking" with words. If you're feeling joy, articulate your emotions to your loved ones. "What a beautiful day! Another opportunity to serve Hashem!" Your expressions of *simchah* are more meaningful to your husband than the most lavish meal, and to your children more than the most colorful candy spread.

Look around your *mikdash me'at* and communicate to your loved ones how blessed they are to share these quarters with such special people. Find the joy in the little things, in the small spaces, and you will become that magnet of *simchah*.

When Are You Most Alive?

In *Parashas Tetzaveh*, we are introduced to layers and layers of clothing: the detailed wardrobe of the Kohen Gadol and his assistants. The High Priest was required to don eight different vestments before starting his service. Otherwise, any service he performed was invalid. When the Kohanim wore their vestments, they were transformed into people of a higher caliber. Just wearing them already gave them this distinction.

These same garments are alluded to in *Megillas Esther*, notes the Kli Yakar. The holy garments were taken with the nation to the Babylonian exile, where Achashveirosh himself seized them and wore them at his infamous party. How he wished for these clothes to transform him into a person of the caliber of the High Priest, with all his sins forgiven! How he craved that position! But for him, the holy clothes were a mere costume.

Yet another person joins the masquerade in *Parashas Tetzaveh*. Indeed, Moshe Rabbeinu wears his mask so well that we don't see him at all. Starting from the Torah portion that depicts his birth, *Shemos*, until the end of the Torah, Moshe Rabbeinu's name is found many times in every *parashah*, except for this one. "I'm hiding," he says to Hashem. "I'm nonexistent. *Mecheini na misifrecha asher kasavta* — 'Erase me now from Your book that You have written' (*Shemos* 32:32)." What motivated Moshe to make this strange request? Following the sin of the golden calf, Hashem threatened to destroy the nation. Moshe subsequently offered to make an exchange: instead of erasing them, erase me.

Because Moshe's name does not appear in this Torah portion, does that imply that he doesn't exist? Of course not. In essence, he was very much alive. When a person negates himself in order to enable someone else's existence, he can't be more alive than that!

As Jewish women, we often fall into the role that Moshe Rabbeinu fills in *Parashas Tetzaveh*. Whether willingly or not, it happens very often that we must sacrifice our comfort, our needs, our wishes, to enhance the quality of another's life. Women sometimes ask me, "I'm erased, totally depleted. I have no essence and no voice. All I do all day, every day, is tend to other people's needs. Where am I in this picture?"

Dear sisters, you must understand this: a woman has a *kiyum*, an existence, when she is *mekayeim* others, when she provides *them* with the tools for existence. When you're raising children, you're not erasing your essence. You're at the height of your existence. You will never be more alive! The thrill and pleasure a woman's essence absorbs when she gives others the ability to exist are what spark her soul and fill her lungs with air.

Queen Esther sacrificed her life for her nation. When Mordechai instructed her to have an audience with Achashveirosh on behalf of *Klal Yisrael*, she cried to him, "But then I will risk being erased!"

When she understood that she would be performing a perilous deed, she said to Mordechai, *V'cha'asher avadeti avadeti* — "If I perish, I perish" (*Esther* 4:16). Esther knew that she was only one in a million in Achashveirosh's eyes. The chance for her to be recognized and called for an audience was minimal. *Va'ani lo nikreisi*, she admitted. He hadn't summoned her for thirty days (ibid 4:11).

But what happened when this pious woman chose to be ready to be erased, to give her life for her nation? Miraculously, Achashveirosh invited her for an audience. *Vayehi chir'os hamelech es Esther haMalkah omedes bechatzer nasah chein b'einav* — "When the king noticed Queen Esther standing in the court, she found favor in his eyes" (ibid. 5:2). Just when she thought she would cease to exist, the peak of her existence came to be.

I want to share with you a most magnificent *gemara* (*Megillah* 15b) that speaks volumes of the place a Jewish woman has in the eyes of Hashem and His heavenly servants. Three angels, tells us Rabbi Yochanan in the *gemara*, appeared before Esther at the time that she stood in front of the king. One extended her neck. One lit up her face with *chein*, charm. And what did the third one do? He stretched out the scepter.

Esther says, "I'm done. I'm erased. It's over." Then comes Hashem and says, "Angels, get to work!" And they do the job for her. *Vatikrav Esther vatiga b'rosh hasharvit vayomer lah hamelech mah lach Esther HaMalkah u'mah bakashaseich ad chatzi hamalchus v'yinasein lach* — "And Esther approached and touched the tip of the scepter. The king said to her, 'What is it for you, Queen Esther? And what is your petition? [Even if it be] until half the kingdom, it shall be granted to you'" (*Esther* 5:2–3). What a miracle!

Just when a Jewish woman thinks that she has no more strength left to wait for her miracle, He makes it happen. He brings the redemption toward her. Only when you are completely erased, completely aware of your inability to make things happen on your own, does the miraculous intervention occur. That's when someone will finally see you, recognize your value, and appreciate you for that. That's when you reach the peak of your existence.

HaKadosh Baruch Hu, too, plays the role of the Hidden One, so to speak, in our generation. This *hester panim* is the reason for the darkness we live in. Originally, our Sages didn't deem it necessary to add *Megillas Esther* as a *sefer* of *Tanach.* Queen Esther, however, persisted. *Kisvuni l'doros* — "Inscribe my words for the generations!" (*Megillah* 7a), she pleaded. Esther, in her deep wisdom, perceived that until the coming of Mashiach, this would be the *sefer* that would comfort the nation. It's the *sefer* that reminds us that even if we don't see the Guiding Hand of HaKadosh Baruch Hu, He is very much in our lives.

The Rebbe of Kotzk tells us the famous parable of the son who traced the path he had taken with his father. At the beginning of the journey, he saw four footprints in the sand. "I understand," he said. "Two are mine and two are my father's as he guided me along the way."

Further down the path, he only discerned one set of footprints. Assuming that they were his own, he said, "Here is where you left me, Father. You left me all alone."

"No, my dear child," answered the father. "Where you see only two footprints is where I lifted you upon my shoulders and carried you to safety."

It's true that Hashem is hiding from us, but *Megillas Esther* reminds us that just when we think that He doesn't exist, G-d forbid, He is indeed most involved in every aspect of our lives. When you don't see the footprints, know that Hashem is even more present. He is carrying you on His shoulders.

VaChamushim Alu: Revving Up the Spirit

Commenting on the first verse of *Parashas Tetzaveh,* the Sfas Emes writes that the word *tetzaveh* is an expression of *zerizus,* enthusiasm. Hashem commanded that the nation fulfill His instructions swiftly and with enthusiasm, says the Sfas Emes, because only deeds that are done in this manner are everlasting. These are the deeds that ascend to the heavenly throne. If you perform an action without passion, on the other hand, nothing remains of it.

The Jewish nation is particularly blessed with the positive attribute of *zerizus*, doing things quickly and efficiently, which the descendants of Amalek tried in vain to eradicate. They understood that only the eager ones from among the nation escaped the exile, as it says, *Vachamushim alu Vnei Yisrael mei'eretz Mitzrayim* — "The Children of Israel were armed when they went up from the land of Egypt" (*Shemos* 13:18). The Sfas Emes translates *chamushim* as *zeruzim*, the swift ones. Thus, Amalek focused on deflating our spirit of *zerizus*.

Only those who perform deeds with enthusiasm and spirit are the ones who have an eternal existence. So how can we ensure that we are among those who operate with this *zerizus* that brings true joy and meaning to our deeds? Let's take an example from the High Priest.

The Kohen Gadol was reminded of his exalted position every moment of his service thanks to his garments. First, the layers of clothing were quite heavy. He couldn't possibly forget that he was wearing these special vestments. The special clothes were intended to ensure that he would perform his duties with dignity and enthusiasm. Even more so, notes the *Sefer HaChinuch* (Mitzvah 99), with every step that the Kohen Gadol took, he saw his clothes that reminded him, "You are an esteemed being. Your deeds have profound ramifications. Make sure to take every step with humility."

In essence, what was the work of the Kohen? What were the holy deeds he performed on behalf of the nation that deemed him one of the most esteemed members of *Klal Yisrael*? He prepared the animals so they would be offered on the Altar as a *korban* to Hashem. Using a special trowel, he cleaned the Altar. And all this time, he remembered, "I'm on duty now. Carefully, carefully. With enthusiasm. With my whole heart."

How can we constantly remind ourselves that we, too, are on duty, that we, too, are performing holy work as we clean, as we prepare the meat in our kitchens to feed the holy people living in our homes? When we adorn ourselves with regal clothes, we have this capacity. Then every deed that we perform has the potential to reach the heavens!

When Queen Esther prepared to approach Achashveirosh without an invitation, she dressed in her regal garments. All the onlookers knew that this fateful move conceivably could lead to her execution, as is evident in the conversations that transpired between her servants. Anticipating her imminent death, they drew a lot over her royal clothes — who would get the shoes and who would get the cape... *Yechalku vegadai lahem v'al levushi yapilu goral* — "They divide my garments among themselves and cast lots for my clothing" (*Tehillim* 22:19; see *Midrash Tehillim* there). Because there was no doubt in their minds that this would be the outcome of her seemingly foolish deed, it ate at their hearts that Esther adorned herself so.

This is what Amalek can't stand about our exalted nation. The nations eat their hearts out when they see a Jew in his vestments, proud and royal, despite the trying circumstances.

Vashti could not handle this regal bearing either. Her sadistic mission was to turn the Jewish *bnos melech*, princesses, into servants — from prince to pauper. They have a Shabbos Queen? I'll turn the regal day into a day of labor. They wear fine clothes? I will strip them of any vestiges of royalty.

Unfortunately, this vicious streak of Amalek can even exist in Jewish homes. His desire is to turn the royal day of Shabbos into a harried, exhausting experience. He wants it to become a day of serving, clearing off, cleaning, and anxious scrubbing — for the day to lose its luster. He wants the queen of the home to dress the part of the servant because he knows that *oz v'hadar levushah vatischak* — when a woman is dressed in royalty, she's happy.

You don't have to dress in extravagant clothes to feel regal, but you have to get dressed. "Clothes make the man" may be a cliché, but it is true. When a woman dons clean, pressed, elegant clothes in honor of Shabbos, there is no doubt that she will experience a more regal day. This is why Rabbi Yochanan referred to clothing as what brings honor to the person (*Bava Kamma* 91b).

When you dress like a queen, you act like one: a happy one. Don't let Amalek infiltrate your home. Remember that when you don your royal clothes, like the Kohen, you will be enveloped with a feeling of appreciation for the work you're doing. The mundane work of sweeping and serving will be elevated into a service for the King, and the effects of your enthusiasm will be everlasting.

The Queen in You Never Sleeps

Figuratively speaking, a woman is always dressed for her part. She never strips herself of her costume as the caregiver. On Purim, the menfolk of our nation have an obligation to consume alcohol to the degree that considerably impacts their clarity of mind. During those moments of intoxication, they're not in their usual state of control. A woman, however, is always on duty. She can never risk insobriety because she must always be available to others. If her son's homecoming is delayed one night, she lies in bed, awake. Even when she's finally asleep, when the baby cries, she's at his crib in a flash. We're always dressed for our role. It's an inherent part of who we are, a role that is intricately bound to our souls.

As the caretaker of your *mikdash me'at*, you are always on duty, performing an exalted service. When you dress the part, you truly appreciate its beauty. *Emes mah nehedar* — how breathtaking was the scene of the saintly High Priest, adorned in his exquisite clothes, emerging from the Holy of Holies on Yom Kippur! When he entered the Kodesh HaKodashim, he did so with joy, because that's when he was at the peak of his existence.

Make your home that magnificent scene, dear women. As the caretakers of your loved ones, know that when you feel the most erased, you are indeed the most present.

Salachti Kidvarecha: The Door to Forgiveness Is Never Closed

The Torah portion of the golden calf is so sad. We read about the nation's fright, their great sin, the shattering of the *luchos*, and how the nation returned the crowns they were granted at Mount Sinai. *Vayisnatzlu Bnei Yisrael es edyam meiHar Choreiv* — "The Children of Israel were stripped of their jewelry from Mount Choreiv" (*Shemos* 33:6). How tragic!

Still, this heartrending Torah portion opens with atonement. HaKadosh Baruch Hu instructs Moshe to tell the nation that when a census is taken, every man should give an atonement for his soul, a half-shekel as a portion to Hashem. So even before we read about the destruction and heartbreak that sin engenders, we already find comfort in Hashem's kindness; the door to forgiveness is never closed.

Indeed, the Bnei Yissaschar offers words of tremendous comfort when he says that only two verses in the entire Torah start with the letter *samech*, the first of which we find in *Parashas Ki Sisa*. Hashem laments, *Saru maheir min haderech asher tzivisim* — "They have strayed quickly from the way that I have commanded them" (ibid. 32:8). So fast? They barely accepted the Torah and already they've strayed from the path?

And the second verse? *Selach na la'avon ha'am hazeh* — "Forgive now the sin of this people" (*Bamidbar* 14:19), which is followed by those famous words *Vayomer Hashem, Salachti kidvarecha* — "And Hashem said, I have forgiven because of your word" (ibid. 14:20).

The Hebrew letter *samech* is a complete circle; a shape that has no end. There is no end to sin, but there is no end to forgiveness either. *V'diber Hashem el Moshe panim el panim* — "Hashem spoke to Moshe face-to-face" (*Shemos* 33:11). Only after true heartbreak, after profoundly destructive separation, did Hashem talk to Moshe face-to-face. Why does it have to be that way?

After the momentous "wedding," *mattan Torah*, and the incredible miracles that the nation witnessed, Moshe Rabbeinu ascended to Heaven to bring down the *kesubah*, the marriage contract: the Tablets. Those were moments of intense love! But what happened in the meantime? The nation built the golden calf and danced around their "new" *chassan*. *Eileh elohecha Yisrael!* — here is your god! Indeed, our Sages describe *Am Yisrael* as a bride who was unfaithful toward her husband just days after the wedding (*Midrash Rabbah, Shemos* 46:1).

Kasveim al luach libecha, Shlomo HaMelech tells us. "Inscribe them [the Torah and mitzvos] on the tablet of your heart" (*Mishlei* 7:3). The *luchos* are symbolic of the heart. When Moshe descended with the brand-new *kesubah* and witnessed the betrayal, "he threw down the Tablets from his hands and shattered them at the foot of the mountain" (*Shemos* 32:19). The shattered *luchos* allude to a shattered heart. What could be more deeply painful than that?

A shattering of hearts always hurts: between two friends, two sisters, two business partners, but the saddest case of all is when it's between husband and wife. How devastating it would feel to find out that the one who should treasure you most found a replacement for you!

A Word of Caution: The Child Is in the Tent

It is very important to discuss the individuals whom strife in the Jewish home most deeply affects. When your heart is so broken that you can't focus, this may be hard to grasp, but even when we experience great pain, we cannot forget that our home must be the safe place for our precious children.

What does Moshe Rabbeinu do when he learns the painful truth? In one of the most heartrending verses in the Torah, we read, *U'Moshe yikach es ha'ohel v'natah lo michutz la-machaneh harcheik min hamachaneh...* — "Moshe would take the tent and pitch it outside the camp, far from the camp..." (*Shemos* 33:7). Our Sages explain that Moshe told the nation, "You distanced yourselves from the G-dly source? Then you've also distanced yourselves from me," and he moved his tent outside the camp.

And imagine what happened next! The nation watched in silence as Moshe distanced himself from them. And then, *V'diber Hashem el Moshe panim el panim ka'asher yedabeir ish el re'eihu v'shav el hamachaneh* — "Hashem spoke to Moshe face-to-face as a man would speak with his friend; then he would return to the camp" (ibid. 33:11). Hashem, in His infinite kindness, begged Moshe to return.

If these words are hard to understand, what follows next makes the verse even more incomprehensible: *U'mesharso Yehoshua bin Nun na'ar lo yamish mitoch ha'ohel* — "And [Moshe's] servant, Yehoshua bin Nun, a lad, would not depart from within the tent" (ibid.). What was HaKadosh Baruch Hu cautioning Moshe about and what message do we deduce from these words? "Just a moment," said Hashem to Moshe, "there's a young man right near you. Yehoshua, your loyal servant, what will be with him? When you picked up your belongings and decided to resettle, did you not remember the young lad who lives with you?"

When we decide to "pick ourselves up" and do our own thing, to distance ourselves from a situation, do we remember that our children never leave our tent? This is his home; where should *he* go? He's right there, listening to every word, soaking in the strife and animosity with way more comprehension than we'd like to imagine. When we express anger or disappointment unpleasantly, our children don't magically disappear. They remain right there, at our sides, even if we're so enmeshed in the battle that we don't even pay attention to their presence. Watch out for them, dear sisters. Your home must always be the first safe place for them.

The Three Phases in Every Marriage

Parashas Ki Sisa is so incredibly sad. The newly minted nation decided to turn its back on the G-d Who only weeks before crowned them as His exalted people. However, *Parashas Ki Sisa* later becomes a joyous *parashah*. This Torah portion teaches us that every salvation transpires in three phases. First comes the initial excitement. The shofar blasts at the adorned mountain! You're so incredibly sure that everything will work out just fine. Next comes the breaking apart. Something will always break, always. How sad. But what follows next is breathtaking: the joyous reunion.

When the Torah describes the people who were qualified to build the Mishkan and its instruments, it repeatedly calls them *chachmei lev*, "wise-hearted people" (ibid. 28:3). What's the connection between wisdom of the heart and the ability to construct the Sanctuary?

The skill it took to create a resting place for the *Shechinah* was more than technical. It was a special wisdom, an emotional wisdom. Jewish women are blessed with this same kind of wisdom so that they can build their own *mikdash me'at*. While some people are intellectually brilliant and others are kind but lack intelligence, the builders of the Tabernacle had to have both qualities. This is the ideal balance of thought and emotion that we must achieve as the builders of our homes, dear women.

Our Sages teach us that, as in the case of *mattan Torah*, every marriage has three stages. The first stage is the wedding — so beautiful! Next come the mistakes: *v'hinei hi Leah* — "and behold, she is Leah" (*Bereishis* 29:25), not Rachel. It's not what we expected. We start to argue, to disagree, to find fault. The third stage is *Pesal lecha shnei luchos avanim* — "Carve for yourself two stone Tablets" (*Shemos* 34:1) — the two people make a new commitment.

Why was the first set of *luchos* broken? Our Sages answer that it was because they were given with such great ceremony and splendor. *Ayin hara*, the evil eye, ultimately led to disaster (*Midrash Tanchuma, Ki Sisa* 31).

Pesol means "to sculpt." In Lashon HaKodesh, it connotes molding oneself into a new person. You have to remove some *pesoles*, waste, to fit the new mold. When Rav Shach, *zt"l*, would give premarital guidance to *chassanim*, he would say that the worst characteristic a spouse can have is stubbornness: "This is me, and you must accept me as I am." A person who refuses to resculpt himself when conflict arises is not marriage material. After the initial excitement breaks down, the new *kesubah* that the couple draws up, like the new set of Tablets, is the real one.

A Jewish man marries his wife with the words *Harei at mekudeshes li...k'das Moshe v'Yisrael* — "You are hereby married to me in accordance with the faith of Moshe and Yisrael." What is *das Moshe*? The fact that things can break down but will be renewed. That's the legacy we've attained from our saintly leader.

After the incident of the broken *luchos*, Hashem commanded Moshe, *Pesal lecha shnei luchos avanim* — "Carve for yourself two stone Tablets" (*Shemos* 34:1). Despite the shattered heart, HaKadosh Baruch Hu chose to forgive, to rebuild, to give us another chance. *Davka* from the deep, dark hurt, HaKadosh Baruch Hu's mercy was awakened. When you look at a child and think, *Lo al hana'ar hazeh hispallalti* — "This child is not what I had in mind when I prayed," and from that pain, you choose a new path, a slightly different, more accepting, more forgiving route, you are following in the ways of G-d.

When you accept that the husband you envisioned is not the husband you're living with and choose to focus on the harmony that could envelop your home, you are following the ways of Hashem. As a woman of Moshe's faith, you have the capacity to gather chips of stone and sculpt something beautiful. You understand with your emotional wisdom that life will bring challenges and that not every day will be bright and sunny. But you also know the principle *Mitzvah gedolah liheyos b'simchah tamid* — "It's a great mitzvah to be joyous always" (*Likutei Maharan* II:24). You have a constant obligation to sculpt, to fix, to make your home the beautiful place you want it to be.

Simchah Takes Effort

Let's talk about one hindrance to this joy. It is essentially a childish pattern of behavior that many don't outgrow, one that wreaks much havoc in every area of our lives: instant fulfillment of your wishes. The word *miyad* is a terrible thing. If you don't have what you want *miyad* — immediately — life is awful. If your husband doesn't buy you that gift *miyad*, if your son isn't accepted into the yeshivah *miyad*, if your married daughter isn't expecting *miyad*, the world is a horrible place. You must have what you want instantly or you're miserable.

As Jewish women, we don't want *miyad*. We want *miyadcha*

hamelei'ah hakedoshah v'harechavah, to receive directly from the Hand of HaKadosh Baruch Hu. We want what's right for us, but we also don't want to fall along the way: *shelo neivosh v'lo nikaleim*. We want the capacity to feel *simchah* always, to have the ideal balance of emotion and logic.

Let's learn from Moshe Rabbeinu, who was a paragon of joy. The one time he showed sadness was when he shattered the Tablets. *Am Yisrael*, who was dancing around the golden calf, looked at him and said, "We made Moshe Rabbeinu so despondent?" That's when they removed the crowns they had been given at *mattan Torah*. They couldn't bear his sadness.

Rebbi Levi Yitzchak of Berditchev says that when a woman tries to work on *simchah*, even when the circumstances aren't rosy, and Hashem sees that a certain situation makes her brokenhearted and sad like Moshe Rabbeinu, He says, "I will mend her pain. I will sculpt for her new *luchos*. I will make her life beautiful again." But this only happens when *simchah* is a priority in her life. If she follows the faith of Moshe, she will merit experiencing the novelty of that new set, the exquisite opportunity to forget the old and bring on the new.

And if we feel we can't handle the hurt on our own — it's just too unbearably deep — what can we do? As Hashem says to Moshe, *V'ra'isa es achorai* — "Then you will see My back" (*Shemos* 33:23). Rashi explains that Hashem showed Moshe the knot of His tefillin, so to speak: the *kesher* of *tefillah*, the connection we make through our prayers. When you find that you're not living the life of your dreams, remember that you can always turn to G-d, the One Who faced the greatest disappointment of all time. With your broken heart, you have the ability to connect to Him, to beg, to feel the warmth, and if you bring the Third Partner into your home, you will merit *ish v'ishah Shechinah sheruyah beineihem* — "a husband and a wife, the *Shechinah* settles among them." By choosing to turn to Hashem, you're doing your part in welcoming the Divine Presence into your home.

Women Standing Strong

*P*arashas *Vayakheil* bears witness to the power of the masses. In *Parashas Ki Sisa*, we read how the Jews sinned as a group: *Vayikaheil ha'am al Aharon* — "The people gathered around Aharon" (*Shemos* 32:1). "Make for us gods that will go before us!" they cried.

Now, how can they rectify that grave wrongdoing? They gather once again; this time to hear words of Torah: *Vayakheil Moshe es kol adas Bnei Yisrael* — "Moshe assembled the entire assembly of the Children of Israel" (ibid. 35:1). The entire nation assembled to listen to Moshe because they so wanted to improve their deeds.

When people gather together, or, better yet, when *women* gather together, and they say, "Hashem, I want to leave this lecture a better woman," the mercy that rains down on them from the heavens is infinite. In *Parashas Vayakheil*, Hashem looked down from Heaven as Moshe transmitted the Torah to them. *Torah tzivah lanu Moshe morashah kehillas Yaakov* — "The Torah that Moshe commands us is the heritage of the Congregation of Yaakov" (*Devarim* 33:4). *Kehillas Yaakov* refers to the women (*Rashi, Shemos* 19:3). How the angels dance when we gather to learn Torah!

Mirrors of Purity

Parashas Vayakheil offers insight on the profound power of the Jewish woman. Prior to the construction of the Mishkan, the nation was instructed to bring contributions. Every man whose heart inspired him came. "The men came with the women; everyone whose heart motivated him brought bracelets, nose rings, rings, and body ornaments…" (*Shemos* 35:22). According to Ramban, this implies that the men were secondary to the women. Since the jewelry enumerated in this verse was worn mainly by women, the Torah pays tribute to them, for as soon as they heard that precious metals were needed, they immediately removed their most valuable possessions and rushed to bring them.

Imagine! As soon as these pious women heard that their materials would be used to construct the resting place of Hashem's *Shechinah*, they were there. One woman gladly donated her beautiful engagement bracelet and another her tenth-anniversary necklace — all for the sake of beautifying the House of Hashem.

Additionally, the women eagerly brought their copper mirrors to be used for the *Kiyor,* the Tabernacle basin. "Here," they said. "These were the mirrors we used to assist us in charming our husbands in Mitzrayim."

Moshe was repulsed by them, our Sages remark. "Mirrors? In the Mishkan?" he asked.

And then Hashem intervened. "Accept them," He instructed Moshe, "because these are more beloved to Me than everything else" (*Rashi, Shemos* 38:8).

What was so special about these mirrors, which the women used to adorn themselves in Mitzrayim? And what can be revolting about mirrors that Moshe was at first loath to accept them?

Moshe Rabbeinu was a mirror himself. The Sages call him an "aspaklaria hame'ira," a crystal-clear glass that lit up the world. When he spoke, it was as if he didn't exist. He reflected the words of Hashem with the utmost transparency.

Every teacher transmits the Torah according to his understanding and style. When I teach Torah, for example, I teach it Yemima-style, with my feminine understanding. L'havdil, Moshe Rabbeinu taught Torah from a different place altogether. He wasn't there at all. It was just Hashem and the students. To him, a person who so much as peered into a mirror did just the opposite. It was her way of acknowledging and emphasizing her existence. "Me. Me. Me. How do I look today? What can I add to enhance my appearance?"

Moshe Rabbeinu, the humblest of all men, was repulsed by egoism. He understood that the goal of every person should be to negate himself to the extent that he doesn't exist at all. But how did Hashem counter his argument? *Kabeil*, He said to him. Accept those mirrors! If these women would have turned into transparent beings back in Mitzrayim, there would be no *Am Yisrael* today. While the Jewish men, exhausted from their backbreaking labor, didn't see a reason to perpetuate the generations in the darkness of the exile, the assertive *bnos Yisrael* stood their ground. They used their copper mirrors to adorn themselves for their husbands because they didn't waver from the will of Hashem.

The Ramchal explains that because a man's inclination for *kavod* is immense, his work in life is to surrender. But a woman, he notes, who is innately more submissive, must develop a staunch and unwavering determination to stick up for what she knows is right. She must make Hashem's will her will and remain steadfast in her decision. What special blessing do we women say in *birchos hashachar* every morning? *She'asani kirtzono.* We thank Hashem that He created us according to His will. It was this strength of character that gave *Am Yisrael* its chance for perpetuation in Mitzrayim. And it was the beauty of the women's willpower that Hashem wanted to incorporate into His holy resting place.

Eizer Kenegdo: Assertiveness as an Ideal

So what is the ideal for a Jewish woman? Is it capitulation to her husband's demands or is it clinging firmly to her beliefs? When women approach me and say, "Rabbanit, bless me with *hachna'ah*," I have a conversation with them. In Judaism, it's not about subservience. In Judaism, a woman must ascertain the will of Hashem. Pray that you and your husband be blessed with the clarity to surrender to His will as a team.

An illuminating midrash reveals that when Adam HaRishon went to name the animals, he realized that each and every one of them had a mate and he was alone. He asked Hashem for a wife. When he saw the woman Hashem gave him, he said, *L'zos yikarei ishah* — "This I call a wife" (*Midrash Rabbah, Bereishis* 17:4).

What was unique about the woman? When Hashem created her, He gave her one explicit command: that she would be her husband's *eizer kenegdo*. And this is what Adam saw in her, the Maharal tells us. In her, he saw her capacity to take a stand, her power to assert her argument. The Jewish woman has the strength of *negidus. Negidah*, in Lashon HaKodesh, is another word for *malkah*, queen. This is your royal ability, dear women, to stand your ground in fulfilling Hashem's will.

Of course, in Judaism, considering another person's side is commended. Yes, we should be empathetic, understanding human beings. It's not okay to be stubborn and unyielding when you're deciding where to spend your summer vacation or whom to invite for Shabbos. It's not okay to be unforgiving and staunch in your request that he be home at a certain time for dinner. But when it comes to *retzon Hashem*, stand strong, dear women. Follow the example of the women in Mitzrayim who used their royal capacity to bring Hashem true joy.

For what purpose were their mirrors used in the Mishkan? The copper frames were melded together to form a *kiyor*. This copper basin, which stood at the entrance of the Mishkan, was used by the Kohanim to purify themselves in preparation for their holy work. Representing purity, the basin served as a reminder of the profound power of the Jewish woman's insistence on doing what's right.

Forget Nature: It's All for Hashem

The display of the Jewish women's righteousness that emerged when they delightedly contributed their jewelry for the construction of the Mishkan was not the first one of its kind. In *Parashas Ki Sisa*, the women refused to give their jewelry toward the formation of the *eigel hazahav*. (Some commentators say they did give it in the end, while others hold that their husbands took the jewelry by force.) No matter how much their husbands begged them to play a role in the sin, they tried to stay out of it. If that would have been the only incident involving women and their jewelry, we would be able to assume that their main motivation for their reluctance was their natural attachment to their jewelry. Which woman wants to part from such precious and sentimental assets?

However, *Parashas Vayakheil* teaches us otherwise. Not only were these *tzidkaniyos* willing to donate their finest toward the elevated purpose of building the Mishkan, but they did it even before their husbands who, only a short while earlier, had to force them to do the same deed! Who is as righteous as you, dear women? Look what you are able to give up — for Hashem.

From those women's righteous deeds, we learn an important concept: *Ma'asim shel adam mochichim zeh es zeh* — the actions of a person in one area can reveal something about his actions in another area. The women's willingness to part with their jewelry for the Mishkan revealed their pure intentions when refusing to do so for the *eigel hazahav*. They weren't stubborn about keeping their jewelry because they loved the pieces; they were stubborn because they loved Hashem.

Sometimes it's hard for us to perform our duties *l'sheim Shamayim*. When we do something special, it feels good for us to know that others are aware of our good deeds. As human beings, we like to feel recognized and appreciated. But sometimes the spotlight is so far away. You're scrubbing that cupboard for Pesach inside and out, refolding all the sweaters into a neat pile, and breathing a deep sigh when you're done. The next morning, your toddler decides that tower of sweaters would make a perfect trampoline. Or your adolescent daughter rummages angrily through the pile because she has *nothing* to wear. How natural it would be for you to lose yourself. You're human! But this is the time for you to ask yourself: Am I doing this because I want to have a clean house, or am I doing this in order to fulfill the mitzvah of cleaning for Pesach?

When we do something *l'sheim Shamayim*, it reflects on all of our actions. And only if we do it purely for Hashem's sake will we reap the positive results and satisfaction. When the women during the sin of the golden calf said no to their husbands' request, they didn't say it because they loved their jewelry too much. They said no because they loved Hashem, and their later eagerness to part with their jewelry proved that.

Why are you performing the mitzvos, dear women? Why do you cook for Shabbos? Are you looking to impress the guests? If an ulterior motive is involved, the joy will be short-lived, but if you are doing it for Hashem, you will do it with a smile. You will do it gladly because you know that this is Hashem's will. And you'll also know that it's Hashem's will to have your sick toddler at home while you want to get the cooking done. In the same vein, with every inch that you clean for Pesach, you're making the *Shechinah's* resting place more and more ready for that special *chag*. But if you do it for yourself, if you do it because you're forced to do it, it will be a burden.

When we do things *l'sheim Shamayim*, nature doesn't come into the picture. As much as the women were naturally attached to their jewelry, doing Hashem's will was more important to them. And as much as it's natural to get frustrated during the cleaning process, if we realize that we're elevating our mundane acts into a spiritual *avodah*, the tension and anxiety will fade away.

The women of Mitzrayim used their simple mirrors to build their solid Jewish homes. The women in the desert used their jewelry, symbols of the physical world, to build the Mishkan. May we Jewish women merit elevating the seemingly mundane tasks to which we tend into a happy, stress-free process that will welcome more and more of the *Shechinah* into our homes.

The Grand Finale:
Hashem Can Make It Happen

Where are your hands when you daven?

In the verse that follows the haftarah to *Parashas Pekudei*, we read that King Shlomo held up his hands as he uttered his beautiful prayer in front of the Beis HaMikdash. In the same vein, in *Megillas Eichah* it is written, *Nisa levaveinu el kapayim el Keil baShamayim* — "Let us lift our hearts with our hands to G-d in Heaven" (*Eichah* 3:41).

Our Sages speak a lot about the victorious gesture of raising our hands toward the sky. This is a wondrous form of prayer, a vehicle that generates its acceptance. Furthermore, this is the kind of prayer that even succeeds in crushing our most heinous enemy: Amalek. *V'hayah ka'asher yarim Moshe yado v'gavar Yisrael* — "When Moshe lifted his hands, the nation triumphed" (*Shemos* 17:11).

How does a prayer with our hands raised high pierce the skies? This is how the angels pray. The Torah teaches us that *kenafayim l'ma'alah*, the wings of the Cheruvim are directed upward (ibid. 25:20). This gesture speaks more than a thousand words. It's a sign of surrender to a Higher Power, a motion that conveys a sense of subservience to His will. That's the essence of a true prayer (*Tiferes Shlomo, Bereishis* 3:24).

When a woman prays with this sincerity, she prays because she truly believes in Hashem's power to intervene on her behalf, and that she will see salvation. The end of the story may not be what she had envisioned, but her reliance on a Higher Power will change her perspective and give her the blessed opportunity to appreciate the path Hashem chose for her.

VaTischak L'Yom Acharon:
Looking Back When It's All Over

The Shabbos of *Parashas Pekudei* is known as Shabbos Chazak. But it doesn't seem to be the extraordinary Torah portion you would expect to see as the conclusion of *Sefer Shemos*. It's not the grand finale, as we call it. For the fourth time, after reading the portions of *Terumah*, *Tetzaveh*, and *Vayakheil*, the content once again revolves around the garments of the Kohen, the Mishkan, its furnishings and its utensils.

What added message does this *parashah* come to impart? At the conclusion of *Sefer Shemos*, our Sages explain, Moshe Rabbeinu stood outside the exquisitely constructed Mishkan. Above this magnificent structure a cloud of Hashem hovered, and the *Shechinah* rested inside the edifice. Imagine the scene!

I like to imagine if Yocheved, Moshe's mother, and Miriam, his sister, had been there to witness the scene. I can envision Miriam turning to her mother and crying, "Do you remember? Do you remember the beginning: how you and Abba felt about building a family? And I, the little girl, convinced you to come together for the sake of the nation. And do you remember baby Moshe's premature birth? How we placed him in a little box in the water and we were sure that this would be the end? And then Pharaoh's daughter came to save him. And then came the *makkos*, and the Exodus, and the splitting of the sea! Oh, and then this same Moshe brought us the *luchos* from Hashem. Look at the milestone we've reached. At the end of the long, long day, this little child of our family merited building this fortress of holiness."

And like parents at the wedding of their child, the mother and sister of Moshe would cry tears of joy.

Look, dear women, how things turned out for that mother Yocheved, who years earlier saw no hope for the future. When she placed her precious child in the river, she didn't dream she would ever see him again, let alone that he would light the way for the nation and serve as the messenger for so much blessing, such redemption.

When King Shlomo assumed the throne as king after his father's death, *Yaseim kisei l'eim hamelech,* he commanded, "A chair should be granted to the mother of the king" (*Melachim I* 2:19). Commenting on this verse, the Gemara explains that the chair was especially designated for the king's great-great-grandmother, Ruth (*Bava Basra* 91b). Yes, she was still alive to witness her descendant sit on the throne of all of Israel.

Again, imagine the scene: The proud elderly Ruth sitting on that chair and reminiscing, "I remember when I was married to Machlon, and he died. Oh, do I remember the days when I clung to my mother-in-law, Naomi, how I converted, how I gathered the bales of wheat in the field, how I bore a child to Boaz. And then David was born, and then Shlomo, and now my very own great-great-grandchild has become king and will soon merit building a home for the *Shechinah*!

"How the people laughed at me," Ruth remembers. "They said, 'What are you thinking? How can a convert merit holiness?' And here I am today, my heart swelling with the pride of the mother of the king." Oh, how Ruth waited for this moment!

Especially in *Parashas Pekudei,* our Sages tell us, Hashem remembers His nation. The word *pekudei* itself means "remember," as we are told in *Parashas Vayechi, Pakod yifkod Elokim eschem* — "Hashem will surely remember you" (*Bereishis* 50:25). This is the time when HaKadosh Baruch Hu remembers all those who feel they've been forgotten. This is the time of your redemption, dear sisters. You may have fallen countless times, but now is your chance for *chazak chazak v'nischazeik!*

All those who've given up on their dream of building a Jewish home, of meriting *nachas*, of having a decent livelihood — your time has come. What relief this *parashah* offers! Now, at the close of the *sefer*, is your chance for *vatischak l'yom acharon*, to have the last laugh. Like Ruth and Yocheved, you will very soon look back at those memories and smile as you recall the unlikely steps toward your salvation.

Seven Attempts, and Then the *Yeshuah*

At first, Moshe Rabbeinu was instructed to erect the Mishkan, then to take it apart each day of the Seven Days of the Inauguration of the Mishkan. After seven such constructions, an exasperated Moshe could have said, "How many more times must I try?" *Shidduchim, shalom bayis*, fertility specialists, therapists — how many more times can we do this?

But my dear sisters, I look around and I see a downpour of *yeshuos* wherever I turn. This week, I was at the bris of a student of mine by the name of Aliza. For twenty years Aliza and her husband waited for a child, and suddenly there I was, celebrating at the bris of her precious child. This woman came to hundreds of my *shiurim*, and she couldn't even sit because of the procedures she was undergoing. And look at the gift with which Hashem blessed her. *Pakod yifkod*, He promised. I will not forget you, my dear child. At the age of forty-six, another student of mine found her *bashert*. Hashem does not forget, dear sisters.

Why does it have to be built so many times, only to be dismantled yet again? It is because Hashem is waiting for the right moment. The *sha'ah tovah*, the propitious moment.

What was one such propitious moment? It was the hour in which Yitzchak was born, the Midrash teaches us (*Midrash Rabbah, Shemos* 52:2). The first of Nissan, the day that the Mishkan was finally inaugurated, is indeed Yitzchak Avinu's birthday.

What's the connection between Yitzchak and the Mishkan?

Hashem asked Moshe, "What are you afraid of? Are you afraid that people will mock your speech because of your stutter? That they won't believe you when you bring them a message from Me?"

Indeed, the presence of cynics in Moshe's generation was not scarce. They stood and sneered, "His motive is to take our money and our jewelry under the supposed promise that Hashem will send down a cloud to rest in that place. What nonsense!"

Said Hashem, "I will enter the Mishkan on the first of Nissan, the day Yitzchak was born; the day that saw the greatest laughter of all time."

On the day Sarah gave birth to Yitzchak and Avraham was one hundred years old, the skeptics said, "Don't tell me that this man is the father of this child. Avimelech is the child's father." When they saw the baby, the spitting image of his father, they knew who was talking nonsense. It was the day the cynics were proven wrong (*Rashi, Bereishis* 25:19).

How far we must stand from the cynics! Scoffers are among the four groups who will not merit greeting the *Shechinah* (*Sanhedrin* 103a). They have the power to extinguish our flame of hope, our deepest dreams in our hearts.

Let's understand cynicism. In essence, it's a defense mechanism. Instead of facing the loneliness of singlehood, some young (and older) women build barriers around themselves. They start by being skeptical about the boys they meet and then about the concept of marriage altogether. We see this all too often in today's world. Stand-up comedians ridicule the basic systems of human life, a sad reality that has led to the steady decline in the appreciation of moral values in the eyes and hearts of people everywhere.

The Gemara in *Sanhedrin* (63b) teaches that every type of mockery is prohibited, except for one: scoffing at *avodah zarah*, idol worship. But who gave you permission to scoff at your chances for salvation? That's *assur*. Believe that you will see your salvation and you will. Arm yourself with an environment of positive people, positive thoughts, positive words, and you will believe that you will get there.

Expounding on a verse in *Parashas Pekudei*, the Midrash notes that before a fetus descends to this world, his entire future is predetermined: if he will be poor or rich, smart or stupid, etc. (*Midrash Tanchuma, Pekudei* 3; see also *Niddah* 16b). The one characteristic that is not fixed is whether he will be a *tzaddik* or a *rasha*. A *tzaddik*, explain our Sages, is a person who accepts G-d's will. He is able to say, "It will be all right; I'm only going through a rough phase." A *rasha*, on the contrary, is one who says, "I have no hope. There is no chance that I'll still see the light at the end of the tunnel."

When Moshe Rabbeinu finally saw the Mishkan standing in all its glory and the *Shechinah* resting inside after assembling and disassembling it seven times, it was a moment of intense joy. It was a moment that disproved the cynic's prediction in every sense of the word. Here was Moshe, the baby that almost didn't make it, leading the nation toward greater holiness, bringing the *Shechinah* into their hearts. A culmination of the entire *sefer*, *Parashas Pekudei's* message is so profound. What a grand finale for the *Chumash*!

The day will come, this *parashah* teaches us, when you will have the last laugh. *Even ma'asu habonim hayesah l'rosh pinah* — "The stone that was despised by the builders became the cornerstone" (*Tehillim* 118:22). Hang in there, my dear sisters, because very soon you will prove all the skeptics wrong. When you pray with intensity, with the understanding that everything is in the Hands of Hashem, you will merit your salvation. The day will come when you will show the naysayers that, yes, you too can stand under the *chuppah* in a white gown. You too can hold a child of your own in your arms. You too can see *nachas* from your child. *Chazak chazak v'nischazeik!*

Sefer Vayikra

The Secret of Closeness to Hashem

Sefer Vayikra is so hard to understand. To our human eyes, the entire *sefer* is filled with commands and obligations that seem incomprehensible. All those *korbanos*, the blood, the details. How hard! This *sefer* is so enigmatic to us.

Let's try to better comprehend sense of the confusion that surrounds the passages in this *sefer* and at the same time, the confusion that surrounds the difficulties we encounter in our daily lives.

The latter chapters of *Sefer Shemos* discuss a very exalted period in the life of the Jews in the desert. They finally completed the construction of the Mishkan. Moshe Rabbeinu stood beside the majestic edifice, "*Sof, sof!* Finally! We've made it!" But there was one caveat: *V'lo yachol Moshe lavo el Ohel Mo'ed ki shachan alav he'anan* — "Moshe could not enter the Tent of Meeting, for the cloud rested upon it, and the glory of Hashem filled the Tabernacle" (*Shemos* 40:35).

What a disappointment! After all his hard work, the Mishkan

was finally complete, but he couldn't set foot in the *Ohel Mo'ed* when the *Shechinah* rested there.

And with that, we commence *Sefer Vayikra*, where Hashem calls out with affection to Moshe Rabbeinu and brings him close. The miniature *alef* in the word *vayikra* transmits a powerful message to us: When you feel super small, tinier than a worm, zero zero, that's when Hashem calls to you. That's when He invites you in. Now you may enter, my dear child. At the moment you're feeling tiny, you experience a blast of greatness.

The Way to Hashem Is Through the *Shelamim*

Parashas Vayikra introduces four categories of *korbanos*:
1. The *olah*, the burnt offering
2. The *shelamim*, the peace offering
3. The *chatas*, the sin offering
4. The *asham*, the guilt offering

Rav Shamshon Rafael Hirsch (*Vayikra* 3:1) tells us something enlightening: the *shelamim* is a specifically Jewish offering.

The *shelamim* was exclusively to draw closer to Hashem, and therefore, according to most opinions, a non-Jew could not bring a *shelamim*. Only a sense of satisfaction and peace, posits Rav Hirsch, is the eternal bridge between Hashem and His nation.

Rav Hirsch is telling us, dear women, that the way to draw close to Hashem is through a *shelamim*. This was a *korban* that was generally not mandatory. It was the offering you brought when you were at peace with life and seeking a connection with Hashem.

Wage the *Simchah* War

In the era in which we live, we have to fight our way to *simchah*. *Milchamah laHashem ba'Amalek midor dor* — "Hashem maintains a war against Amalek, from generation to generation" (*Shemos* 17:16). It is a lofty *madreigah* for a Jew to experience *simchah*: an exalted level, indeed. If only we'd be satisfied with what we have, but Amalek gets in the way. He constantly manages to point out that there's no hope for us, that we just won't make it. Amalek is about sowing doubt and despair. Show Amalek he is wrong: fight your way to joy!

When a Jewish woman is content with what was given to her, she attains the highest level of *simchah*: one that can only be experienced by virtue of her lacking something. Rav Eliezer Papo notes in his holy *sefer Pele Yo'etz* that when a person works toward feeling this joy when she's lacking — be it a husband, children, *parnassah*, health, *nachas*, or *shalom bayis*, G-d forbid — the reward she receives is "indescribable." You have no idea what rewards you reap when you pull yourself together in a moment of sadness and make a conscious decision to feel joy.

To be happy when you're lacking: that's true *emunah*.

"Rabbanit," women ask me, tentatively, "am I allowed to feel joy when the situation is hopeless?" They want to know, "How can I be *b'simchah* when my son is making such trouble? When we're taking treatments to bear children? When I am so lonely?"

Due to their profound anxiety, many women are afraid to experience joy. Know that it's okay to smile. It's okay to laugh! It's even pious and *chareidi* to laugh, I tell them. This is what shatters the power of *din*, judgment, in Heaven.

Which of our forefathers personified the attribute of *din*? Yitzchak: which is why his name means "laughter."

I want to share an incredible story with you, dear Jewish women.

Rabbi Yochanan, quoting Rabbi Shimon ben Yochai, once issued a command: *Assur l'adam sheyemalei sechok piv b'Olam HaZeh* — "No one should fill his mouth with laughter in this world" (*Berachos* 31a).

One day, Rabbi Yehudah HaNasi, who was known as Rebbi, was preparing to celebrate his son's wedding, and he told Bar Kappara, the comedian, "Please do not make me laugh, and I will pay you forty bags of wheat."

Bar Kappara agreed to the deal.

During the wedding, Bar Kappara suddenly arrived wearing an empty sack on his head. When Rabbi Yehudah HaNasi saw him, he burst into laughter and said to him, "Didn't I warn you that you should not make me laugh?"

Bar Kappara retorted, "I just came to claim the wheat debt" (*Nedarim* 50b–51a).

The Maharsha comments that Rebbi had many problems and suffering in his life. Bar Kappara felt that it was best that Rebbi should laugh and be happy, since through happiness, he would merit a share in the World to Come (*Ta'anis* 22a).

The Secret Behind Her Success

For the past century or so, the secular world celebrates International Woman's Day on March 8. Yes, International Woman's Day! The feminists on this planet decided that we deserve one, not 365, days of recognition.

And what exactly happens on this day? The focus is on the unfortunate plight of the female gender, how much the woman has endured over the years. This is the supposed day to celebrate her "freedom." I would have thought that this would be a day that focuses on success, on the women who've triumphed. Instead, it's a day of brooding.

If you look around, you'll realize that even in the secular world, truly successful women are women who are happy.

They're not the women who ruminate over problems of the past. They look toward the future with happiness and joy. These are women who have broken barriers, who have achieved success in areas that were otherwise off limits to them. And for them, every day is a celebration.

On a still more exalted level stands the Jewish woman who has broken the barriers in her heart. A successful *frum* woman is one who juggles her home and work with joy and excitement, who transmits *simchah* to her precious children despite the hectic elements in her life.

To me, a successful woman is one who fills her day with joy, tackling her duties with the necessary burst of energy. A successful woman organizes her home even when she knows that an hour later it will be in disarray again. She's the one who lovingly prepares dinner for her picky brood even after they turned their noses up at yesterday's menu. This is the woman we should celebrate every day.

There are so many women in our midst who deserve to be celebrated! The mothers of children with special needs, the women who have yet to be called "Mommy," the girls who trek on date after date, hopeful, smiling.

I remember when a student of mine who had been on the dating scene for a long while called to inform me that at long last she was engaged. At her *vort*, she said something incredible.

She said, "I see all the young men I went out with as a chain of *shelichim*, messengers from Hashem. The first boy I went out with at the age of twenty held on to my engagement ring and passed it on to the next boy, who passed it on to the next. This is how it was transmitted until I finally got my chance to receive it."

As we all clapped and danced for her, she continued, "Today, I would like to thank that very first boy, wherever he is. Thank you!"

Oh, how we rejoiced at that engagement! This is the story of success, of finding joy in every situation.

The True Warriors:
Smiling Behind the Tears

I'm privileged to meet countless successful women every day. Every day.

I once went to Tel Aviv to be *menachem avel* Chupit, a former student of mine, who lost her baby son, Hillel. The child, all of a year and a half, was at the babysitter when he decided to stroll out of the house. Before the sitter had a chance to look for him, her husband drove up in his car and accidentally killed the child.

He was Chupit's oldest child. What a beautiful child!

At the shivah, I sat near Chupit, trying to console her with words of *chizuk*.

And what did she say to me?

"Yemima, can you do me a favor?"

"Sure. What is it that you want, Chupit?"

"Go to the sitter and talk to her. I can't stop thinking about her — what she must be going through. Go and tell her that I forgive her with every fiber of my being, that I understand that it's all from HaKadosh Baruch Hu."

Following the instructions of my dear student, I went to the babysitter and sat with her too. The sadness in her husband's eyes was greater than the sadness in Chupit's.

When I sat with these people, shattered to pieces, I turned to Hashem and cried, "Look what a *dor* we're living in — a generation that does not seek revenge, that seeks only to offer consolation!" What successful women our generation has!

Several years ago, I participated at a gathering for a noble organization that helps women who are struggling with infertility. As I usually do, I suggested a moment of silent prayer at the end of my *shiur*.

During that quiet moment, I was suddenly reminded of the story of Rabbi Yose in the Gemara (*Berachos* 3a). He tells of the time when he entered one of the ruins of Jerusalem to pray and he heard the harrowing cries of the *bas kol*, which sounded eerily like the cooing of a dove. Rabbi Yose understood that it was the voice of HaKadosh Baruch Hu, Who was saying, "Woe is to Me that I destroyed My home!"

One may ask, "Since the *Shechinah*, Hashem's Presence, cries at other times as well, why did Rabbi Yose hear these piercing cries only when he entered the ruins?"

The answer of the Aish Kodesh is profoundly illuminating. He explains that only when you yourself stand amid the ruins can you feel what *churban* truly means.

At those moments, as we sat, enveloped in the silent prayers of women longing to be mothers, I felt that I could hear the harrowing cries of a dove. I had never in my life heard such piercing cries before. How deep the cries were! And I heard in my ears the voice of Hashem: "Woe is to Me that I destroyed My home!" I heard *churban*.

And yet, a split second later, these courageous women rose and erupted into dance. How we danced and laughed that evening! Who are like the daughters of Yisrael? Who? These are the true *nashim tzidkaniyos*, pious women who are *matzdik*, who graciously accept, Hashem's *din*. As we were twirling in a circle, I thought that this must be what the *machol*, the dance of the *tzidkaniyos* in Gan Eden, looks like.

Our Avodah Today

What's the ultimate sacrifice you can bring to Hashem? Hashem doesn't want you to do your *avodah* with *kor*, coldness. He wants your connection. How do we achieve that?

Hashem wants your joy. *Ivdu es Hashem b'simchah* — "Serve Hashem with joy." That's your *avodah*, dear women. Do it with grace, whether you have what you need, or you don't. Through *simchah*, things will clear up for you. Like the sun, your joy will melt away the fog. It will give you the clarity you crave, the close-ness you seek.

This is your entry ticket to the *Ohel Mo'ed*, from where Hashem is calling your name with affection, with love, as he called to Moshe Rabbeinu so many centuries earlier.

Waiting for the Light

et's look into *Parashas Tzav* to understand the meaning of
the *korban olah*, the burnt offering.

*Zos toras ha'olah hi ha'olah al mokdah al haMizbei'ach kol
halailah ad haboker...* — "This is the law of the burnt offering:
It is the burnt offering that [stays on] the flame, on the Altar,
all night until the morning..." *(Vayikra 6:2)*. The Ohr HaChaim
explains this verse to mean that until Mashiach comes, we're
in a world that's referred to as "night." And in the days before
the coming of Mashiach, HaKadosh Baruch Hu will take those
people of *yichus*, of distinguished quality, as offerings. He will
take *olos temimos*, innocent, pure offerings.

How many *olos* He's already taken from us! How many pure,
flawless *korbanos* we've brought!

But what happens next? Then the morning comes. At the
darkest part of night, the new day begins.

We don't understand the ways of Hashem. We have no way
of making sense of the tragedies that befall us. But in this generation, when we no longer have a Beis HaMikdash, we can still
offer our prayers: *U'neshalmah farim s'faseinu* — "And our lips
will compensate for the calves" *(Hoshea 14:3)*. Please, Hashem,

we don't want to bring another *korban* — not until we have a Holy Temple in which to bring it. Accept our sincere prayers instead.

How can we make it through the darkness of the night?

The Sun Will Rise Again

In another commentary on the *korban olah*, the Ohr HaChaim asks, "For which sin was a Jew required to bring a burnt offering?" For impure thoughts: thoughts that reflected diminished *emunah*, thoughts of a despairing spirit.

The Ohr HaChaim gives an example of the kind of thought that required an *olah* offering: "Ribbono shel Olam, this exile is too great for us. As much as You think that I can handle this — one more day and one more day and one more day of telling myself that very soon the light will come — how can I do this?"

This thought is oh, so human, but it is tainted thinking nevertheless. It reflects a lack in *emunah*, and for that we're required to bring a *korban*. But despite this lack, the Ohr HaChaim tells us, Hashem says that with a bit of *simchah* we can repent for a lot of sadness.

The Ohr HaChaim expresses this idea so beautifully. "This entire Torah portion," he writes, "offers symbolism of the last exile, the *galus* we're in. It serves to console us, to soothe our saddened souls, because every Jew seeks solace in this long and endless *galus*. Is it even possible to compare this *galus* to any other? *Galus Mitzrayim* lasted 210 years. *Bavel*, 70 years. And today, it's been 1,672 years! How much longer will we have to wait?"

This is the "*Toras ha'olah*," the Ohr HaChaim consoles us. This is the story of a nation who has been persecuted and suffering for thousands of years, a nation grappling in the darkness.

Exile is compared to night, he notes, as in the verse *Lini halailah* — "Stay the night" (*Rus* 3:13), where Boaz requests that Rus stay with him overnight. When Boaz requested that

Rus stay with him, he told her to "stay and wait." And she did. She believed in his goodness, and what happened? She waited until the morning, and, incredibly, she became the matriarch of Mashiach. The matriarch of Mashiach! We Jewish women, like the pious Rus, believe in Hashem's goodness, despite the suffering, the darkness of night, and we wait hopefully for the day to dawn again.

This touching *Ohr HaChaim* brings tears to my eyes. It majestically expresses our deep yearning for the redemption, but also our strength to carry through with positive thoughts until *alos hashachar*, the rising of the morning star. Then the morning will come.

"Yafah KaLevanah": How Is the Jewish Woman Like the Moon?

Let's learn from the example of another woman in *Tanach* who is referred to as an *olah*, a woman who knew how to focus not on the night she was in but on the day ahead. *Mi zos olah…* — "Who is this coming up…?" (*Shir HaShirim* 8:5). . . *Yafah chalevanah* — "Beautiful as the moon" (ibid. 6:10). Who is *levanah*, the moon? The Midrash tells us that this is Esther HaMalkah (*Shemos Rabbah* 15:6; see also *Midrash Tehillim* 22:10; *Yalkut Shimoni* there, 685).

How did Esther resemble the moon? On the most frightening day in her life, before she was to approach Achashveirosh without an invitation, her heart was gripped by fear, but her face shone with joy. That's what the Midrash reveals to us.

You, too, dear women, can be that *olah*. You, too, can be the moon that lights up the world in the darkest hours of the night. You can hold up even when your heart is filled with anxiety and fear. You can wait out the *shachor*, darkness, in anticipation of the *shachar*, morning: *ha'olah al mokdah al haMizbei'ach kol halailah ad haboker* — "the burnt offering that [stays on] the flame, on the Altar, all night until the morning" (*Vayikra* 6:2).

When you remember that there is day ahead, when you look forward to the light and believe that it will come, you, dear Jewish women, are like the moon.

Rav Shimshon Pincus, *zt"l*, offers an exquisite understanding of how the Jewish woman is like the moon. "Just as the sun is an independent source of light, energy, and heat," he says, "the man is like a generator that produces greatness. He radiates from within himself Torah and mitzvos — *succah*, *lulav*, and all the commandments a woman is not obligated to fulfill. A man is the generator of all forms of holiness.

"The woman, on the other hand," explains Rav Pincus, "is like the moon. She has no light of her own; she is like a mirror. Fewer commandments were given to the woman. But what power does she have? She has whatever she reflects. If she turns to the One above, to Hashem, like the moon, she reflects the greatest holiness. She is elevated to a much higher level than her husband!" (*Nefesh Chayah*, p. 29).

If you turn to Hashem like the moon, dear women, you ascend to a greatness that no man can reach. This is what the moon desired. She had no interest in being a self-sufficient being. All she wanted was to receive her light, her sustenance, directly from Hashem.

Drawing Closer

The purpose of a *korban* is to draw us *karov*, near, to HaKadosh Baruch Hu. When we learn *Sefer Vayikra*, we're filled with a deep yearning for the days when coming closer to our Father seemed so simple. The *kirvas Elokim* was so tangible!

When Hashem remembers the *korbanos*, He starts to weep over the destruction of the Beis HaMikdash. I remember when I used to participate in gatherings of comfort for the women whose homes and lives were uprooted in the Gush Katif expulsion. They would sit and cry, "Do you remember the sea? Do you remember how your husband would plant those beautiful lilies in your garden? How the children ran on the golden sand?" Oh, how they'd cry from longing.

In *Sefer Vayikra*, Hashem begs us, "Don't give up on this closeness to Me!" HaKadosh Baruch Hu's love for us is boundless. We can reciprocate: like the moon, we must turn our eyes Heavenward and seek to reflect His greatness in our hearts.

Boundless Love

We learn about the true love Hashem feels for us in Shlomo HaMelech's majestic composition, *Shir HaShirim*. In the very first verses, Shlomo begins with lyrical praises: *Al kein alamos aheivucha* — "And therefore have the maidens loved You" (*Shir HaShirim* 1:3).

Let's examine the depth of the words *alamos aheivucha* to grasp the profundity of Hashem's love for us. Our Sages tell us that we should read the word not as *alamos*, "maidens," but rather as *alumos*, "hidden" (*Avodah Zarah* 35b). The verses are saying: That which is hidden from us is revealed to Hashem.

Rav Chaim Zeitchik, *zt"l*, explains that no Jewish soul is lost before the eyes of Hashem. Every Jew, no matter how far he's strayed, stands before the eyes of Hashem and is deeply precious to Him. His every deed is noticed, his every gesture of closeness appreciated. To our eyes, it may seem that we're forgotten; but to Hashem, we are never lost.

Nothing is concealed from the eyes of Hashem, dear women. He observes our every deed, our every desire to draw closer to Him. He watches us struggle from on High, and His love for us is stronger than we can ever imagine. To HaKadosh Baruch Hu, we are flawless. *Kulach yafah ra'yasi u'mum ein bach* — "You are entirely beautiful, My beloved, and without blemish" (*Shir HaShirim* 4:7).

The Moroccans have an interesting custom; they celebrate Mimouna, a *chag* of *emunah*, on *motza'ei Pesach*. They invite friends and family and reinforce their *emunah* over fresh doughnuts and goodies. Why is this a time to proclaim and strengthen their faith in Hashem?

On Pesach, when we read about the redemption from Mitzrayim, of the plagues that struck the evil Egyptians and spared the Jews, it is easy to have *emunah*. On *Shevi'i shel Pesach*, the day on which the vicious Egyptians went down at sea and the Jews emerged unscathed at the other end, it is easy to see the Hand of Hashem. But what happens after? What happens when night comes again? That's when it is crucial for us to reconfirm our faith, to remember that Hashem is there, His loving Hand holding ours even as we stumble in the dark.

Yes, it's hard. Sometimes we look Heavenward, desperate for a sign that Hashem is looking down at us, tending to our needs. Let me assure you that He is there. Through prayer and connection to Hashem, you will feel His presence in your life. The sun is waiting to rise for you, dear women. Very soon, the sun will rise again.

The Opposite of Blame

arashas Shemini should have been one of celebration and joy. After all, it centers around one of the nation's most anticipated days in the *midbar:* the *chanukas haMishkan,* the inauguration of the Tabernacle. This was a day the nation looked forward to with much excitement. Rashi tells us (*Vayikra* 9:1) that ten holy things transpired on this day. What a moment!

Finally, after seven days of inauguration, HaKadosh Baruch Hu invited Moshe to enter the holy edifice. What a sight! What a beautiful milestone! This occurred on Rosh Chodesh Nissan: the day that heralds a season of beauty and rebirth even in the Wilderness.

And what happened? Tragedy struck. Aharon entered, adorned in the magnificent *bigdei kehunah,* flanked by his two pious sons, Nadav and Avihu, whom Moshe described as the most outstanding sons of the nation (*Rashi, Vayikra* 10:3). He offered *korbanos.* The sanctity was palpable. And suddenly, *Vateitzei eish milifnei Hashem vatochal osam vayamusu lifnei Hashem* — "A fire came forth from Hashem and consumed them, and they died before Hashem" (*Vayikra* 10:2).

The Sages and commentators offer a wide range of

interpretations regarding the actual deed of Nadav and Avihu that caused their death. Most follow *Sifra*, contending that they erred by bringing their own incense into the Holy of Holies, the area where even the Kohen Gadol may enter only on Yom Kippur. Others, like the Ramban (*Vayikra* 10:2), disagree and say that they offered the regular daily incense upon the Inner Altar in the Kodesh, but they did not do so with the proper intentions.

Rav Dessler, *zt"l*, notes that when so many sins are attributed to such exalted men, the flaws must have been so minor that the Torah doesn't even feel the need to mention them. These were giant men! Hashem found in them the minutest of the minutest sin.

We find something incredible in the verse that follows this tragic story. What was Aharon's reaction to his sons' untimely death? *Vayidom Aharon* — "And Aharon was silent" (ibid. 10:3). Throughout *Tanach*, the commentators generally build their discussions on dialogue: what Moshe said, what Hashem commanded. This is the first, and perhaps only, time in *Tanach* that Chazal deliberate over silence. Aharon's acceptance of Hashem's justice is awe-inspiring. Even asking a question, a minuscule reflection of a wavering of faith, did not occur to him.

Banish the Guilt

I would like to address a silence that was perhaps even greater: the silence of Elisheva, the wife of Aharon and the mother of Nadav and Avihu. Her silence, which isn't even mentioned in the Torah, speaks volumes.

The Midrash (*Yalkut Shimoni, Shemini* 524) tells us that, on that day, Elisheva was to experience the pinnacle of joy. It was on Rosh Chodesh Nissan that this prestigious woman celebrated four milestones: her husband, Aharon, was the Kohen Gadol; her brother-in-law, Moshe Rabbeinu, was like the king; and two of her sons, the *seganei kehunah*, entered the Kodesh in their fine garments. How much pride she must have felt!

The Midrash tells us, *ma me'urav hasechok she'sachakah Middas HaDin al Elisheva* — "How mixed is the laughter that the Attribute of Strict Justice laughed at Elisheva!" Just as she was basking in the joy of her family, calamity struck in the worst of ways. Her sons entered the Kodesh with *pe'er*, glory, but they emerged lifeless.

How could this be? And how were these bereaved parents able to exercise the strength to remain silent? There's a lesson here that's so pertinent for the mothers and fathers of our generation. The silence that Aharon and Elisheva exercised was not only in relation to Hashem and His ways, but also to *themselves*. The tragedy didn't generate a barrage of self-blame. "If only I…" "This happened because I…" "Where did I go wrong?" No. They didn't even start! They remained silent from the very first moment. To remain silent even when the worst happens to our children requires true *emunah*, true strength.

My dear sisters, the *Tanach* is saturated with the pain caused by children. Our *Avos*, Avraham, Yitzchak, and Yaakov — how much *tza'ar* they experienced from their offspring! Aharon, the one who personified peace, who brought people closer to Hashem — how did this happen to his very own children? Every mother who has a child who's going through a rough period knows the terrible pain. She carries her child with her wherever she goes, and it weighs heavily on her heart. The torment is unbearable. It doesn't let go.

Still, she can turn to Aharon and Elisheva and heed their advice: silence. After their tragedy, they didn't sit down and think, *Hashem, why are You punishing us like this?* It was a silence that came from true acceptance, an acceptance of Hashem's justice that looked for no one to blame, including themselves.

The Rebbe of Slonim writes that Hashem took the Jews into Mitzrayim as a *gezeirah*, not because of any sin. He stresses that from this *galus*, Hashem wanted to impart a message to *Klal*

Yisrael for generations to come: we are not meant to understand why things happen as they do. Our commemoration of the redemption from Mitzrayim is to see a situation that doesn't seem to make sense to us, and to accept it. Don't go down the path that leads to self-blame, guilt, or idle regrets. Rather, follow the example of Aharon. No questions, no blame.

Banishing the guilt is a direct result of *emunah*.

Fighting the Feminine Urge

Elisheva's silence speaks volumes of her faith particularly because she was a woman. We women are a very special species. We really are. And we also tend to blame ourselves, to put ourselves down, as often as we can. "I'm not good enough." "I'll never succeed." "Only in my house things don't go the way they should." Don't even go there. Aharon and Elisheva reached their place only because they were silent. The opposite of blame is *emunah*.

After the nation sinned with the golden calf, their chance for atonement came through the red heifer. *Midrash Tanchuma* (*Chukas* 26) explains the relationship between the sin and its atonement. It's comparable to the child of a servant who defecated in the palace of the king. Says the king to the child's mother, "Come and clean up your child's filth." That's what HaKadosh Baruch Hu says to the *parah adumah*: "Come and atone for the sins of your child."

What should a mother do when her child messes up? She's not commanded to start the "Who did this?" dance. She simply comes and cleans up.

The commandment of the red heifer is one of those that has no *ta'am*, no explanation. It's here to teach us to stop seeking explanations for the things that occur around us. There are times in our lives when we simply have to stand by silently. *Vayidom Aharon.*

Banav HaNosarim:
Focusing on What's Left

We Jewish mothers have the indescribable power to move on. How do we do it? We focus on what we still have. That's exactly what Elisheva did; she looked at her two remaining sons, Elazar and Isamar, and forged on. When the Torah mentions their names, it refers to them as *banav hanosarim* — "his remaining sons" (*Vayikra* 10:12).

When Michal Gross's two precious daughters tragically died after inhaling toxic fumes from an extermination chemical in their Jerusalem apartment, she said to me, "What a gift that our two sons were also in mortal danger. If they would have been unharmed, and I would have 'only' lost my two daughters, I would have forgotten that *simchah* exists in this world. But now that Hashem left me what to fight for, I found comfort in my plight."

The power of a Jewish woman! [*Baruch Hashem*, her two sons survived, and she has since given birth again.]

After I lost my dear son, Yosef Chai, to a heart condition, I remember standing at the *levayah* and the *chevrah kaddisha* said to me, "Move forward, Giveret Mizrachi. Say, '*Hashem nassan, Hashem lakach. Yehi Shem Hashem mevorach.*'" Hashem gave, Hashem took. Blessed is Hashem's Name.

In my intense grief, I only said, "*Hashem lakach! Yehi Shem Hashem mevorach.*"

Later, when I read the holy words of the Ben Ish Chai, I understood. He writes that only when Hashem takes do we realize what He gives us. Why is it that we only see what we had once it's gone? Why do we realize our gifts only after they're taken from us?

I remember getting ready to leave the house for a *shiur* one night soon after the *petirah*. When my husband saw me all dressed up and ready to go, he looked at me, confused. I said to him, "I'm just a corpse with makeup."

The Torah tells us that Nadav and Avihu were removed from the Sanctuary by their tunics. Rashi (*Sanhedrin* 52a) explains that their bodies and clothing were intact. The heavenly fire that killed them had entered their nostrils and burned their souls, as it were, but did not affect their bodies or their clothing. That's exactly how I felt when I stood at the door that evening. The sick feeling of losing a precious child almost consumed me inside, but I found the courage within to move on.

After the *petirah* of Yosef Chai, we were blessed with another son. We named him Natan. I wanted to be able to wake up in the morning and remind myself, "*Hashem nassan, Hashem nassan.*" Since Yosef Chai's passing, my entire language changed. I can't tell my child, "Leave me alone." There's no such thing as "Ima can't talk to you now!" Because I've lost something so precious, I've learned to focus on the gifts that remain.

We know that *ein chacham k'ba'al hanisayon* — "there is no one as wise as one who has been tested." Those who've been tried, those who've experienced the intense grief of Elisheva, know what it means to focus on what's left.

Yes, we tell the Ribbono shel Olam, thank You very much. I'd rather not have this wisdom. *Al tevi'eini li'yedei nisayon* — don't test me! But those who've already endured it know what *simchah* means; they know how to appreciate the minutest gifts. When a woman experiences a tragedy of epic proportions like the pious Elisheva, she knows what's important. Her silence is so majestic, it speaks volumes.

No Place for Logic

It's hard to understand how we can push the questions away to the deepest crevices in our minds. After all, we live in a time when everything needs a reason. But some things cannot be explained with logic

It's hard logically to understand how mothers and fathers can suffer so much, how fine, upstanding people spend thousands of sleepless nights agonizing over the whereabouts of their teenage son. In the generation in which I grew up, "the apple doesn't fall far from the tree" was a given, and yet to say that children today follow the behavior that their parents modeled for them is clearly false. But then again, the wisest of all men, Shlomo HaMelech, says regarding the commandment of the red heifer, *Amarti ech'kamah v'hi rechokah mimeni* — "I said, 'I will become wise,' but it is beyond me" (*Koheles* 7:23; *Yoma* 14a). The logic was lost to him too. As smart as I think I am, and as smart as I really am, I can't understand why a pure mother must come and clean up her child's mess, why she must live with the mess at all.

Even Shlomo, wisest of all men, couldn't understand the ways of a heifer, the calf's mother, cleaning up what her child had dirtied. It was the aspect of motherhood that was hard for him to grasp.

On the verse *Vateirev chochmas Shlomo michochmas kol bnei kedem* — "Shlomo's wisdom was greater than the wisdom of all the people of the East" (*Melachim I* 5:10), the *Zohar* posits that Shlomo's brilliance is accredited to his mother, Batsheva. In essence, the entire *Sefer Mishlei* depicts the gentle rebuke with which she guided him: *Mah beri u'mah bar bitni u'meh bar nedarai. . . Al lamelachim sheso yayin…* — "What is it, my son? And what is it, O son of my womb? And what is it, O son of my vows?. . . it is not proper for kings to drink [much] wine…" (*Mishlei* 31:2–4).

Sefer Mishlei is filled with verses of the maternal appeal from Batsheva to her child. "My child," she was saying, "I am coming to clean you up, and I can do this because I believe in your purity. I always believed in you." That was Batsheva's message to her son. *Bar nedarai*, she called him lovingly. Even before I was expecting, I promised that I would have a righteous child. *Bar bitni* — and when I finally conceived, I would tell your father's wives, "I'm carrying a *tzaddik*." From such pure intentions, I'm sure a holy and righteous child will emerge.

Is there a mother who doesn't have the best of dreams for her child? Is there even such a thing? Of course not. No logic can possibly explain why things would turn out differently, why this sulky teenager whose parents lavished so much love on him, and said so many prayers on his behalf, did not grow up to be another Shlomo HaMelech. And yet, it happens often, so often. And when it does, silence is the only sensible response. Silence and, of course, *tefillah*.

Silence is the only sensible response for young women who still haven't found their destined partners in life. It's not because they haven't tried hard enough. Silence is the only sensible response to women who dream of the day they'll hold a child of their own in their arms.

Being silent doesn't mean you can't cry. Of course you should mourn your loss! It's so painful. *Va'acheichem kol beis Yisrael yivku es hasreifah asher saraf Hashem* — "And your brethren the entire House of Israel shall bewail the conflagration that Hashem ignited" (*Vayikra* 10:6). That's what Hashem promises Aharon and Elisheva. But at the same time, Hashem cautions, *Rasheichem al tifra'u u'vigdeichem lo sifromu* — "Do not leave your heads unshorn and do not rend your garments" (ibid.). Now is not the time for a guilt trip.

The Third Partner

We've established that according to the Torah, silence is golden and blaming is not: we don't blame Hashem, and we don't blame ourselves. And we also shouldn't blame our husbands.

This is an important topic I'd like to address because there are three partners in the creation of man: HaKadosh Baruch Hu, the father, and the mother (*Kiddushin* 30b). We have to constantly maintain this sacred partnership in order for the child to thrive.

Let's analyze a most beautiful verse in *Parashas Shemini* that provides insight on this subject.

Vayavo Moshe v'Aharon el Ohel Mo'ed vayeitzu vayevar-chu es ha'am vayeira chevod Hashem el kol ha'am — "Moshe and Aharon came to the Tent of Meeting, and they went out and they blessed the people, and the glory of Hashem appeared to the entire people!" (*Vayikra* 9:23). In *Koheles* (4:9), it is written that two is better than one. In *Midrash Rabbah* (*Koheles* 4:9), the Sages explain that the verse refers to Moshe and Aharon. When Moshe blessed the nation on his own, Hashem's glory didn't appear before them; it only appeared when the two blessed the nation together.

This is simply astounding. You can be as great as Moshe Rabbeinu, but if you don't work in a partnership, the blessings can't ascend to your dear children. One of the explanations as to why Nadav and Avihu perished in the Sanctuary was because they didn't consult with Moshe before performing the deed (*Eiruvin* 63a). They acted on their own. The lack of partnership, of teamwork, wreaks havoc.

When tragedy struck in Aharon's home, no fingers were pointed. Both Aharon and Elisheva accepted Hashem's judgment in silence. Our Sages tell us, *Zachu Shechinah beineihem lo zachu eish achaltam* — "If they [husband and wife] merit harmony, Hashem's presence rests among them; if they don't, a fire consumes them" (*Sotah* 17a). Rav Yitzchak Ginzburg interprets the word *zachu* as *hizdakeichu*, which connotes to purify. If they seek to purify themselves, to yield to each other, they merit Hashem's presence in their home.

As Jewish women who want only the best for our children, we must strive to work together with our husbands to create a Sanctuary in our homes. The minutest lack of this integral building block in the relationship can't be tolerated in such a holy place. By consulting with our husbands and ensuring their solid roles in our home, we're bringing blessing into our walls.

Badad Yeisheiv:
Why It's Not Worth It
to Speak *Lashon Hara*

In *Parashas Tazria*, we learn that *tzara'as*, a skin condition that afflicts the body, was the punishment for anyone who uttered a negative word against his fellow Jew (*Arachin* 15b). When we engage in *lashon hara*, we perform a deed that's in direct contrast to what the Torah stands for. We find the verse *Zos tihyeh toras hametzora* — "This is the law of one afflicted with *tzara'as*" (*Vayikra* 14:2) five times in the Torah, because of its profound importance. This mitzvah deserves a Torah of its own. Especially today, when bashing others has become an ideology of sorts ("The *klal* must know about this!"), we must understand the importance of this reiteration.

Silence Is Worthwhile

The damage evil speech inflicts on its speaker is immense. First, the prayers offered by a tongue that is besmirched by evil speech are not accepted. The Torah instructs the *metzora* to be quarantined from the community and to announce, "I am contaminated! Pray for me, please!" Why can't he pray on his own behalf? The answer is that in this case, because he tarnished his tongue with negative speech, his own prayers won't be effective.

What's the connection between the acceptance of prayer and evil speech? In order for someone to truly pray and appreciate the words she says, she has to acknowledge the good of another. *Mah rabu ma'asecha Hashem* — "How wondrous are Your deeds, Hashem!" (*Tehillim* 104:24) she says. *Hanosein sheleg katzamer* — "He provides snow like wool" (ibid. 147:16). How can she praise Hashem's deeds when she just finished a verbal barrage on the weather? "What terrible weather! This heat is getting to me." It's hard to believe the praise of a negative, critical person. Her words of prayer, explains the *Zohar* (*Metzora* 53a), have no true meaning.

In this vein, the Gemara declares that the world continues to exist because of the Torah study of children (*Shabbos* 119b). Listen to the words of the saintly *gaon* Rabbi Yehudah HaNasi: "This world exists in the merit of the mouths of young children." Said Rav Pappa to Abaye, "Excuse me, what of your words of Torah and mine?" Abaye answered, "The words that emerge from the mouths of children cannot be compared to those of an adult." Since children (under bar mitzvah age) are not accountable for their sins, it is as if they haven't sinned (see *Maharsha* and Maharal's commentary there).

In essence, Abaye was saying, "We sinned more than a young child. For this reason, the power of words of Torah from their mouth is greater than ours." How profoundly destructive sins are, especially the consequences of *lashon hara*, which includes so many sins (see the introduction to *Chafetz Chaim*)!

A second ramification of evil speech was that the *metzora* was commanded to sit in solitude. *Badad yeisheiv michutz lam-achaneh moshavo* — "He shall dwell in isolation; his dwelling shall be outside the camp" (*Vayikra* 13:46). Despite the fact that his contamination was manifest in a change on his body, it was caused by his degraded spiritual state and it was not contagious. Nonetheless, he had to be quarantined. The connection between evil speech and isolation is logical. People are scared of a gossipmonger! You sit with the woman who finds pleasure in cracking deprecatory jokes, and you may even find yourself enjoying the entertainment. But then it hits you. One minute. If she's sitting with me and talking like this about *her*, when she sits with her she talks like that about *me*!

Yes, that's exactly what happens. A person who engages in evil speech can't differentiate between one victim and the other. And in no time, people don't only isolate themselves from her, but also from the people with whom she surrounds herself. The connection between evil speech and seclusion is simple indeed.

The third negative consequence frightens me most. It's the reason why I refrain from engaging in this pastime. *Lashon hara*, our Sages tell us, leads to a deficit in our merits — and worse. It's not easy to control the tongue, especially for a person who finds such pleasure in sharing and analyzing and then repeating a juicy piece of gossip, but there's one result that makes the silence oh so worthwhile. Here it is.

Do you *really* hate her? the Chafetz Chaim asks.

Yes. I can't stand the woman.

With your whole heart?

Yes, with my whole heart.

Okay. If so, then I'd advise you not to speak ill of her because the moment you open your mouth to speak against her, all of your merits are transferred to her account.

How incredibly brilliant are the ways of Hashem! If you see all the faults in the world in this person, the last thing you want her to have is your lot in the World to Come. After growing hoarse from all of my *shiurim*, I wouldn't want this tactless woman to go up to *Shamayim* and be told, "Shalom, Rabbanit Yemima Mizrachi, and thank you for your merits!"

With this understanding, we can grasp the meaning of David HaMelech's words when he says, *Yasichu vi yoshvei sha'ar u'neginos shosei sheichar* — "I was the topic of discussion at the gates of the city, the talk of drunken men" (*Tehillim* 69:13). Why are only the drunkards and boors talking about me? The few merits I acquire from them aren't worth much. At least if a pious person would speak ill of me, I would stand to gain something!

Of course, I want my prayers to be accepted. And *I* want to be accepted. But if this transference of merits doesn't stop me from turning my tongue into an evil weapon, I don't know what will.

The Secret to Glowing Skin

Keil na refa na lah — "Please, Hashem, heal her now" (*Bamidbar* 12:13). On whose behalf was this heartfelt prayer said? For Miriam, when she was stricken with *tzara'as* upon committing the sin of *lashon hara*, evil speech.

How many millions of people invest in the smoothness of their skin! Botox, treatments, procedures — all to emerge completely flawless. The Ramban (*Vayikra* 13:47) tells us that it's okay for a Jew to be concerned about the details of her appearance, her clothes, her home, and even about the beauty of her skin. Beauty, he says, is a sign of Divine Presence in the Jew.

What suggestion do our Sages offer as the most wondrous anti-aging solution? Do you want to have beautiful skin? Your *or*, your skin, spelled with an *ayin* the Torah tells us, is dependent on your *ohr*, your light, spelled with an *aleph* through which you view others. When you choose to see others in a positive light, you merit brilliant skin, to evince the glow of His Presence on your face.

How do we know this to be true? From David HaMelech's famous words in *Tehillim, Mi ha'ish hechafetz chaim oheiv yamim liros tov netzor leshoncha meira u'sfasecha midabeir mirmah* — "Who is the man who wants to live, who loves to see good all his days? Guard your tongue from evil and your lips from speaking deceit" (*Tehillim* 34:13-14). David HaMelech teaches us that if we want to live, to truly live, we must learn to love our days, to embrace the beauty in them, to seek the good. That's the ultimate cure for the skin: to see everything in a positive light. You want to look good? See the good.

The haftarah for *Parashas Tazria* centers around Na'aman the *metzora*, whose skin looked abhorrent. After he immersed in the Jordan River, he emerged without a trace of *tzara'as*. *Vayashav besaro kivsar na'ar katon* — "His flesh became like the flesh of a young boy" (*Melachim II* 5:14). Young children have beautiful skin. They don't have sins for which they are accountable.

From the Kohen's two-word proclamation *Tahor atah* — "You are pure" — a *metzora* was rendered pure (*Vayikra* 13:13; Rambam, *Hilchos Tumas Metzora* 9:3). Good words will give you a lot more than smooth skin. With a good word, you have the ability to build worlds.

Time and again, I am amazed at the positive influence encouraging words have on others. I will never forget a letter I received from a student of mine, who had approached me the previous year and had admitted that she'd fallen prey to watching indecent videos online. "You looked at me," she wrote in her letter, "and you said to me, 'You're so pure. You can't be truly connected to it, and so you'll see how easy it will be for you to disconnect.' It's been a year," she continued, "and I haven't touched the Internet. Your words healed me."

The power of positive speech! I didn't say to this young woman, "It's *assur*! You should be ashamed of yourself!" I didn't even launch into a speech on the dangers of the Internet. Only two words: "You're pure."

Although expressing positive words is a nice thing to do, it's more than just a suggestion. It's an obligation we have as Torah Jews. *Am zu yatzarti li tehillasi yesapeiru* — "I created this nation for Myself so they could extol My virtues," says Hashem

(*Yeshayah* 43:21). We received the power of speech in order to say positive words, words of praise.

The *Bnei Yissaschar* writes that the Hebrew word *tenufah*, "lifting up" (one of the steps in bringing the Omer offering), is derived from two words: *tenu peh*, "give your mouth." He notes that in the days of counting the Omer, when we seek to repair the world through repairing our relationships, we should use our mouths to say only good words. The *Bnei Yissaschar* also points out that when the *ayin* of the word *omer* is switched to an *alef*, the phrase *sefiras ha'omer* reads as "the counting of words." In order to increase peace as we prepare to receive the Torah, we must be meticulous with our power of speech. Count your words, dear women, count your words. That's the secret to true peace — and to glowing skin.

Find Hashem Amid the Pain

In addition to the lengthy discourse on *tzara'as*, *Parashas Tazria* tackles the laws regarding a woman who has just given birth. This wondrous power was given to us women only, and it is a gift that we should take pride in: carrying our offspring for nine whole months and then playing an integral role in the miraculous emergence of an entirely new being into this world.

The Torah instructs every new mother to offer a *chatas*. Which sin did this fragile woman commit? Between the feedings and changings and catnaps (if she's lucky!), when was she able to squeeze a sin into her schedule? Rabbi Shimon ben Yochai tells us that during the birth process, a woman curses her husband, blaming him for the pain she's enduring (*Niddah* 31b). "We don't have enough children?" she cries. "I'm done." To repent for the negative speech she expressed, she is obligated to bring a *korban*.

Rav Shamshon Rafael Hirsch offers an enlightening explanation for the woman's obligation to offer a *chatas*. A woman who experiences such an utterly astounding miracle and yet allows the pain to obstruct her sight of HaKadosh Baruch Hu in this process must offer a gesture of repentance. Hashem was right there with her in the delivery room, and she chose to get distracted by the birthpangs. Only we women understand how intense the pain of childbirth is, but only we women have the opportunity to appreciate the G-dliness that envelops us during those fateful moments. For allowing the pain to distract us from remembering that this is only part of a journey that will ultimately bring us immense joy, we bring a *chatas*.

How often does it happen that we allow the pain to distract us from seeing Hashem in our lives? On this sad phenomenon cried Iyov, *Mi yitneini cheyarchei kedem* — "If only I could be as in the earlier months" (*Iyov* 29:2). Oh, how I wish to remember the wonders along the journey, and not fall prey to the fleeting moments of pain and suffering that draw me away!

A woman once told me that only now, after she's raised her brood, does she understand why the eldest child inherits a double portion of his parents' assets. When her oldest son cracked a dozen eggs on the kitchen floor ten minutes before her parents were coming to visit, the punishment was, shall we say, not pleasant. When the same thing happened with her youngest child two decades later, and this time her in-laws were due to arrive (!), she ran to get the camera. It's only a journey, she realized, and the end is so beautiful. Why fret over the uncomfortable distractions along the way?

Rav Hirsch explains the depth of a woman's impure state following childbirth. Don't think that it's a physical impurity as an effect of what your body experienced, he cautions. This is an impurity that emanates from the woman's attitude during the height of her pain. "I give up," she says. "I will not emerge from this alive." For thinking impure thoughts that there's no hope, for losing sight of the true reality, she is rendered impure.

Sometimes, the going gets tough. One woman waits with no end in sight, for her *shidduch*, another to carry a child. The journey is not smooth sailing for anyone. But when the pain seems too intense to bear, remember that this is part of the birthing process. To give up hope, to declare defeat, is *tumah*, impurity. You will get there, dear sister, you will get where HaKadosh Baruch Hu wants you to be.

I get messages from formerly suffering women all the time. "I got engaged." "I'm expecting." "Yemima, I gave birth." Take this opportunity to find His Presence amid the agony, because He is right there with you, at your side.

The Gift in the Spots

Tzara'as, in general, was a frightening affliction. Imagine waking up in the morning to find that your body has a peculiar spot, or that your garments are sporting red or green stains, or that the walls of your house have red or green marks on them.

But how does Hashem introduce the surprise that we know as *tzara'as habatim* (the affliction of houses)? In a celebratory tone! "When you arrive in the land of Canaan that I am giving you as a possession, and I will place a *tzara'as* affliction upon a house in the land of your possession" (*Vayikra* 14:34). My children, I have news for you. When you arrive from the Wilderness to the Land of Israel, I will give you this offering that we call *tzara'as*. If you find a spot on the wall of your house, you will approach the Kohen and have him examine it. If he deems it a case of *tzara'as*, the house will be closed for seven days, after which it will be examined again, and if it persists it will be reexamined the following week. If it still remains, the mark will be removed. If the mark returns after the mark removal, the house will be demolished.

"What kind of gift is this?" ask our Sages. What's the excitement in this reality? One way to understand the celebratory element in *tzara'as*, in general, is that its external presentation meant that the inner harm was in the process of repair. The white hairs on the outside, which is the sign of outer impurity, at the same time reflect the potential of purity on the inside. The Gemara tells us that Mashiach will only come when the entire kingdom will turn agnostic (*Sanhedrin* 97a). When all is soiled, it's a sign that the cleansing process has begun.

We women understand this very well. How does your home look when you want to do a thorough cleaning? The first phase of the process generates more chaos than you'd like to see, but you know what's coming next. When a man walks through the door and finds the chairs on the table, he may wonder what the mess is all about, but you know that it's all a part of the process. We understand that in order to reach purity, we first have to undergo a phase of discomfort (which is why only women can do a good Pesach cleaning!).

Parashas Tazria commences with the words *Ishah ki sazria v'yaldah* — "When a woman conceives and gave birth" (*Vayikra* 12:2). According to the semantics of Lashon HaKodesh, notes the Ohr HaChaim, the word *sazria*, "conceives," is written in the future tense and *v'yaldah*, "gave birth," in the past tense. The correct language would have been *vateileid*, "and she will give birth." Doesn't giving birth follow conception? He answers that the thoughts upon conception are going to profoundly impact upon the child who is born.

A woman operates in much the same way: Before she conceives, she's already giving birth. That is, even before the process of birth begins, she knows the beautiful result that will follow. To her, the discomfort and pain are a sign that the gift is on its way.

The external sign of *tzara'as* reflected an inner cleansing, the first step toward purity — a substantial cause for celebration.

The Gift of Knowledge

Our Sages tell us that another great gift lies hidden in this seemingly unwelcome consequence. It's the gift of knowledge.

To know why you're suffering, dear women, is an incredible merit.

When a man woke up to find his a suspicious spot on his body, he immediately knew, "I sinned." He approached the Kohen, the Kohen quarantined him for seven days, after which he examined the spot, and then quarantined him for another seven days. Often, the man emerged healed from the process.

Now imagine that you awake one morning to find your walls covered in spots. "Oh my! I sinned!" you cry. *Tzara'as* on the home emerged as a result of stingy behavior (*Arachin* 16). "Yesterday she came to borrow my mixer, and I told her I don't have one." What happened when a house contracted *tzara'as*? It was demolished. As the house goes down, you beg forgiveness for your sins, and then you're never miserly ever again.

But today, do we know why we're suffering? The *parashiyos* that discuss *tzara'as*, *Tazria* and *Metzora*, are indeed celebratory because they offer clarity. They provide crystal-clear reasons for every kind of spot that afflicts a person or his home or his clothes. If a person found *tzara'as* on his skin, he knew he'd spoken *lashon hara*. Spots on the walls? A consequence for his miserly behavior. Do you realize what comfort this provided? They knew what they needed to repair, what went wrong. What a gift!

On Seder night, when we recount the story of the Jews' redemption from Egypt, it's easy to see the hand of Hashem. The evil ones were stricken by the plagues while the righteous ones emerged unscathed. The wicked ones drowned at sea, and the pious ones walked their way to the other side. It's only logical to confirm our faith when we read about those miracles. But what happens when we enter the *sefiras ha'omer* period? Suddenly, the righteous ones are afflicted. Why? The answer is not so crystal clear.

Think about the story of Nadav and Avihu. What saintly men they were! Their tragic deaths shook up the nation. The *talmidim* of Rabbi Akiva were Torah giants. Because they didn't greet one another, they deserved such severe punishment? What about the millions of *kedoshim* who perished in the Holocaust? If only we'd know what a gift the awareness of cause and effect was indeed.

Before we explore faith in a time when we don't have the clarity of a Kohen and a Beis HaMikdash, let me emphasize that there is one positive difference between affliction in the times of the Beis HaMikdash and affliction that we suffer today. It's true that in those days the knowledge of the pain's reason provided comfort for the sufferer. However, in the times of the Beis HaMikdash, a Jew gleaned from his *tzara'as* that he had committed a sin. He lived with the understanding that *ein yisurim b'lo avon* — "a person only suffers as a result of sin" (*Shabbos* 55a). The good news is that since the destruction of the Beis HaMikdash, this concept does not apply anymore.

No, dear women, the pain you're experiencing is not a result of any wrongdoing on your part. Your suffering is part of HaKadosh Baruch Hu's grand plan, and you're merely playing the role that's destined for you. It's tough to be in the dark, but to be in the dark and to think you were the one who snuffed out the light makes it an unbearable place to be. Don't go there, dear sister.

Like a Strand of Hair: We Do Know One Thing

Iyov, the exceedingly righteous *tzaddik* who suffered innumerable tragedies in his life, asked Hashem, "What did I do to You, what? Why did You inflict all of these calamities upon me?" When did he ask this question? Not when his sons were sick, only when all of his challenges were behind him. I heard a magnificent thought on this topic from a Holocaust survivor. She said, "It was easy to believe in Hashem during the Holocaust. It was much harder to believe when it was all over." At the time of the challenge, Hashem grants the person special strengths to survive it. Afterward is when the true challenge of faith begins.

Rabbi Ezriel Tauber, *shlita*, once shared that during the war, he and his brother were ordered to extract bodies from the gas chambers. When going from chamber to chamber, they got accustomed to seeing the holy *perochos* that the Nazis removed from shuls and brazenly hung as curtains across the shower rooms. Inscribed on those holy curtains were the words *Zeh hasha'ar laShem tzaddikim yavo'u vo* — "This is the gate of Hashem through which pious people pass through." How many holy men and women walked through those very curtains to their deaths, leaving the Tauber brothers to handle their bodies.

When the war ended, Rabbi Tauber recounted, he and his brother boarded a ship to Eretz Yisrael. When they arrived at the port in Haifa, their first question was, "Where is the *beis knesses?*"

They were directed to the nearest shul, and when they walked in, remembers Rabbi Tauber, "There, before my eyes, I saw those same words, *Zeh hasha'ar laShem tzaddikim yavo'u vo.* And I passed out. What I was able to handle at the time of the Shoah, I couldn't deal with afterward."

This happens often. After the challenge is over, we wonder, *Why do good people have to suffer?* That's exactly what happened to Iyov. "Hashem," he cried, "*Atah medakdeik iti kechut hasa'arah* — 'You are strict with me down to a hairsbreadth.' You're so meticulous with me! I'm suffering needlessly."

What does Hashem answer him? "Iyov, aren't you ashamed of yourself? For every hair in your head I assigned a pore, and you think that I don't keep track of what I challenge you with?"

Did Hashem provide Iyov with a direct answer to his question? No.

The Midrash (*Vayikra Rabbah, Tazria*) offers a beautiful tale on this topic. It tells us a story of a woman whose husband was a Kohen. All day, every day, people would come to consult with him. "Is this *tzara'as?*" And he would determine their status based on the color of the protruding hair.

This Kohen was very poor. One day, the Kohen said to his wife, "Listen, my dear wife. We don't have food to eat. I'm leaving for *chutz la'aretz* to find a livelihood."

"But what will happen to the many people who come to have you examine their *tzara'as?*" she asked.

"I will teach you the laws" was his reply. "It's as simple as this: Every single hair has a pore from which it emerges. If you see a white hair, a dead hair, you know that the pore dried out, and that is a sign of *tzara'as.*"

"Don't you hear what you are saying?" the wife asked her husband. "If for every single hair HaKadosh Baruch Hu created a specific pore from which it is nourished, do you think He can't provide for our children?" And she didn't allow her husband to leave.

Did this woman give her husband a solution to his destitution? No.

Both of these midrashim refer to hair. Let's understand the unique quality that hair possesses to gain insight on this subject.

The Gemara tells us (*Sotah* 49) that from the day that Rabbi Akiva died, the respect for Torah was destroyed. Rebbe Pinchas of Koritz explains that Rabbi Akiva taught his students the deep meaning of every crown on every letter of the Torah. His *talmidim*, however, didn't conduct themselves with respect to one another. They would say, "What innovative thought can my friend offer already?" Says Rebbe Pinchas, "Because they were inattentive to the hair, we're prohibited to cut our hair during *sefirah.*"

When Moshe Rabbeinu ascended to the heavens in preparation for the giving of the Torah, he saw that HaKadosh Baruch Hu was, so to speak, binding crowns to every letter, like hairs. And Rabbi Akiva's *talmidim* disgraced this very Torah. They devalued the holy Torah words of their peers. "So he added another adornment to this letter, so what? The main thing is the letter in itself."

The strand of hair symbolizes the scrupulous attention that HaKadosh Baruch Hu pays to every word of the Torah and to every creature in His world. When we refrain from cutting even one hair from our head, we are reminded of the weight every Jew carries. If every hair is so important in the eyes of Hashem, how much more so the heart of every Jew!

Hashem's message to us is very clear. To us, a strand of hair may seem insignificant. But to Hashem, every single detail in the world is important. The comfort of this knowledge is the answer to Iyov's question, and the answer to the Kohen who thought he had a better plan for generating an income. "Iyov," HaKadosh Baruch Hu tells the *tzaddik*, "do you realize what you just said? You cried that I'm scrupulous with you like a strand of hair. How right you are! That should give you comfort." "We don't know why we're suffering," the brilliant wife of the Kohen told her husband, "but we do know one thing: Hashem is meticulous with every detail." Although we can't understand the ways of Hashem, the thought that He runs every tiny detail of this operation provides us with true solace.

V'Lo Yamus: Get a Life

et's talk about life. *Parashas Acharei Mos* teaches us: After death there's always life. The *parashah* commences, *Acharei mos shenei bnei Aharon* — "After the deaths of Aharon's two sons" (*Vayikra* 16:1). It continues with the instructions Aharon received regarding his sacrificial service in the Sanctuary on Yom Kippur.

After Aharon buried his two precious sons, Nadav and Avihu, the jewels of the family, Hashem said to him, "Now back to life. Let Me describe to you your main duty as a Kohen Gadol." One of Aharon's obligations on Yom Kippur was to don a sacred tunic: "Put on your beautiful attire," Hashem commanded him (ibid. 16:4).

This is so hard! But the Torah begs of us, "Please, live! Even if something so painful happened to you, there is a future ahead of you, stand up and live." Hashem asks of Moshe, *Dabeir el Aharon achicha...v'lo yamus* — Talk to Aharon, your brother... so that he should not die" (ibid. 16:2).

Later in this *parashah*, the verses list various practices that one shouldn't engage in because they could endanger a person's physical health. Why do we have all these commandments? Because Hashem wants us to live! *U'shemartem es chukosai v'es mishpatai asher ya'aseh osam ha'adam v'chai bahem* — "You shall observe My decrees and My laws, which man shall carry out and by which he shall live" (*Vayikra* 18:5). The Sages derive from this expression, *v'chai bahem*, that the commandments were given for the sake of life, not death. Therefore, if the performance of a commandment may endanger life — such as the familiar case of a patient who must be rushed to the hospital on Shabbos — the need to preserve life supersedes Shabbos observance. Hashem says to us, "I really want you to live." He commands us to desecrate the holy Shabbos for the sole purpose of sustaining life (*Yoma* 85b).

One moment. Is the choice of life in our hands? According to the Ramban (to *Vayikra* 18:5), the answer is yes. He writes that your life span is dependent on you. It is in your hands to decide if you want to live a short life, a long life, or not die at all (which is what I, for one, would opt for!). Who's the proof? Eliyahu HaNavi and Chanoch, says the Ramban. These were two people who ascended to *Shamayim* while still alive.

Even if it's hard for us to understand how we have the power to prolong or shorten our own lives, we do understand that the quality of our lives is largely affected by our choices. And to truly *live*, we must make that choice. Are we just going through the motions, leading a meaningless existence, or are we cherishing every breath and actively involved in the life we were granted? As Jews, we are obligated not only to *survive*, but also to *live*.

Dear sisters, remember that HaKadosh Baruch Hu is a *Melech meimis u'mechayeh u'matzmiach yeshuah* — "a King Who brings death, then life, and makes salvation sprout." When you recite these words during the Amidah, let them fill your heart and soul with the comfort you're craving. At the moment of death, of darkness and despair, it may seem that life will never happen again. When a person gets *that* diagnosis, that no from the *shidduch* that looked like it would finally be the one, yet another job rejection, she may think that it's all over. But keep praying, dear sisters. Read the words that come after "death" and you will be comforted by them: soon, very soon, salvation will spring forth and life will happen.

How is it possible to live after death? How can a person who experiences a tragedy of such intensity, like Aharon, pick himself up and move on? By focusing on what remains, we find the courage to persevere.

Face the Rising Sun

It's easy to speak about life after death, but, oh, so hard to fulfill. I will never forget the words I heard from Miriam Peretz, a woman whose husband passed away from the dreaded disease and who had two sons killed in battle. In my talk with her, she reminisced about the fateful moment when she heard the knock on her door. They were coming to tell her that her son was gone. At that moment, she shared, she thought it was the end of the world, that she would never find the strength to rise up again.

The second and third time the Angel of Death seized her loved ones from her side, the words that came to her mind were those uttered by David HaMelech when he learned that Avshalom, his son, had died. *Mi yitein musi ani tachtecha* — "If only I could have died in your place!" (*Shmuel II* 19:1). Her situation looked so bleak that she couldn't fathom how she'd wake up the next morning and face the rising sun. But then, shared this pious woman, she came to the realization that life is a choice. It was up to her to see what still remained, and to cherish that.

Look at how the trees blossom so beautifully in spring even after the harsh winds of winter rendered them fragile and bare! This could be your life, dear women. After a disappointment, even after a tragedy, you can choose to remain bereft of your former spark or to bloom once again, filling your branches with beauty and color. How magnificent! What a righteous woman you can be!

The opposite of bringing death upon yourself is making a choice to live with what you do have, with the circumstances Hashem sent your way. If you train your eye to find those gifts, you will see them. As long as you focus on what is going well for you, you will be filled with a true desire to live.

Rebuilding: Rabbi Akiva and Rabbi Shimon

The Maharal of Prague tells us that there's one day in the year that's called "Chai B'Iyar," the eighteenth of Iyar, the celebratory day we know as Lag BaOmer. The word *iyar* has the same numerical value as the word *orech*, longevity. Citing the verse *Orech yamim biminah bismolah osher v'chavod* — "Longevity is in its [the Torah's] right hand; in its left are riches and honor" (*Mishlei* 3:16), the Maharal says that whoever is connected to the Torah merits a long life. Even when tragedy — and even death — strikes, someone who is connected to the Torah is able to rise up again and again, with the resilience of Rabbi Akiva after the death of his students.

When we count the Omer, we don't count the days that remain until the "wedding," *mattan Torah*; we count the days that have passed, and not the days that have yet to come. One day, two days, three days… The profound reason for this is that if you live your life in anticipation for something to happen ("When will I get engaged?" "When will we have a decent livelihood?" "When will I lose weight?"), you're not really living, because you're living with the reality of *ayin*, with what you're lacking, instead of living with *yesh*, what you do have.

Living with *ayin* is like not living at all. It's a kind of death that doesn't allow you to appreciate your breath, your gifts, your life. *Omer* has the same numerical value as the word *yesh*, 310. In the Omer, we count what we have, what we've gained from the days that have passed.

This is what we learn from Rabbi Akiva, who lost 24,000 beloved *talmidim* but forged on. After one death, and another, and then another, he exerted all his energies to remain connected. He focused on what was left, the *yesh*. He gathered five worthy *talmidim*, and he rebuilt an empire of Torah, the wisdom of which remains with us until today (*Yevamos* 62b).

I shared the following fascinating story at an evening for women who were still waiting to bear children. Seventy women sat in the room: some who had been waiting for six years, some for ten, and one for twenty (who ended up giving birth to twins!).

A childless couple who lived in the city of Sidon came to consult with Rabbi Shimon ben Yochai about their situation (see *Alshich, Vayeitzei* 30, quoting the Midrash).

"Listen," said the husband, "I'm married to this woman for ten years already, and we don't have any children. It seems to me that we don't have a reason to live together, so we would like to divorce."

"All right," said Rabbi Shimon. "But before we move ahead with the proceedings, I would like to ask you something. When you got married, did you throw a party?"

"Yes," said the husband, "we did."

"So I would like for you to throw another party now, a divorce party. Okay?"

"Okay," they answered, baffled at Rabbi Shimon's strange command. After all, how does a wedding compare to a divorce? Weren't the two events inherent contrasts?

Rabbi Shimon was indeed a brilliant scholar. Beneath his puzzling words, perhaps he was delivering a crucial, if unspoken, message to the couple:

"When you got married ten years ago, did you have children?"

"No."

"Did you know at all if you'd be blessed with offspring or not?"

"No."

"Did you know each other well? Did you know if you'd be truly happy together?"

"No."

"Am I right that you felt joyous at the wedding?"

"Yes."

"Today, do you know if you will still have children together?"

"No."

"And do you know each other well?"

"Yes, much better."

"So you're in the same situation as you were back then! Then you didn't have offspring, just like you don't have today. And then you were happy and today you're sad. What seized the simchah from your hearts? The anxious waiting."

What happens when someone focuses incessantly on what she's missing? She starts to lose sight of what she does have — and that is a kind of death. What did Rachel Imeinu say to Yaakov when she was desperate for a child? *Havah li banim* — "Bring me children." *V'im ayin meisah anochi* — "For as long as I focus on what I don't have, I am simply a dead woman" (*Bereishis* 30:1).

This was Rabbi Shimon's message to the couple: What a sad home you have! A home that is focused on the wait, on the lack, kills its inhabitants. For many women, life is all about waiting. First to conceive, then to give birth, then for the children to grow up, and then and then and then... When do they *live*?

Now back to the couple, who is waiting for you to learn the end of their story. Heeding the words of the holy Sage, they returned home and got the celebration preparations underway.

"It's been years since we were happy," said one to the other. "When was the last time we celebrated?"

At the celebration, the husband, who'd imbibed a bit too much whiskey, said to his wife, "You know what? In honor of our divorce, I let you take the most valuable asset in our home to your father's house."

And she, who thought her sense of humor had gone dry from all her years of misery, said, "Hmm… He lets me take whatever I want to my father's house? I'll make a surprise and take *him*."

So it was. In his intoxicated state, he followed her home. In the morning, when he awoke in her father's house, he turned to his wife, "Didn't you say that we were divorcing?"

"But you said I could take what was most dear to me to my father's house!"

When he heard that, he said to her, "My wife, let's give this another chance."

Together, they returned to Rabbi Shimon bar Yochai. "Rebbe," they said, "we're so ashamed but we're back."

"Now," Rabbi Shimon said, "you're happy people. You appreciate what you have. Now I can bless you."

Only a happy person is a vessel for blessing. Only a blossoming tree grows beautiful flowers.

Give Her a Chance to Mourn

When it comes to your pain, you must learn to move on. But what happens when it's the pain of someone else? Rabbi Yochanan ben Zakkai had a son who passed away in his youth. His *talmidim* came to console him.

When they saw him sitting in silence, they knew that halachically they weren't permitted to console him (because silence is a sign that the mourner's grief is so great that no words of solace would be of benefit). So they asked him gently, "Do you permit us to speak with you?"

He gave them permission.

Said Rabbi Yehoshua, "Rebbe, may I say one thing?"

"Yes."

"Adam, the first man on earth, had two sons and one died. And he allowed himself to be consoled."

"My suffering isn't enough? Why are you bringing up the pain of someone else?" asked Rabbi Yochanan.

Rabbi Yose joined the conversation and said, "Aharon was a *tzaddik* of your caliber. He lost two sons and allowed himself to be consoled."

Rabbi Yochanan cried again, "Isn't my suffering enough?"

Then Rabbi Shimon remarked, "Iyov was a *tzaddik* and his sons died..."

"Don't talk to me about Iyov's pain," Rabbi Yochanan interjected.

That's when he looked to Rabbi Elazar ben Aruch, his choicest *talmid*, the one who proposed that a good heart is more important than any other virtue, for his input.

"Rebbe," said Rabbi Elazar, "the king left a *pikadon* in the hands of his servant. Every day, the servant looks at it and thinks, *When will I be freed from the burden of taking care of something that belongs to the king? I hope I return it in perfect condition!* You, Rebbi, had a son who learned Torah and Mishnah, and he left this world without sin. You should be consoled by the fact that you returned the *pikadon* in perfect condition."

Said Rabbi Yochanan to Rabbi Elazar, "Rabbi Elazar, my son, how beautiful are your words of comfort. You have consoled me."

What bothered Rabbi Yochanan so intensely about the consolation of his other *talmidim*? May you never know, but when it comes to the death of a loved one, the concept of *tzaros rabim chatzi nechamah*, the knowledge that others also suffered offers half the solace, doesn't take effect. The mourner can't take comfort in the fact that others are also suffering. The person wants you to feel the loss of *his* child, *his* pain. In the Torah, this concept is called *V'ahavta l'rei'acha kamocha* — "You should love your friend like you love yourself" (*Vayikra* 19:18).

Just like you see yourself as a unique being, your friend's pain is unique as well, unlike the pain of any other person who suffered before him.

During our own hard times, we have a duty, dear women, to emulate the resilience of Rabbi Akiva, of the trees that choose to blossom despite the heavy winter that stripped them bare. But when it comes to another person's suffering, remember the words of Rabbi Akiva: love your friend like you love yourself. Validate her, and give her a chance to mourn.

Sefiras Ha'Omer:
The Sefiros of Chesed,
Gevurah, and Tiferes

We all want to believe that we're *kedoshim*, holy women who are doing Hashem's will. However, when we observe the gap that sometimes opens between what we want to be and how we feel inside, we are ashamed. Sometimes we feel angry. At other times we feel jealous. Even hatred worms its way into our hearts from time to time. And we wonder: Are we really *kedoshim*?

The Ohr HaChaim offers us encouragement when he notes that the verse *Kedoshim tihyu* — "You shall be holy" (*Vayikra* 19:2) means you *will* discover how infinitely holy you are, when you work on finding the holiness within.

It's normal for you to look at yourself from time to time and have the urge to take a bottle brush and scrub it all out. The seven weeks between Pesach and Shavuos — in which *Parashas Kedoshim* is read — are designated for purifying us from the inside out in preparation for *mattan Torah*. It is in this time that we put our efforts into becoming vessels of holiness — or, rather, into discovering the *kedushah* within us.

Mere Manners or Real Honor?

During the days of *sefiras ha'omer*, the 24,000 *talmidim* of Rabbi Akiva were *niftar* because *lo nahagu kavod zeh lazeh*, they didn't conduct themselves with respect for one another. The *kavod* the Torah speaks of isn't just manners, *nimusim*. *Nimus* in Hebrew has two definitions: it can mean "manners" and it can mean "to melt." A person can put on a beautiful face when she talks to someone. She can smile brightly and exhibit incredible patience. But if she's only well mannered, the facade will melt away soon after. As soon as the person she encountered is out of sight, she'll take a deep breath and go back to her normal behavior.

Kavod comes from the *kaved*, the liver. It must come from a deep, real place inside of you, a place that really appreciates and loves your fellow man.

Rabbi Akiva treated his wife, Rachel, with the utmost *kavod*, a word that also means "heavy" in Lashon HaKodesh. What was important to her carried *weight* in his eyes, more weight, even, than his own wants and needs. If something is important to your husband, even if it means nothing to you, respect that. *This* is the definition of *kavod*.

The *talmidim* of Rav Shlomo Zalman Auerbach, *zt"l*, relayed story upon story of his dealings with his wife. As their neighbor in the Jerusalem neighborhood of Shaarei Chesed, I too had the exceptional merit of absorbing the respect with which they treated each other.

Before entering his home, he would make sure to straighten his suit. "I'm going to meet the *Shechinah* now," he would say. (Conceivably, he used these words when arriving home, because if there is peace between husband and wife, the *Shechinah* is with them — *Sotah* 17a.)

Kavod means that you don't do what's comfortable for you, what you'd prefer. You think the way he thinks and feel the way he feels. When young women tell me, "I can't get along with my mother," I tell them, "You're not *supposed* to get along. You're supposed to give her *kavod*, as it says in *Parashas Kedoshim, Ish imo v'aviv tira'u* — 'Every man shall revere his mother and his father' (*Vayikra* 19:3)."

The *talmidim* of Rabbi Akiva couldn't emulate that essential element of *kavod* in relationships from their teacher, who was away from his wife for over two decades (*Kesubos* 62b–63a).

V'Al Yavo V'Chol Eis: A Delicate Balance

So how do we do this? How do we become *kedoshim* and find the holy spark in every human being — including ourselves?

We find the definition of *kedushah* in Hashem's command about Aharon: *V'al yavo v'chol eis el haKodesh* — "He shall not come at all times into the Sanctuary" (*Vayikra* 16:2). You can't be too close all the time, but you can't be too far either. A delicate balance of every characteristic is ideal. It's all in the measurements, the *middos*. The paradigm of sterling *middos* is Rabbi Akiva, who possessed two contradictory characteristics: he was both *tzanua*, humble, and *me'uleh*, elevated. While feeling content with his current status, he also strove to reach higher. While he said, "Thank You, Hashem, for what I've achieved," he prayed, "Please, Hashem, help me attain greater heights." That's the work of *sefiras ha'omer*.

Let's take a brief look at three of the *sefiros* to get a better idea of how to achieve that delicate balance.

Chesed, Gevurah, Tiferes

The first of the seven *sefiros* is *chesed*, kindness. Rav Shimshon Pincus, *zt"l*, tells us that the greatest kindness we can bestow on someone is to give of our time, to make ourselves available. The Chafetz Chaim teaches that if we listen to someone share his story for the hundredth time, Hashem will listen to our prayers even if we've begged a hundred times. It's not always easy to be available, but that's true *chesed*.

Of course, charity begins at home. More than the lavish meals and extravagant clothes you work tirelessly to provide for your loved ones, what they need most from you, dear wife and mother, is your *time*. How available are you for your family? Does your child know that Mommy can't wait to hear about her *morah's* new baby? How open are your ears when your husband wants to talk about his day, especially if he wants to share every seemingly insignificant detail of the latest deal? They feel it, dear women, they feel it. Your ultimate kindness is to truly be there for your family. Only then comes your obligation to be there for others.

We find that people who do lots of *chesed* are often also those who are sensitive not only to the needs of the poor, the lonely, and the sad, but also about other things. They may be sensitive if they weren't invited to that bar mitzvah, or if that neighbor didn't smile at them. That's where the second *sefirah*, *gevurah*, comes into play.

Gevurah, strength, is all about overcoming our negative emotions, of quieting the anger. The best tip for this achievement is from the Ramban, who writes in his letter, *L'olam yihyu kol devarecha b'nachas.* When you feel the anger surging inside, speak *very* quietly. Because it's not satisfying to scream in a whisper, you are guaranteed your rant will ebb soon. Rebbe Nachman of Breslov suggests that every time you allow your anger to control you, give a designated amount to charity, to remind yourself that every time you overcome that evil inclination, Hashem will bless you with riches.

Beware, though: There's something that can be missing in a *gevurah* home, and that's warmth. Because those who exemplify *gevurah* exercise immense control, they count their words and expressions of love. That's why the next *sefirah*, *tiferes*, is so crucial.

Tiferes, beauty, is the capacity to say good, warm, encouraging words, to let them flow freely. *Eizo hi derech yesharah sheyavor lo ha'adam? Kol shehi siferes l'oseha v'siferes lo min ha'adam* — "What's the straight path that a person should choose? He should do everything that's beautiful to Hashem and beautiful to his fellow man" (*Avos* 2:1). We must exercise our power of speech in a positive way, in a way that makes others glow. Why are your words of positivity so crucial to others? Even a good person needs to be reminded constantly of his positive qualities.

The Ramak, Rav Moshe Cordevero, writes in his acclaimed *sefer*, *Tomer Devorah*, that if a person doles out compliments and positive words to others when she herself is empty of fuel, when she is lacking encouragement from others, Hashem will give her the energy she needs. In the same way we are punished for the negative words we speak, we are punished for the positive words we didn't say.

Our Sages explain the power of *tiferes*, of heaping encouraging words upon others, is so immense that for this reason alone HaKadosh Baruch Hu granted us the power of speech. *Ish es rei'eihu yazoru u'le'achiv yomar chazak* — "A man would help his friend, and to his brother he would say, 'Stay strong!'" (*Yeshayahu* 41:6). Hashem gifted the woman with nine measures of speech (*Kiddushin* 49b) so she can stand at her husband's side when he struggles with the issues that challenge him most.

The primary curse for the man following the sin of Adam and Chavah was that he would toil for his bread. The primary curse for the woman was childbearing and childrearing. Let's draw a parallel here: How much encouragement do you need for your work with the children? How desperate are you to hear that you're raising them right? How validated we women feel when we receive even the slightest positive feedback on our child-rearing efforts! And even more so, how much a woman craves to bear children!

In some ways, a man who doesn't manage to provide for his family is like a childless woman, or a woman whose children did not turn out as she had envisioned. The worst thing a woman can do is degrade him even further, to blame, to sulk, to distance herself. At his time of fragility, when he needs your support most, be there for him. Shower him with your innate ability of *tiferes*, of offering glowing words of encouragement and faith. Only a man with a wife like Rachel can manage to transform himself from an *am ha'aretz* to the Torah giant of his generation. With her constant encouragement and expression of faith in Rabbi Akiva, she merited seeing his growth.

Every time I meet a mother who lost her young child, *Rachmana litzlan*, the line I hear most is "Why didn't I tell him more often how much I loved him? Why didn't I say more?" As mothers, we have an obligation and opportunity to utilize the power of *tiferes* while raising our precious offspring. Oh, how they blossom from positive words! Your sincere compliments and expressions of love are their sunlight and water. Be generous, dear women. Tell them how much you love them, how much you believe in them, how happy you are to be their mother, until you see their backs grow straighter. Even then, never stop.

When Rav Shlomo Zalman Auerbach, *zt"l*, would go to the house of mourning of parents who had lost their child, he would always ask to speak to the mother. "Tell me about him," he would request gently. "What would you have wanted him to do if he'd still be here with us?" he'd then ask. Of course, the woman would say that she'd want him to learn Torah, do mitzvos.

"How would you react if the child would say, 'I'm leaving the house for the next few years so I can learn undisturbed'? Would you agree to that?" And the mother would reply that for the Torah, she'd agree.

"And what would you put in his suitcase?" Rav Shlomo Zalman would continue. If the mother said food, he'd answer that food could spoil; it can't last him through his journey. If she'd say clothing, he'd answer that the child would soon outgrow them. And then the mother would say, "All my *tefillos* — that he should grow up to be a *talmid chacham*, to go under the *chuppah*, to grow up to be an *ilui*," to which the Rav would reply, "Your child has gone to the *best* yeshivah — the *yeshivah shel ma'alah*. There, he needs no food and no clothing. There, he learns under the *chuppah shel tzaddikim*. And there, he's having an *ilui neshamah*."

When Rav Shlomo Zalman would leave the house of mourning, he'd turn to his *talmidim* and say, "This I say to the bereaved mother. *Acharei mos kedoshim emor* —after the death, we should speak of holiness. But what about *lifnei mos*, before the passing? Yes, food and clothing are very important, but what our children need most are our warm words. They need our words of love more than anything else."

When a mother loses her child, she wishes she could say, "I love you," one last time. Why don't we do it now? Why don't we exercise *chesed* today — right now? Why don't we use our *tiferes*? And why not exhibit *kavod* to our husbands, parents, and children?

In this merit, our homes will be filled with holiness and happiness, always, and we will, indeed, find the holiness within us.

Finding Hashem in This Obscure Reality: The *Sefiros* of *Netzach* and *Hod*

The *shalosh regalim*, Pesach, Shavuos, and Succos, are *chagei re'iyah*, the holidays during which the entire nation is seen in the Beis HaMikdash. The Torah commands us: *Shalosh pe'amim bashanah yeira'eh kol zechurcha* — "Three times during the year shall all your menfolk appear before Hashem" (*Shemos* 23:17). Imagine the scene! The nation trekking together toward Yerushalayim, the epicenter of the world, to celebrate the holiday together. What motivated the masses to leave their homes, their businesses, their routine, and hike for miles? And then they had to set up quarters in homes of people they didn't even know. How can this mass migration be understood?

When these *olei regel* arrived in Yerushalayim, tired and famished, the Kohen moved the curtain aside and said to them, "Look! See how Hashem loves you!" (*Yoma* 54a). He showed them the form of a man and woman, the *keruvim* that rested upon the *Aron*, their wings touching each other, and he would say, "Do you see this? Such is the love HaKadosh Baruch Hu feels toward you, His dear nation."

Hard as it was on the feet, if I would have that opportunity today, I'd be off and running. I'd do anything to hear Hashem say, "Yemima, I love you."

That's the question of this generation. In the obscurity in which we live, we wonder, *Does Hashem really love me?*

True Faith Defies Logic

How do we see Hashem in this darkness? Rabbi Ezriel Tauber once said that he remembers two Seder nights of his youth. The first was a splendid occasion. His father sat at the head of the regally set table, made Kiddush on wine, and handed out large portions of matzah to the many children who sat like princes around him. He also has stark memories of another Seder that transpired only a few years later, this time, in the camps. This time he sat with his father once again, but they had no clue of where his mother was, or if she was even alive. His father raised his meager piece of matzah and said, "Ribbono shel Olam, You commanded us to eat a *kezayis* of matzah. But there is an even greater mitzvah that you commanded that we call *v'chai bahem* — 'and you shall live by them [and not die by them]' (*Vayikra* 18:5). I'm lifting up this measly *kezayis* of matzah because this is all I have." He then recited the *berachah* of *hamotzi* and ate in silence.

At that moment, recounts Rabbi Tauber, two appearances of the word *anochi* sprang to mind. The first Seder was in the realm of *Anochi Hashem Elokecha asher hotzeisicha me'eretz Mitzrayim* — "I am Hashem, your G-d, Who took you out from the land of Egypt" (*Shemos* 20:2). The regal celebration reflected the reality of freedom and exodus. The second Seder, however, brought to mind *V'anochi hasteir astir panai bayom hahu* — "And

I will conceal My face from them on that day" (*Devarim* 31:18). Hashem was present at the first Seder, said Rabbi Tauber, and He was also present at the second. At the first one, he explained, he saw His Presence so clearly because he was basking in the beauty and royalty and freedom. In the second one, it was so hard to see Him, but He was there nevertheless.

Now that we are living in the dark, when the absence of the Beis HaMikdash is so glaring, who will tell us that Hashem loves us? It's hard to understand why good people are suffering and there's so much pain all around us. How do we keep from drowning?

This is the first commandment in *Parashas Emor*: *Vayomer Hashem el Moshe emor el haKohanim bnei Aharon v'amarta aleihem l'nefesh lo yitama b'amav* — "Hashem said to Moshe, 'Say to the Kohanim, the sons of Aharon, and tell them: Each of you shall not contaminate himself for a [dead] person among his people'" (*Vayikra* 21:1). The message? Don't become contaminated by all this death, by all this tragedy. Don't see the world through the prism of *hester panim*, concluding that Hashem isn't present.

How do we do this? How do we ensure that we don't become contaminated from death, from the *tzaros*, the suffering that we see? How do we remember that Hashem is with us, always? The saintly Rebbe of Piaseczna, who perished in the Holocaust, writes in *Aish Kodesh* (pp. 84–85), that there are *yissurim*, pains, that are in the realm of *mishpatim*, laws whose purpose we understand. However, there are other *yissurim* that are in the realm of *chukim*, laws whose reasoning is obscured. We can't possibly fathom why they came upon us. On the contrary, it seems to our human eyes that they're only causing harm. Like these *chukim*, says the Rebbe, *emunah* also defies logic. Therefore, when we connect ourselves with true faith in Hashem, to a level that goes beyond logic, the challenges we face become easier.

Netzach: Reciprocating the Love

How do we emerge victorious, with *nitzachon*, from the pain? We exercise the fourth *sefirah* of *netzach* when we reciprocate Hashem's love for us. We find this concept in the Torah portion of *Emor*: the idea of serving Hashem with unconditional love. Hashem commands us, *V'lo sechalelu es shem kadshi v'nikdashti besoch Bnei Yisrael* — "You shall not desecrate My holy Name; rather, I should be sanctified among the Children of Israel" (*Vayikra* 22:32). Elucidating this verse, Rashi notes something magnificent: A Jew should devote himself to sanctifying Hashem's Name to the extent that he's willing to sacrifice his life, because anyone who devotes himself to Hashem in the hope that a miracle will save him won't merit a miracle. When you do something for Hashem's sake, do it with all your heart and soul.

The Sfas Emes adds a beautiful thought that will fill you with a powerful desire to serve Hashem with love. He says that whoever fulfills Hashem's command not in the expectation of experiencing a miracle, but only because "I love You, and if this is what You want, I want it too," *will* merit a miracle. In his holy words: "The truth is that genuine sanctification of Hashem's Name is when a miracle does occur at the end to those who dedicate themselves to the will of Hashem, but the condition should be that you don't expect it to happen."

In truth, Hashem does want to perform miracles for you, dear women. He sees your pain and aches for your suffering. But instead of waiting for that miracle, start living. Accept your life with love, serve Hashem with joy, and the miracle will suddenly happen.

Kiddush Hashem is not only created through sacrificing our lives for Him. It's not only about jumping into a fire or drowning in sea. It's also about living the life Hashem handpicked for you. It's about saying, "Hashem, right now I don't really want these circumstances. I know exactly what I wish could be different, but my desires are nothing when it comes to Your will. If this is what You want from me, Ribbono shel Olam, this is what I'll learn to love."

I find it incredibly awe-inspiring to meet women who actually live by this credo. These are women who, to the human eye, have all the reasons in the world to question the ways of Hashem. Women like Tammy Karmel, may she live and be well, who is imprisoned in a body that's debilitated by ALS, but whose soul is soaring. "His will is my will," she often expresses through the eye movements that operate her computer. Even at the most difficult moments, her face shines, her smile never wanes, because she so clearly understands that this is what Hashem wants from her at that very moment.

There are women who live for years with difficult spouses, rebellious children, or no children at all. Still, they live — and they make themselves a happy life, because their clarity is brilliant. They know that Hashem loves them, and their mission in life is to reciprocate that love.

Such paradigms of *emunah*, who create a *kiddush Hashem* with every breath they take, exemplify the *middah* of *temimus*, wholeness. Let's talk about this oft-misunderstood attribute.

Parashas Emor contains many references to wholeness. Every offering must be whole. The Kohen Gadol, as well, had to be physically free from blemish. And the weeks that we count toward the Omer must be complete as well: *Sheva Shabbasos temimos tihyenah* — "Seven weeks, they shall be complete" (*Vayikra* 23:15).

The Sfas Emes (*Emor* 5644) notes that the Jews in *dor hamidbar* possessed this endearing *temimus* as well: the *temimus* of the children who live in the here and now. He says that Hashem reminisces of their submissiveness when He says, "Your following Me in the Wilderness, in an unsown land" (*Yirmiyahu* 2:2). The nation followed Hashem blindly, surrendering their will to the will of Hashem. They were true *temimim*! They had no idea where they were headed. If only we could emulate that humility in this generation.

We must learn to live with *temimus*, to emulate the young children who excel in this attribute. We have all heard tales of young Holocaust survivors who escaped the camps to hunt for a morsel of bread. *Temimus* is the ability to live in the now. It's about not asking, "Why did this happen to me?" or "How will I deal with this later?" It's about right now: "What I will eat for my next meal?"

After she received her diagnosis of ALS, Tammy Karmel was told that she would eventually need a respirator in order to survive. "When I first heard that," Tammy related when she still had the ability to speak, "I thought that that would be the end of the world. How would I communicate with my children? To my husband? How would I *live?* But in a flash, my clarity returned to me. Hashem is giving me the *kochos* to carry through my challenge right now. I don't need the *kochos* for a respirator just yet. Why should I worry about what will be then?" Like a beautiful young child, she chose to live in the now. What *nitzachon*!

Hod: More Than Meets the Eye

What is the fifth of the seven *sefiros*, the *middah* of *hod*, splendor? It's the inner ability to understand that there's a deeper reason for everything that transpires, that nothing is the way it seems at a superficial glance. As Jewish women, we must harness this ability to scratch beneath the surface, to find potential where no one sees it, to empower our loved ones with the confidence that only we can imbue.

It's interesting to note that a woman's ability to breastfeed her child is referred to as *hod yafyah*, the splendor of her beauty (*Maharsha, Berachos* 10b). We have an internal ability that's not immediately apparent from the outside, which gives us the capacity to nourish another person. *Hod* personifies the inner power we all possess, one we must seek to bring to the fore in our loved ones.

When I attended the convention that was held for women at the *sheloshim* of Rav Wosner's passing, I was awed by the tales his daughters and granddaughters shared of his greatness. His daughter recalled that, on the one hand, her saintly father was focused inward. He led a remarkably private life for the most part. During his lengthy learning sessions, no one interrupted him. If he was learning in the dining room, the family tiptoed around him because they understood that their father was engaged in an otherworldly task. But if there was a knock at the door and a woman was standing there with a halachic quandary, or an impoverished man asked to speak with the *rav*, he would instantly emerge from his deep state of concentration and welcome the visitor with a shining countenance.

Only someone who understands that every occurrence in this world is orchestrated from Above with utmost precision can straddle two worlds so seamlessly. As Jewish women, we have the unique ability to fill multiple roles at the same time. It is our mission to see the multiple layers in others as well, to look beyond the layers of dust to unearth the brilliant essence of every Jew.

The *middah* of *hod* also gives us the incredible ability to understand that even when a situation seems hopeless, there's more to the story than meets our human eyes. Through finding Hashem's Presence even when it seems so obscured and connecting to Him in times of challenge instead of turning away, we're emulating the holy *keruvim*, who were looking at each other (*Yoma* 54a).

As we return Hashem's love, as we look at our challenges through the prism of *emunah* and *temimus*, we are gifted with an unmatched feeling of comfort and security, one that gives true purpose and meaning to our suffering.

Climbing Upward

*A*t this time of year, during *sefiras ha'omer*, we're engaged in an intense hike, climbing up toward the mountain, Har Sinai, preparing to accept the holy Torah from the hands of Hashem.

In *Parashas Behar*, we read about the mitzvah of *shemittah*, the sabbatical year. The famous question of the *Sifra*, cited in Rashi (*Vayikra* 25:1) is: *Mah inyan shemittah eitzel Har Sinai* — "What's the connection between *shemittah* and Sinai?" Let's try to understand.

Where the View Is Clear

Oh, how I wish to ascend the mountain! Oh, how I wish to reach the top! *Mi ya'aleh b'har Hashem u'mi yakum bimekom kadsho* — "Who merits ascending the mountain of Hashem and who to remain at that holy place?" (*Tehillim* 24:3). The answer is in the next verse: *neki chapayim u'var leivav* — "one with clean hands and pure heart." Not only a *bar leivav*, but a *nishbar leivav*, a broken heart, as it says, *Karov Hashem l'nishberei lev*

— "Hashem is close to the brokenhearted" (ibid. 34:19). Only one whose heart is broken can reach the top of the mountain.

This, my dear readers, is the connection between *shemittah* and Har Sinai. Only one who feels that all that she depended on is crumbling — *nishmatim*, slipping (similar to the word *shem-ittah*), between her fingers — only one who feels like a barren sabbatical field will reach the heights.

Let's look back at the story of Rachel and Rabbi Akiva, the story that takes center stage during the *sefirah* days, to understand what it means to watch life slip away between the fingers.

When Rachel's father, Kalba Savua, heard that his wonderful daughter wanted to marry the illiterate shepherd Akiva, he told her, "You won't see a shekel from me. You don't have my consent for this arrangement."

What did Rachel, princess of all the riches, do? She sent her husband, at the age of forty, to learn the holy words of Torah for an indefinite amount of time, and she lived like a pauper. After twelve years, having amassed a kingdom of Torah, he was ready to return home. When he approached the vicinity of his home (or shack), he overheard a poignant conversation between Rachel and a tactless neighbor.

"Those Torah-scholar husbands!" the neighbor lamented. "How much longer will you live like a 'widow' whose husband is alive?"

"If this arrangement would depend on me," answered Rachel simply, "I would send him away for another twelve years."

And Rabbi Akiva heard every word. "Oh, that's what she said? So I have her permission?" And he hurried to learn for another twelve years.

After a total of twenty-four years of being far from home, it was time for Rabbi Akiva to return. This time, when the pious Rachel was already aging, he returned with 24,000 students. "You should know," Rabbi Akiva addressed the throngs of people who came out to welcome him, "that everything that is mine and yours belongs to this woman. It's all to her credit."

Thereafter, for one year, in the days beginning from the first night of Pesach and lasting until Lag BaOmer, Rabbi Akiva's students began to die. Approximately 700 deaths every single day! Can we even begin to imagine the pain? Can you fathom the heartache? In thirty-three days, 24,000 *talmidim* were snatched away by a rare plague. His beloved students — and his lifework — were snatched away. His world was now, indeed, a barren one.

Yet Rabbi Akiva looked past his broken heart. He traveled to the south to recruit new students, to build a house of Torah anew. How many men did he gather? He started with only five. Only five men, but they turned out to be Torah giants: Rabbi Meir Ba'al HaNes, Rabbi Shimon ben Yochai, Rabbi Yehudah bar Ilai, Rabbi Yose, and Rabbi Elazar ben Shamua.

How did you do this, Rabbi Akiva? How did you have the strength to start anew? He didn't ask, "Why did You give me 24,000 *talmidim*? Just so You can take them from me?" He understood that when a Jew experiences such monumental heartbreak, Hashem carries him to the pinnacle of the mountain, all the way to the top. From there, from that vantage point of view, all man can say is "Wow!"

How do I know this? I, too, was there. I, too, stood at the tip of the mountain, observing the view that took my breath away. On Lag BaOmer several years ago, I gave birth to a child with a broken heart. The *tefillos* we cried for him! Oh, how we begged, the *kabbalos* we undertook. From this saga alone I aged by fifty years.

It was easy to fall into a rut, to wonder why Hashem gave; just so He'd have what to take? But the answer came all too soon. At the height of the pain, when I was ordered by the *chevrah kaddisha* to rip my shirt, I thought I wouldn't be able to bear it any longer. I couldn't bring the words *Hashem nassan v'Hashem lakach* — "Hashem gave and Hashem took" — to my lips. But it was then that I truly acknowledged, *Yehi shem Hashem mevorach* — "May the Name of Hashem be blessed."

May we never know of challenges, but when they strike, there's a concealed beauty in them. From the depth of the pain emerges the clearest view.

Psychology 101

How do we rise after a fall? It's impossible to do so without a helping hand. Only together can you climb up the mountain: holding hands, in friendship.

"Enough is enough," women tell me. "I don't have what to look forward to anymore."

That's how Naomi felt. That's how Ruth felt. Even our Sages teach us that our willpower and burning desire to grow close are not enough. You must have a hand at your side, someone to encourage you, "Come, dear. Rise up and I will help you." When Naomi and Ruth embarked together, only then could they move ahead.

Parashas Behar is extremely brief. In general, it is read together with the following *parashah*, *Bechukosai*. This is also the Torah portion that contains the word *yad*, hand, multiple times, commanding us to support our brothers in need. It teaches us, *Ki yamuch achicha ... u'va go'alo hakarov eilav v'ga'al eis mimkar achiv* — "If your brother becomes impoverished…his redeemer who is closest to him should come and redeem his brother's sale" (*Vayikra* 25:25). When you see someone in need of support, extend your hand toward her. Whether she's in physical or emotional pain, be that companion for her along the way.

The numerical value of *yad* is 14; when two hands join together, you empower each other with *ko'ach*, whose numerical value is 28.

What does it mean to lend a hand? True friendship is more than spending happy times together. It's also about truly being there for another person when she's in desperate need of support: to carry through on your promises until the very end.

When the challenge first strikes, many people jump in to offer their services. But what happens when the trek starts to take weeks, months, even years? Are you still there?

I see in my own life how hard it is to be there for someone over a stretch of time. Often, women whom I've guided through a challenge will reach out to me at a later time with the same story. My first thought can sometimes be, *I've helped you already, now what?* And the woman will say, "But Rabbanit, he's making me nervous again."

Oh, so just take the conversation we had then and replay it in your head. I don't have ko'ach to go through it all over again! Hadn't I already worked out the issues with her then? But Hashem tells me that there's no such thing. True kindness is extending my hand for as long as a fellow Jew needs me.

Take my hand as I walk you through a fascinating interpretation of the Sfas Emes (5641) on the words *Vehechezakta bo* — "And you should support [your fellow Jew]" (*Vayikra* 25:35). Commenting on this commandment, the Sfas Emes notes that every day HaKadosh Baruch Hu provides every creature all of its needs, for his body and soul, as we affirm in Birkas HaMazon, *hazan es ha'olam kulo* — "He provides for the whole world." However, in order for all of us to receive what we need, we must hold each other's hands to enable the blessing to flow, to extend hands from one person to the next. The dependence we have on one another is only in order to remind us everything we have is from Hashem — that we will never find perfection in one human being. Through holding hands, notes the Sfas Emes, we enable the flow of Hashem's blessings to reach others.

Imagine! Every single day, Hashem fulfills our collective needs with exquisite perfection, but we must acquire them from others through giving and receiving.

Even when you extend your hand in greeting, offering "*shalom*," you're giving your friend *peace* of mind. With one "Hi!" that truly exhibits your happiness to see her, you're lighting up her world.

Accept the Hand

As hard as it is to always be there for your friend, it's even harder to be the one to accept. This is the *middah* of *netzach*, victory. Rebbe Nachman of Breslov tells us that we wash our hands first thing in the morning, as if to say, "Hashem, cleanse me from the thought of *kochi v'otzem yadi*, that the work of my hand will accomplish what I must do today." As we embark on a new day, we ask Hashem, "Please, I want to be of those who are able to make do with the fact that he can't do everything" (*Likutei Maharan II*).

Sheish shanim tizra sadecha — "For six years you may sow your field" (*Vayikra* 25:3), we read in this Torah portion regarding the mitzvah of *shemittah*. What happens after six years of toil? Allow yourself to take a step back. Sometimes life shows you that no matter how much you try, no *hishtadlus* will keep you from having to take that break.

It isn't easy, but it's impossible to give all your life, to always be the strong one, the independent one. This drains you, in the same way the Torah teaches that we're prohibited to work the land year after year nonstop. It's okay to let go, to loosen your grip over your life and allow yourself to be on the receiving end.

I'm embarrassed to admit that for many years I didn't particularly admire Ruth. Why did a woman who seemed like a simple follower merit being the center of our attention during the *chag* that celebrates the giving of the Torah? Where was Sarah Imeinu, or Rivkah: foremothers who initiated heroic feats? Ruth merely said to her mother-in-law, Naomi, "Wherever you go, I'll go; wherever you will sleep, I'll sleep..." (*Ruth* 1:16). What was so special about her attitude?

Hashem teaches us a powerful lesson here. Ruth was the consummate Jewish woman; she knew how to be a vessel, to allow herself to accept from others, to have them plant the seeds in her heart. When we stop wanting to conquer the world, we're able to truly accept the Torah.

There isn't a person in the world who hasn't experienced the consequences of her humanness. Sometimes we just need a reminder, a year of *shemittah*, to remind us that as much as we were created in the image of G-d, we're not G-d and we never will be.

On a wall in my home there is a large picture of my beautiful son, Yosef Chai, *z"l*, taken on a day when he looked healthy, without the oxygen mask blocking his tiny mouth and nose. My mother used to ask me why I don't remove it from the wall, and I would tell her that I'm holding on to this photo because it serves as a constant reminder of humility. How convinced I was that I was capable of everything, including saving his life; that if I would tell him, "Don't die," he would listen. Hashem showed me that there's no such thing, that there's *shemittah* in this world.

Shemittah is a profound concept in Judaism. So many women are afraid to let go. They must constantly reconfirm their faith in their ability to charge forward. They want to fight City Hall in their desire to take control, but it doesn't happen. It can't happen. That's another powerful blessing in the challenges Hashem sends our way. Only when we relinquish control, when we realize Who is running the show and we allow ourselves to accept counsel, advice, even favors, from others, can we become vessels of G-dliness and serenity.

Ameilim BaTorah: It's the Effort That Counts

*P*arashas *Bechukosai* contains many verses of despair, referring to seeds that will be sown in vain. *Rashi* (*Vayikra* 26:17) notes that these "crops" refer to the sons and daughters in whom we invest our hearts and souls and then a sin come along and wipes our efforts away. How dispiriting it feels! After all the hope, the prayers, the toil. We must therefore keep in mind the words of solace: there is always a Pesach Sheini, always a time to rectify. You always have a chance to start anew. *Lo me'astim v'lo ge'altim* — "My dear children," Hashem says to us. "I will not have been revolted by them, nor will I have rejected them to destroy them, breaking My covenant with them, for I am Hashem, their G-d" (ibid. 26:44).

Look at our precious children. Before Lag BaOmer, I am always in awe at the efforts they invest in constructing the most gigantic bonfire in the neighborhood. I stop to observe their toil, wondering, *How do they do it?* The answer is because they have a bonfire in their hearts. Their passion burns with intensity.

For a few moments of celebration, they're ready to invest so much.

But for a flame to continue burning, it must constantly be fueled. Otherwise it will gradually diminish, shrinking to tiny embers that will eventually be snuffed out. This is the secret to the perpetuation of the Jewish home. Only with passion that is continuously reignited can the Jewish marriage — the Jewish family — and the Jewish nation flourish.

This is what we learn in *Parashas Bechukosai*, which opens with the words *Im bechukosai teileichu* — "If you will follow My decrees" (*Vayikra* 26:3). Commenting on this verse, Rashi notes, *Shetiyhu ameilim* — "They should toil" — that we must continually toil in Torah. That's Hashem's decree. In *Yiddishkeit*, we don't measure how much we've achieved, but how much we've toiled. It's truly the effort that counts.

How did Naomi know that Ruth's conversion was indeed valid? *Vateire ki misametzes hi laleches* — "She saw that she determined to go" (*Ruth* 1:18). That's the sign of a Jewish woman. From Ruth's attitude, Naomi understood that this woman would push herself day by day, again and again, in order to light her own torch.

It isn't easy to constantly reignite the flickering faith within, to exert ourselves when we don't see the results we dream of. It isn't easy to work on our *middos*. But that's our work here on earth. Let's talk about how we can do this.

Sheli V'Shelach Shelcha Hu:
The Secret to an Everlasting Bond

What makes forging relationships and maintaining them so difficult? Every human being, no matter what his status or position, possesses a flickering spark that demands *kavod*, honor. And the work incumbent upon us is to provide this spark with the nourishment it craves. How do we do that? This is where the tough work lies: Humans thrive on sensitivity.

Rav Yechezkel Levenstein offers an enlightening explanation as to why the *talmidim* of Rabbi Akiva committed the sins that brought about their tragic deaths. It's hard for us to understand how the students of the one who preached and practiced *V'ahavta l'rei'acha kamocha* — "And you shall love your friend as you do yourself" (*Vayikra* 19:18; *Yerushalmi, Nedarim* 9:4) — engaged in inconsiderate behavior toward one another. But Rav Yechezkel explains something very powerful. He says that these *talmidim* were also raised with another principle: You should not do for your friend that which you loathe (*Shabbos* 31a).

To Rabbi Akiva, *kavod* was a detestable thing. He taught his *talmidim* by example to stifle their egos, to rid themselves of anything faintly related to providing *kavod*. They abhorred arrogance, aspiring to attain the level of humility of their teacher. Thus, they not only despised receiving compliments, but they also chose not to give them. After all, they cared as deeply for their friends as they did for themselves. If I hate to be greeted or stood up for because it feeds my ego, why should I perform this detestable deed for my friend?

This was their mistake, notes Rav Levenstein. To think that what is good for you is good for your friend is erroneous thinking. There is no greater fallacy than this! Our task is to find the language of the other person and speak it to him. Things that are hard for you may not necessarily be hard for your husband and vice versa. If you want to foster a true relationship, you must exercise sensitivity, find out his specific needs, and provide what he needs to make him thrive.

The same is true for our sons and daughters. We invest so much in *chinuch*. We try so hard to give it our all. But is your "all" the child's "all"? I'm no proponent of waiting on children hand and foot, but when you do something for your child, whom do you have in mind? Every human being has his own spark of *kavod*, his individual needs that must be fulfilled in order for him to flourish. By giving someone the feeling that you are there to make that happen, you're fostering a true relationship.

The Mishnah cautions that "what's mine is mine and what's yours is yours" (*Avos* 5:13) is an average attribute, and some say that it's a negative one. "What's mine is mine and what's yours is mine" is a wrong approach. "What's mine is yours and what's yours is yours" is a positive approach, because it means you understand that the other person carries more weight than you do. It is with this attitude that relationships can truly flourish.

For twenty-four years Rabbi Akiva's students drank his words of Torah, but they didn't see his interactions with his wife. They saw only his modesty and lack of interest in worldly pleasure, and they sought to emulate those traits. What they didn't know was that although he loved his wife *k'gufo*, like himself, he respected her *yoser migufo*, more than himself (*Yevamos* 62b). That's the secret to a true relationship: the love may be equal, but the respect for the other party must overshadow the respect with which you treat yourself. Indeed, Rabbi Akiva, who took no pleasure in worldly possessions, gave his wife a piece of jewelry (*Shabbos* 59b). Does a man so immersed in Torah even appreciate something so earthly? To him it held no interest, but in his sensitivity, he understood that it interested *her*. And to him, that's what counted.

Regrettably, the *talmidim* never merited seeing this compassionate side of their leader, this intuitive ability to truly consider the needs of the other person.

One of the blessings of *birchos hashachar* is *she'asah li kol tzarki* — "Blessed is the One Who provides me with all my needs." What are our needs? They vary from person to person. I've met too many mothers who don't understand the needs of their daughters.

"When I was growing up, I didn't need everything you need. We lived in a tiny apartment and even had our grandmother move in with us when she grew old. I was the one to cook her meals! Why are you so particular?" But wait a minute. Those were *your* needs when *you* were growing up, not your child's.

"I was happy with two sets of clothes — one for Shabbos and one for weekday," or, better yet, "In our house, we sisters shared one Shabbos dress. I wore it in the evening, my sister in the morning, and my other sister for *seudah shelishis.*" Wonderful — but this is a new generation! Let us emulate the ways of Hashem, who provides each of us our precise needs.

If we want to enjoy satisfying relationships, we must work at them. And as we're exerting our energy to make it happen, whether in our spouse or child, we must ask ourselves this question in all honesty: "What does the other person really need?"

Light the Fire in Your Heart

Just like that young child who's dragging the twigs and branches into the night, exert yourself to light up your passion. It's so much easier to say, "Let him do the work," "Let the kid listen to the rules." Yes, it is easier. But is it worthwhile? If we choose to close our eyes to the pain of those around us, to ignore the calling of those *kavod* sparks in our loved ones, we lose the opportunity to light up our homes. With cynicism and a critical eye, we're giving the crops a chance to wither away, robbing them of their potential to blossom.

Stop being hard — on yourself, on your life, on others, on Hashem. It's so hard to be hard! By nature, Rabbi Shimon ben Yochai personified *din*, judgment. With one stare from his eyes, he had the potential to turn a live person into a heap of bones (*Shabbos* 34a). This saintly *tzaddik*, however, toiled to exercise sensitivity. When he met a simple Jew running on his way with two bouquets of myrtle, he asked him, "Why two bouquets? Isn't one enough?" The Jew replied simply, "I prepare two myrtle leaves in honor of the Shabbos, one for *zachor* and one for *shamor.*" How touched Rabbi Shimon was when he heard that! Rabbi Shimon remarked to his son, "See how beloved the Shabbos is to the Jewish people."

HaKadosh Baruch Hu demands from every single one of us to stop being tough. In *Parashas Bechukosai*, we read a frightening line. Hashem says to us, "If you behave toward Me with *keri*, I will behave toward you with a fury of *keri*" (*Vayikra* 26:27–28). Onkelos explains that *keri* means *kashyu*, hard. When we are hard on others, on ourselves, on Hashem, the consequences are dreadful.

What happens to a tough woman? I know this is stuff we don't like to hear, but sometimes the fear of the consequence helps us keep things in perspective. In *Parashas Bechukosai*, we read about the curse that's especially designated for tough people: "I will bring weakness into their hearts... The sound of a rustling leaf will pursue them" (ibid. 26:36). *Rashi* explains the punishment to mean that the person will be stricken with anxiety. What a scary word!

Sifra (*Bechukosai* 2:4) elucidates this verse with a story that happened to Rabbi Yehudah ben Karcha. He and some other men were once sitting among the trees when a gust of wind caused the leaves to rustle. They got up and ran away, saying, "Woe is to us if the Roman cavalry catches us." After a while, they turned around and saw no one, so they returned to their places and said, "Woe is to us, for through us the verse 'And the sound of a rustling leaf' has been fulfilled."

Anxiety, our Sages tell us, may come from a lack of sensitivity. Don't go to sleep angry and negative about someone, dear friends, because you may wake up feeling fearful. It's not pleasant to be afraid of every shadow in the dark, of the ghosts lurking in the closet. It's the punishment for those who engage in *lashon hara*, a result of judging others harshly. The *Kli Yakar* (*Vayikra* 26:36) explains that one who speaks negatively against others will be afraid of her own voice.

Anxiety is not a good place to be. We find the cure for it in this very *parashah*: *shetiyhu ameilim*. When you keep busy and lead a satisfying, fulfilling life, you're not so preoccupied with the negative aspects of life. You end up cherishing your relationships, the time you spend with your loved ones, and you have less time to dwell on symptoms, real and imagined! When we fill our time wisely, we nourish our hearts and minds and lead a confident life. It's one great step toward being a pleasant person, someone others enjoy being around.

Let's learn to be more sensitive, more attuned to the needs of others. If this is the powerful message we cull from *Parashas Bechukosai*, we will merit solid, loving relationships in our lives.

Sefer
Bamidbar

Every Jew Is Precious – Including You

If there's a *parashah* that seems to be centered on dry facts, it is *Parashas Bamidbar*. In essence, this Torah portion is loyal to its name, stating facts and stats in a systematic matter, dry as a desert. But actually, as always, we can find a wealth of deep emotional truths in this seemingly arid *parashah*.

In this *parashah*, Moshe Rabbeinu counts the nation, which is why this *sefer* is also known as *Sefer HaPekudim*, the "Book of the Counts." In his work *Ohr Chadash*, Rav Chaim Zeitchik offers an insight that simply brings me to tears. In the desert, he tells us, head counts of the nation were never performed directly. Instead, a total was ascertained by counting the number of half-shekels that had been collected. Rav Zeitchik's explanation for this practice is nothing less than magnificent. Whenever someone counts even one person in *Am Yisrael*, he notes, he must stop and concentrate deeply on the greatness of the person he is about to count, because every single Jew is infinitely valuable. And when he wants to count him, he should peer into his eyes and remain cemented in his place from the depth of his admiration. So captivated will he be that he won't be able to continue the count. For this reason, Hashem instructed Moshe to count the nation with coins.

Expounding on this point, Rav Zeitchik offers the example of his two sisters, who survived the Holocaust together and merited emigrating to Eretz Yisrael and meeting their third surviving sister there. When they met at the airport, the sister who was awaiting their arrival embraced one sister for a long, long time. As much as she wanted to hug her other sister, she simply couldn't let go. Such was her passionate depth of emotion toward one human being.

This is the love we must feel toward every single Jew, declares Rav Zeitchik. So overwhelmingly touched must we be by his significance that counting directly should be an impossible feat.

Later, when Moshe is preparing his final words to his beloved people, he tells them, *Yoseif aleichem kachem elef pe'amim* — "[May Hashem] add to you a thousand times yourselves" (*Devarim* 1:11). What a profound message! I love you as you are, said Moshe to the nation. Every single one of you is so infinitely valuable that the greatest blessing is that there be more of what you already are.

True *ahavas Yisrael* is exactly this. It's not "I love you, but…" It's simply, "I love you as you are."

What a Nation!

The truth is that it's impossible not to love every member of *Am Yisrael*. I'll share just two stories to validate my premise.

One Shabbos several years ago, I took my children to a large park in the area, Gan Sacher. (I do this once in about every thirteen years as compensation for running off overseas.) We found a perch on top of a small mountain, and I parked the empty stroller with my *Chumash* in its basket right nearby. Suddenly, the stroller started rolling down the hill, scattering the *Chumash* and all the notes that had been tucked inside. (Me and my precious notes…) In no time, a teenage girl in leggings, a tank top, and a nose ring ran over to help out. She picked up the *Chumash*, collected the scattered papers, and kissed the *sefer* before putting it back into the basket. Then she continued her run. *Mi k'amcha Yisrael.*

The second story took place when I once delivered a lecture in New York to a group of women who were affiliated with a very insular chassidic sect. The organizers of the event gave me one warning: "Listen," they said, "here you don't say the word *Israel*. It doesn't sit well with us." And here my husband always tells me that my travels to *chutz la'aretz* should be to give women a desperate longing for the place!

Anyway, I didn't mention the *I* word in my talk. I spoke about Obama instead, about "Yes, We Can." Apparently, however, someone who hails from Yerushalayim exudes the spirit of Eretz Yisrael. The next morning, I met a very sweet woman, a mother of twelve children, from that chassidic sect. She said to me, "How I dream about Eretz Yisrael! I've always wanted to visit, but I've never been there. I long for the day."

And so we parted ways. And I realized that there's no way we can extinguish the love.

The heart that throbs for purity in every Jewish woman is infinitely valuable. Every member of *Am Yisrael* has a slice of the *Shechinah* resting within her. If we truly internalize this reality, there is no Jew with whom we can't fall in love.

The word *Yisrael* is an acronym for *yeish shishim ribui osiyos laTorah* — "the Torah contains 600,000 letters." Every single Jew is represented by a letter in the Torah. And if you ask the classic question "Rabbanit, aren't there more than 600,000 Jews?" let's listen to the answer from the Pri Tzaddik.

You're right, he says. There may be more Jews than letters, but every letter can be doubled and tripled. For example, the letter *yud* is comprised of the letters *yud, vav,* and *dalet*. Every person, like every letter, is infinitely valuable. Without every Jew's input, the Torah is not complete.

Eretz Lo Zeru'ah: From a Desert to Gan Eden

The Midrash (*Midrash Rabbah, Bamidbar* 1:2) states that after *Am Yisrael* was in the desert for forty years, Hashem said to them in anger, "You should be ashamed of yourselves that you call this a *midbar. Hamidbar hayisi l'Yisrael im eretz mapeilyah* — 'Have I been a wilderness to Yisrael or a land of deep darkness?' (*Yirmiyahu* 2:31). How do you have the audacity to call this a desert when I've supplied you with all your needs? You were protected by a hovering cloud. You did not outgrow your clothes. You had an abundance of food and water. This you call a desert, a land of darkness? You had forty years of wining and dining in a place where you would least expect it!"

Why did Hashem choose to perform these miracles in a desert? The Midrash tells us that only when a place is entirely barren can Hashem fill it with a bounty of gifts.

Who understood this reality better than anyone in the world? Upon the death of her husband and sons, Naomi, Ruth's mother-in-law, cried, *Ani melei'ah halachti v'reikam heshivani Hashem* — "I was full when I went away, but Hashem has brought me back empty" (*Ruth* 1:21). When she left Beis Lechem, Naomi had it all. She had a family and riches and respect and beauty. Our Sages tell us that her life was a veritable bed of roses. However, after she lost everything, only then could she finally play a role in the emergence of Mashiach. Mashiach, your salvation, dear women, will arise from a place of total emptiness.

From the place of true barrenness, the salvation happens. Where there's a *midbar*, there will be a Gan Eden. If you're so full of yourself and so sure you have everything, is there room left for more?

The desert is not a place of permanence; it's a place that people traverse in order reach a destination, complaining about the heat while trampling its soil. Who builds a house there? The Midrash says, don't worry. *Mi yitneini bamidbar melon orchim* — "Who will give me a guesthouse in the desert?" (*Yirmiyahu* 9:1). The exploited desert will still house a hotel for guests, two special guests: Mashiach ben Yosef and Mashiach ben David.

Do you feel like a desert, dear women, a place where nothing grows, where the stillness is deafening? Even a woman with a houseful of children can experience this emptiness. It's the excruciating reality of no growth, no joy. It's when you feel like an *eretz lo zeruah*, a barren land, unable to experience the beauty of life. Do you feel like an exploited being whose supply has simply dried out?

Hashem says to you, dear women, *Zacharti lach chesed ne'urayich ahavas kelulosayich lechteich acharai bamidbar b'eretz lo zeru'ah* — "I remember the kindness of your youth, that you followed me in the *midbar*, a barren land" (ibid. 2:2). When you feel this emptiness — the "now what?" — whether you are in midlife, your youth, or in your golden years, cling to Hashem. With Hashem at your side, you will find the beauty in everyday life. You will cultivate an appreciation for yourself and your gifts.

In the place of utter emptiness, Hashem plants hope, but you must first allow Him into your heart. I am always amazed by Naomi, a woman old enough to have grown children and a daughter-in-law, and how she got a new lease on life. Her husband died. Her two sons died soon after they had married non-Jews, Moabite women. And the instructions she gives to her daughters-in-law are most puzzling of all: "Don't come with me. Go home."

"Why?"

"Just go."

"No," persisted Ruth and Orpah. "With you we will return to your nation" (*Ruth* 1:10).

And what did Naomi answer them? "Return, my daughters. Why should you go with me? Do I still have sons in my womb who will be your husbands?" (ibid. 1:11).

She continued to expound on her hopeless situation, telling her daughters-in-law that even if she would still merit giving birth, it would take a while for the children to grow into adulthood. "No, my daughters, for it is much more bitter for me than for you, for the Hand of Hashem has gone forth against me" (ibid. 1:13).

Was that what Naomi was concerned about: that she won't be able to provide the young women with husbands? Clarifying Naomi's seemingly odd response, the Chida explains that a woman feels most frightened when she comes to the conclusion that nothing awaits her in the future. It is the anxiety a barren woman feels when she's about to give up hope. It's the anxiety an older single experiences when the lineup of siblings under her grows longer and longer.

Because Naomi deeply understood the pain of being in that trap, of losing everything she lived for and looking out to a bleak future of no change, she wanted to spare her daughters-in-law that pain. In her kindness, she was willing to part from her faithful companions so they could build a life for themselves.

One who feels the constriction, the lack of a flourishing future, which Naomi experienced — and from the depth of her pain she connects to Hashem — will, like Naomi, merit true salvation. When you pursue spirituality, dear women, when you seek to be connected to a reality that is greater than the one you've known, you find such beauty, such light!

So how can you experience growth? Only a woman who understands the value of a Jew can truly appreciate herself. If you realize, like Moshe Rabbeinu, how infinitely valuable you are and how much Hashem values your closeness to Him, you will find joy in your growth. You will take pleasure in the garden flourishing in your heart.

Who Is a Faithful Wife?

*P*arashas *Naso* discusses the procedure that was employed in the Beis HaMikdash to confirm the loyalty of a married woman who was suspected of being an adulteress. A woman's faithfulness is of paramount importance in a Jewish home. It is the cornerstone of its existence. Let us understand how faithfulness, a quality so overtly lacking in today's relationships, is cultivated.

The foundation of a Jewish home is the woman's purity, which is exhibited through her *tznius*, her modesty. *Tznius* is not only a matter of dress; it is a demeanor that speaks volumes of the woman's priorities, a demeanor that reflects on her faithfulness to the Torah and to her husband. Incredibly, the more *tzanua* a woman is, the more she will attract the attention of the right party, our Sages teach us. The two women who were most concealed were the ones who were most noticed. "Where is she?" the angels inquired about Sarah (*Bereishis* 18:9). And Boaz, as well, from among the sea of girls that roamed his field, inquired specifically about modest Ruth: *L'mi hana'arah hazos* — "To whom does that young woman belong?" (*Ruth* 2:5).

Especially for single girls who anticipate building a home of their own, it is hard to understand how being *tzanua* will help them achieve their goal. However, tells us the Midrash, *ein lecha yafah min hatzenius* — "there is nothing more beautiful and becoming for a woman than her modesty" (*Midrash Tanchuma, Ki Sisa* 31).

So how does a woman acquire this trait that will reflect on every aspect of her demeanor? Rav Yerucham Levovitz, zt"l, the *mashgiach* of Mir, advises that a woman should think one thought always: *What I'm doing now is the most important thing in the world.*

What's the connection? The true reason for a woman's lack of modesty is her lack of a sense of self-worth. When her internal realm craves recognition, she turns to the external to provide it. *I will attract attention from the outside*, she reasons subconsciously, *to receive the respect and recognition I desperately need.*

Sadly, this is the disease of today's world. The concept of sharing details of your personal life with people whose names you don't even know is a direct repercussion of this deep inner lack. It reflects on a severe deficiency of self-worth and self-esteem. Whenever a mother cries to me about her daughter's lack of boundaries, I always tell her, "Mother, dear, there is something your child is lacking. Fill that for her and she won't even need a telephone."

So how can a woman develop her sensitivity to *tznius* in today's provocative world? The first condition for growing in *tznius* is to tell yourself at every moment that you are a highly valuable human being. This idea is not coming from your therapist or life coach. It's Rav Yerucham's advice to you. If you don't like yourself, you will be dependent on the likes of others. When you appreciate yourself, you won't have a desire for external recognition. There will be no urge for unfaithfulness.

Of all pious individuals in the Torah, Yosef HaTzaddik is considered the paradigm of faithfulness. Let's examine his demeanor.

Even when he worked as a slave in the home of Potifar, Yosef valued his work. Our Sages note that in every hot drink that he prepared for his master, he invested his efforts to do his best. *Einenu gadol babayis hazeh mimeni*, he said. "There is no one in this house who is greater than me" (*Bereishis* 39:9). As a person who valued himself, his accomplishments, and his responsibilities, he knew how important it was for him to protect his *tznius*.

As Rav Yerucham says, continuing his advice for modesty, a Jewish woman must also dress pleasantly. A woman who values her internal world will make it her business to dress with dignity. Look at the Kohen Gadol, the paradigm of *tznius*. The High Priest was truly aware of the significance of his task and he dressed accordingly. Your work, dear woman, is infinitely valuable, and you should dress the part. It is not for naught that the woman of valor is extolled with the virtue of *Oz v'hadar levushah* — "Strength and majesty are her garments" (*Mishlei* 31:25).

David HaMelech was Ruth's crowning descendant. When David was preparing to fight Golias, King Shaul observed that his own royal garb fit David, and he asked, "Whose child is this young lad?" It's not that the king didn't recognize David, whom he knew well; the king, seeing that his own kingly clothes suited David so well, suspected that he was destined to be a king (*Yevamos* 76b).

When a woman has genuine self-respect, she dresses and conducts herself in a way that reflects her inner dignity. And only a woman who has faith in herself can be a faithful wife and mother.

Achieving the Balance

Parashas Naso lists the three prohibitive commandments a person must adhere to as a *nazir*, but it also teaches us that Hashem prefers a wholesome, balanced Torah way of life. Judaism mandates that a *nazir*, one who disconnects from physical practices like drinking wine or cutting his hair, bring a chatas-offering upon completing his term. It's not the ideal choice for a typical Torah Jew. Be *tzanua*, but don't look like a drab. Wear tasteful, clean clothes, but don't dress to call attention to yourself. It's vital, but not easy: balance is one of the hardest things to achieve in life.

How can a Jewish woman achieve this balance of *gashmiyus* and *ruchniyus*, between the physical world and the world of the *neshamah*? No, you're not meant to be a *nezirah*, to cast aside your feminine uniqueness and beauty. On the contrary, you should use your intrinsic beauty in order to bring the *Shechinah* into your home. When you put yourself together to look presentable and pleasant in your home, you're teaching your children a most powerful lesson. You're teaching them that you care more about the *Shechinah* than you do about your neighbor. You're making your home a pleasant place, a place your husband and children want to be.

I remember traveling on a lengthy journey from the Israeli town of Migdal HaEmek with the daughter of Rebbetzin Grossman, the wife of the *rav* of the city, Rav Yitzchak Dovid Grossman. She said to me, "Our mother is a queen. I never in my life saw her come out of her bedroom not looking put together. There was no such thing! She is the queen of our home."

Do we look very different in our homes from the way we appear on the street? Do we wear dowdy robes inside and designer dresses outside? This was the problem of the *ishah sotah*, the faithless wife: her focus was outside the home. Dear women, it is our duty to turn the focus inward, to turn our homes into a sacred place that holds all the value in the world. The more we invest in making it a secure place, the more holiness it will contain.

The woman Kimchis was a role model in maintaining the holiness of her home. The Gemara tells us that when she was asked how she merited raising seven holy sons who became Kohanim Gedolim, she answered, *Mei'olam lo ra'u koros beisi sa'aros roshi*. This pious woman proclaimed that the ceiling beams of her home never saw the hairs on her head (*Yoma* 47a).

How did she do this? The answer is a profound insight on what true *tznius* means. This is the work of *sheleimus*, of wholeness. A woman who has inner *sheleimus* conducts herself in a Kimchislike manner. She sees her true essence as a holy entity and treats it as such. It's her pleasure and joy to safeguard her beauty for the *ruchniyus* it craves. It's not easy to acquire this level of wholeness, but this should be our goal (see Rav Tzadok HaKohen, *Likutei Ma'amarim*, p. 125).

V'Yaseim Lecha Shalom: Let Peace Reign

When we achieve the delicate balance of employing our feminine traits for the right purpose, we have a beautiful life in this world and the World to Come. How can we merit this wholeness, this ideal balance of *gashmiyus* and *ruchniyus*?

The Sfas Emes (*Naso* 5650) tells us that we can merit this combination through the power of the priestly blessing, which we find in *Parashas Naso. Yevarechecha Hashem v'yishmerecha... v'yaseim lecha shalom* — "May Hashem bless you and safeguard you...and establish peace for you" (*Bamidbar* 6:24–26). True peace reigns in the home when its inhabitants seek to protect its sanctity, when the focus is on keeping it a sacred place.

In the haftarah of *Parashas Naso*, we read about a childless woman, Manoach's wife, who was informed by an angel that she would soon bear a child who will begin to save the Jewish nation. The angel then proceeded to teach her the laws of *nezirus*, because her child would be a *nazir* from birth. Indeed, this woman, whom our Sages call Tzlelponis, merited giving birth to Shimshon HaGibbor.

Why did the angel appear first to Tzlelponis and not to Manoach? Answering this question, the Kli Yakar provides us with a powerful insight regarding the importance of peace in the Jewish home. Manoach and his wife had an ongoing conflict over who was at fault for their childlessness, with each blaming the other. Only when peace would reign between the couple, the angels knew, would they be worthy of being blessed with a child. Thus, the angel appeared to Tzlelponis and informed her that she was the barren one.

Look at the power of *shalom*, dear women! If the angel had appeared to Manoach to confirm that he was right, it would have only exacerbated their quarrel. By appearing to his wife instead, the angel taught us how sensitive we must be in maintaining the peace in our home.

As part of the *sotah* procedure, the Kohen was commanded to inscribe the curses for an unfaithful woman, which included Hashem's Name, on a scroll and erase it in water. The woman was then instructed to drink the water, and if she were indeed guilty it would cause her to die a horrible death. This procedure was performed only to confirm one thing: the wife's loyalty to her husband. To create this sacred peace, *shalom bayis*, Hashem allowed His Name to be erased (*Shabbos* 116a).

So much depends on the *akeres habayis*, the Jewish woman. Especially in today's world, when few things remain sacred, we must work hard to ensure that not everything that happens in the home becomes public knowledge. Sometimes, if we just stop to think, we can hold our heads and wonder, *Where has the concept of privacy flown off to?* No, not every gift should be displayed, and not every family moment must be shared. The more we work to build strong walls around our home, the safer a place it will be.

Our Sages ask, "How can a woman assist her husband?" And they answer that a man brings home wheat, and the wife grinds it and bakes bread, and he eats from it; he brings home flax, and she spins it and sews clothing for him and he wears it (*Yevamos* 63a). What does this mean? The woman has a unique role in the Jewish home: she is here to take whatever comes through the door of her home and turn it into a homemade creation, an item that is used in the household in order to nourish and serve its inhabitants. When a woman makes her home a central place, the place where *gashmiyus* is used for *ruchniyus*, our Sages tell us, she "lights up his eyes and stands him on his feet" (*Yevamos* 63a).

Imagine the power you have, dear women! With your innate ability to create, to adorn, to make this world a more beautiful place, you have the capacity to bring *shalom bayis*, true peace, into this world. And when your home is a peaceful cocoon, it will be the safe haven for you, your husband, and your precious children.

The Nation's Litany of Complaints

In *Parashas Beha'aloscha,* we observe a tragic decline in *Am Yisrael's* respect for both Hashem and Moshe Rabbeinu. The nation complains incessantly, first about the quality of the manna and then about the conditions in the desert.

It's hard for Moshe Rabbeinu when the nation complains. He cries to Hashem, "Did I conceive this entire people or did I give birth to it that You say to me, 'Carry them in your bosom as a nurse carries a suckling, to the Land that You swore to its forefathers?' (*Bamidbar* 11:12). What am I, their mother? From where do I have meat to sustain them all? I can't do this alone," he cries. "If this is how You deal with me, then kill me now" (ibid. 11:13–15).

Moshe Rabbeinu was clearly at a loss. Parenting is never easy, especially not when dealing with a hungry, angry brood. (I sound a bit like this at the end of summer vacation.)

Moshe had a tough role to fill. He was dealing with adults. Mitzrayim was the breeding place of the nation, *Yetzias Mitzrayim* symbolized the birth, and the years in the desert was its adulthood. The Jews gave Moshe no rest. When Moshe provided the Jews with the manna, he hoped that they would be happy. Imagine! They were getting food that required no preparation and tasted like whatever they fancied. What a blessing! Still, instead of seeing the food as *kal*, light, they saw it as *kelokel*, inedible.

Nothing Moshe offered appeased his "adult children." Why was this so hard for Moshe Rabbeinu? Why couldn't he handle the nation's complaints? Because he was an *ish tov*. From when Moshe was born, his mother perceived the goodness in him. *Vateire oso ki tov* — "And she saw that he was good" (*Shemos* 2:2). He couldn't handle the negativity.

The Power of Tov

"Come with us to Eretz Yisrael," suggests Moshe to his in-laws. "We just left Mitzrayim, we received the Torah, and very soon we'll arrive in the Holy Land. It will be so good for us! *V'hayah hatov hahu asher yeitiv Hashem i'manu v'heitavnu lach* — "With the goodness with which Hashem will benefit us, we will do good to you" (*Bamidbar* 10:32).

In his request to his in-laws, Yisro and his wife, Moshe repeated the word *tov* five times. It will be so good, he kept saying. He didn't yet know that it wouldn't be so good, that it would take many more years before the nation would finally enter — without him.

The words of Rav Chaim of Volozhin on this topic, dear sisters, will take your breath away. In his *sefer Ruach Chaim* he says that on the day a person says the word *tov* five times, his prayers will be accepted. And on the day a person says the word *ra* three times, his prayers will not ascend.

Why didn't the nation merit entry to Eretz Yisrael soon after they received the Torah? Because they sullied their mouths with evil speech. Look at the damage the tongue can do.

Moshe's Greatness: Positive Speech

A good person like Moshe knows only one thing: *tov*. Complaints don't exist. Even when she doesn't yet see the good, a good woman knows it will come. Life is just *good*.

"Yemima, it's so hard!" you say. "Stop with the 'no complaints.' Look at how the nation suffered!"

It's true that it was hard for *Am Yisrael*. They wandered like nomads from place to place, finding no peace. When they thought they would have a chance to settle down, the hovering cloud signaled their departure once again. "But we just got here!" they cried. "Can we know what You want from us?" Sometimes, in our heart of hearts, we may suspect that Hashem's ways aren't good for us. Life gets uncomfortable, circumstances are trying. "Why are You doing this to me?" we want to cry. But even when you have doubts, dear women, speak only good words. When you speak good words, when you think good thoughts, the goodness will penetrate into your soul.

When you change your perspective, you change the reality. Even when the nation received food directly from Hashem, they weren't appeased. How do you feel when your children complain about the supper you worked hard to prepare? "But I wanted chicken!" they cry when you make what you thought was their favorite supper, lasagna. Chicken? When do children ever want chicken?

When it comes to complaining, there is never a dearth of reasons. Especially during summer vacation, women the world over brace themselves for the onslaught of complaints that seem to always accompany this break in routine. *Can't everyone just be happy?* you want to scream. That's the motto we should hang on our walls — not only for our children but also for ourselves. What message do your children get from you? Is the bungalow too dumpy? The pool too cold? Your husband comes out too infrequently — or too often? The heat is unbearable? It doesn't take much to make negativity feel right at home.

Beha'aloscha es haneiros — "When you kindle the lamps" (*Bamidbar* 8:2) — light up your home with your positivity, with your smile. Be that candle even in the dark, dingy bungalow. A happy mother who doesn't look to complain is a good mother because she gives her children an invaluable tool for life. If you want to be a good person, speak good words.

Siblings and Speech

The name of the Torah portion, *Beha'aloscha*, alludes to growth. *Beha'aloscha es haneiros*, when you light up the candle, its flame rises upward. At the same time, this is the parashah that discusses the Jews' unfortunate descent: their ingratitude to Hashem and Moshe, their incessant complaints. After the incredible greatness they experienced at *mattan Torah*, what a downfall.

And what happens toward the end of the *parashah*? "Miriam and Aharon spoke against Moshe regarding the Cushite woman he had married" (ibid. 12:1). What kind of *lashon hara* did Miriam speak? Not realizing that Hashem had instructed Moshe to separate from Tzipporah, and feeling that it was an unjustifiable affront to Tzipporah, Miriam shared the news of the separation with Aharon. She did so out of a sincere desire to correct what she was convinced was Moshe's error, because she, too, was a prophet and yet she wasn't required to withdraw from normal life. But even with the best of intentions, she was punished.

According to other commentators, Miriam's sin was the reference she made to the color of her sister-in-law's skin. I once had the merit of traveling with the daughter of Rebbetzin Grossman of Migdal HaEmek. She shared that her mother once said to her, "Listen. Today a new student is arriving at our school. Go pick her up from the Central Bus Station. She'll be wearing a white skirt."

The daughter went and looked around. Which white skirt there would be their new student? This one? That one? One young woman gestured to her, so she picked up the phone and called her mother. "Is she Ethiopian?" she asked.

"Yes."

"Why didn't you tell me that?"

"Why would I describe someone according to the color of their skin?" the *rebbetzin* asked, incredulous.

This is the kind of *lashon hara* that Miriam spoke. The slightest of the slightest, but Hashem punished her for that. For seven days, the verse tells us, she was forced into isolation, quarantined outside the camp.

What was Aharon HaKohen's prayer after Miriam was stricken with *tzara'as*? "Let her not be like a corpse, like one who leaves his mother's womb with half his flesh being consumed!" (*Bamidbar* 12:12). On whose behalf did Aharon offer this *tefillah*? His sister! "Hashem," he cried, "Miriam and I were born from the same womb. If my sister is suffering, the other half of her flesh, I am dead. Dead! I can't see my sister in this unfortunate state."

When Moshe joined his brother in prayer (ibid. 12:13), at that moment, our Sages reveal, though Miriam was still obligated to be quarantined for the remainder of the seven days, from thereafter she was completely healed (*Avos D'Rav Nassan* 9:2 and *Midrash Tanchuma, Metzora* 2). Aharon and Moshe's heartfelt prayer, their true display of brotherly caring that Hashem expects from every sister and brother, brought about her much-awaited miracle.

Because our sisters and brothers are the closest people to us on the planet, and we may be spending lots of time in each other's presence, the opportunities for negative speech can come too easily our way. But why would we want to cause damage to them with our most precious tool, the power of our tongue? When you pray for your sister, dear women, you are giving her a priceless gift that only you can offer. It is your sincerity, your deep empathy that is so precious in the eyes of Hashem. Please, Hashem says, I want to see you caring for one another, begging Me on their behalf.

"Cast Your Bread Upon the Waters"

The very *pasuk* that tells of Miriam's unfortunate consequence ends with a most incredible statement: "And the people did not journey until Miriam was brought in" (*Bamidbar* 12:15). What is so profoundly incredible about these words? The Torah uses many verses in *Parashas Beha'aloscha* detailing the journey that the nation took: how they traveled "according to Hashem's command" and rested "according to Hashem's command." Whenever Hashem instructed them to move on, they packed their bags and trekked onward for days on end, destination unknown. When Hashem ordered that they stop, they encamped right then and there; sometimes for as little as a day before they were once again instructed to journey. "According to the word of Hashem they would encamp, and according to the word of Hashem they would journey" (ibid. 9:20), the verse in this Torah portion states. Only once in their entire forty-year trek did the nation say to Hashem, "We are not budging from here for seven whole days." They did not move until Miriam was able to join.

The holy Ohr HaChaim tells us that although the decision when to journey depended solely on when the pillar of cloud lifted, this time the nation decided to honor Miriam by remaining at the camp until she could join them.

In what merit was Miriam honored in this remarkably unique way? The Mishnah (*Sotah* 1:9) tells us it was because she too waited for her brother. After baby Moshe was placed into the sea, she stood from a distance and observed to see what would happen to her beloved brother. Her deep concern for her brother did not allow her to take her eyes off him. She cared for him then as the nation cared for her later.

An act of kindness, dear women, is never forgotten. It may take years before you see it come full circle, but in the end, it will. Until then, stay strong. You can do it.

A Long Way Home

Without the use of Waze, the Torah estimated that the journey from Mitzrayim to Eretz Yisrael should have taken eleven days. But in *Parashas Shelach*, those eleven days turned into an arduous trek of *forty* whole years. And the truth is, the journey did not last forty years. It's been lasting for thousands. We are still on our way home.

When the *meraglim* returned from their espionage, they were baffled. "Oh, my," they cried, "what a land! Frightening. Giants live there." What happened on that very night, after the spies depicted what they'd witnessed? "The whole nation wept all night" (*Bamidbar* 14:1). The night they protested that they don't want to enter Eretz Yisrael is the night of Tishah B'Av. What did Hashem say to them? "You cried in vain. I will establish this day as a day of tears for generations" (*Sanhedrin* 104b). How sad!

In the entire *Parashas Shelach*, we don't find one reference to a woman. Not one. It's all about the menfolk, their tears, and their punishment. Women, Rashi tells us (ibid. 26:64), did not share the fate of the men, who were sentenced to die in the desert rather than enter Eretz Yisrael, because the women loved the Land.

Imagine those pious women, dear sisters. They were the ones who said, "Yes! We *do* want to come home. We are not afraid to enter Eretz Yisrael."

Let's talk about the woman's power that gives her the courage to trek homeward, even when she's so, so far. When we're thrown so far away, we're not unlike a yo-yo. How frightening it is to be thrown into the distance: for forty years, for thousands of years. But what can you do once the yo-yo is thrown? You have the opportunity to slowly, slowly wind the string back and come closer. *Parashas Shelach* is the string of that yo-yo.

Long before yo-yos became popular, the Midrash offered a similar parable (*Midrash Rabbah, Bamidbar* 17:6). It compares the nation to a person who is drowning in deep water. When a rope is thrown his way, the rescuer warns him, "Hold on tight to this rope and do not let go. If you let go, your life will be sucked out of you."

We, too, dear women, have a *chevel*, a rope that we must grip tightly during our long journey home. The Hebrew word *chevel* is an acronym for three qualities of women, beautifully woven to form a tight rope: *chibah*, *bechi*, and *lashon* — love, tears, and speech.

We cry on Tishah B'Av because we mourn the destruction of the Temples. Why was the edifice of beauty and sanctity destroyed? For three reasons: there was no brotherly love among the Jews (during the Second Temple era — *Yoma* 9b), they cried in vain when the spies came back with their negative report (*Sanhedrin* 104b), and because the *meraglim* had spoken badly against Eretz Yisrael.

So what must we hold on to in order to finally come home? We must hold on to the rope of love, the rope of real tears, and the rope of positive speech — all of which women are renowned for. Love? Oh, how the women loved the Land! And if you thought you were the only woman who enjoys a good cry, our Sages have already established that women are known for their tears (*Bava Metzia* 59a). And the tongue! Nine of the ten portions of speech were sent our way when the world was created (*Kiddushin* 49b).

Let's hold on to our three unique abilities to finally come home. When we love more, when we cry more real tears, and when we will strive toward purity of speech, we will get there.

The Power in Our Hands

During the week of *Parashas Shelach* in the year this book was written, I got a phone call from a young woman who was visiting from America. She was in her early thirties, she shared with me, and she was sick with the *machalah*, with a tumor in her brain that could not be removed. "I will be in the Waldorf Astoria before I leave," she told me, "and I would really appreciate if the Rabbanit could come and give me *chizuk*."

I entered the hotel and spotted her immediately. Her eyes were looking out for me, the pain of her search for strength so overwhelming. What could I tell her? When I sat down next to her, she shared with me how painful it was for her when her hands suddenly stopped moving. Such beautiful fingers she had, but they were completely immobile. Oh, how she wanted to hold on to the rope, the rope that would bring her home, but she had no strength in her hands.

So I said to her, "Let's say *Eishes Chayil* together. It is full of references to the woman of valor's hands: *yadeha, kapeha, zeraseha*. Every day when you sing it, say, 'HaKadosh Baruch Hu, what do I really want? To be a woman of valor. That's what I want my hands for.'"

Then I said to her, "Listen, my dear, *Parashas Shelach* discusses the mitzvah of challah. Lift your hands up and knead challos this week. Show Hashem the challos that you've made for Him."

The beautiful young woman straightened her back. "Thank you so much," she said. Her husband shed tears at her side.

But when I left, I said to myself, *Yemima, what's up with all*

*the shtuyot you spoke to her? Where is your seichel? Just take a
look at her medical records, at what the doctors are saying. Are
you nuts? Woman of valor? Bake challos? How can she?*

That's when the holy words of the Pri Tzaddik came to my
mind. He says that when life is truly frightening (may we never
know of this), one should stop being smart. If this woman would
follow only logic, and live according to the results of the tests,
she would die on the spot.

The final letters of the words *Shelach lecha anashim* — "Send
men for you" — spell the word *chacham*. The spies were incredibly brilliant, and that is why they saw a frightening land. They
said, "No way in the world. According to logic, we will never be
able to conquer this country."

Logic can kill us, dear women. Fear can kill. So what can you
do when you're truly afraid? Take all that fear and translate it into
simple *yiras Shamayim*, fear of Hashem. Simply talk to Hashem
and say, "Ribbono shel Olam, You put me in a frightening place.
Help me. Please!"

First comes the deep desire to connect to Hashem and do
His will, and the *chachmah* will follow. What do we remind ourselves every morning? *Reishis chachmah yiras Hashem* — "The
predecessor of wisdom is fear of G-d." And only after that follows the *seichel tov l'chal oseihem* — the "good understanding"
to those who do the mitzvos.

Yes, dear women, of course there is a place for logic and wisdom in our lives. But when fear enters your mind or heart, the
wisdom lies in your *yiras Shamayim*.

Yachol Nuchal: Kalev's Eternal Message

The Rebbe of Piaseczna, the Aish Kodesh, was no stranger
to fear. He stood before hundreds of his *talmidim* during the
Holocaust, their worried eyes pleading for his guidance and
support. Many of them had already lost their families, and

others feared for the day they, too, would join that cursed fate. And what did he tell them? Look into *Parashas Shelach*, he advised. Look at the words of Kalev ben Yefuneh, the spy who stood before the frightened nation and said, *Aloh na'aleh. . .ki yachol nuchal lah* — "We will ascend, we will prevail" (*Bamidbar* 13:30).

"Let's understand," said the holy Rebbe. "The spies' report was based on logic and common sense: the land's inhabitants were tough, surrounded by tough, strong walls. Why did Kalev argue with their eyewitness accounts? He did so in order to contradict those who lost their hope to logic."

Don't you see? Don't you see the condition your son is in? How can he ever come back to the path of truth? How can she ever be healthy again? How can they ever bring a child into this world? How can she ever find a shidduch, with her background? That's the wicked voice of logic that withholds the salvation.

The words of the Aish Kodesh are invaluable. Shut your ears, dear sisters, to the words of logic that fill your mind. Open them wide to Kalev's timeless message, one that proved to be correct.

The test of *emunah* is not when the road to salvation is clear. On the contrary, says the Aish Kodesh, when her chances of salvation are defied by logic, the person must say, "Yes. It's all true. They are tough inhabitants surrounded by tough walls. Nevertheless, I believe that Hashem is beyond nature. He will help. We will persevere."

The Torah portion that is one of the most frightening is also the Torah portion with the most *segulos*, deeds that defy logic. First is the string of *techeiles* that men wear on their clothes. *U're'isem oso u'zechartem es kal mitzvos Hashem* — "And when you see it, you will remember all the commandments of Hashem" (*Bamidbar* 15:39). Next is the *segulah* of the mitzvah of challah. (Getting more and more popular: Here in Eretz Yisrael, it's rare to find a *shiur* that does not conclude with bowls of dough and heartfelt *berachos*!)

The third *segulah* in the *parashah* is to visit *kivrei tzaddikim*.

"Wait one moment," Kalev said to his fellow spies. "I found a *kever* here. I want to spend a few minutes there" (*Rashi*, *Bamidbar* 13:22, quoting *Sotah* 34b). The spies, in their logic, could not understand the importance of this practice. After all, they were on an important mission together! Perhaps this *segulah* was what gave Kalev the remarkable strength to remain steadfast in his *emunah*, in his *yachol nuchal*.

How We Long for Home!

We find something fascinating in *Parashas Shelach*. All of the commandments it contains center around the concept of longing. The mitzvah of tzitzis, for instance, serves to awaken a yearning toward Hashem. *U're'isem oso u'zechartem* — "And when you see [the tzitzis], you will remember." Our Sages explain that *techeiles*, the color of some of the tzitzis strings, resembles the color of the sea, the sea resembles the sky, and the sky reminds a person of the heavenly throne (*Menachos* 43b). When a man has an urge to sin, as soon as he spots his holy tzitzis, he remembers Whom he must long for, always.

The mitzvah that embodies the emotion of longing is the mitzvah of challah: *Reishis arisoseichem challah tarimu serumah* — "The first of your dough you shall apportion a portion" (*Bamidbar* 15:20). Rebbe Nosson, the disciple of Rebbe Nachman, expounds on the intrinsic beauty of this mitzvah. In our long *galus*, he writes, we've been experiencing untold pain of many sorts, for which there is almost no hope, G-d forbid. For this reason, we're left with almost no desire to live, except for the hope we hang on to that Hashem has a desire for us, as it says, *Mah ta'iru u'mah te'oreru es ha'ahavah ad shetechpatz* — "If you [the nations] dare provoke G-d to hate me or disturb His love for me while He still desires it" (*Shir HaShirim* 8:4).

Humans have a natural desire to be longed for, to be appreciated. We seek it out in every relationship. But how does this longing lead to a substantial existence? We find the answer in the mitzvah of challah.

Essentially, the apparent reason for the mitzvah does not apply today. In the times of the Beis HaMikdash, when the Kohen received the challah offering as one of the gifts for his Temple service, it had a purpose. Why did our Sages command that we maintain this practice even now that there is no more Temple service? Rebbe Nosson teaches that through the mitzvah of challah, the food experiences a modification. By performing the mitzvah, we fill ourselves with a longing for the Kohanim's service in the Beis HaMikdash, for the ultimate redemption, and this elevates the food to a level of immense holiness. For this reason, he notes, there is no *shiur d'Oraisa*, there is no fixed amount given in the Torah, regarding how much challah one must apportion. There is no *shiur* to longing and desire.

The whole purpose of challah, dear women, is to arouse our yearning. How does food do this? The very first sin in history was committed through food, the fruit of the *eitz hada'as*. "I allow you to eat from anything you see," Hashem said to them. "Only one tree will be the tree you will crave. One corner of Gan Eden will remain off limits so there will be something outside your grasp" (see *Bereishis* 2:16–17). When the first man and woman committed the sin, they acted upon the negative side of longing.

For this reason, when we recite Birkas HaMazon upon consuming bread, we say, *Posei'ach es yadecha u'masbia l'chal chai ratzon* — "Open Your hand and satisfy the desire of every living thing." A Jew's satiation is his *ratzon*, a manifestation of his longing. Yearning, like every other emotion, can be good or evil. When a woman stands over her challah dough and experiences true yearning for her salvation and the salvation of her fellow Jews, she elevates the bread to an exalted level, one that will permeate the very body of those who will enjoy her challah.

The foundation of the mitzvah of challah is essentially a rectification of the sin of the *meraglim*. Hashem said to them, "If you can't see yourself living in this blessed Land, I can hear that. But not even to long for it?" A Jew must always yearn. Sometimes we experience fear of the unknown: about the days of Mashiach, about life after a commitment. But we should never stop yearning. Never stop longing for the ultimate closeness, the ultimate salvation.

Life could get supercomfortable in this dark *galus:* in the sunny summer home, in the cozy winter abode. But where is the longing? Where is the desire for closeness to our Creator? To finally inhabit His Holy Land? To live in peace with our brothers and sisters? Knead it into your dough, pray for it, long for it. Do something about it! That will be the *tikkun,* the rectification for the sin we've been crying about, for so many centuries.

Festering Under the Surface

arashas *Korach* is not a simple portion, but its message can't be simpler: don't fight. Perhaps it's actually not so simple, indeed, to distance ourselves from every crumb of discord or animosity, but peace must be the cornerstone of every Jewish home.

It is the week that makes our nation *keirei'ach*, bald. True to his name, Korach shaved so many good people from *Klal Yisrael*, sending them into the belly of the earth. We don't want to lose more. Fighting eats us up from the inside and out, bringing out the worst.

The Meshech Chochmah, Rav Meir Simchah of Dvinsk, asks, Why was being consumed into the earth the ideal death for Korach and his crew? Wouldn't it be more powerful if they would have left behind some sort of sign that would remind the nation of the ramifications of discord: a place for people to pass and say, "Here's where Korach, the king of conflict, lies"?

He answers that death by being consumed into the earth *is* the sign. It is immensely symbolic because it teaches people that when a fight breaks out, it did not happen overnight. The final outer display is only a sign that animosity had festered deep inside for a long, long time. It's a sign of a deep-rooted illness that only came to the fore at this point, to a concealed hatred that finally exploded.

That's exactly what the Lashon HaKodesh word of *machlokes* implies: it has in it the word *machalah*, illness. An argument is the final result of a deep-seated illness that eventually explodes like hot, angry lava from inside a volcanic mountain. For this reason, the punishment of *bliah*, being swallowed up by the earth, is the most ideal and powerful one of all. From the surface, the earth looks calm and quiet, but once a month, on Rosh Chodesh, a cloud of smoke rises from the ground. And from underneath, Korach and his crew scream, *Moshe emes v'Soraso emes* — "Moshe is truthful and his Torah is truth!" That's what Rabbah bar Chana reveals to us in the Gemara (*Bava Basra* 74a).

The Ramban teaches us that Korach had always been abnormally jealous of Moshe and Aharon, but he wasn't able to speak against them because the nation revered them so much. After the sin of the spies and the ensuing punishment, he jumped at the opportunity to finally incite the despondent masses. In other words, all that time that he kept his mouth shut he merely maintained a facade, awaiting an opportunity to instigate the Jews. The final fight, dear sisters, was only a display of what festered inside his heart for years.

Remember that a fight does not happen overnight. If we bear a grudge against someone, it will eventually surface to the fore. The longer we let it fester, we're merely allowing it to boil a bit more until the lid will pop. It's like the cloud that will soon burst into a turbulent storm. Don't ignore your feelings; deal with them properly. When you address your hurts in a soft-spoken honest manner, you will bring the sun back to your heart and home.

Why Were the Babies Swallowed Up too?

Let us talk about Korach's exalted children, however, whom the Torah refers to as "roses": *Lamenatzei'ach al shoshanim livnei Korach* — "For the conductor on the roses, by the sons of Korach" (*Tehillim* 45:1). They were swallowed up alive for sins they didn't commit only because they were in the vicinity of the catastrophe, in the vicinity of discord. They're screaming from under the ground, but nobody can hear their cries! Listen to them, dear women, how they beg of you to rid your home of discord, to clear your heart of animosity.

On the day that my toddler son was *niftar*, he sat on my lap as I prepared a *shiur*. While I read my notes, he scribbled on the *Chumash*. That evening, he passed away, and until today I try to decipher what he scribbled there, what his final testament to me was. I think what he wrote is "Ima, please tell everyone that my *tzava'ah* is not to fight." If there's a sin for which young children who haven't yet sinned are torn away from us, it's *machlokes*. Rabbeinu Bachya describes the horrific consequence of *machlokes*: Korach's children suffered for his sins. Even a baby from Korach's *eidah* was dragged toward the crater and into the earth!

Why? What sin did that baby commit? The Chida teaches that if a child is meant to die, *lo aleinu*, there's a big probability that it will happen in the week of *Parashas Korach* because discord kills young children. They simply cannot handle fighting. They've ascended from such a pure place, a place of true peace, and they just can't bear the tainted environment of animosity. What are we doing to our children?

As parents, we make the common mistake of thinking that when the grown children are around, we don't want them to hear us argue so we'll do so under lock and key. But when it comes to the little ones, we think that fighting in their presence is okay. It is not. Standing in front of the baby and tossing harmful, flammable words at each other causes untold harm to the young child. At that time, Hashem says to us, "Ima, Abba, remember: Innocent children were swallowed by the earth as a result of Korach's fight."

A child comes from the place of ultimate respect. In the

upper spheres, the angels *nosnim reshus zeh lazeh* — "give permission to one another." That's how Hashem is *oseh shalom bimromav* — "makes peace in His heights." A baby is still deeply connected to the upper worlds, where serenity permeates everywhere. His soul can't bear the acrid smell of *machlokes*.

Even if you're arguing in a language you think the child doesn't understand, even when the children are sleeping, know that their souls hear every word. They are very sensitive, our precious children, and we must do our best to guard their purity, dear sisters.

The Power of an Evil Woman

If *machlokes* is so terrible and Korach was an intelligent person, *mah ra'ah lishtus zeh* — "what did he see in this nonsense?" (*Rashi, Bamidbar* 16:6, quoting *Midrash Rabbah, Bamidbar* 18:8). What was the source behind his behavior that caused him to lose *everything*?

His wife. The Midrash (*Midrash Rabbah, Bamidbar* 18:20) attributes Korach's demise to the verse that says that the construction and destruction of the home belong to the woman: *Chachmos nashim bansah veisah v'iveles b'yadeha sehersenu* — "The wisdom of the woman built her home, and the foolish one with her hands will destroy it" (*Mishlei* 14:1).

I want to give you an IQ test, dear woman. It's a very simple IQ test, but it's more than enough to let you know how intelligent you truly are: Are you at peace with others? If you're picking a fight with everyone who comes your way, listen to what our Sages are telling us. It is the brilliant woman who manages to maintain the peace and the not-so-smart one who destroys it. If you don't fight with anyone, you're a genius.

Let's understand the *chachmos nashim*, the wisdom of the woman. What does the word *build* mean? To us, it's adding another floor, another room, another brick. And to destroy means to remove that which was built. But our Sages tell us otherwise. Adding more floors, they warn, can be true destruction. That superfluous building is destructive they learn from *mattan Torah*. "Don't dare ascend the mountain," Moshe cautioned the nation. "I know you want to be very spiritual, but be careful."

The words Hashem uses to warn Moshe are *al yehersu la'alos* — the nation must not *destroy* through its ascent (*Shemos* 19:24). When a person attempts to reach heights where he doesn't belong, Rashi notes (ibid. 19:21), *hanifradin mimatzav anashim horsim es hamatzav* — she separates herself from the position of the people and brings on destruction. Who is the woman who destroys? The one who wants more and more. The woman who is a *bonah*, a true builder, on the other hand, is the one who has *binah;* she is able to extract insight from that which she already possesses.

A woman who is always seeking more is only bringing destruction upon herself and her home. It is this desire that could lead to the deepest, most hurtful quarrels. Some women I know will stand on their porches when chaos reigns inside their home, and they imagine, *One day, I'll be able to go on a luxury cruise. One day, I'll be happy.* Of course a woman needs the refuge of dreaming sometimes, but Hashem tells us, "No, dear. Go to that living room, straight to the battlefield. Separate the combatants, dress the wounded, and put them to bed in peace, please." A woman who doesn't seek too much has the capacity to bring the ultimate peace to her home. When she is at peace with herself, she has the potential to spread that quality to every crevice of her *mikdash me'at.*

Let us analyze the deeds of Korach. The Torah tells us, *Vayikach Korach* — "Korach took" (*Bamidbar* 16:1) — to which Rashi asks, "What did he take?" He answers, *Lakach es atzmo* — "He took himself." From where? From himself. What happened here? Hashem told Korach, "You're so good as is." And he replied, "I don't want to be who I am. I want to be like Moshe or Aharon. Anyone but me."

Ispaleig, he split himself, Onkelos tells us. "I'm separating myself from myself. I'm dividing myself into two others. I want to be them, not me."

How many women distance themselves from themselves — some even with the intention of building — which leads to destruction? "Maybe I'll take another job," they say. Or "Maybe I'll clean above the curtains; it's been a while." "I should really make another eggplant dip for Shabbat (because I only have Turkish and Bulgarian eggplant; not enough)."

What are you removing yourself from? Your very self. What's wrong with what you already have? A destructive woman sets impossible expectations for herself, for her husband, for her children. By adding, she's essentially destroying. To her son, she says (or hints), "Why aren't you like your friend? You're wasting your potential."

Our Sages name such a woman: *iveles*, stupid. The Malbim (to *Mishlei* 5:23) explains that *iveles* is derived from the root *ulai*, perhaps. Instead of bringing satisfaction and peace into her home, she fills it with doubt and suspicion ("Perhaps you should learn more hours, make more money, be a better student. Perhaps we should move, switch schools, redo the kitchen").

When a woman sees the world through such a perspective, the person in the house who suffers most is her husband. The children, they'll grow up and move on, hopefully to build more nurturing, positive relationships. But her husband? He's doomed to live with her forever, gradually absorbing the negative, destructive poison. In the *Tanach* list of the least smart people, the first three medals are earned by women.

Korach's wife took the gold.

When her husband returns home bald from his inauguration as a Levi, she says to him, "What is this?"

"I'm a Levi," he says proudly.

"You're a fool. They're playing a trick on you! Tell me, did Moshe shave like that too?"

"No, he sat at the table with long hair and jewels."

"You baldy," she murmurs under her breath, injecting a strong dose of frustration into her husband.

The silver medal goes to Zeresh, whose name can be read as *zeh rash*, "this pauper." "You're pathetic," she says to her husband, Haman. "Everything you have — the position, the title, the riches — is all worthless if Mordechai doesn't bow down to you."

And Izevel gets the bronze prize. When she sees her husband, the king Achav, she says, "*Zevel*, manure! Look where you are and look where I am. I'm the daughter of the king of Tzidon; you're supposed to be *worthy* of me, but look how lowly you are!"

These women, whom our Sages see as unintelligent, dragged their husbands out of this world. Each of these men had the potential to be the greatest of their time, but because their destructive wives had impossible expectations of them, they lost everything in the worst of ways.

Dear Jewish women, you are the greatest builders of your home. The responsibility and honor lie in your very hands: to construct, to build, to create a home that is saturated with peace, satisfaction, and true happiness. May you merit utilizing the gift of your *binah* to make constructive decisions, always.

A Mother Is a Mother
Is a Mother

*P*arashas Chukas discusses the enigma of the *parah adumah*, the red heifer, the commandment that the Jewish nation received as an atonement for the sin of the golden calf. Rashi explains the connection: *Tavo imo u'sikanach hatzo'ah kach tavo parah u'sechaper al ha'eigel* — "Let the mother come and clean up her child's filth. So shall the heifer come and atone for the sins of the calf" (*Rashi, Bamidbar* 19:22).

The heifer, the mother of the calf, is recruited to right the wrong of her child. The Aish Kodesh asks an obvious question: "But the red heifer is not at all the mother of that calf. How can this heifer atone for the sins of a calf it doesn't even *know*?" How does one connect to the other?

The answer the Aish Kodesh provides offers insight into how we mothers operate. A woman, he notes, can wake up in the morning with a tight knot in her stomach, anxious about someone else's child. A mother can think about someone else's child all day, all night, praying and hoping and losing sleep over him, as if he were her own child. When we hear about the plight of another woman's child, we cry for the child like he or she were our own. A mother can do that.

I remember the tense period after the three boys were kidnapped in Eretz Yisrael two summers ago. Which woman had a decent Shabbos that week? Which woman didn't spill tears for the well-being of those precious children? We didn't feel joy in anything. We're like the *parah* that comes and says, "I want to help out. I'm here."

When I spoke with Rachel Frankel, Naftali's mother, during those fateful days when she was still unaware of the whereabouts of her son, she said to me, "Tell the women that if I'm able to sleep at night it's only because somewhere someone is not asleep; someone is poring over the *sefer Tehillim* on behalf of my son."

In my community, we have what's called a "*gemach sheinah*," a *gemach* for sleep. How does it work? When a mother has a new baby and she's desperate for a stretch of sleep, she calls and they send someone to tend to the needs of the baby while she gets her much-needed rest. When we are up at night thinking about another mother's plight, we are giving her an opportunity to sleep. We are that "*gemach sheinah*" for her.

As mothers, as Jewish women, we have the capacity to help others carry the burden. Like the heifer, we can clean up the mess of someone's else's calf — even if he's not our own. No, it is not our job to educate other mothers' children, to take on the helm. If we are truly concerned about their well-being, we will do what we do best: pray, empathize, and truly feel. By sharing the pain of our fellow Jews, by minimizing our gossip over someone else's heartache, we will merit true *achdus*.

The Uncharacteristic Display of Emotion

If we look closely at the words of Torah, we realize that they often don't convey emotion. For instance, we read in *Parashas*

Beshalach that *vayeilchu sheloshes yamim bamidbar v'lo matzu mayim* — "the Jews traveled for three days in the desert, and they didn't find water" (*Shemos* 15:22). Can you imagine what that means? Walking in the scorching desert for days, feeling the burning thirst, believing that there is no water available. What fear, what despair, could they have been feeling? Yet the Torah doesn't tell us how the nation felt.

Another example: *Vayashlichu oso haborah* — "And [the brothers] threw him [Yosef] into the pit" (*Bereishis* 37:24). How did Yosef feel when he was thrown into the deep, dark cavern? Only when his brothers confessed to him twenty-two years later do we finally get the answer: *Aval asheimim anachnu al achinu asher ra'inu tzaras nafsho b'hischaneno eileinu* — "We confess to our wrongdoing when we saw our brother's pain as he begged to us" (ibid. 42:21), the *shevatim* finally admitted. We didn't hear anything about Yosef's cries in the Torah portion that discusses his traumatic descent into the pit.

The Torah, we see from such examples, doesn't always communicate the emotional facet of the episodes it conveys.

It is interesting to observe the sheer display of emotion we find in *Parashas Chukas*. First Aharon HaKohen was *niftar*. "When the entire assembly saw that Aharon had perished, they wept for Aharon thirty days" (*Bamidbar* 20:29). What a tragedy to lose the peace-loving, pious leader!

And then, *Vayisu meiHor HaHar* — "They journeyed from Mount Hor" (ibid. 21:4). They wanted desperately to enter Eretz Yisrael, but when they arrived on one side of the border, the Edomim said to them, "No, no, go around this way and enter from there."

How did the nation feel when they heard this? In an exceptionally uncharacteristic portrayal, the verse states, *Vatiktzar nefesh ha'am badarech* — "The spirit of the people grew short on the way" (ibid.). In reading the Torah, we've already found that the Jews were hungry or thirsty or even that they screamed, but an explicit description of their emotions is a rarity. On these words, Rashi offers a most profound portrayal of how the Jews felt, one that makes me cry when I read it.

From the strain of the journey, says Rashi, their spirits diminished, and everything that is hard on a person leads to a depletion of the spirit. Listen to his next words, dear sisters: "It's like a person whom a stress befalls and he doesn't have the capacity to handle it; there's no place in his heart for that pain to reside there." What words! No place in the heart. How often do we feel like that, dear women? How often do our fellow suffering women feel the way Rashi so aptly describes the tired nation?

Just Believe!

What happens when a Jew feels the way our brethren felt in the desert?

On the opening words of the *Chukas* portion, *Zos chukas haTorah* — "This is the decree of the Torah" (*Bamidbar* 19:2), Rashi comments, *Chukah gezeirah hi milfanai ein lecha reshus l'haraher achareha* — "It is a statute, I have decreed a decree, and you aren't permitted to second-guess it" (*Rashi*, ibid. 19:2). What does second-guessing mean?

At that point in the Torah, *Klal Yisrael* reached a breaking point. After the passing of Aharon HaKohen, they cried, "What will happen now? Who will comfort us? We're all on our own!" At his moment of death, they saw Hor HaHar, Mount Hor, whose name alludes to the word *hirhur*, doubtful thoughts. Upon the demise of Aharon, the nation entertained the kind of thoughts that we sometimes have when we lose a loved one, when we're stricken with a challenge, when we don't know where to turn. At those times, we're at the greatest risk of falling prey to *hirhur*. It is then that we're prone to think, *What will happen now? All of my efforts were for naught. Life is terrible!*

Parashas Chukas discusses one of the most mysterious mitzvos: the *parah adumah*, whose ashes purified those who've been defiled by contact with death. Rav Shamshon Refael Hirsch notes that the red cow was meant to cleanse the person of the great impurity associated with death, that of the *hirhurim*.

Says Hashem to His dear nation, "Remember, there is no bad that isn't followed by good, and there is no defilement that isn't followed by purity." Although we may not see this at times, this is a fact. And it's crucial for us to remember this reality and to ingrain it in our dear children. The commandments are not meant to make our lives miserable. They aren't a code of laws that we are forced to keep as we gag and retch. They are all good. *That's* the message of *Parashas Chukas*. Every challenge that makes us feel weary is good in its essence.

Rav Elyah Lopian used to say that when a mother tells her daughter, "Listen, my child, I know the heat is suffocating today and it's tough to dress modestly, but that's what Hashem wants from us so we'll suffer through this together," she has it all wrong. This is certainly not a manifestation of her faith!

So what is? Shlomo HaMelech writes in *Koheles* that all *gashmiyus*, materialism, is *hevel*, futile. He confesses that he tried everything and found it to be worthless. *Sof davar hakol nishma es haElokim y'ra v'es mitzvosav shemor ki zeh kal ha'adam*, he concludes in the penultimate verse of *Koheles* (12:13). "In the end of the matter, after everything has been heard, fear Hashem and keep His mitzvos, for that is the entire man."

Rav Elyah asks, what would have happened if Shlomo HaMelech would have found materialism to be of value? Would he still arrive at the same conclusion regarding the mitzvos? He obviously means something deeper: As soon as a person chooses to accept the mitzvos and the will of Hashem, it *will* be best for him. Once a person reaches that state of happy acceptance of the mitzvos, everything else will automatically prove futile to him. As long as a person feels shackled to the mitzvos, he feels that he's losing out, his *Yiddishkeit* won't be real. The only real faith is when a Jew comes to the belief that Hashem's will is always good for him.

Let's Practice the Drums: Miriam's Legacy

So why don't we truly believe and express that everything will be good? One reason is that we're afraid that if we predict that something will work out but then it doesn't, we could cause a *chillul Hashem*. We see this in the case of Moshe, when he sinned at Mei Merivah. What were his thoughts during those fateful moments? The nation was thirsty and came crying to him for water. Moshe spoke to the rock, but when water did not begin to gush forth, he became concerned; *What will happen if water doesn't end up pouring out of this rock? What will they say about Hashem and His powers?* Because he was so anxious about making a *chillul Hashem*, he hit the rock instead of speaking to it. However, the episode teaches us that a Jew must not be concerned about Hashem's reputation in a way that prevents him from saying and doing the right thing. We should all truly believe and express *Hashem ya'azor* as our manifestation of our belief in His power.

From *Parashas Chukas* we learn a most fundamental principle. If we say something good, believe in good, and pray for good, even if the good doesn't come to be, we'll be better off than someone who says, "It'll be terrible. Life is tough!"

Let's look at the story of Miriam, the prophetess whose passing is discussed in this Torah portion. She was the one who had asked her father to return to her mother because she had a *nevuah* that they'd have a son who would save the nation (see *Sotah* 12a). Didn't her thoughts sound completely illogical in an exile-ridden era? Later, when Amram remarried Yocheved and Moshe was born, the family was once again in distress as they took their precious baby to the Nile. This time, too, Miriam said, "Father, just wait. I know it will turn out good." She was right.

Later, she gathered all the women in the nation and said to

them, "We're rehearsing with our drums in preparation for the redemption." The women, exhausted and depleted from the shackles of Mitzrayim, looked at her with pity. But once again, she was right.

The Gemara (*Shabbos* 35a) tells us that Miriam's well can be seen until today as a bubbling sieve from Mount Carmel. How interesting is that? Can a sieve hold water at all? No. But that's only true when the sieve is on the *chol*, sand. If that same sieve is in water, the more holes it has, the more water it holds. Hashem says to us, his dear children, "When your attitude is *chol*, mundane, your faith can hold no water. But if you're in a sea of faith, and your entire life you're thinking and talking positive, even if your sieve is full of holes, the water will remain with you."

Dear Jewish woman, is there something better that you could ask for? How beautiful it would be if we could stay with our steadfast faith, always. All it takes is belief. Just believe. That's the power of our prophetess Miriam. She had the power to interpret every situation to see only the best. The milk spilled? It won't ruin the tiles forever. The machine broke? I could get a new one. This son is making trouble? His exceptional potential will bring him to the greatest heights one day.

Miriam is personified by the words *Rachash libi davar tov* — "My heart overflows with a goodly matter" (*Tehillim* 45:2). Even in the face of tragedy, even in the face of death, keep the faith! This is what we must remember: that every impurity is followed by cleansing, that everything HaKadosh Baruch Hu does is *tov, tov, tov*. And if we truly believe it, may we merit seeing it.

Off to a Good Start

In the devastating aftermath of the kidnapping that took place during the summer of 2014 in Eretz Yisrael, I went to speak with the three grief-stricken mothers. When I asked Rachel Frankel, mother of Naftali, what I could say to the women, whose hearts and ears were open, she said to me, "Tell them that now I understand that the simple role of a mother is to wait for her child."

All our lives, we mothers wait: first, for the child to be born; then, for him to develop, to learn to read and write, to foster friendships, to grow, grow, grow. When the time is ripe, we wait once again: for him to find his *shidduch*, for her to be expecting, for the child to be born. It's a waiting game that mothers play, from the start until the end.

As Rachel and the other mothers waited on edge, I sat and cried with them. We cried and cried until there were no more tears left. And that's the role of the mother: to wait for her children.

Even if your child is kidnapped by the *yetzer hara*, by negative influences, by a lack of *emunah*, you sit and wait. And when he comes back, what type of reception will he receive? Will he hear, "Why are you so dirty? Why do you look the way you do?" Or will you simply hug him, the way Rachel and the others yearned for that embrace?

All Rachel dreamed about during those terrifying days was to hug her son, to tell him, "The main thing is that you came back." The last thing on her mind was the dirt on her son's feet, the disheveled hair. And when we return to Hashem, He does just the same: He simply hugs us, no questions asked. "Just come home," He begs. "Just return to Me." Although He may not approve of our every action, He accepts us nevertheless.

The *berachah* that we are bestowed with in *Parashas Balak* is *Mah tovu ohalecha Yaakov* — "How good are your tents, Yaakov!" (*Bamidbar* 24:5). When a child returns to his mother's tent, he must feel welcome, loved. "You're good as you are" is what he needs to hear. The outside world is engulfed in a tempestuous storm that rages with the *ayin hara* of Bil'am, with an ungenerous eye, but in the cocoon of his home, a child must feel secure. And even when he leaves the nest, his ears should always ring with the sweet sound of his mother's whisper: *Mah tovu* — how good you are, my child.

I remember that during that difficult saga in Eretz Yisrael, everyone was amazed at the *achdus* of *Am Yisrael*. Even the secular politicians tried to preserve the peace in the aftermath. HaKadosh Baruch Hu was pleading with us, "Please, My children, remember this *shalom* even when everything goes as you wish."

When we bless a *kallah*, we say to her, *Bo'i b'shalom ateres ba'alah gam b'simchah u'vetzahalah* — *Kallah*, dear, remember the peace and love you're experiencing now, in times of *simchah* and joy. Even when there's *parnassah*, when there's health, keep the peace. Why wait for a tragedy to strike, G-d forbid? Remember this *shalom* and don't lose it.

The Secret to a Happy Home: Good Morning!

From the *berachos* of Bil'am we learn a wonderful secret for a happy home, which is especially relevant during vacation season. When Bil'am said, *Hen am k'lavi yakum* — "They're a nation who arise like a lion cub" (*Bamidbar* 23:24) — he intended to curse us that we should wake up late. Bil'am understood the secret: a happy home is where the parents and children rise early.

Who saved us from the curses of Bil'am? The one who awoke even earlier than he did: Avraham Avinu, of whom it says, *Vayashkeim Avraham baboker* — "Avraham rose early in the morning" (*Bereishis* 19:27). Bil'am, too, awoke early on the day he set out to curse the nation, but Hashem said to him, "*Rasha*, someone who awoke even earlier than you will save them."

The Pele Yo'etz writes that waking up late ruins the entire day. The later you awake, he explains, the more lethargic you will be. Let's understand why this is so.

The Gemara tells us, *V'Keil zo'eim b'chal yom* — every day, Hashem is angry at His world for a fraction of a second (*Berachos* 7a). Bil'am knew when that very second was, and that's when he planned to curse the nation. This short bout of anger, says the Gemara, happens sometime during the first three hours after dawn. When we awake early, before this moment of wrath, and we say, "*Modeh Ani*," the positive act has the power to prevent negative *kochos*.

If a Jewish woman wants her home to be a happy place, she must not only wake up early, but also start off her day with love. Rabbeinu Yonah advises us "to tear out the hatred from your heart every morning." Explains Rav Chatzkel Levenstein, from Rabbeinu Yonah's words we understand that within you lies an inherent hatred toward the new day and toward everything around you. In other words, it's only natural and human for you to wake up in the morning and see the gray clouds in the sky. However, it is also within your capacity to abolish this hatred, to quash those negative voices that beg you to stay under the covers and reject the new day. You, Jewish women, have the ability to arise with a jump, to recite the words of "*Modeh Ani*" with an appreciation and excitement for the day ahead.

How can you accomplish this feat? Here's where love comes into play. *Ahavah mekalkeles es hashurah*, our Sages tell us (*Midrash Rabbah, Bereishis* 55:8). When you wake up and expect everything to go your way, according to the *shurah*, the line you drew for yourself, you won't love anyone or anything, because the reality will always surprise you. Expectations will always lead to disappointment. Even Bil'am's donkey was smart enough to understand this. It exhibited a surprising change in nature when it recognized that something unusual was occurring: it opened its mouth and started to talk! Love is all about being flexible. Step out of the straight lines and you will learn to love the new day and everything within it.

From when we're in the first grade, we're taught to write only inside the line. An exception to this rule is the letter *lamed*, which represents *limud*, learning. The Ben Ish Chai explains a beautiful reason for this: the *lamed* is composed of three lines: the top line represents the capacity to cope with those who are above you, such as your parents and teachers; the horizontal line symbolizes those who live beside you, such as a spouse, sibling, or business partner; and the bottom line refers to those who are under your care, your children and students. For all of these relationships, going out of the line is necessary in order to cultivate a loving relationship. A part of the learning process in life is to know when to write outside the line, when to exhibit flexibility on behalf of a greater purpose.

Do you sometimes wonder how a person can be so overwhelmingly dedicated to an incapacitated or unwell child or spouse? How does she do it? Does she not have her own needs? you may wonder. But the fact is that when we love, there is no line. *Ahavah mekalkeles es hashurah* — the love simply erases the line. There's no such thing as "But what you're doing is not normal!" because when there's love, there is no normal.

In the story of Kamtza and Bar Kamtza (*Gittin* 55b–56a), no one was willing to be flexible. Your servant didn't invite the right person to your party, so what? You weren't invited to the big bash, so what? Step out of the line! That's the true love we need to exhibit if we want to foster true relationships.

If your child went out of the line, if he or she was, *Rachmana litzlan*, kidnapped by the *yetzer hara*, step out of the line as well. If you don't especially appreciate a certain characteristic in your husband, or a specific gesture irks you to no end, cultivate the love. Because when you truly love, you will have no problem looking away. You will have no problem accepting him as he is. True love, true *shalom bayis*, is when you love the whole of the person; you may be aware of his faults, but because you love, you're flexible with your expectations.

The Time Will Come

But what if it's just too hard for you to truly love? It's so painful for you to see the child who was once the apple of your eye disappoint you time and again. When life gets too difficult, the heaviness weighs you down to the extent that you can't find it in your heart to love. How can you bear the pain and learn to love again? Give it time, dear sisters. Give it time.

As members of the Jewish nation, dear women, we have a unique capacity for patience: a characteristic Bil'am sought in vain to eradicate. When he attempted to curse *Am Yisrael*, his jargon included words like *ka'eis* — "right now" — *kvar*, and *harega*. He was not one for patience. Just do what I want right now! *Ka'eis yei'ameir l'Yaakov u'leYisrael mah pa'al Keil* — "Even now it is said to Yaakov and Yisrael, 'What has G-d wrought?'" he declared (*Bamidbar* 23:23). What was his intention? He wanted to turn us into an impulsive people, people who want immediate answers, immediate clarity. He wanted us to lose our patience for waiting. Bil'am was no fool. He understood that without this ability to wait it out, we would fall apart.

Bil'am's special ability was that he knew the moment Hashem gets angry and wanted to curse at that moment so that the curse would be effective (*Berachos* 7a). *Tosafos* asks, What could Bil'am have said in that tiny span of time? And *Tosafos* answers, he could have said the word *kaleim*, "destroy them," G-d forbid (*Berachos* 7). Explains the Chasam Sofer that *kaleim* is an acronym for *kaveid, lev, mo'ach* — liver, heart, and brain. What did Bil'am want? His dream was for us Jews to begin talking from the liver, the kishkes, to turn into an impulsive nation. Only after we would utter the impulsive comment would we start to feel in our hearts that what we said was unkind or improper and then think in our minds, "I'm not normal. I can't believe I actually said that." He wanted to "bless" us with the harmful trait of impulsivity.

Rabbeinu Bachya (*Bamidbar* 23:21) writes that instead of saying the word *kaleim*, Hashem scrambled the letters of the word to form the word *melech*: *Lo hibit aven b'Yaakov v'lo ra'ah amal b'Yisrael Hashem Elokav imo u'seruas melech bo* —"He perceived no iniquity in Yaakov and saw no perversity in Yisrael; Hashem, his G-d, is with him, and the friendship of the *King* is in him" (*Bamidbar* 23:21). Oh, how Bil'am wanted to turn us into an impulsive people, that we should join the nations who fall in and out of love, who act immediately upon their impulses and emotions. Instead, he blessed us to become a kingly nation, a nation that has patience, a nation who thinks things through rationally, who makes decisions from a place of clarity.

It's not always easy to stop and think. When you're hurt, when you're in pain, you just want to scream, you want to tear the aggressor apart. But you're a *bas melech*, dear sister. You have the true capacity for self-control. Your child, your husband, your friend may test you time and again. It may be so difficult to continue loving, to remain accepting, when you're being tried. But this is your chance, *bas melech*, to exhibit royalty, to show what you can do. How does a queen conduct herself? She may have the perfect retort at the tip of her tongue, but she thinks, she waits, she contemplates her actions.

When you truly love someone, dear women, you will learn to wait. You will learn to have patience, to let things develop as Hashem sees fit. And as you wait from your regal place, remember that the King is waiting to hear from you. Turn to Him with your sorrows, with your pain, and He will help you love again. He will help you see the *mah tovu* in every day, in every moment of your life.

The Daughters of Tzelafchad: Their Legacy

We all struggle to have *emunah*, especially the *emunah sheleimah* that the Rambam discusses in his Thirteen Principles. It's not easy to wait and wait without knowing what will happen, but still the faithful Jew knows that *v'af al pi sheyismamei'a* — although Mashiach's arrival is delayed — we are meant to wait patiently. And so much of life is about waiting, dear women, whether it is for a child, for *nachas* — or for one's soul mate.

Shidduch Prospects

In *Parashas Pinchas*, we women find great role models of *emunah*: the daughters of Tzelafchad — Machlah, No'ah, Chaglah, Milkah, and Tirtzah — were five strong women who wouldn't do well, to say the least, had they been set up for a *shidduch* interview today.

Let's imagine the scene: These five older singles sit before the matchmaker. "So let's start with the basics," she says. "How old are you?"

The youngest, her hair already turning gray, says, "I'm forty."

The oldest answers, "I'm sixty."

Not off to a great start.

When the *shadchan* then inquires about their *yichus*, all they can muster is "Our father died in the desert. He was the first *mechallel Shabbos*" (*Shabbos* 96b).

To add salt to the wound, because all five of his offspring were female and unmarried, Tzelafchad's daughters had no plot in Eretz Yisrael. Plus, they had a reputation for being very meticulous regarding every mitzvah and *chumrah* (*Bava Basra* 119b), something that was not most appreciated by the menfolk in those times. If we look at their circumstances, what chance did they have to ever find their *zivugim*?

Still, the daughters of Tzelafchad did not compromise. They waited patiently, with the utmost *emunah*, for husbands who would share the same unwavering appreciation for the Torah that they had maintained throughout all of their single years, and they truly believed that they would merit building holy homes one day.

The attitude of the *bnos Tzelafchad* was one of "Yes, we can!" Although their circumstances seemed dire, they were filled with positivity, says the Midrash, and their belief was what kept them going. Because they always said, *Tov Hashem lakol* — "Hashem is good to all" — they merited bearing children until the age of 130 (*Yalkut Shimoni, Pinchas* 773).

Another virtue that the Midrash mentions about these women is *Vatikravnah* — "They drew near" (*Bamidbar* 27:1). This not only means that they approached Moshe to discuss the acquisition of a plot in Eretz Yisrael, but that they also "kept close to one another." Many times, older singles run away from one another, and understandably so. Their unmarried peers remind them of their loneliness. But the daughters of Tzelafchad were in the challenge together; they infused one another with encouragement and spirit.

The daughters of Tzelafchad, says the Midrash, were heroic in other ways as well. They would often examine their actions and discuss how they could improve together. In doing so, they came to the conclusion that they were lacking in respect for their father because they didn't do enough to clear his name. Tzelafchad was a pious man whose righteous intention in desecrating Shabbos was to show the rest of the nation how severe the punishment would be. Although he received that punishment, he didn't deserve to be vilified for his actions, because his motives were pure. Thus, his daughters embarked on a mission to polish his reputation.

It's sometimes hard for a single woman who is already an adult and who lives with her parents to show them the honor and respect the Torah demands. But I have witnessed time and again that when single women take *kibbud horim* upon themselves, like the daughters of Tzelafchad, this virtuous step opens their *mazel* in finding their *zivug*.

In addition to being learned in Torah, as the question they posed to Moshe with regard to the acquisition of their plot attests, the daughters of Tzelafchad also had the keen sense to know *when* to approach Moshe. They understood when the time was right. The Ben Ish Chai says that the months of Tammuz and Av are the opportune time to ask for a home, because then is the time when Hashem mourns His House. At the time of year when Hashem mourns the destruction of His own home, He understands the depth of a single woman's pain.

Often, women who wait like the daughters of Tzelafchad say to me, "There's a *tefillah* for every type of *nisayon*, but there's no *tefillah* for someone like me. What should I say?" And I say to them, "Your *tefillah* is *U'venei Yerushalayim* — 'May Jerusalem be rebuilt.' Your *tefillah* is '*V'liYerushalayim ircha b'rachamim tashuv* — 'To Jerusalem, Your city, may You return.' When you daven with such pain, when you share HaKadosh Baruch Hu's anguish, He will want to help you build your home."

Cover Up to Discover

The last virtue that the Midrash lists of the daughters of Tzelafchad was their unwavering *yiras Shamayim* even in times when they could have let go. When they held on tightly to the Torah principles and their *tznius*, they didn't feel that they were losing out. Unfazed by those who suggested that perhaps "taking it a bit easy" would bring their *yeshuos*, the *bnos Tzelafchad* carried on.

At the time of the infamous kidnapping of the three boys in 2014, I learned a powerful lesson. Hashem punished us in an area in which this generation is most lax. We live in a time of information hunger. We must know everything there is to know, about everyone, *all* the time. Suddenly, with the story of the boys, we had no clue. Zilch. The entire IDF was on an intense search for eighteen days, during which they didn't stumble upon even a trace: not a sock, not a pair of glasses, and to everyone's surprise, no organization took responsibility for this horrific act either. We experienced the curse of *V'anochi hasteir astir es panai bayom hahu* — "I will conceal My face on that day" (*Devarim* 31:18). Hashem hid His face from us to the highest degree.

The Maharal from Prague says that when Hashem hides so well, like He's doing in our times, only the hidden ones of the generation, the *tzanua* women, can save us. Citing Queen Esther as an example, the Maharal discusses how bleak the situation was for the Jews in the times before the miracle of Purim. The letters decreeing their destruction were already signed! And then came along Esther, the modest, hidden one, and she saved them all.

In the haftarah of *Parashas Balak*, we read, *U'mah Hashem doreish mimcha ki im asos mishpat v'ahavas chesed v'hatznei'a leches im Elokecha* — "What does Hashem request of you? To perform acts of justice, to love *chesed*, and to walk modestly with your G-d" (*Michah* 6:8). Our Sages surprise us by expounding on *v'hatznei'a leches*, being modest, by explaining that these words refer to the mitzvos of *halvayas hameis*, escorting the dead, and *hachnasas kallah l'chuppah*, bringing a bride to her *chuppah* (*Succah* 49b). Aren't these public events? What is their connection to the mitzvah of *tznius*, which obligates us to be modest and out of the limelight?

Explains Rav Shlomo Wolbe, *zt"l*, in his *mussar sefer Alei Shur*, that it is at such public events where the real test of *tznius* lies. Can you, at public occasions, when you want to look your best, remain *tznius*? When your daughter or sister is getting married, and you want to look especially beautiful, what are your priorities?

I was faced with this *nisayon* before the wedding of my eldest daughter. I had just bought a most exquisite long, ankle-length dress for myself when I was speaking with the *chassan's* mother. She asked me, "Yemima, are you going to be wearing a long dress at the wedding?" When I replied that I would, she said that she had bought a short one for herself, and I sensed that she wouldn't feel comfortable if I would look more elaborate than she.

It was hard for me, very hard, but I went out and bought myself a shorter and less elegant dress. The long one is still hanging in my closet, and anyone who wants to wear it for her special *simchah* is welcome to borrow it. I know this is an immodest story because I'm bragging about my *tznius* and my wonderful *middos*, but I felt on my own skin how hard the *nisayon* could be. This is the challenge the daughters of Tzelafchad did not fall prey to. They fiercely held on to their principles despite the pressure they received to "chill" because they understood what was truly important.

The more we cover up, the more Hashem will help us

discover. In a time when the *hester panim* is so great, what more can we ask for?

A Deeper Look

What was the secret that kept the daughters of Tzelafchad going all those years? For decades, they were single and alone, orphaned and without a property to call their own. How did they do it? We find an illuminating answer in a stunning *Ohr HaChaim* in *Parashas Pinchas*, when the *yahrtzeit* of the Ohr HaChaim usually takes place. This beautiful explanation cures the soul and fills us with *emunah*.

In *Parashas Pinchas*, Hashem instructed Moshe Rabbeinu to ascend Mount Avarim, *u're'eih es ha'aretz...v'ra'isah osah* — "and see the Land...and you shall see it" (*Bamidbar* 27:12–13). Commenting on this verse, the Ohr HaChaim asks why Hashem used a double expression of sight. He answers that the first glance a person takes is natural. It's a physical view. The second look is with spiritual eyes; it's a view that's taken with a special light that he calls *ohr hachaim* — "the light of life." At that point in time, Moshe Rabbeinu was deeply saddened by the reality that he would not merit entering Eretz Yisrael. The second passage promised him that he would attain a deeper vision, one that would enable him to grasp the Land's inner, spiritual essence even without stepping foot there.

Hashem's message to Moshe Rabbeinu is profoundly pertinent to our daily struggles, dear women. If you succeed in envisioning your salvation with spiritual eyes, if you look beyond the superficial world you see before you, you will get there. When women cry to me that they're desperate for a *yeshuah*, I say to them, "The dream is still yours. The moment you stop wishing, it's not yours anymore."

What did the daughters of Tzelafchad have going for them? To our physical eyes, they had nothing, but our Sages teach us that they were dreamers. These pious women held on fiercely to their dreams, to their vision of a better tomorrow. They never gave up hope.

Dare to dream, dear women. Unleash your imagination and allow yourself to enter the territory you never believed you could conquer. This is a trait that's been transmitted from woman to woman since the Jewish nation's existence. Why is the Jewish woman called an *Ivriyah*? While the Egyptian women got absorbed in the pain of their *metzarim*, contractions, the Jewish woman saw an *ibur*, a fetus. They already saw a child. This is the power inherent in every one of us.

It's called dreaming, this ability to use your spiritual eyes to envision a brighter future. Follow the example of the daughters of Tzelafchad, and start dreaming today.

The Secret to Winning the Battle: Harmony

$\mathcal{I}$n *Parashas Mattos*, we read about the Jewish soldiers who went to war with Midian in order to take vengeance against the Midianites, who were responsible for the Jewish sins of immorality and idolatry that resulted in the deaths of 24,000 Jews. Moshe commanded that each tribe, except for Levi, send one thousand men, amassing a legion of twelve thousand soldiers. (Efraim and Menasheh were considered two tribes.) Incredibly, not one man was lost in the battle (*Bamidbar* 31:49).

When Moshe conveyed the commandment to the Jews regarding the reason for war, he did not relate the message that Hashem had given him: this war would serve as a vengeance for the harm that was done to the nation. Instead, he spoke only of avenging the slight to Hashem's honor that resulted from their actions. The Midrash explains Moshe's reasoning. "Had we been idolaters," he presumed, "they would not hate us or persecute us. Therefore, the vengeance is for Hashem" (*Midrash Rabbah, Bamidbar* 22:2).

Rashi's comment on this explanation offers profound insight on the value of our nation: one who wrongs *Am Yisrael*, he notes, is regarded as if he had wronged Hashem. This is the level of holiness of every Jew!

Putting the Pieces Together

Before the nation went out to war, trumpets were sounded (*Bamidbar* 10:9). What was the purpose of this ritual?

Rav Tzadok of Lublin (*Pri Tzaddik, Mattos* 7) offers an illuminating explanation. At a time of war, he writes, the most important factor toward success is unity. Through the trumpets, this was achieved. The trumpets were sounded whenever Moshe needed to gather the people together. It was a signal for the nation to come together, to unite.

The war against the Midianim, notes the Pri Tzaddik, was a battle against the *medanim*, against strife, against those who judged others: the fighters among the nation. What better way to prepare for such a battle than to bring the people together as one? The sounds of the trumpets, a sound that symbolized unity, reverberated in the heart of every soldier as he headed out to the battlefield: the awareness that only together, as one nation, would they triumph against the Midianim.

This is the way to win the war, dear sisters. The Vilna Gaon says that when Moshe Rabbeinu descended from the mountain with the *luchos* in his hands, he saw that *Am Yisrael* was split apart regarding the golden calf. He knew that they would not be able to build the Mikdash in this splintered state. Like a teacher who tears a paper into several pieces, he took the *luchos* and broke them apart. His message to them was "I'm giving you all the pieces of the puzzle. Go and find the missing ones."

On the 17th of Tammuz, the day he broke the *luchos*, Moshe Rabbeinu taught us the importance of love. Go find your brothers and sisters, he instructed, in order to acquire true Torah.

Only when we bring all the pieces together will the Torah be complete.

For thousands of years, Hashem is begging us, "Stand together, My precious children!" Still, we're fighting. When will we hug each other with our wings like the *keruvim* in the Mikdash? When will we assemble the beautiful puzzle and bring it whole to Hashem?

Personally, I totally detest doing puzzles. I can't even do the oversized, twelve-piece ones. My children do those 1,000-piece Ravensburger beauties, and I sit there in awe. It's quite easy when they're assembling the horse or the cabin, but when they get to the sky, the hard part starts. All you have is blue. I try with all my might to push one blue puzzle piece into the other, but the pieces won't fit.

The Maharal offers a stunning explanation for our constant quarrels, one that will fill you with hope and excitement that the *geulah* is drawing near. During the Three Weeks, he says, we should say to Hashem, "I tried. I tried not to think negatively of others. I tried to refrain from *lashon hara*. But each and every one of your sons is a piece of sky. They are all so holy, such exalted *neshamos*. It's so hard to make a puzzle of the sky!"

The Maharal teaches us that because every single Jew is so holy, sparks tend to fly when we're together.

Why is *machlokes* a Jewish disease? Our nation boasts the highest percentage of lawyers in the world! There should be only peace among us. However, each and every one of us has a *tzelem Elokim*; each of us was created in the Divine image of Hashem, even the ones who petition for the rights of the Palestinians or bash our beautiful Torah. Listen, Hashem, You're asking us to assemble a Ravensburger with seven million pieces! If it would only be a cabin, okay. A horse, we could do that. But the sky? Can You please do it for us? It's so hard to merge holiness with holiness. We need Your help!

But first, before we can fit the pieces together, we must see that holiness. What are you doing to bring the salvation near?

Do you try to see the holiness in your friend, in your neighbor, in your mother-in-law? That's the way to bring the nation together in preparation for the *geulah*. That is the sound of the trumpet that can only happen when we all come together to create a beautiful melody.

Ish Ki Yidor Neder: Your New Torah

The Torah portion of *Mattos* is always read during the period between the breeching of Jerusalem's walls on the 17th of Tammuz and the tragic destruction of the Beis HaMikdash, which took place on the 9th of Av.

This time is known as *bein hametzarim*. The 17th of Tammuz is considered one "*metzer*," boundary, and the 9th of Av another. The days in the middle are *bein hametzarim*, caught between a rock and a hard place. During this period, Hashem gives every Jew a precious gift: the opportunity for concern. This is the time to worry, to ask, "What will be?"

The *Shulchan Aruch* (*Orach Chaim* 1:3) instructs that one must be *meitzar v'do'eig* about the destruction of the Temple. *Meitzar*, our Sages explain, is to lament over what happened, to feel the pain of the loss, whereas *do'eig* is a magnificent word in Lashon HaKodesh that has two implications: to worry, but also to take care of, to do something about the pain.

This is the lesson we learn from *Parashas Mattos*. In this *parashah*, HaKadosh Baruch Hu gives every Jew the right to do something that could not be done beforehand: to create a new halachic status, to sway the reality one way or another in a time of *da'agah*, worry. *Ish ki yidor neder laShem...* — "If a man takes a vow to Hashem..." (*Bamidbar* 30:3). Through the means of a vow that a person takes upon himself in a time of stress, he is able to create a new reality.

On the one hand, when you're in a challenging situation, you want to remain positive, to tell yourself that this will come to an end. But does that mean that you should deny the difficult situation altogether? Of course not. This is the concept of *da'agah*: know that you're in a narrow strait, that you are in a tight place, but remember that you can do something about it.

When a person obligates himself with additional prohibitions or commandments, such as offering more sacrifices, through this vow he creates a new piece of Torah for himself in order to leave the place he's in. This is the concept of taking a vow. When you create a new piece of Torah for yourself, dear women, when you undertake to go that extra mile for Hashem, you are liberating yourself from your pain. At the same time that you acknowledge that the situation is difficult, you also choose to do *something*, something substantial, that will help you make sense of the trying time. By connecting to Hashem from your new *kabbalah*, you are creating a new reality.

The Sfas Emes (5650) teaches us something astounding on this topic. Listen, he says, this is the only way to win a war. You won't win if things aren't a bit tight for you, if you don't experience some distress. What does Moshe say to *Am Yisrael*? *Heichaltzu mei'itchem* — "Take a step out of yourselves" (*Bamidbar* 31:3). Leave your comfort zone, dear women, take a step back from your narrow view of the situation, and you will win the war. Yes, times will be tough. Yes, there will be days when you will walk on very narrow straits. Your *shalom bayis* won't always be perfect. There will be days when you will hit the pillow with a heavy heart. Every mother has a child who makes her feel that her very heart is constricted from the pain he's causing. But from this pain, allow a new piece of Torah to emerge. Take something on; connect to Hashem from your new place and you will win.

The Time for Tears

Must your new undertaking be something lofty? Does this mean that you must make it to the Kosel for forty consecutive days or change so completely that you become unrecognizable? Not at all! It only takes something small, something a little extra, to take you out of your tight place. But first, dear sisters, you must know how to cry.

After HaKadosh Baruch Hu destroyed the Temple, the Midrash tells us (introduction to *Eichah* 24), He said to Yirmiyahu, "I destroyed My city and you're not in pain?! Turn to Avraham, Yitzchak, and Yaakov, who know how to cry." What kind of knowledge did our forefathers have that Yirmiyahu was lacking? What kind of education do we need to be well versed in how to cry?

Yirmiyahu did not shed a tear because he made a logical calculation. As a prophet, he understood that the destruction he was observing was rightfully deserved. He was the one who warned the nation, who begged them to repent, but they didn't heed his words. To him, the destruction was a rational result of their conduct. And so, he did not cry.

It's easy to come to logical conclusions, but that is not what Hashem prefers. Instead, instructs Hashem, look at our forefathers, who know how to cry. They were not part of a bureaucracy that makes intricate conclusions regarding every occurrence. No, they simply knew how to cry because they were fathers. Emerge from the logical state and allow yourself to cry. Now is the time for tears.

Dear women, let the tears flow from your heart and connect to Hashem from the depths of your pain. Go that extra step for His sake. Say that kind word to the child who brings such heartache. Smile to the one who's causing anguish. Extend yourself in that tiny way that will show Hashem how much you care about His precious children. When you do for Hashem, dear women, you never lose. Even during those difficult moments, the closeness you will experience will expand that suffocating tightness in your heart.

When you take upon yourself that additional vow, a new, beautiful reality will unfold; a reality that no one can take away from you because it is your very own Torah.

Is There a Way Out?

I f there is one thought that will keep you going no matter what you're encountering in your life, dear women, let it be the holy words of the Aish Kodesh that I am about to share with you. What a balm for the soul and spirit!

Parashas Masei opens with an intriguing verse: *Eileh masei vnei Yisrael asher yatzu mei'eretz Mitzrayim...vayichtov Moshe es motza'eihem l'maseihem al pi Hashem v'eileh maseihem l'motza'eihem* — "These are the journeys of the Children of Israel, who went forth from the land of Egypt...and Moshe wrote their goings forth according to their journeys at the bidding of Hashem, and these were their journeys according to their goings forth" (*Bamidbar* 33:1–2).

The word *motza'eihem* refers to their starting points, and the *maseihem* refers to their destinations. Moshe kept a "diary" of the departure points along the way. But essentially, the route was the other way around; it was one chain of journeys bringing them toward their destination. Why did Moshe write about their journeys in such a way, focusing on their departures?

The Aish Kodesh offers a most comforting answer. The verse, he notes, should have read *maseihem l'motza'eihem* — that

Moshe Rabbeinu wrote of their journeys, focusing on their destinations. But Moshe Rabbeinu wanted to provide us solace. He wrote how the nation left the frightening journeys, how they departed from the forty-two journeys that they endured, and reached their next destination. By this Moshe wanted to impart a valuable lesson to us: there is no journey without a *motza*, an exit, if we traverse it *al pi Hashem* — according to Hashem's bidding. And, continues the Aish Kodesh, Moshe Rabbeinu wrote *Parashas Masei* at the conclusion of the travels, after the Jews had endured the struggles of the journey and they had all observed how they finally found the way out, because when a person is still in the midst of the journey, he thinks he will stay in the pain forever.

How powerful are these words of the Aish Kodesh! How true! When you're in a dark cave, all you see is darkness. You can't imagine that there is light somewhere, even just a few feet away. During the three weeks of mourning, when we lament the destruction of the Temple and the ramifications we suffer until this day, this is especially true. But always during this trying time, Moshe's words of comfort convey a profound message to us. Listen, he reminds us, you are on a journey right now and there will be an end. You will emerge from this, dear.

Know Where You're Coming From

Parashas Masei is generally read on the same Shabbos as *Parashas Mattos*, so I end up focusing more on the latter. When *Parashas Masei* is read on its own, I find it hard to teach the Torah portion that is one chain of *Vayisu...vayachanu, vayisu... vayachanu, vayisu...vayachanu* — "they traveled...and they rested, they traveled...and they rested, they traveled...and they rested.

Furthermore, tells us Rav Shteinman, in his stunning *sefer Ayeles HaShachar*, that Moshe Rabbeinu lived many years ago.

It is true that the journeys of the desert all had an ending, but all that occurred in the distant past! Perhaps his statement that to every travel there's a destination does not hold true today.

Rav Shteinman cites a passage from the *Zohar* that clarifies this confusion for us and makes *Parashas Masei* so incredibly powerful. The name Moshe is an acronym for *mah shehayah hu [sheyiheyeh]* — that which was will be. If Moshe felt it was right to record the forty-two seemingly redundant destinations — places that were downright dangerous and problematic for the nation — and he tells us that they emerged safely from them, this tells us that we, too, will emerge, with Hashem's help.

Furthermore, cautions Rav Shteinman, we are only able to cull lessons from the past, from that which we've already endured. It is impossible to know what the future will bring. If you've experienced a challenging time, it is incumbent upon you to take a message from what happened before, instructs the *gadol hador*.

What is the message we can take from our journey? When you're in the midst of your travels, dear women, ask yourselves, "Is this *al pi Hashem*?" Is this the way Hashem wants me to go? As long as you're on the right track, know that there will be an end. And the way to know whether you're there or not is to take heed of the following parable that the Chafetz Chaim teaches us.

Think of a person who is on a trail, when he suddenly encounters a fork in the road. Confused and lost, he doesn't know which path to take, until he sees a sign in the distance. One arrow on the sign points in the direction of the city he departed from, and the other to the city he wishes to reach. He has one problem, though: the sign is on the ground. How will he know which direction to follow?

The Chafetz Chaim tells us that if this traveler holds up the sign with one arrow facing his point of origin, the other arrow will guide him toward the trail he seeks. Do you know where you're headed? No. You're no angel, and that is not the point. Of genuine importance are your values, that you know where you're coming from. This is what will give you the *kochos* to traverse the winding roads that will come your way. If you set yourself up with a strong connection to the Torah and mitzvos, a commitment to what's truly right, your journey will eventually come to its happy end.

Our Children Need Their Heritage

Why was it important for Moshe Rabbeinu to list all of the forty-two travels in the Torah? Why do we need to know the precise details of *Am Yisrael*'s never-ending travails? We find our answer in the days of *bein hametzarim*, the period between the 17th of Tammuz and the 9th of Av: without having a past, we as a nation cannot have a future. If we don't know what we endured, if we don't know even the minute details, then we can't fully appreciate the depth of what the future holds for us.

Often, we want to spare our children the pain and fear engendered by discussing our angst-filled past with them. We think, *Why do I need to horrify them with the details of the Holocaust? Why do I need to overwhelm those little souls with the traumatic tales of the Churban?* But in *Parashas Masei*, Hashem teaches us that there are things you must tell your children. You cannot expect them to yearn for our future when they know nothing about our tumultuous past.

When I teach my secular students about the *Churban*, I often find that they are clueless about even the basic timeline. I once asked them, "How come you know nothing about this?" And they told me, in all honesty, that because there's no school during the summer, they had no other source from which to receive this vital education.

Sadly, this is the case in many religious communities. Perhaps the calendar is arranged especially so in order for parents to fulfill their obligation to tell their children. We parents must realize that the responsibility to transmit the details of *Am Yisrael*'s journeys is ours, and ours only.

I remember sitting on the floor of our living room as Abba captivated us with the tales of the *Churban*, not sparing any details. Even as a young child, I yearned for the *geulah* because I learned what we'd lost and how much we'd suffered. Only children who know of their past can properly yearn for the rebuilding of the Beis HaMikdash. Oh, how we need the *tefillos* of these innocent children!

The *Menoras HaMaor* (11) tells us that sometimes children can be a burden on their mothers. Especially during vacation season, not a moment goes by that they don't voice their requests. First they want to eat, then they want to drink, then they want us to take them places. And before we know it, they want to eat again. The *Menoras HaMaor* says that during this time, when the sweet, high-pitched voice of your child fills the room and he tugs relentlessly at your skirt, immediately use this opportunity for *tefillah*. In your mind, take advantage of this special moment to beg for anything you're yearning for. Why? Because the soft voice of a child is sweet in the ears of Hashem, and this is what He hears as you pray.

The *Menoras HaMaor* brings testimony to this suggestion from a verse in *Mishlei*: *V'lashon rakah tishbar garem* — "A soft tongue can break hard bones" (*Mishlei* 25:15). He says, don't read it like that. Instead, see the words as *Lashon rakah tashbar garem* — "The soft voice of our *tinokos shel beis rabban* [which is the acronym of *tashbar*], our young children, is *garem*: *gezeiros ra'os mevatlim* [which is the acronym of *garem*], to eradicate harsh decrees." What their sweet voices can do!

The more we talk to our children about the Beis HaMikdash, the more we educate them about what we've lost and endured, the more heartfelt their *tefillos* will be. Hashem is so moved by the prayer of these children; why should we prevent them from utilizing their power?

When the Beis HaMikdash was destroyed, the Kohanim went to *galus*, but the *Shechinah* did not accompany them. The same was true of the holy Sanhedrin: the *Shechinah* did not go with them. Only when the babies and young children were exiled did the *Shechinah* go with them into exile. As we read in *Megillas Eichah, Olaleha halchu shevi lifnei tzar vayeitzei mibas Tzion kol hadarah* — "When her babies went into exile, Tzion lost all her beauty [the *Shechinah*]" (*Eichah* 1:5-6, based on *Midrash Rabbah, Eichah* 1:32). The *Shechinah* knows that if she remains at the side of the innocent children during their harrowing journey, they will daven for her. In the same way that we, their mothers, can't turn down their requests no matter how outlandish they may be (hot chocolate with marshmallows at 4 a.m.), HaKadosh Baruch Hu fulfills every request of these sweet-tongued children.

There's a beautiful *kinah* we say on Tishah B'Av titled "*V'Es Navi Chatasi,*" with the refrain *Miyamim yamimah...* (based on *Gittin* 58a) that tells the story of the two children of Rav Yishmael Kohen Gadol. The girl was as beautiful as the moon, and her brother was as beautiful as the sun. When the Romans captured Yerushalayim, two soldiers each took one of these young children into captivity.

One day several years later, the two Roman masters of these children met. One said to the other, "You know, I have a servant who is as beautiful as the sun." Said the other, "You know, I have a maiden who is as beautiful as the moon." Together, they came up with a brilliant plan. They would marry off the two servants to each other, and the beautiful children the marriage would undoubtedly produce would engender greater income on the slavery market. Several nights later the Romans gathered to celebrate the arranged marriage of the two servants, and led the boy and girl into a secluded room and called it a night.

As soon as they were left alone, the boy, huddled in one corner, cried out, "I am the grandson of Aharon the Kohen Gadol. How can I marry a non-Jewish slave?" From the other corner, the girl cried out, "I am the granddaughter of Yocheved. How can I marry a non-Jewish slave?" In the morning, they recognized each other, and they immediately fell on each other's shoulders and cried until their souls departed. In the morning, the Romans opened the door to find their two lifeless bodies on the ground.

Why is this heart-wrenching *kinah* so beautiful? It teaches us a profound lesson in *chinuch*. These precious children were saved from sin because instead of focusing only on the future and present, they thought of their past. They didn't think, *We must move on. How else will we build future generations?* Instead, they thought of their lineage, where they were coming from, which prevented them from sinning.

Sadly, we see today that those parents who wanted to "move on," to provide for their children lives of too much comfort and to get away from our tumultuous past, lost the opportunity for a *nachas*-filled future. It is our duty, dear women, to ingrain in our children a deep appreciation of what our nation has gone through, to let them feel it in their bones so they will want to carry on the legacy.

We find this powerful parenting lesson in the first verse of *Parashas Masei. Eileh masei vnei Yisrael* — if you want your children to be *banim*, children, of *Am Yisrael*, tell them, *Eileh masei*, these are the travels. Don't spare them the pain. Don't try to raise them in a new world, disconnected from our rich heritage that is also rich in blood and *mesirus nefesh*, because it is these tales that will help them overcome obstacles in the future, and bring them to use their incredible power of *tefillah* to bring the *geulah*.

Sefer
Devarim

The Chumash of Rebuke

The entire *Chumash Devarim* is filled with words of rebuke to the nation. This is an entire *sefer* that our Sages viewed as a book of *mussar*, says the Pri Tzaddik. It's not easy to accept admonition. *Eileh hadevarim…* — "These are the words…" (*Devarim* 1:1), the *sefer* opens. *Davar* is something that is hard to digest, our Sages explain. One of the hardest things for a human being is to listen to, and then accept, rebuke. It's not pleasant for anyone to hear his faults being highlighted and to be made aware of his imperfections by another party. Do you like it when someone points out your issues, even in the kindest, gentlest way?

It's enlightening to note that Chapter 94 of *Tehillim*, which the Levites sang once each week (on Wednesdays) on the *duchan*, is composed entirely of rebuke: *Hayoseir goyim halo yochiach hamelameid adam da'as* — "He Who chastises nations, will He not rebuke? It is He Who teaches man knowledge" (*Tehillim* 94:10). *Da'as*, knowledge, is the human's ability to differentiate between good and evil, which is what rebuke is all about. As much as it's hard to receive *mussar*, it's important for a person to accept it in order to come to that objective understanding.

The Three Conditions to Delivering *Mussar* Your Child Will Accept

Parashas Devarim starts with the words *Eileh hadevarim asher diber Moshe el kol Yisrael...baAravah mol Suf...acharei hakoso eis Sichon...v'eis Og...* — "These are the words that Moshe spoke to the nation of Israel...concerning the Aravah, opposite the Reed Sea...after he had smitten Sichon...and Og..." (*Devarim* 1:1–4). The passage then launches into the words of rebuke that Moshe delivered to *Klal Yisrael* shortly before his death. *Parashas Devarim* is all about reprimand, and the very first verse already serves as a guide for us in showing the way for giving proper rebuke.

Although humans are generally loath to receive rebuke, sometimes, especially in parenting, there is a place where it is necessary. Contrary to today's liberal theorists, our Sages believe that a child who was never reprimanded cannot grow up to be healthy and mature. As the adults in their lives, we have an obligation to show them right from wrong, to point out their errors in a way that will build them into fine, upstanding adults. But how can we ensure that our children will listen to our *mussar*? What conditions must our rebuke fulfill in order to accomplish what we want to achieve?

We find the answer in the first verse in *Devarim*, in the brilliant way that our leader, Moshe Rabbeinu, gave *mussar* to *Klal Yisrael*.

The first clue to how we can give *mussar* that will be properly accepted is *baAravah*, which comes from the Hebrew word *me'urav*, involved. Only when a child sees that you're involved in his life on an intimate level will he accept rebuke from you. If he only hears from you when he's making trouble in yeshivah, it just won't work.

It's so sad to hear from broken girls and boys who cry, "Where were they when things were okay?" These children want to know, "Where was my father when I was learning Gemara? Did he know which *masechta* we were learning? Did he even care to know who my *chavrusa* was?" And the girls want to know, "Did my mother know the name of my teacher? Did she know what that change of seating meant to me, how I suffered sitting near the class bully?"

If you want to be an involved parent, you must constantly inquire about your child's life. Children don't always offer information on their own. Are you aware of your child's daily successes and struggles? Do you know how he spends his time and with whom? What are his favorite foods and activities? If you only get involved when things go awry, how will the *mussar* ever find its way to your child's heart?

The second condition necessary for *mussar* to reach its target is *mol suf*: before the end of his days. Moshe Rabbeinu chose to reprimand the nation only shortly before his death because he wanted to avoid repeating his messages again and again. If your *mussar shmuess* is one that keeps going in circles, your child won't listen anymore. He'll just assume that the tape recorder has been rewound and that the recording will soon end. If you want your rebuke to be accepted, you must give it rarely, not on a constant, repetitive basis. When all a child hears from her parent is "No" and "Don't," her ears will simply stop absorbing those messages. Make it a rare occurrence, and your children will heed your words.

The third condition that leads to optimal results is when *mussar* is given *acharei hakoso eis Sichon ... v'eis Og* — "after he had smitten Sichon ... and Og." Only after Moshe Rabbeinu gave *Klal Yisrael* the tremendous gift of killing Sichon and Og, thus ridding them of their enemies, did he sit down to deliver his rebuke. Commenting on this verse, Rav Shteinman notes that before a parent gives rebuke to his child, he has to have given him five compliments on that same day. If your child knows that spending time with you automatically equals a critical conversation, why would he want to do that? If all that ever escapes his mother's lips are words of negativity, doesn't it make sense that he would choose to spend his time elsewhere?

Compliments and criticism must operate on a ratio of five to one. If we want our children to truly accept the criticism we hand them, they must first be prepped with hefty doses of good words: words that let them know how proud we are of them, how highly we think of them, and how much they mean to us.

Only when your rebuke fulfills all three of these conditions, and it is given with a light hand and a soft demeanor, will it reach the ears and hearts of your dear children.

The Pain of the *Galus* Children

Sefer Devarim is filled with the unfortunate circumstances that befell the nation from the Exodus from Egypt until they finally entered Eretz Yisrael. It's not easy to read all of this heaviness, to absorb the intensity of the pain. However, only someone who doesn't possess *da'as* lives in denial; only someone who doesn't grasp the true reality that says, "It will be good, it will be good." A Jew knows that, yes, there is evil, but there is also good. And it is up to us to choose that path. Only *Sefer Devarim* contains a commandment of repentance: *V'shavta ad Hashem Elokecha v'shamata b'kolo k'chol asher anochi metzavcha hayom atah u'vanecha b'chol levavecha u'vechol nafshecha v'shav Hashem Elokecha es shevuscha v'richamecha v'shav v'kibetzcha mikol ha'amim asher hefitzcha Hashem Elokecha shamah* — "And you will return to Hashem, your G-d, and listen to His voice, according to everything that I command you today, you and your children, with all your heart and all your soul. Then Hashem, your G-d, will bring back your captivity and have mercy upon you, and He will return and gather you in from all the peoples to which He has scattered you" (*Devarim* 30:2–4).

What a powerful message!

The last generation before the redemption will experience such pain: the pain of disconnection. These *galus* children will feel the intensity on their skin; they'll feel scattered and alone. But when they repent, Hashem will shower them with benevolence and love.

It is not easy to be a *galus* child. It is not easy to suffer the pain of loneliness, to feel that no one in the world understands your sorrow. Be there for your child, dear mother. Be there in a way that only you can: with a warm, loving heart that only gives rebuke in the proper way. Because we live in a rapidly changing world, today's parents will not always understand the challenges that their children endure, but if you show your child that he is your first concern, and that you believe in him, he will feel it. Believe me, he will feel it.

Children are not dumb, dear women. Sometimes they are far more brilliant than we would like them to be. How you feel about your child is not only expressed in words. Only when you truly believe in your child, which will come through naturally in your gestures and words, will your words of rebuke reap success.

Parashas Devarim serves as a reminder of this reality. After the *meraglim* returned from Eretz Yisrael, the Jews complained that *b'sinas Hashem osanu hotzianu mei'eretz Mitzrayim* — "because of Hashem's hatred toward us did He take us out of the land of Egypt" (ibid. 1:27). This totally false charge against Hashem, explains Rashi, is a classic illustration of how someone with ill will toward someone else assumes that that person has the same feelings toward him. Because the nation did not love Hashem properly, they assumed that Hashem hated them as well. And look how far this phenomenon took them! They actually claimed that the Exodus itself was proof of their contention, because if Hashem truly loved them, He would not have taken them out from fertile Egypt.

Look how far the power of feeling unloved goes, dear mothers. If your child feels unloved, no matter how hard you will try to help him, he will see the situation from his negative, twisted viewpoint. You have the ability to serve as a model of positivity for your child. And this starts when the child is still in his youth. Our children pick up on our cues all too well. How you feel about your husband, about your mother-in-law, about the neighbor is the message you give your child about the world. A mother who views situations with a positive, noncritical approach secures for herself an environment where love and happiness blossoms.

The Sfas Emes (5643) teaches us that a simple sentence can contain the key to *geulah* or destruction. Instead of saying, "He hates me," say, "He loves me," and that will change the reality for you and your children. The key to the *churban* was evil speech: *eretz ocheles yoshveha* — "a land that consumes its inhabitants" (*Bamidbar* 13:32) and *b'sinas Hashem osanu* — "because of Hashem's hatred toward us." That's when the seeds of the destruction were planted. The key to the redemption, then, is positive speech. Give your children the gift of a positive environment, and you will reap the benefits when they grow up.

And what else can you do for your precious child, the one who constricts your heart with pain? *Parashas Devarim* gives us a clue. Before the nation arrived in Eretz Yisrael, they reached the mountain of Esav. *Rav lachem sov es hahar hazeh, penu lachem tzafonah!* Hashem said to Moshe, "Enough of your circling this mountain. Turn yourselves northward!" (*Devarim* 2:3). Stop trying to win over Esav, Hashem tells us. The *yetzer hara* is too powerful for us little people to win the bloody war against him. But what can we do? We can turn upward; we can raise our eyes to the Heavens, rely on the One Who is in control of it all.

You, dear mother, you have the ability to cry like no one else. You have the ability to express your dependence on Hashem through *tefillah*, to arm yourself with the ammunition that will help you wage any war, come what may, and to emerge victorious.

Lashon Hara:
The Culprit of All Our Pain

Parashas Va'eschanan is always read around the time of Tishah B'Av, the saddest day of the year on which we mourn the destruction of the Beis HaMikdash and all the *tzaros*, all the suffering, that ever befell the nation as a result of that catastrophic calamity. The Second Temple, our Sages tell us, was destroyed due to *sinas chinam*, baseless hatred between the Jews (*Yoma* 9b), which we must rectify in order to bring the third and everlasting Temple. In *Parashas Va'eschanan*, we find one way to repair this destructive behavior.

As is known, the original sin that led to the eventual destruction on the Ninth of Av was the sin of the *meraglim*, the spies, who spoke negatively about the Land (*Taanis* 29a). The punishment for everyone who engages in evil speech is isolation: *Badad yeisheiv michutz lamachaneh* — "He shall dwell in isolation, outside the camp" (*Vayikra* 13:46; see *Arachin* 15b) — and it was this isolation that the Holy City experienced after the *Churban*. *Eichah yashvah vadad* — "How did it happen that the city of Jerusalem sits alone?" cries Yirmiyahu in the opening verse of *Megillas Eichah* (1:1). In essence, every widow, every divorcee, every older single, everyone who suffers is suffering from this very isolation that befell us then.

The *Zohar* tells us that *lashon hara* is not considered a *ta'avah*, a desire, because every desire can be fulfilled. If a person has a desire for food, he can eat. If he wants money, he can steal, G-d forbid. Then he appeases the craving, albeit for a short while. *Lashon hara*, he states, emanates not from a place of desire but from a place of routine. The more a person engages in evil speech, the more he will want to carry on. *Lo ragal al leshono*, says David HaMelech (*Tehillim* 15:3). If you train your tongue to be accustomed to evil speech, that's what you'll have to feed it every day, all day. For this reason, many *rabbanim* recommend learning two halachos regarding speech every single day. By replacing a bad habit with a constructive one, you can ensure that you've truly uprooted the hateful behavior.

The greatest pain of all is when *lashon hara* is spoken about HaKadosh Baruch Hu, G-d forbid. For this, we must cry. When we see that His Name is being desecrated by the nations, or by His very own wayward children, how can we not?

In the Talmud (*Gittin* 58a), we read a heartrending story of the beautiful Tzofnas bas Peniel, the daughter of the Kohen Gadol, who was violated and then put up for sale at a slave market. Her beauty was so dazzling that she wrapped herself in seven layers of clothing.

One uncouth man approached and said that he would only buy her once he saw her beauty. So it was that the daughter of the holy Kohen Gadol was stripped of her clothes in the marketplace. When only one layer of seven was left, she herself tore it off and screamed, "Ribbono shel Olam, if You haven't had mercy on us, why don't You have mercy on Your own holy Name?"

This is the cry of our generation. Perhaps we deserve what we were given, but all of these *tzaros* lead to the besmirching of Hashem's Name! How can He allow this? When the nations of the world see what we're going through, when those who've turned their backs to the Torah see what we're enduring, we cry, "Hashem, please defend us for Your sake if not for ours!"

I once went to console Liza, a bereaved mother who lost her precious eight-year-old daughter, Noa. The child's last request was, "Ima, take me to the Kotel." That's what she wanted. Her mother said to me that Noa wanted so badly to observe Shabbos, but her father wouldn't hear of it. When I heard those words, I wanted to scream to Hashem, "Ribbono shel Olam, if you haven't had mercy on us, why don't You have mercy on Your own holy Name?" How much *lashon hara* will still be spoken against You? This is unbearably painful.

Even here, however, I found comfort. Noa's father hails from a village called Batzrah. Suddenly, a thought popped up in my mind: it is written that Mashiach will come from that city (*Ibn Ezra, Yeshayahu* 63:1). The prophet Yeshayahu asks, *Mi zeh ba me'Edom chamutz begadim miBatzrah* — "Who is the man that comes from Edom with sullied garments from Batzrah?" (*Yeshayahu* 63:1). The clothes of Mashiach, our Sages teach us, will be spotted with stains of Jewish blood that was shed over the centuries, and one final spot will bring on the Redemption. When that one last bloodshed will happen, Hashem will no longer be able to bear the pain of His nation (see *Bereishis Rabbasi, Vayechi* 49:11).

One More *Tefillah*: Your Salvation Is Near

When people ask me what general message I bring to my audiences throughout the year, I answer the one thing that I know everyone is searching for: comfort. *Nachamu nachamu ami* — "Comfort, comfort My people" (*Yeshayahu* 40:1). That's what every woman wants to hear. It's over! Your pain has come to an end. You passed the test with flying colors, and your time of salvation has finally arrived. *V'hayah he'akov l'mishor v'harechasim l'vik'ah* — "The winding roads will become straight, and the pebbled paths will become flat," promises the prophet Yeshayahu (40:4). Suddenly, things will fall into place for you, dear women. And all those confusing parts of your life will become clear. What a solace!

It's not for naught that the word *nechamah*, consolation, is in feminine form. Oh, how we women yearn for the comfort of closeness: to Hashem, and to our loved ones. These are days of intense love. We awaken Hashem's mercy on the eve of Tishah B'Av, and it continues to accompany us through the months of Elul and Tishrei, the months of mercy and forgiveness. In *Parashas Va'eschanan* as well, Moshe Rabbeinu reminds us of the power of prayer: how we can beseech our way to Hashem's mercy.

After Moshe Rabbeinu fulfilled his duty in this world, he begged Hashem *ba'eis hahi* — "at that time" (*Devarim* 3:23): "Hashem, please allow me to enter Eretz Yisrael." The commentators (*Alshich* and *Ohr HaChaim*) deduce from the words *ba'eis hahi* that there are propitious times for prayers: the *eis ratzon*.

Moshe prayed 515 *tefillos* to be granted entry to Eretz Yisrael: three *tefillos* each weekday from the time he thought he might be allowed to enter the land (see *Pnei Yehoshua, Berachos* 32a). How he prayed! And in the end, Hashem said to him, *Rav lach al tosef dabeir eilai od b'davar hazeh* — "Enough! Don't speak to Me about this matter anymore" (*Devarim* 3:26). Our Sages deduce from this conversation that every request has a certain limit of prayers until which it is not answered. The appeal regarding entry to Eretz Yisrael had a maximum of 515. If Moshe would have offered one more *tefillah*, Hashem would have granted his request, because the 516th prayer would have been a *tefillas nedavah* (an extra, non-obligatory prayer).

So why didn't Moshe daven that one more *tefillah*? He was

a true servant of Hashem. If Hashem asked him to stop, he followed the order faithfully. But we are not Moshe Rabbeinu! The moment Hashem "asks" you to stop, the moment that you feel that you've reached rock bottom, know that this is your sign: one more *tefillah*. How Hashem anticipates that prayer from your trembling lips! Gather your strength one last time, and then you'll enter the Promised Land. That's when Hashem will bless you with a *matnas chinam* for your *tefillas chinam*.

Rashi tells us that Moshe prayed to be allowed into Eretz Yisrael not because of his merit and his great deeds, but as a "*matnas chinam*," an unearned gift. The concept of *matnas chinam*, our Sages teach us, should serve as a lesson for us in eradicating the *sinas chinam* that caused this dark and endless exile. How does *Parashas Va'eschanan* show us the rectification of that grave sin? If we think about it, baseless hatred always stems from one place: the "I deserve this" attitude that spurs jealousy, loathing, and animosity.

So what is the antidote that we find in *Parashas Va'eschanan*? If Moshe Rabbeinu, Hashem's closest servant, begs for a free pass, a *matnas chinam*, how in the world can we come with an attitude of "I deserve this"? It just doesn't make sense!

If we truly understand that everything we have is not in our own merit but merely a free gift from Hashem, how can we hate? How can we harbor animosity in our hearts? Imagine someone gets a free pass for a show, and when he enters the auditorium, he pushes people out of his way to make himself more comfortable. How boorish and unappreciative can a person be?

Moshe Rabbeinu teaches us this humility in *Parashas Va'eschanan*. He understood that every breath he took was from Hashem, so how could he hate another Jew?

Understanding that all of life is a gift, dear women, not only enriches our relationship with others but also our connection with Hashem.

All of our conflicts and disappointments with others and Hashem essentially emanate from the "I deserve this" mind-set.

Once we realize that everything is a *matnas chinam*, *sinas chinam* will be eradicated from our midst.

V'Im Ein Atem Ma'aminim: Even if You Don't Believe

How can we draw comfort from our pious leader, the one who sacrificed his heart and soul for his nation? Above all else, Moshe Rabbeinu was the humblest human being on the face of the earth. Only a true *anav* understands that every breath he takes is a gift from the Ribbono shel Olam. And if this is the choice that Hashem makes — to deny him entry to the land he loves — then so be it. The complete subservience with which Moshe Rabbeinu served Hashem allowed him to live a life of true serenity.

But what can we do if we don't believe that the salvation will finally come? What if our situation has gotten the better of us and we're too blinded to see that the *nechamah* is within our reach? Our Sages teach us, and we now know these words in a most touching tune, that when Mashiach will come, he will stand on the roof of the Beis HaMikdash and shout out to *Am Yisrael*, "Your time of redemption has come! *V'im ein atem ma'aminim* — "And if you don't believe Me, look at My light that is reflecting upon you" (*Yalkut Shimoni, Yeshayahu* 499).

Hashem understands the *v'im ein atem ma'aminim*, dear women. He knows the pain of not believing. It's not easy to put one foot in front of the other in this utter darkness. After all, the *yeshuah* has not yet come! How can we turn up the music and be merry at this time?

Dear Jewish women, Judaism is unlike every other belief system. In *Yiddishkeit*, consolation, like mourning, revolves around a specific time. Hashem, in His wisdom, dictates that there be a time of consolation, so there will be one. It's hard to understand how this can happen. How can we go from one extreme to the next just like that?

After the tragic *Churban*, HaKadosh Baruch Hu came to Yerushalayim and said, "Be consoled." The lonely city, stripped of her beauty and glory, cried, "How can I be consoled right now? How can I go from shivah to *shivah dinechemta*, the seven haftaros of consolation?" To which Hashem replied, "Do as I say. Go console *Am Yisrael*."

That's when all the prophets immediately gathered in Yerushalayim, and Yerushalayim said to them, *Eich tanachmuni havel* — "How can you so futilely console me?" (*Iyov* 21:34). My ears are still full of the rebuke you've given me, and now you come to console me?

First, the prophet Hoshea attempted to console her. When she refused to accept consolation, Yoel, Amos, Michah, and even Avraham, Yitzchak, and Yaakov tried, but she refused to be consoled.

That's when HaKadosh Baruch Hu approached Yerushalayim and said, *Biti, kol haka'as hazeh* — "My daughter, why all this anger?" And she said to Hashem, "Master of the world, is my anger not justified? You have exiled me among the nations and cursed me with horrific curses. I have been afflicted until my face became as black as the bottom of a pot. Yet through it all I sanctified Your great Name."

Said Hashem to His precious daughter, *Keneged zechuyos she'asisa chovos alecha she'avarta* — "Your meritorious deeds are canceled out by your iniquitous ones, but nevertheless, the time has come for you to be redeemed" (*Yalkut Shimoni, Yeshayahu* 443).

From this incredible discussion we learn the secret of comfort. We see it in the *gematria* of *yud Av* (the tenth day of Av, the day after Tishah B'Av) — the same as the word *ahavah*: it is to love baselessly. The remedy for all that *sinas chinam* is right here, in this conversation. Hashem says, "You may not deserve it, but now is the time when love is poured into the world, the time to be comforted." Whether your loved ones deserve it or not, whether or not your husband or son or mother-in-law does what has to be done, shower them with this baseless love. And if you treat others with love, you exhibit true *ahavas Yisrael*, Hashem will exhibit an outpouring of love toward you, and you will finally merit your true salvation.

Va'A'heivcha: Hashem's Love to You Is Personal

$\mathcal{I}$n *Parashas Eikev*, we read about the blessing that *Am Yisrael* was promised on condition of their conduct. If they would observe the commandments that were given in the previous *parashiyos*, the Torah tells us, they would merit great *berachah*: wealth, health, and victory against their foes. However, if they would forget about Hashem's existence and of the miracles He performed for them in the desert, He would no longer guard them and they would be lost among the nations of the world. Moshe continues to remind them of the kindnesses Hashem performed on their behalf: the story of the golden calf, the breaking of the *luchos*, etc.

Although *Parashas Eikev* is the *parashah* that contains threats against *Am Yisrael*, it is also the *parashah* that is full of love. The word *ahavah*, love, appears many times in this Torah portion. *V'atah Yisrael mah Hashem Elokecha sho'el mei'imach ki im… l'ahavah oso…* — "Now, Yisrael, what does Hashem, your G-d, ask of you? Only…to love Him…" (*Devarim* 10:12) and *V'ahavta eis Hashem Elokecha v'shamarta mishmarto…* — "You shall love Hashem, your G-d, and you shall safeguard His charge…" (ibid. 11:1) are just two of the many examples.

Hashem's love for us is overflowing, dear women! If we take a look at the opening verse of *Parashas Eikev*, we find what seems to be a grammatical error. *V'hayah ekev tishme'un eis hamish-patim ha'eileh ush'martem va'asisem osam v'shamar Hashem Elokecha lecha…va'aheivcha u'veirachecha v'hirbecha…* — "This will be the reward when you heed these laws and you observe and perform them; Hashem will love you, bless you, and cause you to multiply" (ibid. 7:12–13). When Moshe conveyed the stipulation, he delivered it in plural form, *va'asisem*, but when he informed the nation of the reward, he used the singular form, *va'a'heivcha*. How do we understand the revision in language? The answer offers us insight regarding Hashem's deep love for each of us.

True love, explain our Sages, is a personal thing. It's a one-on-one relationship. If we follow Hashem's command, we won't be rewarded as a group. Every single Jew will merit feeling Hashem's affection as an individual. *Va'aheivcha* — He will love *you*. The entire *Parashas Eikev* is full of examples that prove this phenomenon. *Simlascha lo valsah mei'alecha v'raglecha lo vatzeikah zeh arba'im shanah* — "Your garment did not wear out upon you, and your feet did not swell, these forty years" (ibid. 8:4). Even the clothing was a sign that Hashem was with *Am Yisrael*. How many of your children's shirts last for more than one season? What a miracle! In a comment that stirs emotion, Rashi expounds on Hashem's kindness. The *ananei hakavod*, he notes, would steam the Jews' clothes like steam irons, and their garments grew along with them, remaining clean and fresh.

Look how Hashem took care of every single Jew! He ironed the shirt of every single man, woman, and child so that no one would walk around with a creased garment. Hashem is concerned about each of us, dear women. When it comes to expressing His love, we are not a collective bunch. Like a dedicated mother who devotes herself to the needs of each child, He expresses His love in even the minutest details.

Elul, the acronym for *Ani l'dodi v'dodi li* — "I alone am my Beloved's, and my Beloved is mine," is the month that teaches us to do *teshuvah*, to repent from a place of love because that is the emotion through which Hashem expresses His concern for us. The knowledge that Hashem loves each and every one of us on an individual level is a great comfort.

Kochi V'Otzem Yadi: Why a Lack of Emunah Is so Destructive

The greatest fear that every human being has is that he will be forsaken. Even at my age, I still dream sometimes that my mother left me behind on the bus. A recurring theme in our nightmares revolves around losing a loved one, being left behind to fend for ourselves, G-d forbid.

And that's the fear many of us have in relation to Hashem. "Hashem forgot to create my *zivug*." "When Hashem handed out *parnassah*, He skipped me." "Why did He forget about me when He gave out beauty?" I was forgotten, I was forsaken— that's our deepest fear.

In the haftarah to *Parashas Eikev*, we hear these very cries from Yerushalayim. *Vatomer Tziyon azavani Hashem VaA-donai shecheichani* — "Hashem has forsaken me and my Lord has forgotten me" (*Yeshayahu* 49:14). But Hashem tells us in the very next verse that forgetting us is impossible: *V'anochi lo eshkacheich!* Hashem will never forget you, dear sisters.

We've all envisioned in our minds what it must feel like for a young child to be left in a car, alone. The child cannot grasp how her mother or father forget about her! There is no greater pain in the world. Yes, Hashem tells us, because of the human *ko'ach hashikchah*, the power of forgetfulness, even a mother or father can forget about a child. But, He promises, I will never forget My children.

If Hashem's love is so great and He expresses it to each of us individually, how can it be that we don't always feel it? We find the answer in *Parashas Eikev*, which discusses the outcome of a person who believes that *kochi v'otzem yadi asah li es hachayil hazeh* — "my strength and the might of my hand made me all this wealth!" (*Devarim* 8:17).

Besides being irrational, why is this line of thinking so dangerous? Working our way toward independence from Hashem can lead to dismal consequences. When you feel that you are in control and that you are the one in charge, you are essentially putting yourself in the weakest place.

What happens to a woman who thinks she can do it all on her own? Instead of relying on Hashem, she loses the ability to be comforted. You know those toddlers who are certain they can do everything on their own, right? What happens when they can't tie their shoes? They refuse to ask for help, and trip over the laces.

The only source of comfort is Hashem, dear women. He is the One you want to rely on to feel safe and secure, the most important feeling you long for. He will give you the *ko'ach* to be an *eishes chayil. V'zacharta es Hashem Elokecha ki hu hanosein lecha ko'ach la'asos chayil* — "Then you shall remember Hashem, your G-d, that it was He Who gave you the strength to make wealth!" (ibid. 8:18). Turn to Him for the strength you need to forge through the challenge.

When I pack for our annual family vacation, I always have that moment where I think I'm losing it. An overwhelming feeling washes over me. "How will I do it all? What should I take and what should I leave behind? Where should I begin?" And suddenly I see that the little ones have grown up, and they're stuffing their own belongings into the suitcases and everything is under control. Hashem has not forsaken me. He didn't leave me alone with these empty suitcases. And He doesn't leave us alone when we wait for a *shidduch*, a child, a *yeshuah*. He is right there, showering each of us with His love, remembering us at every moment.

Verbal Declaration: The Antidote to Forgetfulness

The knowledge that HaKadosh Baruch Hu never forgets any one of His precious children is profoundly comforting. What can we do not to forget about Him?

I once heard a psychologist explain the forgotten-baby syndrome, which is where parents leave their child in a car, *Rachmana litzlan*. Of course, no parent in the world would intentionally leave her child to suffocate in the heat of a locked car. So how does it happen that the most dedicated, loving parents commit this catastrophic error?

The psychologist explained that the act of forgetting does not occur when the parent leaves the car; it happens when the parent first brings the child *into* the car. If a parent is cognizant of the child's presence from the moment he fastens the child's seatbelt and sets out on his way, he will remember to take him out when he leaves.

Indeed, in most cases where a child was left in a car, the parent had not remembered the child's presence because the child was generally not with the parent at that time. In other words, it is necessary for parents to create the initial awareness in their mind that the child is in the car in order for them to remember later.

The concept that this psychologist explained so aptly applies to how we can ensure that we don't forget about Hashem's existence and His constant involvement in our lives. *Parashas Eikev* teaches us to recite blessings on our food (ibid. 8:10). The idea of this commandment is that eating is one of the most routine actions that we perform every day, often without giving it a thought. It's just so ingrained in us to eat that we need that extra step of awareness that will remind us to thank, to be cognizant of Hashem's Hand in our provisions.

In order to combat the forgetfulness issue, the psychologist suggested that when a parent secures a child into his car seat, the parent should declare, "I am putting the child into the car now." Before parents leave for a trip, they should announce, "Moshe, Yitzchak, Rivkah, and Rochel are coming with us on a trip now." This explicit declaration that ingrains the awareness into the brain, says the psychologist, can prevent the forgotten-baby syndrome.

Verbal declaration has a tremendous power. Only after a man says, *Harei at mekudeshes li…,* to a woman does she become his wife. For this reason, Hashem commanded us with the wonderful mitzvah that we know as a *berachah.* Before we forget to recite Birkas HaMazon, He warns us, *Hishamer lecha pen tishkach es Hashem Elokecha* — "Take care lest you forget Hashem, your G-d" (ibid. 8:11). Stop for a moment and sort your thoughts in words. *V'achalta v'savata u'veirachta* — "You will eat and you will be satisfied, and bless Hashem, your G-d" (ibid. 8:10).

The well-known verse, *V'atah Yisrael mah Hashem Elokecha sho'el mei'imach* — "Now, Yisrael, what does Hashem, your G-d, ask of you?" (ibid. 10:12) is found in this *parashah.* Our Sages teach us (*Menachos* 43b and *Rashi* there) that we should read the word *mah* as *mei'ah,* "one hundred." Hashem commands us to recite one hundred blessings every day because we need one hundred daily reminders of His involvement in our lives.

Dear women, we cannot fathom the power of even one *berachah.* I have a student who lives in Tel Aviv, a smart woman who has a flourishing career, who suddenly returned to Torah observance and pulled along her husband and children. I once asked her how she managed to accomplish this feat, and she told me, "My story is very simple. We were once on a trip during summer vacation, and we made a quick stop at the gas station. We went into the store, and my kids started pulling me in all directions. 'I want this and I want that!' I spotted a *frum* family in the corner of the store. Their mother was handing out cups of water and then, together, they all said a *berachah*. I looked at those kids and I looked at mine, and I said, 'This is what I want.'"

When this student of mine told me her touching story, I thought to myself, *It is not for naught that Hashem blessed Avraham with the words Veheyeih berachah — "You shall be a blessing" (Bereishis 12:2).* When you make a proper *berachah*, you not only acknowledge Hashem's participation in your own life, but you also inspire others to see His glory. What a blessing to the world!

When you recite a *berachah* loud and clear, dear women, you are making a conscious declaration. You are letting your children know that you are aware of Who the Boss is in your life. What greater blessing can you bring into your home? When children are raised to say *berachos* aloud, how can they forget about Hashem's Presence in their lives?

And take it a step further. Learn to recognize Hashem's existence in your life by verbally stating your acknowledgment in your own words. Talk to Hashem throughout your day, dear women, and You will not forget Him. The more you train yourself to converse with Him about all matters, the more you will feel His Presence in your life.

Alef Before Beis: What Precedes Berachah?

Parashas Re'eh opens with an important message from HaKadosh Baruch Hu. *Re'eh anochi nosein lifneichem hayom berachah u'klalah* — "See, I present before you today a blessing and a curse" (*Devarim* 11:26). *Nesinah* is an expression of *matanah*, a gift. What's the gift that Hashem is granting us? *Hayom:* the day of Rosh Hashanah.

From the start of Elul, we are blessed with the light that this gift of a day exudes. Chodesh Elul, the month that reminds us of our relationship with Hashem, when *ani l'dodi v'dodi li* — "I alone am my Beloved's, and my Beloved is mine" — also has the power to renew our connection with our loved ones after a long and hot summer vacation.

Ask for the Beis

Chodesh Elul has the power to transform a *klalah* into *berachah*. What is *berachah*? It's a huge word. The *Zohar* tells us that before Hashem wrote the Torah, all of the letters came to Him and begged, "Please start the Torah with me."

Said Hashem to them, "I want to start the Torah with the letter *beis*, the first letter of the word *berachah*. Because if I start the world with blessing, it will survive."

If something starts right, it will be a success.

But what happens if it didn't, G-d forbid?

The Rebbe of Gur offers words of comfort (in *Sfas Emes, Re'eh* 5641). Preceding the *beis*, he notes, is the *alef*. That's the first letter of the word *anochi*, the word we find in the opening passage of *Parashas Re'eh*. That's the letter with which Hashem's Name begins and the *Aseres HaDibros* likewise opens with that letter. So even if you look back at the end of a year and you see that it didn't seem to be a blessing — your husband didn't fulfill his promise, your son's *Yiddishkeit* took a fall — remember that before the *beis* comes the *alef*. Simply put, Hashem's will comes before the *berachah*. It is all up to Him. What is left for you to do? To beg.

What should you ask for? Ask for the *beis*, the *berachah*, an abundance of blessing in your home. And for the *alef*, for Hashem's Presence, always in the heart of your husband, children, and yourself. A life centered on Hashem and His Torah is an unparalleled existence. It brings you to another realm, one that no one and nothing in the world can take away from you.

But it's also important to *do* Torah. How do we do that? Let's turn to *Parashas Re'eh* for the answer: *Es haberachah asher tishme'u...* — "The blessing that you will listen..." (*Devarim* 11:27). When will your home be infused with the blessing of Torah? When Torah is *heard* in its walls. Speak to your children in Torah. Yes, dear women, you can do this too. You may think that the official studies are relegated to school, but the true place for *chinuch* is the home. Regale them with tales of *tzaddikim*, stories about the power of mitzvos, the *kippah*, the tzitzis. So many fights can be halted with simple Torah words. "My sweeties, you are all so good. Let me see that you have *ahavas Yisrael.*" "Let's ask Hashem for help."

And what's the curse? What sucks the *berachah* out of the home? *V'haklalah im lo sishme'u...* — "And the curse: if you don't listen..." (ibid. 11:28). Sometimes evening comes around, and I realize how much *klalah* I scattered all over my own house. "If you don't listen to what Ima is telling you..." "If you don't organize your room right now..." "If you don't go to bed..." "Sit up straight!" "What's up with these nails?" "What's going to be with you?"

That's a curse. Instead of blaming your son's inexperienced rebbi or your daughter's teacher's overemphasis on grades, take a serious count of the words of *berachah* or, Heaven forbid, *klalah*, that echo in your house every day. It is up to us to choose if we want to fill the air in our home with blessing or curses. Our words and attitude penetrate the impressionable hearts of our dear children and mold them accordingly. Is it "You're so dear to me" and "I love you more than you can ever imagine," or "When will you stop causing me so much *agmas nefesh*, heartache?" and "Why can't you just be *normal*?"

Which one do you choose?

The Power of a Mother's Story

The Torah portions in *Sefer Devarim* were transmitted to the Jews prior to their entry to Eretz Yisrael. After forty hard years in the desert, the wandering tribes were finally readying themselves to enter the land and conquer the seven nations there. From where did they have that power?

Rav Shamshon Refael Hirsch answers that the nation's power came from their mother's tales. Most of the generation that entered Eretz Yisrael were born in the desert. Those people had not experienced the slavery in Mitzrayim, the miraculous redemption, the miracles at the sea. But when they were young, their mothers and grandmothers would regale them with tales of the plagues. The children would sit on the ground as the sun sank into the sky, listening with wide, glistening eyes to the stories of Hashem's miracles. Throughout the long night, they were thinking, processing the tales that were lovingly fed to them.

And what about us? We put the kids into bed at night and tiptoe out of the room, our feet barely touching the ground, for fear that the kids will ask for a story. *Hashem, please, just don't have them ask for a story. Not tonight*, we pray silently.

And suddenly a small voice pops out in the darkness, "Mommy, can you please tell me a story?"

A good story, dear mothers, is the fuel that gives the child power for life. Tell them of their grandparents: how they sacrificed to observe the mitzvos. Tell them how you've learned to cope with the plagues in your life. Tell them stories of *tzaddikim*, of holy people who gave up everything to live a life of Torah. And don't forget to remind them how much you love them. These stories fill the *berachah* tank in your home.

Re'eh Anochi: He Is Your Moshe Rabbeinu

It is not only important for a Jewish woman to address her children with an attitude of *berachah*. She also has the opportunity and obligation to fill her husband's life with blessing. The Ohr HaChaim writes that Moshe Rabbeinu said to the nation, "*Re'eh anochi* — look at me! I grew up in Pharaoh's palace. When I left, I went to Midian. Considering my background, you'd think I wouldn't have any potential for growth, and look…" Indeed, Moshe Rabbeinu's childhood and even young adulthood was not a harbinger for such an illustrious life.

When your husband seems so far removed from Torah, from *middos tovos*, remember that there's no such thing. He can be Moshe Rabbeinu.

What does the outcome depend on?

The *yiras Shamayim* is every individual's department. At the end of the game, that's his call, but you can play a huge role in this, dear wives. So much depends on how you care about him, how you praise him.

In *Parashas Re'eh*, we learn about the mitzvah of *tzedakah*. *Ki faso'ach tiftach es yadcha lo v'ha'aveit ta'avitenu dei machsoro asher yechsar lo* — "You should open your hand to the destitute person, and you should lend him his requirement, whatever is lacking to him" (*Devarim* 15:8). Rashi explains that *asher yechsar lo*, "whatever is lacking to him," refers to the poor man's wife, as it is written in the verse that discusses the creation of woman, *E'eseh lo eizer kenegdo* — "I will make him a helper corresponding to him" (*Bereishis* 2:18). Everything a man lacks or doesn't is contingent on his wife. She has the capacity to nurture him, to prevent him from sinning, to give him the feeling that he is the spiritual center of the home. Oh, how a man thrives on this! Conduct yourself according to this instruction and see for yourself what happens when you treat your husband like you would Moshe Rabbeinu.

Whether the issue is big or small, run it by your husband. If you have a funny joke to share, call him first. Although they may seem petty, these little gestures will make your husband the central part of your life, where he should be. The more you center your life on him, the more you will cherish the closeness it engenders. So many people whose parents were Holocaust survivors tell of their mother's shining eyes when their father walked through the door after a day of work. "It was as if she hadn't seen him for a month!" And that's because, to these women, the husband was everything: their mother, father, sibling, and friend.

In today's world, we are lucky to be surrounded by an abundance of loved ones, thank G-d, but in spite of this blessing, we must ensure that the husband takes center stage, always. If you want to be the queen, dear women, he has to be your king. The more you believe in him, the more he feels that you see his potential, the more of a Moshe Rabbeinu he will become.

"But I don't want to be his slave!" women complain when I address this topic in my lectures. To them, focusing their lives on their husbands means making him their master and they turning into slaves. Let's understand why this erroneous thinking is so dangerous. Supposed you decide that you're ready to be your husband's slave. You tell him, "Okay, I will do whatever you please." All of your gestures toward him will become emotionless, heartless, like those of a puppet.

How can you know if there is friendship in a relationship? asks the Vilna Gaon. The measuring tape for a true relationship is in how the deeds are done to each other. Are you performing the gestures with kindness? If your thoughts are *I'm drained from this. All day I have to do for him*, then you're a slave. Expressions like "I don't have *ko'ach*," "I'm tired," are all synonymous with "I don't have *ahavah*."

But what happens if you truly are sapped of all energy? You're only human, after all. With true love, you will find that you can give what you even didn't know you possess. And the appreciation for those gestures knows no bounds.

Let me tell you how I've learned this from my own experience. HaKadosh Baruch Hu sent me a gift whom we named Yosef Chai, *z"l*. My precious son was born with a heart defect, and he never slept for even half an hour at a time. Every half-hour I had to wake up for him. I used to see the sun set and the sun rise. Every day. And I didn't complain even once. Why not? Because I loved Yosef Chai. I loved him so much that I found the *ko'ach* to do everything for him.

Yosef Chai gave me the understanding of how much he relied on me. In tending to him, it was crystal clear to me that he was dependent on me for his every need. My other children, I thought, can manage on their own. They don't need me as much. So I don't have that much *ko'ach* for them.

But Hashem taught me otherwise. "Listen," He said, "you're wrong, Yemima. Every morning, you say the *berachah* of

she'asani kirtzono — 'He made me according to His will.'"
What's Hashem's will? To perform good deeds. In the same way
that Hashem lovingly concerns Himself with our every need, we
must do our utmost to extend ourselves to others, especially
our loved ones, who need us most.

And what does your husband need from you most? The
crown. The more you extend yourself to him from a place of
love, the more you will treat him like a king. If it comes from a
forced place, you will be his slave. *Hachaim v'hamaves nasati
lefanecha* — "Life and death I gave to you" (*Devarim* 30:19) —
Hashem lays out the choices for us. *Haberachah v'haklalah
u'vacharta bachaim* — "The blessing and the curse, and you
should choose life" (ibid.). Essentially, you have only one choice:
life. Life means conducting yourself with heart, a heart that
pulses with love.

In your very own home, no matter whether or not you have a
career, you are your children's teacher. You have the capacity to
make your home the best school in the world, to instill in your
children true *middos tovos* and a deep connection to Hashem
and His Torah. The best *berachah* you can possibly instill in their
impressionable hearts is that Abba is the king in the home.

Judges and Officers: Learning Is Not Enough

I am privileged to meet thousands of women every month, sometimes every week, who come to a *shiur*, thirsty to learn and grow. But it's not enough to attend a *shiur*. It's not enough to read a book. What are we doing with this information?

Shoftim v'shotrim titen lecha b'chol she'arecha — "Judges and officers shall you appoint in all your cities" (*Devarim* 16:18) — are the opening words of *Parashas Shoftim*. What is the difference in the implications of *shoftim*, judges, and *shotrim*, officers? The judge tells the officer what to do; the officer fulfills the judge's command. In our lives, *judges* refers to the voice of logic that prompts you to do something good and sensible. *Officers* refers to the actual deed, the result of your logical thought.

The Ohr HaChaim explains it so beautifully. He says, "If there are no officers, there are no judges. If there are no judges, there are no officers." What good is study, the command of the "judges," if it remains in the realm of academia or habit and is never given over to the "officers," if it is not translated into action? Learning is only worth something if we apply it to our lives and truly create change.

When I look around, especially in Chodesh Elul, I see so many people learning. The *batei midrash* are swarming with people like mushrooms after a rainfall. But are they judges without the officers? Rabbeinu Yonah calls learning without translating the knowledge into action, "decorations of the *seichel*, the intellect." If nothing is actually done, it's only a mere adornment.

In order to make our learning count, our *mussar* giants teach us, we must commit to a small change. A very small change, one that we will be able to implement in our lives.

"But how will this small improvement make a dent, Yemima?" women ask me all the time. "Can it really wipe out all of my wrongdoings and give me a chance for a clean slate?"

Parashas Shoftim covers the laws regarding the acceptance and provision of *shochad*, bribery. It's prohibited to bribe and prohibited to accept a bribe in any Jewish court because even if the judge accepts a bribe without obligation, it is impossible for him not to be swayed in the favor of the one who bribed him. There is one exception to this rule: in Chodesh Elul, our Sages teach us, HaKadosh Baruch Hu accepts our bribes with joy and open arms.

On this topic, the Chafetz Chaim enlightens us with an illuminating thought. He writes in his *sefer Ahavas Chesed* that the repentance, good deeds, charity, and acts of kindness that a person performs during these days generate the acceptance of our prayers in Heaven, even though this is not justifiable.

Imagine, dear women! In the month of Elul, Hashem accepts your bribery. It's the time of year when He seeks to help anyone who stretches out a hand. Don't underestimate the power of your small commitment. It may sound like bribery, but at this time of year it is totally proper.

So what can we take upon ourselves when we want to improve? There are two kinds of commitments that we can make, both of which are referenced with the words *Tik'u vachodesh shofar* — "Blow the shofar at the moon's renewal" (*Tehillim* 81:4). The first is *chodesh*, renewal. Commit to doing something new. An example of this would be to start davening *Minchah* every afternoon if you haven't done so yet.

The second is *shofar*, whose root means to revamp or improve. Focus on a mitzvah that you're already observing and make it better, more beautiful. You can do this with any mitzvah. Simply take upon yourself to do it with more joy.

What is greater: a new deed or an improved deed? An improved one, of course. What is the reward for your improved mitzvah? If you take a step in this direction, Hashem says, "I will make you like a shofar, with which one blows in air from one side and the air goes out from another" (*Yalkut Shimoni, Emor*). A shofar emits a sound when air enters from one end and exits from another. The amount of air that exits is directly influenced by the amount of air that enters. If you invest more, Hashem will repay with more.

If you're cooking for Shabbos, remind yourself to do it with joy. You're anyway cooking, so why not? You're anyway bathing the children now, so why not giggle with them in the process? I'm anyway calling my mother, so why shouldn't I listen to her stories with joy and real interest?

With thoughts like these, Elul can become a very happy time. It's the opportunity for you to rectify or embellish a small deed and see huge results.

Fear in Judaism: For Optimists Only

But let's not kid ourselves. Elul is also a time of fear. Of anxiety. What do we know of what the next year can bring? We look around at the world we see today, and the year that has just passed. It's frightening to observe how much can happen in just one year.

Is there a place for fear in Judaism? There is forbidden fear, but there's also necessary fear. Forbidden fear comes from a place of despair, from giving up on seeing the light. It's the voice that tells you, "Nothing good will happen this year. It'll be just another lonely, depressing, stuck circle around the calendar. Nothing will ever get better for me." This kind of fear is unfortunately self-fulfilling, because that's what happens to the pessimist's prophecy.

So what is necessary fear? It's the fear that must grip our hearts in Elul. It's the fear of "Did I do everything in my power to ensure a good year for myself and my loved ones? Did I exploit the potential of Elul, seeking favor from Hashem with my commitments and good deeds?" This is the fear of the pious Jews who are optimistic in their ability to generate goodness into their lives. It is not only a justified fear, but it is also one that we should all feel at this time of year. It's okay to be jittery and feel tense about the upcoming days, but only from this perspective, a perspective of optimism.

In *Parashas Shoftim*, we encounter an interesting law regarding someone who built a new house and hasn't inaugurated it before going to war: "Let him go and return to his house, lest he die in the war and another man will inaugurate it" (*Devarim* 20:5). In the same vein, if a man planted a vineyard and did not redeem it [i.e. in the fourth year, when it is redeemed and the proceeds are eaten in Yerushalayim], he too must return from war to redeem it "lest he die in the war and another man will redeem it" (ibid. 20:6). The same is true with regard to a man who has betrothed a woman and hasn't consummated their betrothal. He too must return home and get married "lest he die in war and another man will marry her" (ibid. 20:7).

The men in all of these situations were allowed to fear because of their optimistic viewpoint. They didn't resist going to war out of a cowardly fear that their life may end. Instead, they looked at their future with excitement. One man saw the new house he just finished building and envisioned a beautiful life in it. The other looked forward to starting a new life with his future wife. And the man who harvested his vineyard thought, *There's a whole year's livelihood awaiting me in the field!*

As long as you're afraid for the future because you know how beautiful it can be and you don't want to mess that up, your fear is permitted, even encouraged. This is the kind of fear that spurs you to invest more, to work a bit harder, because you don't want to lose all that promising potential.

How does the Torah view people whose fear is purposeless; who only fear because they see their future in shades of black and gray? "Who is the man who is fearful and fainthearted? Let him go and return to his house, and let him not melt the heart of his fellows, like his heart" (ibid. 20:8). A person who was uselessly anxious, always predicting the worst, was commanded to return home in order to prevent him from inculcating the others with his pessimism and fear. Unfounded fear has no place in Judaism.

If you're an optimist, allow yourself to fear. It will bring you to good places, to performing good deeds that will help you grow. But if you're a pessimist, stay away from fear. The only outcome it provides, G-d forbid, is a self-fulfilling prophecy.

I saw an incredible response that a *rav* provided to a marriage counselor who asked, "Is it permissible to ask a couple if they want to remain married or to get divorced even before we begin our work?" The counselor wanted to know if he was allowed to plant the idea of separation in the minds of his clients.

The *rav's* answer was wonderful. A couple who enters therapy embroiled in a bitter battle, he noted, should not be offered the way out through divorce. Together with the counselor, they must first exhaust all other options before heading in that direction.

However, when the therapist perceives that the couple he's seeing is operating on a basis of love, the *rav* added, the mere mention of the word *divorce* will have them scrambling for ideas to mend their relationship immediately. Just thinking of separating will have them clinging tightly to each other.

What a brilliant thought! If you're optimistic, allow yourself to fear the worst because it will only generate good. But if you're a pessimist, stay away from it. Fear and anxiety will only pull you further down into the abyss.

Why We Need Kings in the Home

More than the delicious food and clean laundry, your husband wants a wife with a shining face and a wife who crowns him as king.

Som tasim alecha melech — "You shall surely set over yourself a king," the Torah commands (ibid. 17:15). Why do we need a king? Aren't we the subjects of the King of kings? The Sfas Emes explains that before Rabban Yochanan ben Zakkai passed away, he blessed his disciples with the blessing that the fear of Heaven should be upon them like the fear of their fellow man. What was his message to his students? If you don't know how to accept the yoke of Heaven, you will learn how to do so by fearing man.

If you make your husband the king of your home, your children will follow your example, and they will also learn to crown Hashem as their King. They will learn from you what it means to give up your own wishes voluntarily in order to make another person happy. There is no greater lesson you can teach them.

In your home, you have the ability to be the judge and the officer; to preach with your mouth or teach with your actions. Which tool is more potent? The modeling, of course. What you do in reality is what will ultimately impress your values upon them. Even if you improve your mitzvah observance one tiny bit, even if you only change your attitude from cold to warm, they will notice. And they, too, will learn that change is possible, and very, very good.

Ad Derosh Achicha: Someone Is Waiting for You

In *Parashas Ki Seitzei*, we read that if a person finds an object that belongs to someone else, he has an obligation to keep it in his possession *ad derosh achicha oso* — "until your brother seeks it" (*Devarim* 22:2). Commenting on this verse, the Ohr HaChaim notes something profound. We are the lost objects of Hashem, he says. We went missing and Hashem is searching for us. It is as if Hashem is saying, "Where is he? Where is she?"

And what are the halachos of *hashavas aveidah*? The precise words of the Torah are *V'im lo karov achicha eilecha* — "And if your brother is not near you or you don't know him, then bring it [the lost object] inside your house, *ad derosh achicha oso*, until your brother seeks it" (ibid.). The commandment we receive in this passage is not only about mere possessions that somehow end up in our property. It's an obligation regarding the lost children of Hashem! If a child of Hashem, His precious possession, is not near Him, take him under your wing. Take the lost *neshamah* to a place where he will seek Hashem — *ad derosh achicha* — and where Hashem will find him.

The *beis midrash* isn't called a *"beis hadrush,"* a place where people seek Hashem, because it is primarily the place where Hashem is seeking His lost possessions. Take this lost soul to this holy place so Hashem can find him!

When Hashem sees His children gathered in the shul, even if they have no idea what the words of the *tefillos* mean, we cannot fathom the joy He feels. It is as if He is saying, "My child is here in My house!" Hashem looks through the windows, tells us the Ohr HaChaim, and He exclaims, "I knew I would find My *aveidah* here."

The month of Elul is the time of year when we all must seek Hashem. *Dirshu Hashem b'himatzo* — "Seek Hashem when He can be found" (*Yeshayahu* 55:6). This is the time when He is close to us, when we aren't far from where we belong.

When you say the words *Hashiveinu Avinu. . .Lefanecha...* — "Return us, our Father...to You..." in *Shemoneh Esrei*, do you really feel that longing to return to Hashem? You are the precious lost daughter for whom He's searching!

Why is this prayer so important? In the very next paragraph, we ask Hashem for forgiveness. *Selach lanu Avinu...* — "Forgive us, our Father..." We may wonder why we need two blessings in the Amidah dedicated to repentance. The Chida explains that *Selach Lanu Avinu* is the prayer we recite on behalf of ourselves. Who doesn't want a clean slate? The prayers that follow, the prayers about Yerushalayim, about health or peace or Mashiach — they are all requests we make on our own behalf. The only *tefillah* that is not for our sake, says the Chida, the only prayer that tears at the heart of Hashem, so to speak, is the *tefillah* of *Hashiveinu*. Hashem, I want to be close to You, we cry. Oh, how I miss You! Ribbono shel Olam, please return me to You. This is the one prayer where we beg Hashem that He should enjoy closeness to us.

When we say the words of this prayer with true concentration and we internalize its message, our repentance takes on a new level entirely. We realize that Someone is awaiting our return! Someone is seeking His lost possessions.

Do You Wait for Yours?

The path to true *teshuvah* stems from the realization that our Father in Heaven desperately awaits our return. This is the feeling that fills us with a desire to come closer to Him. It is also the feeling we must give to our precious children.

I once gave a lecture at a seminary specifically for girls who had been sent from one school to another. The principal told me about one master teacher on her staff who has the ability to talk even about lofty subjects and still keep the girls entranced. "I once peeked in while she was talking about the *Yamim Nora'im*, and I couldn't believe what I saw," she related. "They sat and listened to every word."

For starters, I asked the teacher how she got the girls to come to class on time. That in itself is no easy feat. And she answered, "I do something very simple. I don't focus on the girls who come late and what punishment to hand them. Instead, the attention is on the ones who come on time. They're the ones who receive coffee and fresh rugelach that I picked up from the bakery that morning."

The truth is that these girls can easily walk over to the nearest bakeshop and purchase the same fare for a few shekels. But it's not the same. It's not the coffee or the rugelach that we crave. It's the feeling that someone is waiting for us.

This is the feeling that changes every person. It's the knowledge that someone is waiting for me, whether it's when I come home from school or when I return to the Torah. I mean something to another being. And this is the feeling that fills us with a desire to get there.

Rav Yitzchok Shlomo Zilberman, a renowned *rav* in Jerusalem's

Jewish Quarter, hails from a family of eighteen children. All of them, one by one, are leaders, *rabbanim,* daughters married to *rabbanim,* the heads of beautiful families. When he was asked, "How did you all turn out like this?" he replied, "Do you want to know how? Our mother would wait for us every day. She wouldn't go to bed until the last of her children would walk through the door. Even in the late hours of the night, she would sit and wait with a cup of tea and some cake to ask about his or her day."

My heart bursts when I hear about this pious mother. She knew what was important in life! There is nothing more true than this: When a child knows that someone is waiting for him at home, he will find his way there.

What earns a woman merits? Not when she waits for the vacation to end. ("Are you sure you don't have school today? Maybe there's a mistake in the calendar!") The merits accumulate when you wait for them to *return.* Only when you tell your child, "I always wait for you to come home."

How do women merit raising righteous children? Not when their children sense the feeling of relief when school starts again.

So many sad jokes circulate during the season when school begins again.

A teacher called a father to say that his child is disturbing the class.

"Listen," she says, "your child is bothering us."

"When my son bothered me for two whole months," the father says angrily, "did I call you?"

When we say, *Hashiveinu Hashem eilecha,* we realize: We are not the children that our Father can't wait to get rid of. How He longs for our return! As long as we know that Hashem is desperate for our return, we are filled with a desire to do *teshuvah.* And as long as our children know how we await their return, they too will be filled with a true desire to bring us *nachas.*

The Power of Being Waited for

Parashas Ki Seitzei discusses the perplexing mitzvah of *shiluach hakein*, in which a mother bird is driven away from her egg-filled nest, which she had worked arduously to nurture. In the merit of fulfilling this commandment, says Rebbe Nachman of Breslov, Mashiach will arise from the place where he sits, which is called "Heichal Kan Tzippor."

When the mother is sent away, she flies to the heavens and prays for her children's well-being. How does this bring Mashiach closer? Let's think, dear women, what this mother bird does all the time that she's away from her children. All she does is wait for their return, for their reunion. And all these baby birds feel is that their mother is waiting for them somewhere, pining for them from the depths of her heart.

If there's anything that will bring Mashiach, it's our longing for him. *Af al pi sheyismamei'ha im kol zeh achakeh lo* — "Even though he may delay, we wait for him nevertheless," we say in the Thirteen Principles of Faith every morning.

Listen to this great story on the power of waiting: what the feeling of being waited for triggers in a person.

A pious man was once offered the rabbinate in a large city, and he declined the offer. "It's too much for me," he said. "Too much."

"But, Rebbe, 250 people are already waiting for you at the train station!"

"Are you serious?" asked the *rav*. He quickly packed his suitcase, and then he began to cry.

"Why are you crying?"

"Listen," he answered. "I didn't want to go to that city, but when I heard that people were waiting for me, I immediately packed to go. If we would truly wait for Mashiach," he cried, "even if he wouldn't want to come, do you think he wouldn't come?"

This is the power of knowing that someone is waiting for you. It brings you to do things you hadn't dreamed you were capable of.

I remember giving a *shiur* once when I was very tired. As I was speaking, my secretary kept gesturing for me to finish.

"What happened?" I asked her.

"We didn't remember that you were scheduled to speak somewhere else tonight," she said to me, "and we have to leave right now."

"I can't go to another lecture now," I protested. "My battery is going."

But then she said to me, "Right now, four hundred women are sitting in an auditorium and waiting for you." Suddenly, I was ready to run — because I was being waited for.

In the haftarah to *Parashas Ki Seitzei*, Hashem promises, *Nishbati miktzof alayich u'mig'ar bach* — "I promise," says Hashem, "that I will refrain from expressing fury and reprimanding you" (*Yeshayahu* 54:9). No matter what you've done, just return. The main thing is that you've come home, My daughter.

Every year, when I share the story of Rav Shalom Schwadron in the month of Elul, I'm overcome again with emotion. In the months following the Holocaust, Rav Shalom used to stand at the ports of Haifa and observe how the survivors would await the arrival of their loved ones. One woman, already old and tired, would stand there for consecutive days and nights, from sunrise to sunset, her eyes looking out at the sea. And every night, she would return home: today, too, he didn't turn up.

One day, after months of desperate waiting, a lone boat arrived. When it docked, a frail and haggard young boy stepped out. And this mother! Her shoulders, slouched for years, suddenly shot up, and he ran toward her. "Mamma, Mamma!"

She hugged him tightly. And then she said to him in Yiddish, "Don't talk now. The main thing is that you've arrived. The main thing is that you've arrived."

This is how Hashem feels about us, especially in the month

of Elul. Don't talk now, My child. Don't worry about what you've done. *Al tiruni she'ani shecharchores sheshzafasni hashamesh* — "Don't look at how black I've become because I was burned in the sun" (*Shir HaShirim* 1:6). Enough, My children, says Hashem. Just come home and all will be forgotten.

If only we could talk this way to all of Hashem's precious children! If only we could invite them home and promise that all will be forgotten. Dear women, every Jewish child — and, yes, every Jew — is so precious, so beautiful.

In my lectures, no matter who the audience is, be it religious or secular, I never request change. No Jewish man or woman has to *change* because our essence is so perfect. We merely have to bring that beauty to the fore. That's all!

Let us uncover the beauty in every Jewish child. Let us give our children the feeling that their home is the place where they are loved, where they are cherished, where they are waited for. And they will never forget their way home.

Advancing Toward Your Days

arashas *Ki Savo* opens with the words *V'hayah ki savo el ha'aretz asher Hashem Elokecha nosein lecha nachalah* — "And it will be when you enter the Land that Hashem, your G-d, gives you as an inheritance" (*Devarim* 26:1). What beautiful words! Hashem offered the nation the gift of a new land. But what must they do to receive it?

They must come.

The only thing we must do to accept Hashem's gifts is to come toward them. Can it be simpler than that? What do we ask for on Rosh Hashanah? We ask for another year, for a long life. In other words, we're begging to be *ba bayamim*, to "come" with our days.

But there's a secret, dear sisters, of how to become a woman of days, even in your youth. You don't have to be of an advanced age to truly be blessed with days. You simply have to become a person who advances toward your days. You have to be a "*ki savo*," someone who looks forward with excitement to every new day. This happens when you learn to truly appreciate the gift that every moment of time is, when you realize that this day in the calendar never was and will never repeat itself, not next year and not the year after.

This is precisely the wisdom we beg for when we say to Hashem, *Zachreinu l'chaim* — "Remember us for life." We are not only beseeching for physical life, but even more so for the ability to make each day alive. To *feel* the day.

"Just come," Hashem says to us. "I will give you the gifts. Are you coming?"

Let It Pour

Let's understand this phenomenon with a parable of a king who set up a most exquisite affair, but not one guest showed up. Toward the evening, several latecomers trickled in. How the king rejoiced with their attendance! If you've ever made a bar mitzvah or wedding (may you all merit this blessing soon), you know what it means to stand in an empty hall, all decked out and ready to celebrate, and the guests have not yet arrived. What anxiety! What will happen if no one shows up?

Our Sages tell us that this is Hashem in the month of Elul. He sets a magnificent table and waits for His precious children to come partake in the celebration. *Ki savo*, He pleads, just come and I will give you. And His promise is just so exhilarating. "If you come to My *simchah*," He says, "I will come to yours this coming year."

I receive many invitations to *simchahs*, and often I simply don't have the energy to attend. But then I think to myself, *That's not nice. She went out of her way to participate in my simchah — how can I not go to hers?*

Do you want to make a wedding this coming year? Do you want a bar mitzvah? A bris? Do you want *simchahs* in your home? Just attend Hashem's *simchah* — and He will make it happen by you. Hashem will remember that you did your part of the "*ki savo*," and He will bring the gift.

Where does Hashem's *simchah* take place? Where do you need to be to attend the affair? In the month of Elul, the Ari HaKadosh tells us thirteen faucets of mercy burst open on top of your head. The *yud gimmel middos* of *rachamim*, the thirteen attributes of mercy, come pouring down in torrents: *Hashem Hashem Keil rachum v'chanun erech apayim v'rav chesed ve'emes notzer chesed la'alafim nosei avon vafesha v'chata'ah v'nakeh* — "Hashem, Hashem, G-d, Compassionate and Gracious, Slow to Anger, and Abundant in Kindness and Truth; Preserver of Kindness for thousands of generations, Forgiver of Iniquity, Willful Sin, and Error, and Who Cleanses" (*Shemos* 34:6–7). It's a heavy downpour.

One day every summer, when all of our trip ideas are exhausted, we take the children to a park in Yerushalayim. The main attraction there is a water fountain that is set to erupt once every hour, sending gusts of water in every direction. It's such fun, if you're in the mood of getting wet. When I take the children there, I urge them to stand directly underneath the stream, while I make myself comfortable at a distance. While their clothes get soaked through, I feel a bit of refreshing mist on my skin. And as I stand there, I think, *This is what Elul must be like.*

Do we want to stand directly under the tap and become saturated with Hashem's mercy, or are we okay with our view from a distance?

Come, dear sisters. Don't stand on the side. Come under Hashem's faucet and allow your life to become saturated with blessing. How do you come toward Hashem? Bring Him into your life, at every moment. Make Hashem a real Presence in your home. *Yiddishkeit* should not be designated for specific times: for when you daven, for when the *chagim* come. *Yiddishkeit* should enjoy a vibrant, central place in your life. That's when you're coming toward Hashem.

The Extent of Hashem's Mercy

The haftaros in the weeks of the *shivah dinechemta*, the seven haftaros of consolation, are so thoroughly comforting, one by one. My husband once admitted to his *rav*, Rav Tzion Bracha, *zt"l*, that he didn't feel happy. The *rav* said to him, "If you look into the haftaros that are read between Tishah B'Av and Rosh Hashanah, it can't be that you won't feel saturated with joy and the sadness will leave you." Our Sages chose these haftaros carefully because they wanted them to serve as a balm for even the saddest soul.

What is the profound comfort in the haftarah to *Parashas Ki Savo? Kumi ori ki ba oreich* — "Arise! Shine! For your light has arrived" (*Yeshayahu* 60:1). Come, My daughter, come already, Hashem begs.

And what happens if you don't come? *Ki yeihafeich ala-yich hamon yam cheil goyim yavo'u lach* — "The waves of the ocean will advance toward you; the troops of the nations will come toward you" (ibid. 60:5).

The Midrash explains that if a person doesn't come toward the ocean, the ocean of mercy will come toward him. What a comfort!

While we're on vacation, the children always scream at me from the water. "Ima, come! We're waiting for you!" They want me to come inside and get wet with them, but I'm in my heels and my hat and…my *Chumash*. So what do they do to drag me in? They spray some water at me. The ocean comes toward me. And then my daughter says to them, "Now just wait. In another minute, Ima will put on her rubber shoes and join us."

Dear sisters, enter the ocean of mercy. And even if you don't, it will come toward you. That's our loving Father's approach.

It's All About the Heart

True *teshuvah* occurs when a change of heart takes place. *U'mal Hashem Elokecha es levavcha* — "Hashem, your G-d, will circumcise your heart" (*Devarim* 30:6) is *teshuvah's* famous reference. It is a pure heart that we beg Hashem to grant us when we cry, *Lev tahor b'ra li Elokim v'ruach nachon chadeish b'kirbi* — "Create a pure heart for me, G-d, and a steadfast spirit renew within me" (*Tehillim* 51:12).

Parashas Ki Savo contains many references to the heart, the organ that gives us the capacity to feel, to express, to make a difference.

First, all curses are caused, G-d forbid, because of the absence of heart: *tachas asher lo avadeta es Hashem Elokecha b'simchah u'vetuv leivav meirov kol* — "because you did not serve Hashem, your G-d, amid gladness and goodness of heart, even when everything was abundant" (*Devarim* 28:47). "Where is the reciprocation?" asks Hashem. "I gave you everything, but you didn't see it as everything."

In another passage in *Parashas Ki Savo*, Moshe Rabbeinu says, *V'lo nasan Hashem lachem lev* — "Hashem did not give you a heart" (ibid. 29:3). For forty years, Moshe Rabbeinu cried to the nation, "I led you through the Wilderness and fulfilled your every request. Every time you sinned, I turned to Hashem and pleaded for forgiveness on your behalf. And every time I begged, Hashem asked me, 'Moshe, what do you prefer? That I forgive you and allow you to enter Eretz Yisrael but the nation dies in the Wilderness, or that I don't forgive you and the nation of Yisrael lives forever? You choose.' And I performed the ultimate sacrifice and surrendered my opportunity to enter the Land I love. 'May Moshe die and a hundred like him, but a nail of *Am Yisrael's* hands should not be damaged,' I said. And Hashem saved you time and again."

What is Moshe's cry all about? "I've begged on your behalf for forty years, and you don't have a heart to pray for me?" What a sad cry! When their leader needed them most, the nation did not reciprocate. One man was able to save 600,000, but 600,000 did not do their duty to save him, explains the Midrash (*Midrash Rabbah, Devarim* 7:10).

HaKadosh Baruch Hu does so much for us, dear sisters. Every breath we take, every step we make: it's all Him. And let's not talk about the *gifts*. The many, many gifts He throws our way. Where is the heart: the heart that should welcome Him in and make Him the most comfortable place? Oh, Hashem — how can I ever make You a nice-enough guest room?

Only with this realization will you be bestowed with the ability to appreciate your every day. It is this awareness that will make your days count. Otherwise, life becomes a row of pages in the calendar, one after the next after the next. You may be asking Hashem for this blessed awareness, but what are you doing to make it happen? The more you learn to appreciate the "small" favors He performs on your behalf, the more you will become a woman with a heart. And the more you will "advance" toward your days.

How to Crown a King

arashas Nitzavim is always read immediately before Rosh Hashanah. This Torah portion opens with Moshe's words to the nation, *Atem nitzavim hayom kulchem lifnei Hashem* — "You are standing today, all of you, before Hashem" (*Devarim* 29:9). Commenting on the word *atem*, the Rebbe of Slonim writes that it is an acronym for the request *Al tashlicheinu milfanecha* — "Please don't throw us away from before You," which we beg of Hashem during the fateful day. But how can we ensure that this prayer will be fulfilled?

The Rebbe says, make sure that you're standing together. Make sure that you're one nation before Hashem. When we come before the heavenly throne on the first day of the year, pleading for blessings, we must remember this: when we stand together, we merit Hashem's Presence in our lives.

Parashas Nitzavim contains many references to *teshuvah*. *Hanistaros laShem Elokeinu* (ibid. 29:28) — the hidden sins are for Hashem, Moshe reminds us. We can't hide our wrongdoings from the Master of the world, and Rosh Hashanah is the time to clean up the mess. *V'shavta ad Hashem Elokecha* — "And you will return to Hashem, your G-d" (ibid. 30:2) — is yet another allusion to Rosh Hashanah. Let us understand what this exalted day is all about.

The Meaning of True Prayer

We have always known that Rosh Hashanah has something to do with *hamlachas Hashem*, crowning Hashem as our King, but what does that mean?

On the first day of Rosh Hashanah we read a story from the Torah, and on the second day we read another quite similar one. In the first story, the son of Avraham and Hagar, Yishmael, is about to die of thirst. Both mother and son cry desperately to Hashem, begging for a miracle. Suddenly, an angel says to Hagar, "Don't worry. He will live." And, indeed, the child survives.

In the second story we read on Rosh Hashanah, we are again reading about a son of Avraham. This time it is the son of Sarah, Yitzchak, who is also about to die, bound on the *mizbei'ach*, his father holding the knife over his neck. Suddenly, an angel comes to Avraham and says, *Al tishlach yadcha el hana'ar* — "Do not stretch out your hand against the lad [to slay]" (*Bereishis* 22:12). And, again, the child lives.

Both stories have similar plots: both involve sons of Avraham who are about to die but are then suddenly saved by the words of a merciful angel. However, in the first story, Hagar and Yishmael daven and Hashem listens. In the second tale, Avraham doesn't daven, and neither does Yitzchak. Hashem Himself is the One to make a request from the *malach*, and the angel listens.

Throughout Rosh Hashanah, we repeatedly mention the coronation of the King, which requires our complete and utter acceptance of His will. The *Akeidah* is all about this: *Hashem says, and I obey*. It is not *I say, and Hashem obeys*. That's the way of Hagar, the way of Yishmael.

A woman once said to me, "I married off three of my children in one year. Do you know how it happened? *Tefillah. Tefillah.*

Tefillah. Every morning for one year I was at the Kosel for Shacharis. I was by Kever Rachel every week. And every month I was by Rabbi Shimon bar Yochai."

Is this what *tefillah* is all about? I fax in my request, Hashem, and You obey my orders. Of course not!

Yes, dear women, turn your hearts to Hashem in *tefillah.* But those words of prayer should not be a shopping list, and you should not look at your Creator as if He were an ATM machine: pop in the card, get out the cash. He is your King, and He will lead you where you must be.

What Is Your *Akeidah*?

Crowning Hashem means that I acknowledge that Hashem is *molich,* He rules. He carries me on His shoulders and leads me in the direction that He deems good for me. I may not like what I see, I may not appreciate the scenes that unfold during this journey, but this is the true meaning of crowning Him as my King.

What better day than Rosh Hashanah to accomplish this glorious feat? At the start of the new year, when we are yet unaware of what the next twelve months will bring, there is no more important focus than *kabbalas malchus Shamayim,* accepting the kingship of Hashem. It is only with this mind-set that a Jew can carry through, no matter how painful the challenges that may befall him: Hashem says, and I obey.

If we take a look at the name Yishmael, the son in the first story, we find the roots *yishma Keil.* Yishmael's mentality is to say to Hashem, "I daven, and You listen to me now." On the other hand, the name of the father of *our* nation, Yisrael, is comprised of the roots, *yashar Keil,* "Hashem is just." As Jews, we accept that whatever Hashem, our King, decides to do for us is for our good, even when our human eyes do not see it as such.

The chapter of *Akeidas Yitzchak* starts off with Hashem's

request to Avraham in which He tells him, *Kach na es bincha es yechidcha asher ahavta...* — "Please take your son, your only son, the one you love..." (*Bereishis* 22:2). When the chapter ends, however, Hashem refers to Yitzchak only with the words "your only son" (ibid 22:16). Where's the description "the one you love"? Why didn't Hashem mention this once again? The Shelah HaKadosh says, it is because Hashem now says to Avraham, "Now, after you were ready to bring your beloved as a sacrifice to Me, I see that you love Me more than you love him."

The Shelah HaKadosh says something beautiful on this topic. On Rosh Hashanah, he advises, every Yid should come to shul for *tekias shofar* with one *akeidah* that he sacrificed in the past year. What did you give up this year because you love Hashem more than you love yourself? That's your true *akeidah*, the greatest merit to your name as you stand before a brand-new year. Think of this before you enter the shul at the start of one of the holiest moments of the year.

Our Sages tell us that when Yitzchak lay before his father on the altar, his concern was "What will you tell Ima after you sacrifice me?" And Avraham answered him, "The One Who helped us before you were born, when we waited for years and years for a child, He will help us through this." Avraham's answer teaches us that the patience it takes to wait for a miracle, to wait for something we feel we can't live without, can be even harder than missing something we've lost. However, a Jew who crowns Hashem as our forefather Avraham did understands that through it all, it is He Who is guiding us.

While Hagar calls the place where her prayers were answered, "Be'er Lachai Ro'i," Avraham calls the mountain on which the *Akeidah* occurred, "Hashem Yireh." The contrast between their relationship with Hashem is clear in these two names: *ro'i* implies, "Hashem, see me *now*," but Hashem Yireh refers to a time in the *future* when we will see. That's *akeidah*: to have faith in Hashem and show Him that we await our salvation patiently.

The true crowning of the King occurs only when we bring a

true *akeidah;* when we choose to love Hashem more than anything else in the world, and there is no greater *avodah* for us on Rosh Hashanah than to focus on achieving this lofty goal.

Achos Ketanah:
The Power of a Mother's Cry

During the last hour before the final sun of the year sets, we recite the poetic words of a most beautiful song in our liturgy, *"Achos Ketanah."* Penned by the master liturgist Rav Avraham Hazan Gerondi of Spain, each clause (except the last one) in this *piyut* ends with the words *Tichleh shanah v'kiloseha* — "May the year and its accompanying curses end."

Who is the *achos ketanah*, the little sister, who is standing and davening for the *geulah* that Rav Gerondi alludes to in his piece? It is our mother Rachel. Why does he mention her now, as we stand at the threshold of the brand-new year? Because our Ima Rachel doesn't daven with words anymore; after so many years of waiting and waiting, after so many *akeidos* that she's sacrificed, she has no words left: only a voice. *Kol b'ramah nishma:* only her voice is heard, like the wordless voice of the shofar. Why doesn't she say anything? Why don't *we* say anything when the shofar is heard?

The Ba'al Shem Tov explains the answer with a parable of the king's children who are lost for many years in a vast forest. At first, they scream to him, "Father, Father, please save us!" But he doesn't answer. Finally, after years of fruitless requests, one of the sons says to his brothers, "I know why he's not answering us. We don't remember his language anymore! Let's shout wordlessly until he finds us."

The Ba'al Shem Tov says: Sadly, we've forgotten the language of our Father. We've sullied our mouth to the extent that it cannot speak the holy language that the Ribbono shel Olam knows.

Only the mere voice of the shofar, the voice of Rachel's cries, can still save us. The voice of the shofar is the voice of all the desperate women in *Klal Yisrael*, who, like our Ima Rachel, are waiting for their redemptions.

The Midrash (*Midrash Agaddah, Vayeira* 22:10) tells us something so beautiful about Sarah's passing. At the moment when Avraham was about to slaughter Yitzchak, the Satan approached Sarah and asked her, "Where is your son?" to which she answered, "He's learning in the yeshivah." The Satan then told her, "You poor woman, your husband took your son to the high hills and put a large knife over his throat." At that moment, Sarah emitted a visceral scream, "Nooo!" This corresponds to the flat sound of the *tekiah*.

Then she broke down and cried. This, the *Shibbolei HaLeket* (Rosh Hashanah 298) writes, corresponds to the shattered sound of the *shevarim*.

She then screamed again: "Nooo!" once again, another long *tekiah*, and then her heart gave out.

The *kol shofar* is the cry of all the mothers from all generations. It is the cry of all Jewish women who are *akudim*, bound to HaKadosh Baruch Hu, even as they wait. It is a moment of maternal anguish and tears.

"Sarah, why didn't you wait?" asks Rav Klonimus Kalman Shapira, the Rebbe of Piaseczna, who served as a spiritual guide to many during the anguished time of the Holocaust and author of *Chovas HaTalmidim*. "If you'd have waited just another moment, you'd have heard the Satan's next words: that Yitzchak was ultimately spared."

His illuminating answer teaches us a most inspiring lesson about our selfless mother Sarah. Sarah was a prophetess, he says, and so she knew that her son would live. However, she wanted her cries to serve as a message to Hashem on behalf of all future generations: "Even if my son will eventually return, even if this Holocaust will ultimately end, even if this woman's cancer will be healed after years of treatment, we *can't* wait!

We mothers don't have the *ko'ach* for this. Even if we know that *yashar Keil*, Hashem's ways are just, even as we wait with *emunah* for that *shidduch*, that child, the return of a wayward son, it's just too hard for us, Ribbono shel Olam. Please bring us the final *geulah* already."

Imagine! This was our mother Sarah's selfless focus during those painful moments. She sacrificed her life in her hopes to spare the anguish of all future mothers.

The Ari HaKadosh tells us that although most *poskim* say that it's forbidden to cry on Rosh Hashanah (we are meant to tremble with joy — *gilu bir'adah*), for those who cry during *tekias shofar* it's a sign that they possess a holy soul. *Tekias shofar* is a time of crying; it is the collective voice of all of our cries for generations.

Also, says the Ari HaKadosh, if a Jew suddenly feels the urge to cry on Rosh Hashanah, he should allow his tears to flow freely during those few moments of inspiration, for this urge is a sign that he is being judged at that very moment, and it is therefore the opportune time for him to repent with his whole heart.

What does Hashem do when He hears our cries? We find the answer in *Parashas Nitzavim. Im yihyeh nidachacha biktzeih hashamayim misham yekabetzcha Hashem Elokecha u'misham yikachecha* — "If your dispersed ones will be at the ends of the heavens, from there Hashem, your G-d, will gather you in and from there He will take you" (*Devarim* 30:4). Rashi (ibid. 30:3) notes something utterly moving on this verse. Hashem will gather every single Jew, he says, one by one. He will gather up the broken hearts, the shattered souls, and bring us out of exile.

Dear Jewish woman, when you stand in shul during the *tekiahs*, remember that this is the time for you to cry: a wordless cry like the *kol b'ramah* of our mother Rachel, like the piercing cries of our mother Sarah. It is the moment when all human voices penetrate the skies.

In the merit of our good deeds, of our desire to be the best we can be, may we be *zocheh* to hear the shofar of Mashiach, and may we shed only tears of utter happiness.

Inscribe Yourself in the Book of Really Living

During the time that *Parashas Vayeilech* is read, we're slowly, slowly entering new territory, the new year. What does a sweet year look like? Let's look into the Torah portion to find our answer.

Unfortunately, we have lived to see the words that Hashem foretells in *Parashas Vayeilech*. What will happen when the Jews will turn away from Him? *V'anochi hasteir astir es panai* — "I will conceal My face" (*Devarim* 31:18). How frightening! The Rebbe Reb Bunim of Peshischa comments that the sin in this verse is that the Jews state that Hashem is not among them. There is no such thing, says the Rebbe, no such thing at all. Although we may not always see His Presence, Hashem is always there; He is only concealed by a mask created by our sins.

No Jew, dear women, ever has the right to feel that Hashem has deserted her. A sweet new year is a year in which we acknowledge Hashem's Presence, a year in which we bring Him into our lives. There can be no greater joy than a spiritual life, a life of connection.

We've heard countless stories of men and women who have suffered through the greatest of tragedies. Parents who lost children, people who lost entire families in pogroms, in the Holocaust, in terrorist attacks. We've heard of women who longed for children, women who longed for a *shidduch*, women who yearned for *nachas*. We've heard it all. But despite the excruciating pain that may have seared their hearts and given them no rest, when these Jews were connected to Hashem, they merited leading lives of sweetness, lives of true peace. This is the year we want for ourselves, dear women. A year that will bring us closer to Hashem, regardless of how He chooses to try us.

A Matter of Perspective

Rebbe Yisrael of Rizhin offers a stunning commentary on the words *Rosh Hashanah*. The *shanah*, year, follows according to the *rosh*, the head, he says. It's all in your head. You have the power to shape this year based on the *ko'ach* of your mind.

"And the Jew," he continues in his enlightening discourse, "who merits sanctifying his first thought as soon as he enters the holy day will have a smooth year all year long. He will remain connected to that first *machshavah* that entire year."

All of the *shiurim* you heard or read during the month of Elul, all of the *Selichos* you recited — they are all a preparation for this very moment, the first second of Rosh Hashanah. What power that moment holds!

So what should you think about at that opportune time? Rebbe Yisrael provides us with the answer. "At the time that the *chag* begins, a person must think that he is being inscribed in the Book of Life. If he thinks at that very first moment that he relies entirely on Hashem and that he sincerely wants to do a full *teshuvah*, he will be inscribed in the Book of Life."

You yourself, dear women, have the ability to inscribe yourself in the Book of Life! In simple language, this is what you should think at the very start of this holy day: This year, I will live, and I will not do any deed that takes away from a good life: no *lashon hara*, and no relationships that aren't good for me (or any other sin that has become second nature to you). I'm going to really live."

Why is that very moment so auspicious in setting the tone for the entire year? Rebbe Yisrael explains the reason beautifully. This is the moment when you light the candles on Rosh Hashanah. On the very first Rosh Hashanah in this world, there was a woman who lit up the world with her candles. Then she sullied her soul by performing the first sin. Because of Chavah's wrongdoing, death was decreed on every future being. *Ner Hashem nishmas adam* — "The soul of man is Hashem's candle" (*Mishlei* 20:27). From then on, every flame would eventually be extinguished. When we light the candles for Rosh Hashanah, we rectify Chavah's sin and we light up the world once again.

What happened when Chavah transgressed Hashem's command? In her mind, she doubted the value of life. She said to herself, "I'm not certain that I'll die if I eat from the *eitz hada'as*. And if I die, so what? It's worth it for me to try." *Oy*, Chavah! Because she questioned the infinite value of life, Rebbe Yisrael teaches, she blew out her candle.

Do You Want to Really Live?

My daughter read a fascinating book on the Holocaust, and she shared what she read in one chapter with me. She said that on the Yom Kippur after the Holocaust, the Rebbe of Klausenberg stood, surrounded by a crowd of survivors, and together, they said the *vidui*.

"*Ashamnu*, we're guilty," said the Rebbe, "but did we do anything that made us so guilty? *Bagadnu* — whom were we able to rebel against in the Holocaust? *Gazalnu* — but did we have what to steal? *Dibarnu dofi* — but we didn't have *ko'ach* to speak *lashon hara!*" When the Rebbe reached the confession of *Latznu*, he closed his *machzor* and turned to the crowd.

"The *vidui*," he said, "is not for us. But there is one confession that we must make to the Ribbono shel Olam. We are guilty, because on many mornings we woke up and wished to die. *Bagadnu*, we rebelled, because we didn't want to say, 'Modeh Ani.' We didn't want to thank Him for another day. *Dibarnu dofi*, we spoke untruth when we said, '*Elokai neshamah shenasata bi*,' because we so wanted Hashem to take our precious soul from us. We're sorry, Hashem, that we didn't value enough the gift that we call Life."

Oh, how we need to treasure life, dear women! The fact that we are around for another Rosh Hashanah — what a blessing. If you enter Rosh Hashanah with this mind-set, with a profound appreciation for the gift of life, and you say at that very moment, "Ribbono shel Olam, I want life!" you will live.

When you stand at the Rosh Hashanah candles, dear women, remember the power of your thoughts. We learn just how important they are from the famous story of Rav Ami. The Sage once said, "Whoever wants to know if he will live that year, should light a candle on Rosh Hashanah. If the candle lights up as it should, he will live. And if not..." (*Horayos* 12a). It's not the candle that determines whether or not a person will be inscribed in the Book of Life. It's the prayer to Hashem that He should bring light into our life (see *Maharsha* there).

Before Rosh Hashanah, which is also called Yom HaZikaron, I usually deliver a *shiur* to mothers who lost their children in battle. I tell them, "Dear mothers, who if not you knows what 'Yom HaZikaron' means? I don't have to explain what happens in that moment of silence, in Israel on Remembrance Day (known as Yom HaZikaron). When people hear the siren, they remember their fallen child and they think, *How tragic! So much could have become of him, but he will always remain twenty years old.*"

On Rosh Hashanah, on this Yom HaZikaron, we gather to hear the call of the shofar, the siren that wakes up the heart. And we think to ourselves, *How tragic! How much potential was wasted. So much could have become of this year, and now it's over.*

But Rosh Hashanah isn't only Yom HaZikaron. It is also *hayom haras olam* — a day of conception. It heralds a new opportunity, pregnant with hope and blessings. It is the day on which we remind ourselves of the famous saying of Rav Yisrael Salanter that he learned from a cobbler who worked late into the night: *Kol zeman shehaneir doleik efshar od l'sakein* — "As long as the candle burns, it is still possible for us to repair."

To the mothers of the fallen children I say, "Every woman in this room knows what it means to mourn. But every woman in this room also knows what it means to give birth. Rosh Hashanah is a culmination of both."

This is the power of Rosh Hashanah. Hold on to it, my friends, and remind yourself of the opportunity that lies before you. Want to live, want to make life a rich, spiritual experience of connection to the truth that your soul seeks, and you will be blessed with a beautiful year.

And the Children

It is not enough, dear Jewish mothers, to have a clear perspective in your own mind. As an *eim b'Yisrael*, you were tasked with the holy role of transmitting this clarity to your precious children. Who was present during *Hakheil*, the gathering that Moshe speaks of in *Parashas Vayeilech*? Once every seven years, on the first day of *chol hamo'ed Succos* that followed *shemittah*, the entire nation was commanded to come together at the Temple to listen to the king read from *Sefer Devarim*. Not only were the men and women commanded to attend, but they were to bring their children (*Devarim* 31:12).

What was the purpose of including the children in this command? Rashi, echoing our Sages (*Chagigah* 3a), explains that the children were present in order to give reward to those who brought them.

Our Sages expound on this commandment that signifies the importance of *chinuch*. The time to inculcate values in your children, dear mothers, is in their earliest youth. We read in the *Talmud Yerushalmi* (*Yevamos* 1:6) of the mother of Rabbi Yehoshua ben Chananyah. She used to bring his cradle to the study hall so he could absorb the sounds of Torah study from infancy. What greater way to demonstrate what is important to you? If you start transmitting your values to your children when their minds are young and open, you leave them with indelible imprints for life. You teach them that you care more about your connection to Hashem than the color of their hairbands.

Closeness to Hashem is not a matter of the words you say. It is a reality that your children can touch with their own fingers. It is their understanding that you are leading a life of focus.

Especially during the times of year when the pressure is on, when you spend days and evenings in the company of family and friends, your children's antennae are alert. Does Mommy care about the stain on my new dress or about the atmosphere in the home? Is the texture of the meat more important than the feelings of her loved ones? It is then that they pick up what's important to you, dear mothers. Give them the message that you know is the truth.

Moshe's Song

In this *parashah*, Moshe chants a song and asks the heavens and earth to witness what he says. On his deathbed, he calls them to bear witness to the calamities that will befall the nation if it sins and the ultimate joy that will come at the final redemption. What beautiful words he sings, but also what frightening words he sings!

The nation, Moshe was telling them, will always have the choice between the two realities he poetically described. Will we want to live in peace or at war? Will we want vengeance and retribution or rewards and closeness? The beautiful conclusion of the song, however, teaches us a powerful lesson, dear women. Toward the end, Moshe speaks of the closeness we will enjoy with Hashem. He does not mention repentance as a condition. Despite the nation's rebellion against the G-d Who gave us so much, we will merit to be reunited when the time comes. What a comfort! Though we have gone far away and we think we're lost, we did not sever the deep relationship we have with our Father in Heaven.

In the End, Hashem's Will Triumphs

After Moshe finished his song, Hashem requested Moshe to take the fateful steps toward his final resting place. The verse reads, "Hashem spoke to Moshe *b'etzem hayom hazeh*, on that very day, saying, 'Ascend to this mountain...Mount Nevo...and see the Land of Canaan that I will give to the Children of Israel as an inheritance, and die on the mountain where you will ascend...'" (*Devarim* 32:49–50). Where else does the Torah use the expression *b'etzem hayom hazeh*, in broad daylight?

Rashi (to ibid. 32:48) cites two other places in the Torah and the identical message we cull from each one is so profound. In all three places, throngs of people were determined to prevent Hashem's word from being carried out, so He ordered that it be done "at high noon," in view of everyone, so they would all see that nothing stands in the way of Hashem's will.

We find the first usage of this term when Noach's compatriots were determined to prevent him from entering the ark. For 120 years, they didn't lend an ear to Noach's pleas, but when reality hit, it was too late (*Bereishis* 7:13). The Egyptians, too, got their fair share of warnings. How many more times could Hashem threaten them about the consequences of their evil deeds? Only when the Jewish nation was finally extricated from Egypt at high noon (*Shemos* 12:51) did they realize Who they were up against: a G-d Whose will would ultimately triumph.

In *Parashas Ha'azinu*, too, the Jewish people were distraught that their devoted leader would be taken from them. They said, "If we sense that he is about to die, we will prevent his death!" They would do everything they could to keep him from ascending Har Nevo, but Hashem commanded him to go up publicly, to show that no one could prevent it.

Until high noon, dear sisters, we have a chance to do everything we can. But when Hashem decides that it's over, nothing can stand in the way of His will. It's too late. Even in broad daylight, despite the opposition of the masses, Hashem can remove an entire nation from exile. Even in broad daylight, He can perform the miracles that He sees fit.

Where else do we find the expression "at high noon" in the Torah? When it speaks of the holiest day of the year, Yom Kippur. Dear sisters, we have until this sacred day to do our duties, to scrub the insides of our hearts until they glisten. And then, when we stand before Hashem on this holiest of days, what is left for us to do? To simply acknowledge that it is Hashem's will that will ultimately prevail.

This knowledge is deeply comforting, but it also places the heavy responsibility of *teshuvah* on our shoulders. Please, dear Jewish women, don't wait for the last minute to clear the accounts, to ask for forgiveness, to make amends. Live every day as if it were *erev Yom Kippur* so that when "high noon" comes around, you will not have to shake your head sadly, thinking that it is too late. Do it for yourself, dear sister. Do it for your soul.

Forgiveness: Can It Really Happen?

To ask for forgiveness is an action that we do for ourselves. Imagine that you have a bag of trash on your back, and when you ask for forgiveness you're getting rid of it. "Take this. I'm free!" Amazing. You've made yourself a woman who has been cleansed.

This happens to me every year. "Rabbanit, I must ask you for forgiveness," young women say to me before Yom Kippur.

"Why? What happened?" I'm curious.

"I said some derogatory things about you this year. I must stop this, but it's not easy. Do you forgive me?"

"Yes," I say with a heavy heart.

"No, you have to say it three times."

"Yes, yes, yes."

Asking for *mechilah* is not the hard part, dear women.

But to forgive is not easy. That's the hard part. And we can't enter Yom Kippur if we haven't forgiven. Hashem can't shower you with blessings if you're bearing a grudge because He must forgive you first. How can He forgive you if you haven't done the same?

So how can we forgive?

Really, says the Malbim, a human being is not capable of forgiving. It's simply a Divine strength that we do not possess: to wipe away a pain that stings the heart and pretend that it never happened.

If so, what does forgiveness mean to us? What are we meant to do in preparation for the holiest day of the year?

HaKadosh Baruch Hu, our merciful Father, is only requesting that we do something human; something that may not be easy, but it is a human ability nevertheless. Hashem is asking us to be *dan lechaf zechus*, to judge people favorably. Does that mean that we should see the bad as good? No. We're smarter than that, and Hashem appreciates that we know the difference between *chaim* and *maves*, between *tov* and *ra* — between life and death, goodness and evil. He doesn't want us to *ignore* the bad that occurred, only to put the good on one *kaf*, on one side of the scale, and the bad on the other, and allow the scale to be weighed down on the good side.

The *mazel* of Tishrei is a scale, rendering it a significant part of this month's work. While HaKadosh Baruch Hu performs the weighing in *Shamayim* to determine what kind of year awaits you, there's work for you on your own scale. It's our duty to decide that we will make the good in our lives outweigh the bad. As the Ba'al Shem Tov said so beautifully, we cannot judge the bad in itself favorably, but we could judge the event *as a whole* to the good.

When a woman divorces her abusive husband, of course she can't judge him favorably. He destroyed her life and her self-esteem! However, if she places the beautiful children the marriage produced on the other side of the balance, and she adds all the lessons learned, the friends she made, the closeness to Hashem she gained, the *kaf*, the scale's pan, of merit and goodness will surely weigh more than the evil.

Disease and death and divorce are not good. They are not meant to be. But it is our obligation to look at the entire picture and focus on the *tov*, to fill that side of the scale until it tips.

I couldn't judge favorably the broken heart my son was born with — the one from which he ultimately died — but I am able to judge favorably the gifts that accompanied this *nisayon*: I discovered *tefillah* I never knew I was capable of, and I gained the ability to understand others who are heartbroken as well. Because I understand what it means to have a broken heart, I can now serve as the *shaliach* to provide comfort to broken young women. I know how hard it is to wake up in the morning, to get dressed, to smile, to work, to come to shul for yet another Yom Kippur with only hope and no joy.

When my son was in the hospital, the doctors taped an apparatus around his finger to measure his oxygen levels. The digits would move up and down, up and down. How hard it was for him to breathe! Today, when I see a woman with a broken heart, I hold her hand and I feel the hardship, the pain of taking each breath. And, oh, how I appreciate her every effort despite the anguish.

I know this well. For months, my baby son wanted to get rid of the thing we call life. To him, it was all about pipes and injections and more pricks. And I knew that he was breathing for Ima, so that he wouldn't cause her any pain. When I once shared this thought at a *shiur*, a woman came over to me with a photo of her handicapped daughter who'd endured a serious traffic accident years before. She said to me, "I know that she's living for me. If it would've been up to her, she would have long been gone."

Countless students say to me, "Yemima, I'll be okay. I want to get married so my mother will finally be happy in the end. So my mother will finally have *nachas*."

Dear Jewish mothers, do you realize what your children are

doing to make you happy? The difficulty they may cause is only one side of the scale. Our sons and daughters who find it hard to breathe take every breath only for their *ima*. How much blessing there is in that!

The Most Beautiful Song

I want to share with you one of the most famous lessons from Rebbe Nachman of Breslov, which is so appropriate for us to internalize at this time of year. In the *devar Torah* so aptly named "*Azamrah*," Rebbe Nachman says that every person is required to find the little dots within him and others in order to create the beautiful music of *tefillah*. What does he mean by that? On Yom Kippur, he says, the *sheliach tzibbur* we choose to represent us must be someone who's an artist at loving people. He must be someone who sees the good in those around him, who believes that there's no such thing as a bad sound.

If we look at the parts of music— do, rei, me, etc.— can we say that one sound is beautiful or bad? Obviously not. The effects of those short dots of music depend entirely on where they're placed. So, too, the *sheliach tzibbur* should be someone who looks at those around him and says, "This spiritually deficient person only highlights the beautiful voice of the one standing near him. Together, we are all beautiful." In order to create magical music, we need all different kinds of sounds: the low, the high, the deep, the soft.

What does Rebbe Nachman want to convey with this deep thought? *Teshuvah* and forgiveness is all about putting the dots in the right place. The actual occurrence may have been terrible, it may have caused you such pain and suffering, but if you connect the dots to the larger picture, you understand that it had a purpose, and only then can you forgive. Judging favorably is not about confusing the good with the bad; it's about choosing to focus on the good only.

Kol hama'avir al middosav ma'avirin lo al kol pesha'av (Rosh Hashanah 17a). Our Sages teach us that one who is *mevater* will be forgiven of all his sins. The commentators offer a beautiful interpretation of this verse. They note that *middah* can also mean "measuring stick." If a person finds the strength within to give up on this measuring stick, to stop looking for the things that bother her in others, Hashem will gift her with a clean slate. What a blessing! Stop trying to find the reasons as to why you're correct and he's wrong. Stop measuring how much you're doing and how little she is contributing. Give up that measuring stick, dear women, and you will merit true forgiveness from Hashem.

Rebbe Nachman of Breslov instructs us to perform a beautiful deed on Yom Kippur. He says that when you, dear Jewish woman, stand in shul and listen as the *sheliach tzibbur* sings the soul-stirring *niggunim* of the *tefillah*, when he cries out the words of *U'Nesaneh Tokef*, all you should ask for is this: "Ribbono shel Olam, *please* give me the capacity to place the events in my life in their proper perspective. Please give me the strength to get rid of my measuring stick. Guide me toward creating a one long, beautiful melody of forgiveness."

That's what Hashem expects of us: to truly understand that the evil we see is only part of one magnificent masterpiece. Just like there are various *tekios*, our lives take us through several phases. At first, we hear the long, smooth sound of the *tekiah;* everything seems so full of hope. Then the *shevarim* come our way; the broken sounds of sadness and anguish. But what follows only adds to the choir of perfection; at the end, we will hear the sweetest sound of all, the *tekiah gedolah* of Mashiach.

May we merit seeing only beauty in our lives, in ourselves, and in others, and in this merit may we very soon greet Mashiach all together, as one nation.

Want a *Yeshuah*?
Ask for It Now!

hat final message do I want to leave you with as we finish the entire *Chumash*, soon to start anew? What message does the Torah leave us with? Let's talk about some of the very powerful ones that the Midrash shares with us at the close of *Sefer Devarim*.

When Moshe Rabbeinu learned that his days were coming to an end, he was filled with an intense desire to live. How he wanted to serve Hashem one more day! How he wanted to lead the nation! So why couldn't he succeed in achieving his dream? The Midrash teaches us something profoundly enlightening.

"Ten deaths were ascribed to Moshe," tells us the Midrash (*Midrash Rabbah, Devarim* 11:10). We find ten references to Moshe's imminent death in the Torah. *Karvu yamecha lamus* — "Your days are numbered" (*Devarim* 31:14) and *Ki anochi meis* — "Soon I will die" (ibid. 4:22) are two. These references, the Midrash teaches, are signs that nine times Moshe Rabbeinu was successful in deferring the decree. Only the tenth time he failed.

Why? How did the decree ultimately catch up with him? The answer brings tears to my eyes. Moshe Rabbeinu said, "So many times I've annulled decrees issued against the nation. So many times Hashem wanted to destroy them and I saved them. If so, when the time will come to enter Eretz Yisrael, I, who have never sinned in my life, will pray on my behalf, and the verdict will be overturned in my favor."

The illuminating Midrash tells us that as soon as HaKadosh Baruch Hu saw that Moshe Rabbeinu did not take the decree seriously and intended to postpone his *tefillah* for a later time, He sprang upon him and promised with His holy Name that Moshe would not merit crossing the Jordan River.

What a Midrash! Hashem said to Moshe, "Do you think that this is how it works? That you can postpone a *tefillah*? Now you will learn that it's not so. You will not enter Eretz Yisrael."

The Midrash ends with words of caution to us, dear Jewish women. At the moment a desire awakens in your heart, whether you want to get married, see *nachas* from your child, have *parnassah*, get thin, or get rich, stop at that very second and translate your desire into a prayer. Don't lose that opportunity! David HaMelech says, *Va'ani sefillasi lecha Hashem eis ratzon* (Tehillim 69:14), which can be interpreted to mean, "When my moment of *ratzon* hits, I immediately turn it into a prayer." This is the way to attain the salvation you're wishing for, dear sisters.

When you're feeling disappointed, lonely, or rejected, don't wallow in the emotions. This is your chance, dear women, to transform your sadness into a heartfelt plea. I've seen too many women translate their pain into a shopping spree, an eating binge, an Internet addiction. That happens because they haven't learned to translate their *eis ratzon*, their desperate moment, into an immediate *tefillah*. "Tomorrow I will go to the Kosel," they say. Why not right now? Why are you postponing this opportune moment?

The portion of *V'Zos HaBerachah* is always read around the time of the exalted day of Hoshana Rabbah. What is our main request on this auspicious day? *Hosha na. Na* means "please," but it also means "right now." Hashem, please help me at this very second, we beg. *Na*, dear sisters, also refers to meat that is "rare," not roasted well (*Shemos* 12:9). On this day of prayer, we plead, "Hashem, I know I'm not ripe for marriage. I know I'm not ready enough for a child. I know I'm not the best person to run a business. But please, help me anyway, in my raw state. Even if I am not fully developed, help me!"

Let us learn from David HaMelech how to turn every desire into a prayer. What makes the words of *Tehillim* so unique is that it expertly translates every kind of emotion into a song for Hashem. That was David HaMelech's exquisite ability. When you find yourself in a moment of *ratzon*, desire, grab the *sefer Tehillim*. It's the gift that David HaMelech created with you in mind. Like David, the guest in our *succah* on Hoshana Rabbah, translate your pain, your sadness, your gratitude, your love, into *tefillah*.

Moshe Rabbeinu's Legacy

Let's touch the very edge of the Torah, the words that conclude the most precious gift we were given thousands of years ago. If we take a look at the last verses of the entire Torah, we realize that they are about the 17th of Tammuz.

U'lechol hayad hachazakah u'lechol hamora hagadol asher asah Moshe l'einei kol Yisrael — "And by all the strong hand and awesome power that Moshe performed before the eyes of all of Israel" (*Devarim* 34:12). What's the strong hand that the Torah is referring to?

On the 17th of Tammuz, Moshe Rabbeinu descended with the set of *luchos* from Heaven. Instead of finding a nation anticipating his arrival with bated breath, he found a nation dancing around a golden calf. In an instant, he broke the holy *luchos*. Our Sages describe this heartrending scene in the *Talmud*

Yerushalmi (*Ta'anis* 4:5). The *luchos*, they explain, were six *tefachim* long. Hashem held two *tefachim* and Moshe held two. Two *tefachim* were in the space between them. When Moshe observed the horrific scene of the Jews dancing around the golden calf, Hashem wanted to take the *luchos* back, but Moshe wanted to give it to the nation. Our Sages teach us that Moshe's hands prevailed, he had the *yad hachazakah*, and he broke the *luchos*. How tragic!

Why does the edge, the very end, of the Torah discuss such a conflict? Aren't the ways of Torah *no'am*, pleasant and peaceful? And why is the 17th of Tammuz the grand finale of the five holy books? Let's learn a beautiful commentary from the Sages to cull profound insight on what really transpired during that fateful episode.

Moshe Rabbeinu, the faithful leader of our nation, broke the object he loved most on behalf of his fellow Jews. When he descended with the majestic *luchos* from Heaven, he held in his hand a treasure, a set of Tablets full of light, full of clarity. On that fateful day, however, he saw that we'd be coming to very dark times. He understood that a time would come when we wouldn't see Hashem face-to-face as the Jews merited in the Wilderness, that there would come a time of *hastarah shebesoch hahastarah*, concealment within concealment, as Hashem says, *V'anochi hasteir astir panai bayom hahu* — "I will conceal My face on that day" (*Devarim* 31:18). This is the sad reality we live in today, the time in which we try desperately to understand the ways of Hashem, but they are hidden from us.

When Moshe realized what the Jews would eventually go through, he said, "This is not the Torah that this nation needs. I have to give them something else, a *broken* Torah." And that's when he shattered the Tablets. "This Torah will hold you during dark times," he told the nation. "Take it with you. The Torah full of light won't speak to you anymore. It's the Torah of the broken people that tells you that Hashem is with you even when you cannot see Him."

When we had the Beis HaMikdash, Hashem was referred to by the Name Nora: "We fear You because *ro'eh*, we see You," as it is written, *Nora Elokim mimikdashecha* — "You are feared, G-d, from Your Sanctuaries" (*Tehillim* 68:36). When we came to the Beis HaMikdash, we felt fear because we "saw" Him. Then came the terrible destruction. The nations came and trampled the place, turning holiness into *chol*. When the lost Jews witnessed this, they said to the prophet Yirmiyahu, "Hashem is not Nora anymore. Look what the nations did to His Temple!" The next morning, when Yirmiyahu davened Shacharis, he omitted the word *nora* from the first *berachah* of *Shemoneh Esrei*. The days of Hashem's open glory had come to a bitter end (*Yoma* 69b).

In his farsighted wisdom, Moshe Rabbeinu was concerned about us, the nation he lovingly led for decades. When we won't have *nora* anymore, no Beis HaMikdash, how would we fare? The letters of the word *nora* can be rearranged to form the word *aron*. "You will have an *Aron* that will go with you to war," Moshe comforted us. What were the contents of the *Aron* that accompanied the nation in the darkest of places? The broken tablets. When you don't feel the closeness like the Jews did in the Mikdash, when you feel that Hashem's glory is hidden from you, take the broken *luchos* with you.

When the *luchos* were shattered, the stone broke, but the letters flew up in the air. Now, said Moshe Rabbeinu to *Am Yisrael*, you can grab them and make them into your Torah. Use the letters to compose a special Torah that will heal your broken heart.

I want to share with you an example of a woman who gathered the floating letters and created a most magnificent Torah for her broken heart. Her son was graduating from an institution that no mother wants her son to be in. He had fallen into a deep abyss of darkness that led to drug abuse and then, ultimately, to rehab. Now that her son finally completed the program, she was called upon to speak at the momentous graduation.

"What did you say?" I asked her.

"Once there was a man whose name was Hillel. He wanted to enter the *beis midrash* because his heart longed for Torah. At the entrance, he was asked, 'Do you have money?' and he said no. 'So you can't come in,' he was told. So he climbed up to the roof to listen from the skylight there, and the teachers wondered, *Why is our beis midrash so dark?* Until one teacher looked up and he saw — a face! He climbed up to the roof and found Hillel lying there, frost-bitten. They brought him into the *beis midrash* and warmed him up by the fireplace. And the light returned to the *beis midrash*. If you won't let him enter through the front door, he'll do it from up there," this holy mother finished her speech.

When I heard this touching talk, I hugged this *ima* tightly. "Who told you this beautiful, gorgeous broken Torah?" I asked her. And I knew it had come from Moshe Rabbeinu. He was the one who gave us the gift of the Torah for broken hearts. "This is what will comfort you," he said to us. "Broken mother, broken father, broken daughter or sister, this Torah will take your frozen ice and melt it. It will make you a princess again."

Dear Jewish woman, there is no Torah more beautiful than the broken Torah. It has accompanied us through the generations, its blood-soaked pages telling the story of a nation that lives for a Higher Purpose, a nation that is ready and willing to sacrifice everything that is precious and dear for the glory of Hashem. Since time immemorial, we have suffered, but suffering is not a blemish. We are a nation that celebrates imperfection, a nation that celebrates a broken heart, because this is what draws us close to our dear Father.

When you are in pain, dear sister, remember the broken Torah. Remember what Moshe Rabbeinu did at the very end of the *Chumash* so you can have a guide during your times of sorrow. When the pain is so deep that every breath is a struggle, please don't forget that the Torah is at your side. It is my deepest *tefillah* that I be blessed with the capacity and opportunity to emulate the holy ways of our consummate leader, Moshe

Rabbeinu, in shedding light on the Torah's ability to heal, to nurture, to bring joy into your life once again.

The Joy of Torah

How can you bring joy into your life when the pain is so great? Fill your life with Simchas Torah, the *chag* that we celebrate when we read these very words. *V'Zos HaBerachah* talks about the end, the finale of Moshe Rabbeinu's life. That is the source of the greatest *simchah*. When you're connected to the Torah, you attach yourself to eternity. Although Moshe Rabbeinu's body died in *V'Zos HaBerachah*, his words live on forever and ever. And then, before we know it, we're learning *Parashas Bereishis* again. In the Torah, there is no finality.

Life is all about learning, dear women. The lessons you learn can sometimes be very painful, but they also provide you with a new start, a new hope. As long as you're connected to the Torah, you live by its sweet words and absorb the lessons it teaches, you will find comfort. You will realize that life is not about the here and now, that the picture is much greater than you can ever fathom.

At the conclusion of the last *Midrash Rabbah* in the Torah (*Devarim* 11:10), we read about how everyone (Hashem, the angels, Yehoshua, and the Jewish people), and everything (*ruach hakodesh*, the heavens, and earth) all cried and briefly eulogized Moshe Rabbeinu when he passed away. Then they all said together, *Zecher tzaddik livrachah*. What is the *berachah*? When will you remember the *tzaddik*? *V'zos haberachah...* — every time you learn these words of Torah. Every time you immerse in the Torah, you don't only bring Moshe Rabbeinu back to life, but also yourself. *Ki heim chayeinu v'orech yameinu* — "The Torah's words are our life and the length of our days" (second *berachah* in Ma'ariv).

A publisher once asked me if I would write a coaching book.

I told him, "I don't need to give any answers. They are all in the Torah. I am only the messenger of its holy, brilliant words."

The Torah, dear sisters, has answers to your every question. It provides comfort to suffering of every kind. And it offers guidance on every matter, be it marriage, parenting, business, and relationships. When you live by the lessons you've learned from the Torah, dear women, every facet of your life will become elevated, enriched, and more beautiful.

Glossary

achdus — unity.

achvah — brotherhood.

adoni — my lord; my master.

ahavah — love.

ahavas Hashem — love of Hashem.

ahavas haTorah – love of the Torah.

ahavas Yisrael — love for fellow Jews.

Akeidah, Akeidas Yitzchak — the Binding of Isaac.

akeres habayis — the mainstay of the home; i.e., the homemaker.

al kiddush Hashem — for the sake of sanctifying Hashem.

alef — the first letter of the Hebrew alphabet.

alos hashachar — sunrise.

am ha'aretz — unlearned, illiterate person.

Am Yisrael — the Nation of Israel.

Amidah — lit., *standing prayer*; the *Shemoneh Esrei*.

ananei hakavod — the Clouds of Glory in the Wilderness.

anav — a humble person.

aron — 1. (u.c.) (in Mishkan) Holy Ark that housed the Tablets (*Luchos*). 2. (l.c.) (in shul) ark where the Torah Scrolls are kept. 3. (l.c.) a coffin.

Aseres HaDibros — the Ten Commandments.

asham — a guilt-offering brought in the Beis HaMikdash.

ashrei — fortunate; happy.

assur — forbidden by halachah.

atzel — 1. reserved. 2. lazy; idle.

atzvus — sadness.

aveirah — sin; transgression.

Avinu — lit., *our father*, usually used in reference to one of the Patriarchs.

avodah — lit., *work; task;* the service of Hashem, whether in sacrifice, prayer, or self-refinement.

avodah zarah — idol worship; idolatry.

avodas Hashem — service of Hashem.

Avos — the Patriarchs; Avraham, Yitzchak, and Yaakov.

ayin — an eye.

ayin hara — an evil eye.

b'seder — all right; okay.

b'shogeig — unintentional.

b'simchah — with joy and happiness.

balagan — a tumult; a chaotic situation.

bar mitzvah — 1. 13-year-old boy. 2. ceremony marking the coming of age of a Jewish boy.

baruch Hashem — lit., *Blessed is Hashem;* an expression of appreciation of Hashem's goodness.

bas — daughter.

bas kol — a voice from Heaven.

bashert — 1. fated. 2. the person one is fated to marry.

Bavel — Babylonia.

bechirah — choice; free will.

Beis HaMikdash — the Holy Temple in Jerusalem.

beis knesses — synagogue; house of worship.

beis midrash (pl. *batei midrashim*) — house of learning or prayer.

ben — *son.*

berachah (pl. *berachos*) — a blessing recited before performing a mitzvah and before and after eating; a formula for acknowledging a gift from G-d, whether material or spiritual.

bigdei Kehunah — the special clothing worn by Kohanim (the priestly class) during their service in the Beis HaMikdash in Jerusalem.

binah yeseirah — heightened intuition; special insight.

birchos hashachar — blessings recited during the morning prayer service.

Birkas HaMazon — Grace after Meals.

bnos melech — daughters of the king.

bnos Yisrael — Jewish girls.

bris milah — circumcision of male infants, generally performed on the eighth day after birth.

chad — sharp and smooth.

chag — a Festival.

challah (pl. challos) — 1. colloquially, loaves of soft wheat-bread traditionally eaten at a Shabbos meal. 2. the portion separated from the dough and given to a Kohen (today it is burnt).

chamas — outrage; anger.

chanukas haMishkan — the inauguration of the Tabernacle.

chareidi — strictly religiously observant.

chassan (pl. *chassanim*) — a bridegroom.

Chassan Torah — lit., *the bridegroom of the Torah*; the one given the honor of being called to the Torah on Simchas Torah when the last Torah portion is being read.

Chassidic — following the customs of a Chassidic leader (Rebbe).

chatas — a guilt-offering brought in the Beis HaMikdash.

chavrusah — a study partner.

chazak chazak v'nischazeik — Be strong! Be strong! And may we be strengthened!

chein — grace; charm.

cheishek — desire; enthusiasm.

chesed — acts of kindness; loving-kindness; charitable giving.

chevrah kaddisha — burial society.

chiddush — innovation; Talmudic or halachic novellae.

chillul Hashem — desecration of Hashem's Name

chinuch — Jewish education; Torah education (of minors).

chizuk — encouragement; strengthening.

chodesh — a month.

chok (pl. *chukim*) — a statute, a Biblical decree; a decree; a Midrashic teaching derived from the Torah.

chol — not sanctified; the six days of the week.

chol hamo'ed — the intermediate days between the first and last days of Pesach and of Succos.

Chumash — one of the Five Books of the Torah; the Five Books collectively.

chumrah (pl. *chumros*) — stringent application (of a halachah); stringency.

chuppah — wedding canopy beneath which the wedding ceremony takes place.

churban (pl. *churbanos*) — 1. destruction. 2. (u.c.) destruction of the Holy Temple. 3. the Holocaust.

chutz la'aretz — anywhere outside of the Land of Israel; Diaspora.

chutzpah — gall; nerve; rudeness; impudence.

da'as — full moral comprehension; knowledge.

dalet — the fourth letter of the Hebrew alphabet.

dan l'kaf zechus — the obligation to judge others favorably.

daven — (Yiddish) to pray.

davening — (Yiddish) 1. praying. 2. prayers.

davka — 1. specifically. 2. spitefully.

derech — 1. path. 2. method. 3. a way.

devar Torah (pl. *divrei Torah*) — a short speech on a Torah topic.

din (pl. *dinim*) — Jewish law; the attribute of harsh judgment; strict justice; law.

dor —a generation.

dor hamidbar — the Jewish people in the Wilderness after the Exodus from Egypt.

duchan — 1. the platform in the Beis HaMikdash where the Levi'im stood to sing. 2. the act of giving the priestly blessing by the Kohanim in the shul.

echad — one; lone.

eigel hazahav — the golden calf.

eim b'Yisrael — lit., *a mother in Israel*; a Jewish mother.

eish — fire.

eishes chayil — 1. woman of valor; a worthy wife. 2. (u.c.) *Proverbs* 31:10-31, traditionally recited before the Friday-night Shabbos meal.

eitz hada'as — the Tree of Knowledge of Good and Evil in Gan Eden.

eitzel — beside; next to.

eizer kenegdo — lit., a helper corresponding to him; term used to denote a man's wife.

Elul — one of the Jewish months.

emunah — faith.

Eretz Yisrael — the Land of Israel.

erev Shabbos — the eve of the Sabbath; Friday.

erev Yom Kippur — the eve of Yom Kippur.

fargin — (Yiddish) not begrudge.

frum — (Yiddish) religious; Torah observant.

galus — the Jewish exile; (u.c.) the Diaspora.

Galus Mitzrayim — the exile of the Jewish people in the land of Egypt.

Gan Eden — the Garden of Eden.

Gan Eden mikedem — the Garden of Eden of yore.

gaon — a revered Torah scholar.

gashmiyus — materialism; something physical.

Gehinnom — Hell.

gemach (pl. *gemachim*) — acronym for *gemilus chasadim*; acts of kindness; system for providing aid of various kinds; e.g., interest-free loans; a service providing goods and services to those in need.

Gemara — (u.c.) the Talmud. (l.c.) a volume of the Talmud.

gematria — the numerical value assigned to each letter of the Hebrew alphabet.

geulah — redemption; the redemption.

gevurah — strength.

gezeirah — an edict; a decree.

giddul banim — lit., *raising children;* refers to the effort involved in bringing up one's children.

hachna'ah — submission to a higher authority.

hachnasas orchim — hospitality; inviting guests.

haftarah (pl. *haftaros*) — the selection from the Prophets read following the Torah reading on the Sabbath, Festivals, and fast days.

Haggadah — liturgy recited at the Pesach *Seder*.

HaKadosh Baruch Hu — lit., *The Holy One* (i.e., Hashem), *Blessed Is He.*

halachah (pl. *halachos*) — Torah and Rabbinic law.

halachic — pertaining to Jewish law.

hamotzi — the blessing said before eating bread.

Har Sinai — Mount Sinai, the mountain where the Jewish People received the Torah.

hashavas aveidah — returning lost articles.

Hashem — lit., *the Name;* a respectful way to refer to G-d.

hei — the fifth letter of the Hebrew alphabet.

hester panim — literally, *hidden face;* referring to when Hashem hides His countenance.

hishtadlus — one's own efforts; the required effort.

hod — majestic splendor.

Hoshana Rabbah —the seventh day of the Festival of Succos, when seven circuits are made around the bimah in shul and special prayers are recited.

hotza'as orchim — escorting guests when they depart.

ilui — a genius.

ima — (l.c.) mother; (u.c.) Mother; Mommy.

Imahos — the Matriarchs.

Imeinu — our mother, usually used in reference to one of the Matriarchs.

ish — a man.

ishah — a woman; a wife.

Ivriyah (pl. *Ivriyos*) — a Jewish woman.

Kabbalah — (u.c.) the body of Jewish mystical teachings. (l.c.) lit., *acceptance;* the act of taking on a specific action to elevate oneself spiritually; an obligation taken upon oneself.

kadosh (pl. *kedoshim*) — holy; holy one.

kal — unexacting; light; easy.

kallah — a bride; an engaged girl.

kasheh — rigorous; exacting; hard to deal with.

kaved — the liver.

kavod — honor, respect, dignity.

kedushah — holiness

Kehunah — the priesthood.

keilim — utensils.

keitz chayah — lit., *the end of life;* the point of death.

keruvim — the cherubim in the Holy Temple.

kesher — a connection; a bond.

kesubah — a marriage contract.

kever (pl. *kevarim*) — a grave.

kezayis (pl. *kezeisim*) — the volume of an olive or half an egg (somewhat more than the volume of one fluid ounce).

kibbud horim — the mitzvah to respect and honor one's parents.

kiddush/Kiddush — 1. mandatory blessing over wine expressing the sanctity of Shabbos or Festivals. 2. (l.c.) a reception after Sabbath morning prayers at which *Kiddush* is recited and refreshments are served.

kiddush Hashem — doing something that brings honor to Hashem; sanctification of Hashem's Name.

kippah — yarmulke; skullcap.

kirvas Elokim — drawing close to G-d.

kivrei tzaddikim — the graves of righteous individuals.

kivui — longing; hope.

kiyor — a laver.

kiyum — ability to last; endurance.

klal — the community.

Klal Yisrael — Jewish people in general; the Jewish nation.

klalah — a curse.

ko'ach (pl. *kochos*) — strength; ability; energy.

Kodesh — see *Kodesh Kodashim*.

Kodesh Kodashim — Holy of Holies; the inner chamber of the Sanctuary.

Koheles — the Book of Ecclesiastes.

Kohen (pl. *Kohanim*) — a member of the priestly tribe descended in the male line from Aaron.

Kohen Gadol (pl. *Kohanim Gedolim*) — the High Priest who served in the Beis HaMikdash.

kol hakavod — lit., *all the honor*; (colloq.) roughly, "you are right."

Kol Nidrei — opening prayer recited at the onset of Yom Kippur.

kol shofar — the sound of the shofar.

kor — coldness.

korban (pl. *korbanos*) — a sacrificial offering brought in the Beis HaMikdash.

korban olah — a burnt offering brought in the Beis HaMikdash.

Kosel; Kotel — the Western Wall.

Krias Shema — three paragraphs of the Torah recited twice daily, beginning with the words "*Shema Yisrael*, Hear, O Israel"; this prayer expresses the essence of Jewish faith.

l'havdil — in contradistinction; often used to distinguish between the holy and the secular.

l'shem Shamayim — lit., *for the sake of Heaven*; a selfless action done solely for the sake of Heaven.

lageshes — drawing near.

Lashon HaKodesh — lit., *the holy language*; the Hebrew of the Bible.

lashon hara — lit., *evil speech*; derogatory speech; slander; gossip.

levanah — the moon.

levayah — a funeral.

lo aleinu — lit., *not on us*; Heaven protect us.

Luchos — the Tablets inscribed with the Ten Commandments.

lulav — palm branch, one of the Four Species taken in hand on Succos.

ma'aser — tithes.

ma'avar — transition.

mabul — a flood; (u.c.) the Biblical Flood at the time of Noach.

machlokes — an argument; a dispute.

machzor — Festival prayer book.

madreigah — a level; a degree (as of piety); a step.

makkah (pl. *makkos*) — 1. a blow. 2. a plague; often used in reference to any detrimental situation.

malach — angel

masechta (pl. *masechtos*) — tractate of Talmud

malchus — kingship; royalty.

malkah — a queen.

mamashus — physical presence; reality; substance.

manna — the manna that miraculously fell in the Wilderness for the Jews.

mar — bitter; bitterness.

mashach — to attract.

mashal — a parable; an example.

masheish — a loving touch.

Mashiach — Messiah, the awaited redeemer of Israel, who will usher in an era of universal recognition of the Kingship of Hashem.

matbei'a — a coin.

mattan Torah — the Giving of the Torah at Sinai.

matzah — unleavened bread.

mazel — 1. an astrological sign. 2. stellar constellation. 3. fortune; fate; luck.

Me'aras HaMachpeilah — the cave that houses the tombs of the Patriarchs and Matriarchs (other than Rachel).

mechallel Shabbos — one who desecrates the Sabbath; the desecration of the Sabbath.

mechilah — forgiveness.

megulgal — to be reincarnated in another body.

mehallel — to praise; to glorify.

meirosh — from the start; initially.

mekaveh — hopeful.

menachem avel — to comfort a mourner; to pay a condolence call.

menuchah — rest; peace of mind.

metzora — one who suffers from the skin disease *tzara'as*.

metzuyan (pl. *metzuyanim*) — (adj.) excellent; (n.) one who is excellent.

midbar — desert; wilderness.

middah (pl. *middos*) — character trait; attribute.

middos tovos — positive character traits or attributes.

Midrash, midrash — homiletical teachings of the Sages.

mikdash me'at — miniature Beis HaMikdash; i.e., a synagogue.

mikveh — ritual bath.

milah (pl. *milim*) — a word.

Minchah — the afternoon prayer service

Mishkan — Tabernacle; the portable Sanctuary used by the Jews during their sojourn in the Wilderness.

Mishkan Shiloh — the Tabernacle housed at Shiloh.

Mishnah — teachings of the Tannaim that form the basis of the Talmud.

mishpachah — a family.

Mitzrayim — Egypt.

mitzvah (pl. mitzvos) — commandment.

miyad — immediately.

mizbei'ach — (l.c.) an altar. (u.c.) the Altar in the Beis HaMikdash

mohel — one who performs a circumcision.

morah — a woman teacher.

motza'ei Pesach — the night following the conclusion of the Passover Festival.

motza'ei Shabbos — Saturday night; the time of the departure of the Sabbath.

mussar — ethical teachings geared toward self-refinement; reproof.

mussar shmuess — a lecture on self-refinement.

nachalah — territory; allotted portion.

nachas — pleasure, usually from one's children; spiritual or emotional pleasure.

nashim tzidkaniyos — righteous women.

nazir — a Nazarite; one who has vowed, for a defined period, to refrain from cutting his hair and to abstain from (a) grapes and grape products and (b) contact with a grave or corpse.

negidus — opposition.

neshamah (pl. *neshamos*) — a soul.

netzach — victory.

nevuah — prophecy.

niftar — (n.) a person who has died. (v.) died.

niggunim — Jewish tunes or melodies, often sung during special occasions.

nimus (pl. *nimusim*)— 1. courtesy; good manners. 2. to melt.

nisayon (pl. *nisyonos*) — a test, esp. a spiritual test.

nishbar leivav — a broken heart.

nishmatim — slipping; be omitted.

nistar — lit., *hidden; the esoteric portions of the Torah.*

nitzachon — *victory.*

ohel — a tent.

Ohel Mo'ed — lit., *Tent of Meeting;* the Mishkan in the Wilderness.

ohr — light.

olah (pl. *olos*) — an offering that is completely burned on the Altar in the Beis HaMikdash.

olei regel — *those who, when the Temple stood, make the pilgrimage to Jerusalem to celebrate Pesach, Shavuos, and Succos.*

Omer — 1. the barley offering brought in the Beis HaMikdash. 2. the count of days between Pesach and Shavuos.

oneg Shabbos — lit., *joy of Sabbath;* a gathering to celebrate the Sabbath; something that enhances one's joy on the Sabbath.

or — skin.

oy, oy v'avoy — (Yiddish) (interjection) what a pity!

parah adumah — the red heifer.

parashah (pl. parashiyos) — the weekly Torah portion; Torah portion; parchment inscribed with Torah paragraphs and inserted into tefillin; Torah portion.

parashas — the Torah portion of ….

parnassah — livelihood.

paroches (pl. *perochos*) — the curtain in front of the Torah ark in a synagogue. 2. (u.c.) in the Beis HaMikdash, the curtain separating the Holy of Holies from the remainder of the Temple.

pasuk (pl. *pesukim*)— a verse of Scripture.

pe'er — glory.

Perek Shirah — The Song of the Universe.

pesol — to sculpt.

pesoles — waste; refuse.

petirah — lit., *departure;* death; the moment of death.

pigua — terrorist attack.

pikadon — a deposit; a pledge.

Rabbanit — Rebbetzin; the Rabbi's wife.

Rabbeinu — our Teacher.

Rachmana litzlan — 1. Heaven have mercy. 2. G-d forbid.

rasha — an evildoer; a wicked individual.

ratzon — favor; desire; good will.

rav — a rabbi; a spiritual leader.

rebbe (pl. *rebbeim*) — a rav; a rabbi or teacher. (u.c.) Hassidic Grand Rabbi.

refuah — cure; recovery.

refuah sheleimah — lit., *a full/complete recovery*; a blessing for a complete/speedy recovery extended to an ailing person.

retzon Hashem — the will of Hashem.

ribbis — interest; the halachic prohibition of charging interest.

Ribbono Shel Olam — lit., *Master of the World*; i.e., Hashem.

rosh bayis — the head of the household.

Rosh Chodesh — the first day of a new month.

Rosh Hashanah — the Jewish New Year.

ruchniyus — spirituality; spiritual growth

samech — the fifteenth letter of the *alef-beis*.

Sanhedrin — 1. high rabbinical court in Jerusalem; supreme judicial body in the Holy Land during the Roman period, consisting of 71 ordained scholars; Supreme Rabbinic Court in the times of the Holy Temple. 2. (l.c.) a lesser court.

Satan — the prosecuting angel.

Savta — Grandmother.

seder (pl. *sedarim*) — 1. (l.c.) a study period in yeshivah. (u.c.) Pesach-night ritual during which the Haggadah is recited.

sefer (pl. *sefarim*) — a book, specifically a book on holy subjects or a learned topic.

sefirah — counting or numbering, generally refers to the counting of the Omer.

sefiras ha'omer — the counting of the seven weeks between Passover and Shavuos.

sefiros — emanations of God's holiness.

seganei Kehunah — deputies of the Kohen Gadol.

seichel — insight; intelligence; common sense; rationality; one's rational side.

Selichos — prayers said during the Ten Days of Repentance.

seudah shelishis — the third Shabbos meal.

seudas hoda'ah — lit., *meal of gratitude*; a festive meal served on the occasion when one wants to give thanks to Hashem.

sha'ah tovah — a propitious time.

Shabbos — the Sabbath.

shachar — morning.

Shacharis — the morning prayer service.

shachor — black; darkness.

shadchan — a matchmaker.

shakran — a liar.

shaliach (pl. *shelichim*) — a messenger; an emissary.

shalom — peace; often said on meeting or leave-taking.

shalom bayis — peace and harmony in the home; marital harmony.

shalosh regalim — the three Festivals when Jews were required to ascend to Jerusalem and the Beis HaMikdash; i.e., on Pesach, Shavuos, and Succos.

Shamayim — Heaven.

shamor — guard; heed; obey.

she'asani kirtzono — Who made me according to His will; a berachah recited specifically by women.

Shechinah — the Divine Presence; the spirit of the Omnipresent manifested on earth.

shefa — abundance; profusion.

shefa berachah — abundant blessing.

shekel — Israeli monetary unit.

shelamim — peace offerings brought in the Beis HaMikdash.

sheliach tzibbur — one who leads the prayer service.

sheloshim — lit., *thirty*; the 30-day period of mourning observed for a close relative.

Shema, Shema Yisrael — Hear, O Israel; this prayer, recited twice daily, expresses the essence of Jewish faith.

Shemittah — the Sabbatical year, occurring every seventh year, during which the land is not worked. This law pertains only to the Land of Israel.

Shemoneh Esrei — lit., *eighteen*; the prayer, originally eighteen blessings but now nineteen, that forms the central core of each weekday prayer service.

sheva berachos — lit., *seven blessings;* 1. the seven blessings recited at a wedding. 2. the weeklong festivities following a wedding. 3. festive meals, celebrated during the week after a wedding, at which the seven blessings are recited.

shevarim —the tripartite shofar blast.

shevet — a tribe; one of the Twelve Tribes of Israel.

shevi'i shel Pesach — the seventh day of Passover; it has special significance since that was the day the Reed Sea split to allow the redeemed Jews to cross on dry land.

shidduch (pl. *shidduchim*) — 1. match, esp. a marriage match. 2. proposed marriage match. 3. one's betrothed.

shirah — a song of praise; a poetic song.

shiur (pl. *shiurim*) — 1. a Torah lecture. 2. the required halachic amount (e.g., of eating prohibited food to be considered a punishable act).

shivah — lit., *seven*; the seven-day mourning period immediately following the death of a close relative.

shivtei Kah — lit., *the tribes of Hashem*; the Twelve Tribes.

shlita — acronym for (Hebrew) "May he live a long and good life."

shul — (Yiddish) synagogue.

siddur — a prayer book

siman (pl. *simanim*) — lit., *symbol*; food traditionally eaten on Rosh Hashanah because of its symbolic implications.

simchah (pl. *simchas*) — 1. happiness, joy; a joyous occasion. 2. a happy occasion; a celebration, esp. a celebration of a family milestone such as a wedding, bar mitzvah, or a birth.

Simchas Torah — the festival immediately following Succos, honoring the cycle of the Torah.

sinas chinam — unwarranted hatred of one Yid for another; unwarranted hatred.

sof — the end.

sof, sof! — (interjection) Finally!

sotah — (l.c.) a woman suspected of an illicit relationship, who, in Biblical times, was subject to the test of the bitter waters (see *Numbers* 5:12*ff*). (u.c.) the Talmudic treatise dealing with this subject.

succah — booth in which Jews are commanded to dwell during the Festival of Succos.

ta'am — 1. reason. 2. taste.

Ta'anis — (l.c.) a fast day. (u.c.) the Talmudic treatise dealing with this subject.

talmid (pl. *talmidim*) — disciple; student.

talmid chacham (pl. *talmidei chachamim*) — lit., *the student of a wise person*; a person learned in Torah and Talmud; a Torah scholar.

Talmud Yerushalmi — the Jerusalem Talmud.

Tammuz — the fourth month of the Jewish calendar

Tanach — acronym for *Torah, Ne'viim, Kesuvim*; the written Torah, including the Five Books of Moses, the eight books of Prophets, and eleven books of Writings.

Tanna — one of the various authorities quoted in the Mishnah.

tav — the twenty-second letter of the Hebrew alphabet.

techiyas hameisim — Revivification of the Dead.

tefillah (pl. *tefillos*) — prayer.

Tefillas HaDerech — the wayfarer's prayer.

Tehillim — 1. (u.c.) the Book of *Psalms*. 2. (l. c.) psalms.

tehillos — praises.

teivah — (l.c.) a basket. (u.c.) Noach's Ark.

tekiah — one of the sounds of the shofar.

tekiah gedolah — the extended shofar blast that completes a set of sounds.

tekias shofar—the sounding of the shofar.

tekios — shofar blasts; the sounds of the shofar blasts.

temimim — people of integrity.

temimus — 1. integrity. 2. naiveté.

tenufah — the act of raising up; lifting.

teshukah — 1. passion; enthusiasm. 2. desire; craving.

teshuvah — 1. repentance. 2. rediscovery of Torah Judaism. 3. an answer. 4. a response to a halachic query.

te'umim — twins.

teva — nature; the natural order.

tiferes — splendor; glory.

Tishah B'Av — [the fast of] the Ninth of Av; day of mourning for the destruction of the Holy Temples.

Tishrei – the first month of the Jewish year, in which are the holidays of Rosh Hashanah, Yom Kippur, Succos, Shemini Atzeres, and Simchas Torah.

todah — gratitude; thanks; to thank.

tumah — spiritual impurity.

tza'ar — pain; suffering.

tza'ar ba'alei chaim — lit., *causing pain to a living being*; generally refers to the commandment regarding prevention of cruelty to animals.

tza'ar gidul banim — the anguish (trouble) inherent in raising children.

tzaddik (pl. *tzaddikim*) — righteous man; righteous person.

tzadeikes (pl. *tzidkaniyos*) — a righteous woman.

tzanua — one who is modest and

refined in both dress and behavior.

tzar — narrow.

tzara'as — a severe spiritual affliction that manifests itself (on people) as white or light-colored spots on the body.

tzaros — problems; difficult, painful situations.

tzava'ah – a will; an ethical will.

tzechok — laughter.

tzedakah — compassion; charity.

tzelem Elokim — G-dly image; lit., *image of G-d*, therefore deserving respect.

tzirim — contractions.

tznius — standard of modesty with regard to speech, behavior, and dress.

vidui — confession of sins recited on Yom Kippur and prior to one's demise.

vort — lit., *word*; 1. a Torah thought. 2. an engagement celebration.

yad — hand.

Yad Hashem — the Hand of God.

yafah — beautiful.

yahrtzeit — (Yiddish) the anniversary of a person's passing.

Yamim Noraim — lit., *Days of Awe*; Rosh Hashanah and Yom Kippur.

Yehi Ratzon — May it be His [Hashem's] will.

Yerushalayim — Jerusalem.

yeshivah — a school of Jewish studies; a Torah academy.

yeshivah shel ma'alah — the Heavenly Academy.

yeshuah (pl. *yeshuos*) — salvation; rescue; remedy.

yetzer hara — the evil inclination; the negative impulse to behave contrary to the Torah's commandments.

yetzer hatov — *the good inclination.*

Yetzias Mitzrayim — the Exodus from Egypt.

yichus — lineage.

Yid (pl. *Yidden*) — a Jew

Yiddishkeit — Judaism.

yiras Shamayim — lit., *fear of Heaven*; connotes reverence for G-d, an all-pervasive attitude of piety.

yishuv hada'as — *calmness.*

yissurim — pains; suffering.

yofi — beauty.

yud — the tenth letter of the Hebrew alphabet.

zachor — 1. remember. 2. male.

zerizus — alacrity; enthusiasm; urgency.

zeruzim — lit., the swift ones; zealots.

zivug — one's destined marriage partner.

z"l — acronym for "*zichrono livrachah,*" lit., *may the righteous person be remembered as a blessing*, appended to the name of a deceased righteous person.

zocheh — to merit.

zt"l — acronym for *zecher tzaddik livrachah*, may the righteous person be remembered as a blessing.

This volume is part of
THE ARTSCROLL® SERIES
an ongoing project of
translations, commentaries and expositions on
Scripture, Mishnah, Talmud, Midrash, Halachah,
liturgy, history, the classic Rabbinic writings,
biographies and thought.

For a brochure of current publications
visit your local Hebrew bookseller
or contact the publisher:

Mesorah Publications, ltd

4401 Second Avenue
Brooklyn, New York 11232
(718) 921-9000
www.artscroll.com